D1452982

EDWARD L. DREYER

Early Ming China

A POLITICAL HISTORY
1355-1435

Stanford University Press
Stanford, California

©1982 by the Board of Trustees of the
Leland Stanford Junior University

Composition in Hong Kong by
Asco Trade Typesetting Limited
Printed in the United States of America
ISBN 0-8047-1105-4
LC 80-51646

Published with the assistance of the
National Endowment for the Humanities

For J U N E, *who asked how I could care so much about what happened so long ago*

Acknowledgments

The writing of this book began under a Fellowship for Younger Humanists of the National Endowment for the Humanities, supplemented by a summer grant from the American Council of Learned Societies. The University of Miami granted me a leave of absence to undertake the project. The library systems at both the University of Miami and Miami University were extremely helpful. I am also indebted to several colleagues who read the manuscript and provided detailed criticisms. Naturally, the aforementioned institutional and individual support cannot absolve the author from sole responsibility for the errors and omissions remaining in his work.

Contents

Maps

Early Ming China

ONE

*The Early Ming Period
in Chinese History*

Late in 1354 the court of the Mongol Yüan dynasty dismissed its chancellor, Toghtō, thereby throwing away its last opportunity to suppress the Chinese peasant rebellions then raging in the Yangtze valley. By 1368 one of the rebel leaders, Chu Yüan-chang (Emperor Hung-wu, r. 1368–98), had grown strong enough to expel the Mongols from the lands south of the Great Wall and proclaim the Ming dynasty (1368–1644). Hung-wu and his son Chu Ti (Emperor Yung-lo, r. 1402–24)—and to a lesser extent the other emperors reigning before 1435—determined the final shape taken by Ming institutions; in so doing they significantly changed the course of development that had been followed by Chinese society before the rise of the Ming. How they did it is the subject of this book.

In principle the founding of the Ming had a transcendent moral significance. For the first time in over four centuries the entire Chinese cultural area was under Chinese rule, so there should have been a thoroughgoing eradication of "barbarian" accretions in dress and language and in culture and institutions. And since the characteristic genius of Chinese civilization had previously expressed itself in political philosophy and governmental organization, reassertion of Chinese values should have implied a reconstruction of the Chinese state on the basis of Confucian principles. Whatever the meaning of the Chinese-barbarian dichotomy, Chinese then and later felt it to be deeply significant. Hung-wu sought to appeal to the Chinese intellectual elite by searching out precedents from Han and T'ang—dynasties that were assumed to be impeccably Chinese—for his policies. When a new barbarian power, the Manchus, conquered China in 1644, they made peace with the Chinese intellectual elite—by then also the ruling elite—by preserving, down to fine points of detail, the Ming structure of civil administration and its supporting educational and examination systems, which by then had come to embody the essence of orthodox Chinese Confucian culture. In very long-term historical perspective, then, the significance of the Ming dynasty appears to be that it revived the Confucian state and its supporting social order—indeed, that it reconstituted both so solidly that they survived a renewal of barbarian rule and endured until the early decades of the twentieth century.

However correct this generalization may be with regard to the Ming period as a whole, it does not apply to the early Ming, herein defined as the period (1352–1435) comprising the wars of the Ming founding and the reigns of the first five Ming emperors. Although the year 1368 clearly marked the substitution of a Chinese for a Mongol ruling elite and was the occasion for a great deal of pious Confucian rhetoric, in most other respects the sense of continuity with the departed Yüan regime was intense. Not only did the Ming retain institutions and practices that were often Yüan innovations, the new Chinese ruling elite itself manifested values and attitudes similar to those of the former Mongol warrior aristocrats, and often did so in contradiction to Confucian prescriptions. The institutional continuities are evident in the formal structure of government organs and the terminology employed in its workings. Attitudinal continuities are harder to pin down, even though they may be more important. However, in the following five general areas the practice of the early Ming leadership betrays significant elements that correspond to Yüan attitudes and practices, and that contradict Confucian prescriptions that had become established by the end of the Sung (960–1276), the last native dynasty:

Military conquest. In the Confucian view, it was legitimate to use military force to unite the Chinese cultural area and to repel invasion or suppress rebellion. Such early emperors as Han Wu-ti (r. 140–87 B.C.) and Sui Yang-ti (r. 604–17), who attempted to conquer non-Chinese territory, however, were stigmatized by Chinese historians.[1] Both of the two great early Ming emperors won the throne by military force, and they went on to incorporate substantial regions of non-Chinese territory into the Ming empire, this last against the advice of their Confucian counselors. Their outward policy was a late reflection of the Mongol ideal of world conquest through military force and of the Yüan dynasty practice of dealing with a difficult frontier by absorbing it.

Foreign affairs and foreign trade. In the Confucian view, fully formulated as of the ninth century, the submission of foreign rulers was a sign of the legitimacy of the Chinese emperor, but foreign trade as such was undesirable since it might lead to imperial preoccupation with strange and useless exotica at the expense of agriculture, the economic foundation of society.[2] Early Ming policy was not uniform in this regard. Hung-wu eventually attempted to seal China off from all foreign influences, while Yung-lo dispatched naval expeditions throughout the South China Sea and the Indian Ocean, establishing trading and diplomatic relationships with all of the countries in those areas. His attitude was nearly identical to that of the Yüan emperors, who eagerly sought relations with foreign countries and employed foreigners in their service. Early Ming Confucians, on the other hand, saw the suppression of foreign trade as a major step in the establishment of orthodoxy.

Preponderance of military over civil officials. The warlordism of the later T'ang and Five Dynasties periods (ca. 755–960) made Confucian opinion permanently suspicious and disdainful of the military, and in the ensuing Sung dynasty this opinion had been inculcated in Chinese society as a whole. Emperors and civil officials agreed that the military should be confined to an instrumental role, and obedience to orders was often preferred to victory.[3] But early Ming practice sharply contradicted this. At the beginning, military men held all the policymaking posts at both central and provincial levels. Military officers were higher in rank and were paid more than civil officials of corresponding degrees of responsibility. Here the immediate precedent of the role of the military in the Yüan dynasty counted for more than the more distant, if more truly Chinese, example of the Sung.

Official appointment based on heredity. Confucian intellectuals emphasized the family-centered moral ideal of filial piety, but politically they stood for appointment to office on the basis of individual qualifications rather than membership in a particular social class. In both the Han and the T'ang dynasties Confucian officials had opposed tendencies to monopolize hereditary office-holding, and in the Sung they had contrived a remarkable personnel system in which original appointment rested largely on educational, and promotion on bureaucratic, criteria.[4] The early Ming in contrast made most military offices hereditary and established a class of military nobles superior to all officials. It was dominated by this hereditary military elite, whose model and inspiration was the Mongol aristocracy that had ruled the Yüan.

Civil service examinations. Under the T'ang and Sung, civil service examinations had done more than merely recruit officials; they also symbolized imperial acceptance of the Confucian ideological order. Thus, the refusal of the Yüan to hold such examinations signaled its rejection of that order, a state of affairs that lasted for most of the dynasty.[5] Hung-wu waited until 1384 before reluctantly establishing the civil service examinations on a permanent basis, and he did so only after his previous methods of recruiting civil officials had proved dangerously unsatisfactory. Like the Yüan emperors, the early Ming monarchs found strict Confucianism too restrictive of their own freedom of action.

The most important institutional expression of continuity with the Yüan was the military system. This had evolved during the long civil war period (1352–68), during which the rebel movement that later founded the Ming empire simply adapted the Yüan structure of local government and military organization to its own purposes. Beginning in 1364 and continuing after he became emperor, Hung-wu rationalized the military system to bring it more tightly under his control, but without altering the main features that had already developed by the time of the most intense phase (1360–63) of the civil war. These features were hereditary enrollment of troops in regiment- and battalion-sized units, each of which was assigned military colony (*t'un-t'ien*) lands that the troops were expected to farm during periods of respite from combat; rather high hereditary rank and status for the regimental officers, who also managed the military colony lands; and limitation of the number of generals, hereditary in practice before 1370 and in principle after 1370 (drawn mostly from Hung-wu's childhood companions, they were later supplemented, and in part replaced, by his sons, who monopolized the most important command positions).

By making the army self-supporting, Hung-wu both prevented it from becoming a burden on the civilian population and gave the soldiers a stake in the system. However, the military system had come into existence in a period of continuous warfare; given a period of protracted peace, its military effectiveness could be expected to deteriorate. This actually took place, and its occurrence marks the watershed between the early and mature Ming periods.

The deliberate creation of a military elite that was set above the civil service was a new departure for a dynasty of Chinese origin. During the Han and T'ang dynasties members of the official elites regularly held both civil and military positions in the course of their careers, and the prime aim of Sung policy had been to maintain the subjection of military officers to the dominant civil service elite. In contrast, the predominant role played by the Yüan-inspired Ming military elite in political decisionmaking gave the early part of the dynasty a military character reminiscent of such Turco-Mongolian empires as the Ottomans or the Mughals, rather than of the native Chinese dynasties.[6] Regimental officers could hope to rise to noble rank and political power through success in battle. This created a vested interest in more or less continuous warfare, a tendency resisted by Hung-wu but actively promoted by his son Yung-lo. Regular campaigning maintained the discipline and effectiveness of the armed forces and made possible territorial conquests, as well as providing an organization for the efficient execution of administrative programs (land survey, resettlement, grain transport, naval building and voyaging, and public works) that otherwise would have been much more difficult.

Nevertheless, like all previous Chinese regimes, the Ming empire required a corps of civil administrators to apply the laws and collect the taxes. Since these tasks required literacy, the recruitment of a civil service in fact necessitated coming to terms with the Confucian literati class. This class had emerged in the second century B.C. and had been the basis of the civil service and educational systems ever since; it attained its greatest prestige and power under the Sung, the last native Chinese dynasty. Since the literati claimed to be the authoritative interpreters of the political ideology and moral theory of Confucianism, it was difficult for rulers who did not share Confucian assumptions to employ them as officials. The Yüan, in consequence, had given the Confucian literati a low social standing and had sought for officials among foreigners, Taoists, and Buddhists. The Ming founder, Hung-wu, was similarly suspicious of Confucian pretensions and willing to employ non-Confucians as officials. But in the end he came to the conclusion that the Confucian literati were the only group in Chinese society sufficiently numerous, competent, and principled to provide a basis for the recruitment of a civil service. From the time of the permanent reestablishment of the civil service examinations in 1384, a Confucian civil service elite grew slowly but steadily in strength, in competition with and in opposition to the military elite.

In 1435 the civil service elite finally won out completely over the military. On the death of Emperor Hsüan-te (r. 1425–35) a child came to the throne under the guardianship of an empress regent who listened only to her civil advisers. Within a few years the armies in the capital had been placed under the authority of the civilian minister of war, and those in the provinces under the civilian governors, while the military colonies had been brought under the jurisdiction of troop-purification intendants drawn from the civil service. Throughout the mature Ming period, which lasted the rest of the dynasty, the attitudes previously described as typical of Confucianism prevailed. Wars of conquest were eschewed, and foreign trade was sharply restricted in volume and confined within the tributary system. A civil service career became the most significant route to wealth and social status, passing the examinations became the best route to a successful civil service career, and an intensely Confucian education became the only way to pass the civil service examinations. Bureaucratic criteria prevailed in the civil service, with heredity playing only a vestigial role. Although nobles and military officers retained their high hereditary status, they either became social parasites or, at best, performed purely instrumental functions under overall commanders who were civil officials. And although the succeeding Ch'ing dynasty (1644–1912) revamped the military system, its rulers did not significantly alter the position either of the civil service in the Chinese state or of the Confucian literati in Chinese society.

In interpreting the early Ming period, two sets of questions naturally come to mind. First, from the immediate perspective of the late fourteenth and early fifteenth centuries in China, one must ask how the rebellions of the 1350's, during which the issue of Chinese versus barbarian had been clearly articulated in both the political and cultural spheres, gave rise to an empire in which attitudes and institutions peculiar to the vanquished non-Chinese rival prevailed over the Confucian tradition. Given that, one must further ask how this situation was reversed, and what factors in early Ming history permitted the triumph of the Confucian world view in the early fifteenth century. Second, from the perspective of the long-range evolution of Chinese society, the question to be asked is whether the structure of the gentry society of the mature Ming and Ch'ing periods is to be attributed primarily to long-term social and economic trends or to significant influences in the political history of the early Ming period immediately preceding. This book argues that the special conditions prevailing in the early Ming period gave the emperors an unusual range of choice in their decisions, that both the creation and the displacement of the distinctive early Ming mix of institutions and elites were to a great extent the consequences of imperial decisions made largely for political and military reasons, and that therefore the choices made in early Ming had the effect of closing off certain options and thereby deflecting China's subsequent social and economic development onto the path actually followed.

If subsequent developments were the consequences (not always intended) of politico-military decisions, then the actual decision-makers become unusually important. Although the gentry-based civil service elite later became dominant, early in the Ming period it was balanced by an interlocked hereditary elite of nobles and military officers, and the ideological monopoly of Confucianism was challenged by heterodox values. As the steadying factor in this conflict of elites and ideologies, the emperors had more policy options than Confucian political theory thought normal or proper, and all of them—though especially Hung-wu and Yung-lo—left an individual mark on the development of the Ming state.

Hung-wu and his son Yung-lo both ascended the throne as a result of hard-won military victory. As rulers they were very different. Hung-wu retired from active military command after 1364 and devoted himself to governing. His iron will shaped the early Ming state and was largely responsible for its administrative successes, but as he grew older his growing distrust of all his subordinates led him to adopt measures that seriously disorganized both the military and the civil elites. Yung-lo in contrast was an out-and-out militarist. Once satisfied that the geographical and institutional bases of his rule were secure and that his foreign policy preferences were being carried out, he was perfectly willing to leave all internal administration to the civil service while he went off on campaign. The unintended result of this practice was the growth in power of the civil service at the expense of the military elite.

Hung-wu's grandson and successor, Emperor Chien-wen (r. 1398–1402), and Yung-lo's son and successor, Emperor Hung-hsi (r. 1424–25), both represent the third generation of the Ming imperial family, and both were products of Confucian training who came to the throne committed to the reversal of their predecessors' policies. In this they had the full support of the civil service. Chien-wen provoked a civil war that led to his own death. Hung-hsi, though more successful, died before he could achieve his major objectives. His son, Emperor Hsüan-te, the last emperor of the early Ming period, tried to maintain an equitable balance between the military and civil elites while he lived, but the unforeseen result of his policies was to position the leadership of the civil service advantageously for their takeover of the state, which followed soon after his untimely death.

The following chapters will treat early Ming history in detail, emphasizing those matters, chiefly political and military, that came to the attention of the emperors and therefore led to imperial decisions. Since the main tension in the early Ming was that between the Yüan inheritance and the Confucian tradition, it is natural that these principal areas of concern correspond closely to the five areas of continuity with the Yüan and conflict with the Confucian tradition (see pp. 2–4). They may also be grouped under five headings:

Warfare. Victory on the battlefield determined that Hung-wu would replace the Yüan dynasty, and military victory similarly brought Yung-lo to the throne. For both emperors, winning power through warfare was a necessary precondition to exercising power in a distinctive manner. Success and failure in the lesser wars of the period also were important in determining what direction Ming policy would take. Thus although the successful conquest of Yünnan was an argument for invading Vietnam, the ultimate disaster in Vietnam gave the civil service a weapon in its battle with the military elite. The importance of military results thus requires an understanding of the military background against which decisions affecting other areas were made.

Geographical basis of power. The early Ming emperors were aware that their power ultimately rested on the secure control of territories capable of fielding armies of sufficient strength. The key to the rise of the Ming was the conquest of the population resources of the central Yangtze region in 1363–65, and Yung-lo was constantly aware that the basis of his personal power lay in the region around Peking. The emperors attempted to construct a military-geographic system in which the troops in the capital under direct imperial control were stronger than any likely combination of regional forces, but in which adequate provision was still made for the security of the provinces and frontiers. Decisions stemming from this concern were made exclusively on politico-military grounds, but some of them, such as the ultimate decision to move the capital to Peking, had profound social and economic consequences.

Military institutions. Hung-wu, after securing his territorial base through victory in battle, proceeded in 1364 to reorganize his military forces, and Ming military institutions thus attained a high level of development at a time when civil administration was still at a rudimentary stage. The emperors responded to the challenges posed by peace, or changes in the geographical balance or type of military operation called for, by restructuring the military system. Thus, despite the prominence of military men in the early Ming, military organization itself was not stable, and analysis of military organizational change illuminates both the conflicts within the early Ming regime and the causes of the displacement of the military elite by the civil service at the end of the period.

Foreign affairs. This area has been of more concern to modern scholars than it was to Chinese of the Ming period. Nevertheless, an account of foreign relations in the early Ming provides added confirmation of the degree to which security considerations dominated the Ming emperors and of the way in which the military could be used to execute policies disapproved by the civil service. Also, it was in foreign affairs that the emerging eunuch establishment scored its first major success.

Civil service and government administration. Most Western works on the Ming are oriented to the mature Ming period and naturally emphasize the dominant role played by the civil service and the degree gentry within the mature Ming state and society, respectively. This dominance did not exist during the early Ming, and the analysis of civil government in that period has two major objectives. The first is to describe the principal administrative achievements of the early Ming and to show that where these were innovative they were often achieved against civil service opposition, as a result of imperial insistence and of their execution through military or eunuch agencies. The second is to show the growth in influence of the civil service from Hung-wu's original distrustful and instrumental conception to his reluctant revival of the examination system, the emergence of a small clique of senior officials under Yung-lo, and the seizure of full power by this clique in 1435.

These concerns are listed above in their order of priority as the early Ming emperors saw them. The survival of the regime depended on military victory, which thus became a necessary precondition to everything else; three of the five emperors in the period (Hung-wu, Chien-wen, and Yung-lo) had to confront this fact directly in the course of their lives. Firm control of sufficient territory came next in priority, with military organization following. Foreign affairs were viewed as an aspect of the general security problem. Civil administration, later the core of the Ming system, came last, and even then it had as its primary task the provision of financial and logistic support for military operations. The early Ming emperors paid lip service (sincerely, in the cases of Chien-wen and Hung-hsi) to the rites and music so beloved of Confucian officials, but they ruled in practice as the leaders of a powerful military system. After 1435 their armies ceased to be effective and the emperors themselves no longer took the initiative in determining state policy. The special characteristics of the early Ming period therefore ceased to exist.

TWO

The Rise of the Ming Empire, 1352–1368

Between 1352 and 1368 the Ming grew from a small rebel band to a new Chinese empire as a result of military victories against rival regimes of similar composition. In this period foreign relations meant diplomatic contacts with other regimes in China, and civil administration meant the logistics of feeding the armies; both served the cause of military victory, which alone could ensure the survival of the regime or permit territorial expansion or army reorganization. In this respect the Ming regime did not differ significantly from its rivals; distinctive characteristics could manifest themselves only after victory in the field.

The Yüan empire in the fourteenth century was undergoing the strains attendant upon its transformation from a province of the Mongolian world empire to a conquest dynasty of traditional Chinese type, while the Chinese peasants were expressing their alienation from Yüan rule by turning to apocalyptic varieties of Buddhism. Drought and famine in the 1340's led to peasant rebellions in the 1350's, which were attacked and nearly suppressed by the Yüan chancellor, Toghtō, a leader in the previous struggle to sinicize the Yüan regime. In 1354 court politics led to the dismissal of Toghtō; his armies disintegrated, and in the end the dynasty failed to create an alternative basis of support.

The fall of Toghtō permitted the rebellions to flourish once again, and by 1360 a precarious balance of power existed in China among several military regimes, some avowedly rebellious and others professedly loyal to the Yüan. Socially and politically, however, the various regimes were similar. Each was controlled by an army of recently enlisted troops enrolled in units led by men they knew and trusted and to whom they were personally loyal. The ruler of each regime had fought his way up from the leadership of such a band, and his relationship to his other military commanders was to some extent that of a first among equals; if he was defeated, his commanders might take their men to a more successful leader. The Ming victories of 1360 and 1363 destroyed this balance. Holding off their enemies in the east, the Ming crushed their rivals in the west. The territory annexed permitted the Ming to raise armies overwhelmingly superior to those of any potential rival. The prestige gained permitted the Ming ruler to rationalize the organization of his armies and bring them more tightly under his control. By 1364 the Ming state was the strongest regional power in China.

In the next four years the Ming conquered the Yangtze delta, and then in 1367 Ming armies drove the Mongols from North China while Ming fleets conquered the South China coast. In 1368 Chu Yüan-chang proclaimed himself emperor at Nanking. The new Ming empire was victorious on the battlefield; its armies were solidly based on the lower Yangtze region and were now tightly under the emperor's control. However, it still had to win recognition among foreign nations, and its civil administration was very rudimentary.

Peasant Rebellion and the Collapse of Yüan Authority

The Yüan dynasty in China in the mid-fourteenth century underwent a crisis contemporary with those in the other Mongol empires in Iran and Russia. Although they differed in detail, these crises shared the common feature of conflict between traditional Mongol culture as embodied in the laws and precepts of Chinggis Qan (r. 1206–27) and the attraction of the indigenous cultures of the conquered lands. This conflict intensified the divisions in the

Mongol ruling elite, already built into the Mongol political system by the lack of a fixed rule of succession among the descendants of Chinggis Qan. However, the crises had different outcomes in the three empires. In Iran the dynasty of the Ilqans collapsed, and the Mongol presence virtually disappeared. In Russia the unity of the Golden Horde was disrupted, although its successors remained individually strong until the mid-sixteenth century. In China the mid-century crisis resulted in rebellions that expelled the Mongols from the country.[1]

The Yüan dynasty had been established by outright military conquest, with very little appeal to the legitimizing modes characteristic of Chinese politics, and Chinese reaction to it had not been unanimously favorable. The campaigns of Chinggis Qan and his successors down to the 1250's were murderous to a degree that even recent history can scarcely equal. Qubilai (r. 1260–94), under whom Yüan institutions took their final form, refrained from massacring the population in the areas he conquered; South China thus escaped the destruction visited earlier upon North China and upon Transoxiana and Khurasan, whose once-flourishing urban cultures never fully recovered from the Mongol invasions. Unified under his rule, China had to support his grandiose military failures in Vietnam, Java, Japan, and Central Asia. Modern historians tend to celebrate the intercultural intercourse that the Mongol empire briefly achieved, a condition that contemporaries in China often saw mainly as an opportunity for Central Asian carpetbaggers such as the famous Ahmad to enrich themselves while enriching the government, both at the expense of Chinese society.[2]

Chinese responses to Mongol rule varied. Surrendered military units were absorbed into the hereditary and decimally organized Mongol military system. Clerks and others whose literacy was not entirely within the Confucian great tradition could receive appointments as officials. The spiritually eclectic Mongol emperors particularly favored Buddhist monks and Taoist priests, many of whom responded positively to Mongol culture as well as Mongol rule, learning the Mongol script and language and adopting Mongol names and dress. The traditional Confucian literati, in contrast, were not favored by the Mongol emperors, since they could offer neither unquestioning obedience nor exotic religious doctrines. Their response to Mongol rule was often to withdraw from political participation.[3] For the peasantry, religion and banditry, both organized around the secret societies, remained the principal escapes from an oppressive regime, and the beliefs current by the mid-fourteenth century offered both political hope and millennial fervor—the first in the form of a movement to restore the native Sung dynasty conquered by the Mongols and the second in the form of the belief that Maitreya Buddha would soon descend to reign on earth.[4]

After the death of Qubilai's grandson Temür (r. 1294–1307), the Yüan empire, in the manner of the other Mongol empires, attempted to accommodate itself to the native orthodox tradition, which implied government more in accord with Confucian prescriptions. Candidates representing the Mongol empire in China—as opposed to those representing the steppe tradition— won out in the struggle for the throne, Confucianism became the accepted vocabulary for political struggles at court, and the civil service examination system was reinstituted. The Yüan empire seemed to be going down the road followed earlier by the Northern Wei (386–534) and later by the Ch'ing that led successively from rule by barbarians who dominated through military conquest to rule by a combination of barbarian and Chinese elements that complemented each other—and then to rule by a sinicized barbarian ruling house presiding over an elite that was largely Chinese in outlook. The famines of the 1340's and the rebellions of the 1350's interrupted this process in midcourse.[5]

The crisis of 1351 that provided the proximate cause of the collapse of Yüan power in the Yangtze area was an amalgam of rivalries within the Yüan ruling group and religious sedition among the peasantry, a mixture that was in turn ignited by natural disasters. In 1344 the Yellow River had flooded, and the resulting silt had wrecked both the Grand Canal and the irrigation system in the Huai area. Droughts in succeeding years had aggravated peasant distress and disaffection with Yüan rule. The silting up of the Grand Canal meant that the capital was dependent on sea transport to bring the grain tribute rice from the Yangtze delta area. Usually more expensive and less favored than the canal, the sea routes had suffered from another problem since 1348, the depredations of the well-organized pirate fleet of Fang Kuo-chen. Fang and his broth-

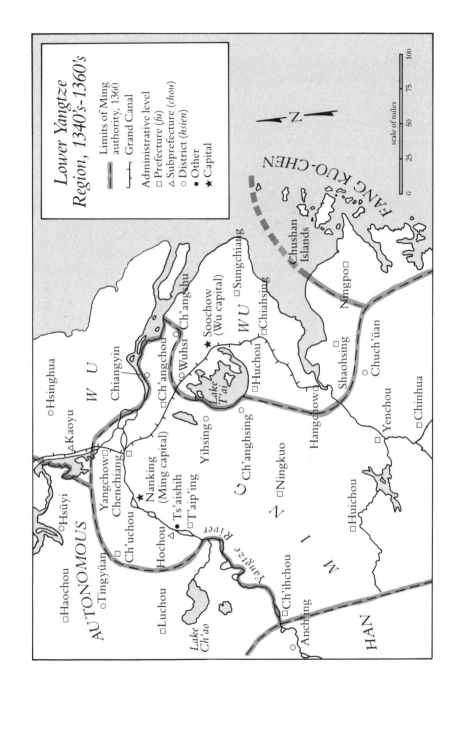

Lower Yangtze
Region, 1340's-1360's

Limits of Ming
authority, 1360
Grand Canal
Administrative level
□ Prefecture (fu)
△ Subprefecture (chou)
○ District (hsien)
● Other
★ Capital

scale of miles
0   25   50   75   100

N

FANG KUO-CHEN

Chushan
Islands

Ningpo

□Sungchiang
W U
□Chiahsing
○Chuch'üan
□Shaohsing
□Huichou
□Yenchou
□Chinhua

★ Soochow
(Wu capital)

□Huchou
Hangchow

○Hsinghua
△Kaoyu
W U
Chiangyin

□Ch'angchou
○Wuhsi □Ch'angshu

Lake
T'ai

Yihsing○
○Ch'anghsing

□Ningkuo

□Hüichou

□Haochou
○Hsüyi
AUTONOMOUS
○Hsüi
○Tingyüan
Yangchow□
Chenchiang
□Ch'uchou
△Hochou

Nanking
(Ming capital)
★
●Ts'aishih
□T'aip'ing
Yihsing○

C H I N

□Luchou

Lake
Ch'ao

Yangtze River

□Ch'ihchou

○Anching
H A N

ers had originally been certified seagoing salt merchants who did some unlicenced salt trading on the side. Denounced to the authorities for this, they murdered their accusers and went to sea, basing themselves on the Chusan Islands off the Chekiang coast and defeating all the government naval expeditions sent against them. Their fleet grew to over a thousand vessels.[6]

Since the government could not destroy Fang Kuo-chen's fleet, restoring the Grand Canal was the only way to ensure the supply of grain to the capital. However, the labor for this had to come from the Huai River area (northern Anhwei and northern Kiangsu), whose peasantry, already affected by food shortages resulting from the drought, were much under the influence of anti-Yüan secret societies. Chief among these was the White Lotus Society, whose origins go back to the fifth-century diffusion of Pure Land doctrines and Amida worship among the peasantry. However, by the fourteenth century the nature of White Lotus doctrines had altered significantly, from political passivity to political activism. Instead of invoking Amida in the hope of being reborn in his Pure Land after death, they prayed that Maitreya, the Buddha of the Future, might descend to earth in their own lifetimes to establish a "pure land" in which his worshipers might rule. In practical terms, this change in doctrine provided a religious justification for rebellion.[7]

Two other doctrines were associated with Maitreya worship in White Lotus propaganda. One of these was Manichaeism, which had spread to China via the Central Asian silk route during the T'ang dynasty and was now represented in many cities of the North China plain. Its eschatology of a universal conflict between the forces of light and darkness led to the portrayal of Maitreya as the "Prince of Light" (Ming Wang) whose victory would end the conflict. The second doctrine was secular in its goal, the restoration of the Sung dynasty. Han Shan-t'ung of Pochou, the leading White Lotus propagandist in northern Anhwei, advertised himself to his followers as a descendant of the artist-emperor Sung Hui-tsung (r. 1100–25), whose capture by the Jurchen invaders had ended the Northern Sung dynasty (960–1126). Han Shan-t'ung and his disciple Liu Fu-t'ung formed secret societies whose members took ritual names and swore blood brotherhood. "They sacrificed a white horse and a black ox and swore an oath to

Heaven and earth, and planned to raise armies with a red turban as their insignia." The monk P'eng Ying-yü raised similar secret societies in the land along the Yangtze River as far west as Hupei. By 1351 a network of secret societies covered the Yangtze valley from the gorges to the sea. Even though, as events were to prove, no one leader could control them, they were in communication with one another and could plan risings in concert.[8]

The Yüan government in 1351 was dominated by the chancellor of the right, Toghtō of the Merkid tribe. In the conflict between the Confucian and steppe traditions that had shaped Yüan politics since 1307, Toghtō represented the Confucian tradition; in the internal Confucian conflict between reformist and conservative wings, Toghtō represented reform, meaning the increase of the state's wealth and power and the alleviation of popular distress through positive governmental action. Toghtō's status as an exemplar of Confucian virtues had been sealed by his retirement from the chancellorship in 1344, a step he took in order to avoid partisan wrangling. In August 1349 he returned to the chancellorship as a result of the personal intervention of Emperor Toghon Temür (r. 1333–70), who desired to end the policy of drift that had been followed by the central government in the face of mounting natural disaster. Toghtō's return to power came a year after Fang Kuo-chen's rebellion, and his attempts to suppress Fang by military action were failures. Toghtō's main concern, however, was the repair of the Yellow River dikes and the Grand Canal. The idea, especially the scope of the project as proposed by Toghtō, aroused conservative opposition, and he was not able to overcome this opposition and announce the project until April 1351. Some 20,000 troops from the Huai area, and 150,000 commoners from nearby villages who provided their own rations, worked on the dike and canal project until its completion in December. The project was technically successful, rerouting the Yellow River to flow into the sea north of the Shantung peninsula.[9]

The original flooding of the Yellow River had created swarms of refugees. Many fled in the direction of the Yangtze, where they swelled the ranks of the White Lotus movement there. The impressment of such a large group of discontented peasants for the construction project risked popular disorders, as Toghtō's critics at court pointed out. Unluckily for the Yüan, the construction sites were near the center of the White Lotus agitation, and by the end of the year rebellions had broken out throughout the Yangtze valley. The received tradition has it that White Lotus adherents spread the superstition that the appearance of a one-eyed man would foretell the end of the empire, and that they buried a statue of a one-eyed man where the construction gangs were sure to dig it up. This may be apocryphal. What in fact triggered the Red Turban rebellion was the arrest and execution of Han Shan-t'ung in the summer of 1351. Liu Fu-t'ung escaped with Han's young son and heir, Han Lin-erh, and the White Lotus societies rose in rebellion. That autumn the societies organized in Hupei by P'eng Ying-yü also rebelled and proclaimed as emperor Hsü Shou-hui, a former cloth merchant whom P'eng had chosen because of his auspicious appearance. The rebel movement in Hupei called itself the T'ien-wan empire and made its capital first in the town of Ch'ishui, north of the Yangtze in eastern Hupei. In Anhwei Liu Fu-t'ung became separated from Han Lin-erh and did not get him back under his control until 1355. Up to that time, although the rebellion had an imperial cause, it had no emperor.[10]

The rebel armies wore red turbans and burned incense in their religious rites, so they were called "Red Armies" or "Incense Armies." At first they were invincible. In 1352 the T'ien-wan armies went west, took Hanyang and Wuch'ang, and then went further up the Yangtze. Another T'ien-wan column took Chiuchiang on the Yangtze and then went on to capture most of Kiangsi, with the significant exception of the provincial capital at Nanch'ang. Liu Fu-t'ung's rebellion began at Yingchou, and in 1352 his armies captured the cities of southern Honan. Meanwhile, rebels under P'eng Ta and Chao Chün-yung rose at P'ei and eventually captured the strategic city of Hsüchou, thus cutting the Grand Canal. By the end of 1352 most of the area originally affected by White Lotus organizing activity was in rebellion. Even though the dynasty retained control of Nanch'ang, Nanking, and Soochow—the greatest cities—government forces failed to hold the smaller cities and therefore failed to hold the countryside.

This degree of rebel success was not entirely due to the decadence of the official armed forces. Although the underlying cause of the rebellions was the effect of White Lotus propaganda on a peasant population afflicted and to some extent displaced by natural disasters, their success at this stage was largely due to the deliberate neglect of city fortifications by the Yüan authorities since the Mongol conquest. Originally a purely cavalry force, the Mongols had been hampered by city fortifications more than by any other military factor, and so they regarded the walled cities as an impediment to their ability to control the country. Sections of walls breached in siege operations during the conquest had been left unrepaired, and city walls in general were allowed to deteriorate during Yüan rule. This policy backfired in and after 1351. Repair of city walls is mentioned frequently in the chronicles of subsequent years, but the cities thus refortified served as power bases of rebel secessionist regimes rather than as bastions of the dynasty.[11]

The flames of the White Lotus rebellion spread through the Yangtze valley and in so doing ignited two other varieties of militarization: disaffected local elements not affiliated with the White Lotus took the opportunity to rebel on their own, and elements that favored the status quo and were threatened by the rebellion raised militia forces to defend their immediate areas. Viewed formally, the first response indicated rebellion and the second loyalty; viewed functionally, both responses resulted in the transfer of military power to regional groups and thus hindered the reimposition of dynastic authority. Chang Shih-ch'eng at Kaoyu is the outstanding example of the first response, and Kuo Tzu-hsing at Haochou, of the second.[12]

Chang Shih-ch'eng's family, like Fang Kuo-chen's, was engaged in both legal and illegal salt trading, though on a smaller scale than the Fangs, and in the Grand Canal region of central Kiangsu rather than in coastal Chekiang. In 1353 certain unidentified "rich families" refused to pay for the (presumably illegal) salt that he had delivered to them, so Chang and his brothers raised a band from among the salt workers and burned down their houses. This was the signal for a general rebellion among the salt population led by Chang and his brothers, who seized T'aichou, Hsinghua, and Kaoyu on the Grand Canal. Spurning the Yüan offer of an official title in return for his surrender, Chang Shih-ch'eng proclaimed himself "Prince Ch'eng of the Great Chou dynasty."[13]

For the second time grain shipments to the capital had been

interrupted by a rebellious salt smuggler. The repair of the Yellow River dikes and the reopening of the Grand Canal had been undertaken in order to circumvent Fang Kuo-chen's control of the high seas, but unless Chang Shih-ch'eng could be dislodged from Kaoyu so that the grain barges could get through, all of this effort would have been in vain.

After their initial setbacks in 1351–52, the Yüan armies had rallied and put the rebels on the defensive. In 1353 Hangchow and the cities of Kiangsi were recaptured from the rebels, and the Yüan armies then went on to take the T'ien-wan capital at Ch'ishui and to recover Wuch'ang and Hanyang. Hsü Shou-hui and the T'ien-wan leadership were reduced to wandering in the mountains of southeastern Hupei for over a year. The Red Turbans of central and northern Anhwei lost ground to Yüan counterattacks and were driven back on their capital city at Pochou. Since recovery of the Grand Canal was the major objective of the Yüan government, Chancellor Toghtō dealt with it personally. Late in 1352 he retook Hsüchou in a lightning campaign, after which only Chang Shih-ch'eng stood between his army and the grain resources of the Soochow area, as yet untouched by rebellion. Still Toghtō continued his careful preparations, spending most of 1353 restoring routine administration in central Kiangsu and readying his army for the Kaoyu operation. Late in 1354 he finally moved, and within a matter of weeks he had Kaoyu completely surrounded and on the point of surrender.[14]

In the spring of 1352 Kuo Tzu-hsing, Sun Te-yai, and three other leaders raised armed bands and seized control of the city of Haochou in north-central Anhwei. Very soon afterwards, on 18 April, an itinerant monk named Chu Yüan-chang came to the city and joined Kuo Tzu-hsing's contingent. By the end of the year P'eng Ta and Chao Chün-yung, in flight from the Yüan reconquest of Hsüchou in October, came to Haochou with the remnants of their forces. The arrival of the newcomers released latent tensions. The original five leaders had styled themselves "commanders" (*yüan-shuai*) and ruled jointly, and their raising of troops had been not so much an act of rebellion as a spontaneous military response to the disorder of the times. Kuo was the son of a fortuneteller who had prospered after moving to Haochou; he had himself been apprenticed to a cattle butcher, and he enjoyed drinking cheap wine in the company of soliders. He was hardly a model of refinement, but his four colleagues are described as out-and-out ruffians who resented his attempts to restrain their looting and lawless behavior. Despite all this, the militia forces they raised were recruited from among what the sources describe as "good people" (*liang-min*), and there is some evidence of gentry support. However, the arrival of P'eng and Chao identified the Haochou movement as rebellious just at the time that the Yüan counteroffensive was developing momentum. P'eng and Chao had fallen out previously, and on their arrival at Haochou P'eng attached himself to Kuo Tzu-hsing, although the other four commanders looked to Chao Chün-yung for leadership. While the rivalries among the leaders escalated, the walls of the city were being repaired to resist a siege.[15]

The situation in Haochou at this time contained elements that were to recur again and again in the Yangtze area during the two decades preceding the establishment of stable Ming rule. Cities that were easily overrun in 1351–52 proved quite capable of resisting assault and withstanding siege later, but they were often ruled by unstable military coalitions, sometimes including troops from outside the area. The resulting instabilities were resolved in two general ways. One leader, a local or an outsider, would eliminate his colleagues and establish a stable one-city regime that might then maintain a precarious independence by carefully playing off the conflicts among the larger powers; or a divided leadership would provide a lever for the capture of the city through treachery, a situation usually exploited by one of the major post-1355 regional leaders.[16]

Chu Yüan-chang (1328–1398) entered the political arena in 1352. His family were peasants, originally from the P'ei area in northern Kiangsu, the birthplace of the founder of the Han dynasty. The family had moved several times, and under Chu's father they settled as tenant farmers in Haochou. Chu was the youngest of four sons. The story of the crimson glow that attended his birth need not be taken literally. From his maternal grandfather he heard stories as a child about the struggle of the Southern Sung against the Mongol conquerors, but he imbibed no particular hatred for the Mongols. Still very young, he was promised by his father to the local Buddhist monastery, the Huang-chüeh-szu. He grew to be tall and ugly in a way that fascinated and frightened his contemporaries; the standard unofficial portrait of him shows beady eyes looking out over a bulbous, protruding nose mated to a jutting chin. After he became powerful he reportedly punished those who punned on his surname with the other word *chu* ("pig"). Like most other martial founding emperors, he is recorded as having played the usual warlike games with other boys of his village, some of whom later became his leading generals.[17]

The shift of the Yellow River in 1344 brought the Haochou area not floods but drought, which combined with a plague of locusts to produce a famine of unprecedented proportions. Chu Yüan-chang watched his family—parents, uncles, cousins—all die of starvation. Owning no land himself, he had to borrow land from a neighbor to bury them. He then entered the Huang-chüeh-szu as a novice, as a servant in effect, but at least he was fed. Eventually the Huang-chüeh-szu itself ran out of grain, and Chu had to take begging bowl in hand and wander for the next three years. Where he traveled is known—northwestern Anhwei and southern Honan—but what he did there is not. These travels have led some of his biographers to suspect Manichaean influence, just as his Buddhist career leads one to suspect White Lotus connections, but there is no real proof of either. When conditions improved in Haochou, he returned to the Huang-chüeh-szu, where he remained for three more years. During his life as a monk he acquired some education and literacy, enough for him to read administrative documents and compose works of his own in a distinctive and vigorous, if unrefined, style. As was true of his most trusted supporters as well, his education lay outside the Confucian great tradition, and in his later life he frequently displayed suspicion, contempt, and hatred towards representatives of that tradition.[18]

Chu was thrown into prison when he first offered his services to Kuo Tzu-hsing, but when Kuo finally saw him he was impressed by Chu's strange physiognomy. He released Chu, appointed him to his guard, and gave him his adopted daughter to be his wife. This was the future Empress Ma (d. 1382). Chu soon recruited twenty-four men from his native area, and by early 1353 he controlled seven hundred men and was Kuo Tzu-hsing's most trusted henchman. One source gives the names of the twenty-four original followers. Although three of them were killed in action (one in 1360, two in 1362) while already holding responsible positions as city commanders or higher in Chu's growing state, the remaining twenty-one all became either dukes or marquises. This group alone thus accounts for one-third of the sixty-four noble titles granted to living men during the Hung-wu reign.[19]

The small-scale successes of Kuo Tzu-hsing and Chu Yüan-chang are recorded only because of their importance for the career of the future dynastic founder. The process of army formation that they illustrate, however, was typical of all China during these rebellions, and is to some extent analogous to the process of militarization in nineteenth-century China in the wake of the Taiping rebellion. Evidence of similar processes at work in the armies of the other mid-fourteenth century military leaders is less detailed but no less conclusive. Basically, in recruiting a military force a leader would look first to his relatives and then to his friends and neighbors. If he emerged as the leader of a larger force, he would then have as his immediate subordinates several men who had recruited their own bands in the same way. Such was the relationship of Kuo Tzu-hsing to Chu Yüan-chang. Conversely, soldiers entered the ranks as clients of their immediate superiors, whom they looked to for protection and repaid with loyalty, and who in turn were clients of those at the next higher level in the chain of command, the links of which were thus bonds of personal loyalty rather than of institutional authority.

Several consequences flowed from the personal nature of military loyalties. Military command, first of all, tended to become hereditary; when a leader died his followers might accept a son or brother or other close relative as his successor, but not someone from outside. Next, military rank did not confer authority by itself; it merely recognized an already existing command authority grounded on personal factors. Furthermore, as a leader like Chu Yüan-chang grew in power, so did the members of his original warband, each of whom became the patron of his own group of client leaders who had joined later. And with loyalty based on personal factors, a leader's trust in his followers tended to be inversely proportional to their "social distance" from him, kin being the most trusted, members of the original warband next, and the most recently joined least. Finally, leaders relied heavily on fictive kinship ties to strengthen personal loyalties. Chu Yüan-chang established marriage links with his commanders, and he also adopted sons who held military positions. In the way he expanded his own military forces under the patronage of Kuo Tzu-hsing, Chu Yüan-chang in 1353 was typical of the numerous middle-rank military leaders then emerging in the Yangtze valley area.[20] The leaders at Haochou soon began to intrigue against one another. Kuo Tzu-hsing was kidnapped by Chao Chün-yung and Sun Te-yai and held prisoner in the latter's house. This happened while Chu Yüan-chang was away; when he returned he went with Kuo's sons to raid Sun's house and release Kuo, who thus became even more dependent on Chu. Haochou was blockaded by Yüan troops for several months in 1352–53, and during this time its leaders were forced to postpone their internecine rivalry.[21]

Meanwhile Toghtō's counteroffensive was under way. Its main operation was the carefully prepared siege of Kaoyu, which by December 1354 was on the point of falling. But Toghtō was permitting it to starve rather than attempting to take it by storm, and the delay that ensued permitted his enemies at court to impeach him. In January 1355 an imperial decree arrived in the camp of the besieging army at Kaoyu dismissing Toghtō from all his offices. Through his return to power in 1349, Toghtō had elevated Emperor Toghon Temür from passive to active participation in Yüan politics, but in the years immediately following, the initiative had passed more and more to the chancellor. Toghtō already held the highest honorific title of grand preceptor (*t'ai-shih*) and was a hereditary prince; it was impossible to imagine any suitable reward for his anticipated success at Kaoyu, short of the throne itself. In its dismissal of Toghtō the court testified to its belief that the chancellor had become a danger to the state and that his work of suppressing rebellion was essentially complete, but the court was mistaken on the latter point. In fact the dismissal marks the point of no return for the Yüan dynasty in its exercise of power in Chinese politics; within a year China was divided into a number of regional military regimes, none of them under the control of the dynasty.[22]

The Rebels Struggle for Power

The dismissal of Toghtō ended the direct pressure on Chang Shih-ch'eng and lessened the pressure on the rebel movements generally. As Yüan army commanders struggled for regional autonomy within the disintegrating dynastic political system, they had little attention to spare for the suppression of rebels. In 1355 Chang Shih-ch'eng and Chu Yüan-chang both crossed the Yangtze and set up power bases south of the river, and in the same year both of the original rebel "empires" revived: in northern Anhwei Liu Fu-t'ung finally regained possession of Han Lin-erh and in 1355 proclaimed him emperor of a restored Sung dynasty, and in Hupei Ni Wen-chün took Wuch'ang and several other major cities, installing Hsü Shou-hui as emperor at Hanyang in 1356. The common theme of the next five years is the emergence of a small number of regimes that among them divided all the lands of the Yangtze basin, in the process destroying or absorbing the military forces that had supported the Yüan. Events in the Yangtze were only one part of the growth of regionalism throughout China, but the process first went to completion there. By 1360 three principal warlords—Ch'en Yu-liang (Han), Chu Yüan-chang (Ming), and Chang Shih-ch'eng (Wu)—controlled virtually all of the Yangtze basin downstream from the gorges, and no one of them could expand his area of control except at the expense of the others.[23]

As Toghtō's remnant forces fell to pieces before Kaoyu, Chang Shih-ch'eng was able to scatter them. He thereupon decided, following the advice of his younger brother Shih-te, to shift his base to the area of the Grand Canal south of the Yangtze, thereby minimizing the risk of another siege by the Yüan armies of the North China plain. Chang Shih-te led the river crossing from T'ungchou in 1355, and in short order the major cities on the south bank of the Yangtze, including Soochow, fell to him. Chang Shih-ch'eng then made his capital at Soochow, while Chang Shih-te marched south in an unsuccessful attempt to take Hangchow. In 1356–57 Chang Shih-ch'eng's armies suffered successive defeats by Chu Yüan-chang's generals, who wrested from him Chenchiang, Chiangyin, Ch'angchou, and Ch'anghsing to add to the emerging Nanking-based Ming state. Chang Shih-ch'eng was failing in his attempt to build a secure power base around Soochow. He first attempted to surrender nominally to Chu Yüan-chang, offering two hundred thousand *shih* of annual grain tribute in return for being left alone.* Chu rejected this offer, and Chang then recalled Shih-te to command the defense against the Ming. However, Ming forces captured Chang Shih-te, who starved himself to death rather than submit.[24]

Before his death Chang Shih-te succeeded in smuggling a letter to his brother advising him to surrender to the Yüan. At Hangchow the Yüan commander-in-chief, Chancellor Dash Temür (a proliferation of chancellors in provincial governments had been one consequence of Toghtō's fall), hated his principal military commander, the Miao general Yang Öljei, and therefore was willing to plead Chang's case to the Yüan court. The court accepted Chang's surrender, and one of Chang's generals in turn helped Dash Temür to murder Yang Öljei. Yang's Miao troops mostly went over to the Ming, while Chang's troops took over Hangchow and Shaohsing and imprisoned Dash Temür. These events stabilized Chang Shih-ch'eng's territories. He now ruled a compact and densely populated territory south of the Yangtze centered on Soochow and Hangchow, and his authority reached far north of the Yangtze as well, into the wartorn and famine-ravaged lands along the Grand Canal as far as Shantung. These territories, combined, had about 10.3 million people according to the census of 1393. The Yüan court granted Chang the honorific title of grand commandant (*t'ai-wei*) and set his grain tribute quota at 110,000 *shih* annually, which was shipped north regularly by Fang Kuo-chen's fleet until 1363. Chang Shih-te's death had dampened the fighting spirit of the Wu regime, and after Chang Shih-ch'eng came to terms with the Yüan court, he was content to enjoy the pleasures of Soochow without seriously bidding for supreme power. Command of the Wu armies devolved on another brother —Chang Shih-hsin, whom the sources describe as pleasure-loving and incompetent—and three lesser generals. Nevertheless, Wu's population gave it great potential military power, and its professed loyalty to the Yüan dynasty—and therefore to the Confucianism practiced by that dynasty in its late phase—made Wu the haven and hope of the scholar-gentry of South China; whatever Chang Shih-ch'eng's faults, the only militarily plausible alternative was

---

* A shih was a measure of volume equal to approximately 107.4 liters. The word is often transcribed *tan* in this usage.

that represented by the explicitly anti-Confucian Red Turban movements.[25]

While the Wu regime was solidifying around Soochow and Hangchow, in Fukien an illiterate militia soldier, Ch'en Yu-ting, who had once been a landless agricultural laborer, became military commander and administrator (*p'ing-chang cheng-shih*) of the province. Ch'en's rise to power had been the result of victories within the authorized militia system, and he also remitted tax grain to the north by sea on Fang Kuo-chen's fleet, so there was no suggestion of rebellion in his career, but once in power he executed those who opposed his autocratic rule of the province. His career is thus another instance of the regionalism that was tearing Yüan rule to pieces.[26]

With the Grand Canal route lost beyond hope of recovery after Toghtō's dismissal, and with the north also either in rebellion or under the control of regional militarists who retained their tax grain for their own use, the court found itself even more dependent than before on the grain shipped by sea from South China. Even though the amounts shipped were small when compared to the peak years of the dynasty (over 3 million *shih* annually in the 1320's), they nevertheless provided the margin of subsistence in this period of vanishing revenues. This situation enhanced the power of Fang Kuo-chen, who from 1356 on established regular rule over his three coastal prefectures of Ningpo, Wenchou, and T'aichou (aggregate population about 2.5 million in 1393). He placed a brother in command in each city and maintained his supremacy at sea. The Yüan court repeatedly rewarded him with titles, ultimately honoring him as duke of Ch'ü and chancellor of the left. In the last analysis, however, even though Fang maintained his influence on the Chekiang coast for twenty years (1348–68), his position rested on the balance of regional power in China and on conditions along the Grand Canal rather than on his intrinsic strength. Realizing this, many of the scholar-gentry of Chekiang were disgusted by the court's willingness to accommodate him after his frequent rebellions.[27]

The revival of the T'ien-wan movement in the central regions of the Yangtze valley also began shortly after the dismissal of Toghtō. Ni Wen-chün was the main leader of the revived movement, but he continued to recognize Hsü Shou-hui as nominal emperor. During 1355 the major riverine cities of Hupei were recaptured from the Yüan, and Hanyang became the T'ien-wan capital. Between 1355 and 1357 the T'ien-wan leaders brought the rest of Hunan and Hupei under their control. In 1357 Ming Yü-chen led a fleet through the gorges into Szechwan, which he conquered. Although he remained nominally loyal to Hsü Shou-hui, Ming nevertheless established his own personal rule there, founding an independent kingdom that lasted until 1371. The rapid expansion of the T'ien-wan area had made its original group of leaders, headed by Tsou P'u-sheng, envious of Ni Wen-chün's preeminence; in response to their intrigues Ni attempted to seize Hsü, but he failed and had to flee from Hanyang. When he arrived at Huangchou, he was surprised and murdered by his own trusted subordinate, Ch'en Yu-liang.[28]

Ch'en, originally surnamed Hsieh, came from a fishing family in Mienyang and was one of five living brothers. He had acquired marginal literacy, and when he joined the rebels, he was placed on Ni Wen-chün's staff. Gaining Ni's confidence, he rose to the command of troops. He was a brave soldier, but impulsive and headstrong, with a streak of brutality. He now amalgamated Ni's remnant forces with his own, assumed a high title that Hsü Shou-hui ultimately recognized, and transferred his base of operations to Chiuchiang on the Yangtze. For the next two years he concentrated on conquering a personal power base in Kiangsi. From 1357 on the T'ien-wan "empire" was in fact trifurcated, with the warlords Ming Yü-chen and Ch'en Yu-liang building up independent kingdoms in the east and west that were attached only nominally to the core of the movement at Hanyang, where Hsü Shou-hui reigned under the tutelage of Tsou P'u-sheng.[29]

In early 1358 Ch'en Yu-liang captured Anch'ing, and soon afterwards Nanch'ang, the key to central Kiangsi, fell without serious resistance. Ch'en then took the remaining prefectural cities of northern and central Kiangsi and detached a force to invade Fukien (it was Ch'en Yu-ting's successful resistance to this invasion that led to Yu-ting's rise to power there). Ch'en Yu-liang's attempt to invade Chekiang in 1359 was also unsuccessful, but by mid-1359 he was in control of all of Kiangsi except the extreme south, as well as eastern Hupei and the Anch'ing area of Anhwei. Expansion to the east was blocked by the consolidation of the two regimes of Ch'en Yu-ting in Fukien and Chu Yüan-chang at Nanking, and conquests westward would have meant civil war within the T'ien-wan empire. Ch'en might not have balked at conflict in either direction, but as it turned out it was the pressure of external events that directed his attention first to the east and then to the west.[30]

Under their leader Chao P'u-sheng, commonly called "Two-Sword" Chao, the fishing communities of Lake Ch'ao in central Anhwei near the prefectural city of Luchou had risen in the original White Lotus rebellion. When another rebel leader, Tso Chün-pi, captured Luchou, however, his military pressure made Lake Ch'ao untenable for the original group of rebels. Some of them joined Chu Yüan-chang, thus making possible his 1355 crossing of the Yangtze and the events that followed, but most went along with their old leader Chao P'u-sheng, who went upstream to join forces with Ch'en Yu-liang. After capturing Anch'ing in 1357, Ch'en put Chao in command there. In 1358 Chao captured Ch'ihchou from the Ming, and from there attempted to conquer all of Anhwei south of the river. The threat he posed to the Ming was so serious that Chu Yüan-chang sent his strongest general, Hsü Ta, against him. In 1359 Hsü Ta recaptured Ch'ihchou. This clash indicated that the no-man's-land between the regimes of Ch'en and Chu had been used up; the two ambitious warlords now had a common frontier. However, Chu at this time was more concerned with assimilating his conquests in Chekiang and with wresting more of the rich delta region from Chang Shih-ch'eng. Ch'en was more concerned with Anhwei, since he probably knew that some of Chao P'u-sheng's men had gone over to the Ming. In any event, Chao was in control of a major city on the Yangtze, and Ch'en no longer trusted him, possibly (as the sources hint) because of Ming espionage activity. In September 1359 Ch'en took his fleet down to Anch'ing and cut down "Two-Sword" Chao as the latter was boarding his flagship to confer. The Lake Ch'ao men could not resist amalgamation with Ch'en's personal forces, but their loyalty was lost.[31]

After the fall of Nanch'ang, Hsü Shou-hui had wanted to transfer the T'ien-wan capital there, but Ch'en Yu-liang wished to keep Kiangsi as a personal preserve and was evasive. Later in 1359, however, Hsü Shou-hui abruptly left Hanyang with his guards and retinue and went downstream. How and why he did this remain unknown; presumably he was maneuvering once again for some degree of independence from the Hanyang generals. Ch'en met him at Chiuchiang and separated Hsü from his guards, whom he slew. Placing him under close confinement, Ch'en proclaimed himself prince of Han. The T'ien-wan leadership in Hupei-Hunan was thus divided, and Ch'en's forces were the strongest united army, so he was able to get his authority accepted in Hupei-Hunan as well, though Ming Yü-chen in Szechwan refused to acknowledge it. These additions meant that by the end of 1359 Ch'en controlled areas whose total population in 1393 was over fourteen million; his Han state was thus potentially stronger than either Ming or Wu. However, Ch'en was a later entrant in the power struggle, and many of the city warlords who acknowledged his authority did so merely for fear of his army and lacked positive grounds for loyalty. He needed a continuing sequence of victories merely to maintain his prestige within his dominions.[32]

The main body of Red Turban rebels revived in northern Anhwei after the dismissal of Toghtō. In 1355 Liu Fu-t'ung proclaimed Han Lin-erh emperor of a restored Sung dynasty at Pochou. Between 1355 and 1357 Liu had to fight both to maintain his position within the Sung regime and to defend Pochou against Yüan attack, one result of these struggles being the transfer of the Sung capital south to Anfeng. Since by 1357 the Yüan regular armies had collapsed on the North China plain and the militia forces that were to defend the Yüan in the 1360's were still very weak, this interlude permitted the Red Turbans to engage in spectacular campaigns in North China. While the main army under Liu Fu-t'ung laid siege to the former capital of the historical Sung dynasty at Kaifeng, another Red Turban army under Mao Kuei conquered most of Shantung. Shansi and Shensi were also invaded. Kaifeng fell in mid-1358, and Han Lin-erh reigned for a year from the actual capital of the Sung. The most striking campaign was conducted by the army that invaded Shansi and Hopei in succession, went north of the Yüan capital to destroy the summer palaces at Shangtu, and then invaded Manchuria, marching as far as the Korean border.[33]

At this point the official *Ming History* (1739) pauses in its narrative to describe the Red Turbans at the height of their power:

Until now peace had lasted for so long that the departments and prefectures were all without military commandants, and when the civil officials heard that the bandits were coming, they at once abandoned their offices and fled. Hence no matter where [the Red Turbans] went, there was no [city] they could not overthrow. When Han Lin-erh first rose in rebellion, the bandits were without any long-range goal but simply followed the orders of Liu Fu-t'ung. [Han Lin-erh] was forced by his followers to accept an empty title. The generals holding commands in the field led without any regard for discipline, and burned and plundered wherever they passed, to the point of chewing up the old and feeble like grain. Moreover, all of Liu Fu-t'ung's old comrades were so wild that not even Liu Fu-t'ung could control them. Though his troops became numerous, his orders were not carried out. Often he would capture a city, but the Yüan commanders following behind would afterwards recapture it. He could not hold the lands he conquered.

Despite the superficially impressive scale of their conquests, the Red Turbans had not created a military machine with enough cohesion to turn these conquests into permanent occupation based on the walled cities. Needless to say, they could not attract scholar-gentry to their cause or establish regular civil administration while they continued to operate as roving bandits. Red Turban operations in North China after 1355 thus contrast sharply with the careful consolidation of regional power—based on military discipline, repair of city walls, and maintenance of internal peace and order—that characterized the regimes of Chu Yüan-chang, Chang Shih-ch'eng, the lesser regionalists, and apparently even Ch'en Yu-liang during this period.[34]

In 1359 the Red Turban position on the North China plain collapsed. The immediate cause of this was the creation of a strong militia army by Chaghan Temür, a Honan chü-jen of Naiman Turkish ancestry who had begun to raise militia forces soon after the original Red Turbans rebelled. Between 1356 and 1358 Chaghan Temür and his boyhood friend and associate Li Szu-ch'i were able to regain their regional power after the Red Turban onslaught by a series of military victories in Shensi. By 1359 Chaghan was strong enough to move his armies eastward onto the North China plain. He defeated Liu Fu-t'ung and laid siege to Kaifeng in the summer. After resisting for over three months, Liu Fu-t'ung escaped and fled to Anfeng once again, taking along Han

Lin-erh and a few hundred soldiers. Kaifeng itself, and the palaces and harems of the rebel leaders, fell to Chaghan Temür, and Kaifeng became his base of operations for the reduction of the rebel holdings in Shantung. The Red Turban Sung empire nevertheless lingered on at Anfeng until 1363; its historical function had been to dominate the North China plain and to hold the attention of the Yüan government for four crucial years during which the Yangtze regional powers grew to maturity.[35]

The last of the Yangtze regional regimes to develop was that of Chu Yüan-chang (here called Ming in anticipation of the name adopted in 1368). When the Yüan siege of Haochou was lifted after the winter of 1352–53, the previously existing tensions in the Haochou leadership reasserted themselves. P'eng Ta died, and the high command devolved on Chao Chün-yung, who took Kuo Tzu-hsing and his men with him and marched down the Huai to attack Hsüyi, presumably with the ultimate objective of recovering his former base at Hsüchou. To break up Kuo Tzu-hsing's following within the army, Chao sent Chu Yüan-chang south to conquer Ch'uchou. Chu took Tingyüan and then Ch'uchou, victories that added over twenty thousand men to his forces.[36] Chao had planned to murder Kuo while Chu was away. When Chu found out about this he got word to Kuo, who extricated his ten thousand men from Chao's control and came to join Chu at Ch'uchou. Chao lost out in the fighting in the north and is not heard from again.

Relations at Ch'uchou were naturally strained, since Chu Yüan-chang now had a larger army than Kuo Tzu-hsing, his former patron. Chu at this stage wished to move further south and take Hochou on the Yangtze. Kuo approved this plan early in 1355 but sent one of his own officers to carry it out. Chu then took over Hochou from Kuo's men in a coup carried out by Chu's childhood friend T'ang Ho and held the city for three months against a siege by Yüan troops. When Chu admitted to the city Sun Te-yai, Kuo's chief rival in the original Haochou leadership, the two leaders moved to the brink of outright conflict.[37]

At this juncture Kuo Tzu-hsing died. The Sung court at Pochou appointed his son to succeed to the chief command, with Chu Yüan-chang and the general who had first taken Hochou as his deputies. The sources tactfully leave some of the events of the next year unclear and represent Chu Yüan-chang as being in command from the death of Kuo Tzu-hsing on. Chu in fact probably was responsible for the decisions to cross the river and take Nanking; at least, whatever the political niceties, most of the troops were his. In the course of these operations, Chu allowed Kuo's heir and his fellow deputy commander both to be killed in battle, and later he executed Kuo's remaining son on a charge of violating military discipline. By the time of his triumphal entry into Nanking in 1356, Chu had thus disposed of Kuo's family and had seized control of his movement.[38]

Chu Yüan-chang wished to transfer his army from the north to the south bank of the Yangtze so as to have a free hand in a region still virtually untouched by war and rebellion, and the Lake Ch'ao fleet wished to escape from the attentions of the warlord Tso Chün-pi of Luchou. The situation thus favored an alliance. In July 1355 Yü T'ung-hai of the Lake Ch'ao fleet came to Hochou, and Chu Yüan-chang in his turn then went in person to the fleet headquarters. These visits established trust between Chu and the faction in the fleet that was led by the Yü and Liao families (leaders of this faction would be second only to Chu's original band in the later distribution of noble titles and military authority). Soon afterwards the fleet left the lake. Chao P'u-sheng led most of them upstream, ultimately to join Ch'en Yu-liang, but the rest came to join Chu Yüan-chang at Hochou. On 10 July 1355 Chu's newly augmented forces left Hochou. The next day they crossed the Yangtze and captured Ts'aishih; then, turning south, they took the prefectural city of T'aip'ing. The principal Yüan commander in the area, Ch'en Esen, attempted to retake T'aip'ing but was himself captured, whereupon he submitted to Chu. Apparently Chu now saw an opportunity to get rid of Kuo Tzu-hsing's heir and former followers. He sent them off in company with Ch'en Esen to attack Nanking. Ch'en betrayed them at a critical moment in the battle, so they were killed. Ch'en himself was mysteriously murdered afterwards.[39]

Chu spent the rest of 1355 expanding the area under his control. On 27 March 1356 he crushed the Yüan river fleet under Manzi Qaya at Ts'aishih. This victory cleared the way for another attempt to take Nanking. When Chu and his army arrived there, Ch'en Chao-hsien, nephew and heir of Ch'en Esen, surrendered with his thirty-six thousand men. After a day of hard fighting, the Ming soldiers broke into the city on 10 April, and most of the defenders surrendered.[40]

Imperial Nanking had been the seat of six dynasties that had ruled South China between 221 and 589, and of the Southern T'ang regime in the tenth century. Protected as it was by the Yangtze to the north and west, and by the Purple Mountain overlooking the city from the east "like a coiling dragon and a crouching tiger," Nanking had been a mighty fortress in times of adversity; the redoubtable Ts'ao Ts'ao had failed to take it, and its later imperial rulers had frequently issued byzantine defiances to besiegers camped on the other side of the river. Looking backward, historians have judged Chu's prescience in choosing Nanking for his capital to be a major factor in his success; looking backward himself, Chu may have wondered at the empire's never having been unified from the south. Nevertheless, Nanking with its five hundred thousand people was a great prize, and Chu, as its possessor and as the only Red Turban warlord operating south of the Yangtze, had become an important figure in the then impressive-seeming Red Turban empire.[41]

On 28 July 1356 Chu Yüan-chang allowed his subordinates to proclaim him duke of Wu, and he took the offices of the former Yüan Branch Censorate (*hsing yü-shih-t'ai*) for Kiangnan as his ducal palace. As a duke he was in a quasi-monarchical position and could appoint officials and give them seals, but strictly speaking the title did not preclude loyalty to the Red Turban emperor Han Lin-erh, whose calendar he continued to use. The reverence of his soldiers for the religious movement represented by Han Lin-erh made it impossible to renounce this symbolism for many years to come, even though the "Sung" empire fell to pieces in the north and the Red Turban association hindered the acceptance of Ming legitimacy by the politically important scholar-gentry. On the same day Chu created a Branch Secretariat-Chancellery (*hsing chung-shu-sheng*) and a Branch Bureau of Military Affairs (*hsing shu-mi-yüan*), both of which he headed personally, to be the highest civil and military organs of his regime. Under Chu's crony Li Shan-ch'ang, who governed Nanking when Chu was away, a small corps of scholars worked to create a regular civil administration, but the early Ming regime was predominantly military in its composition, with the highest positions going to Chu's original followers and the leaders of the Lake Ch'ao group. The conquered cities were placed under military garrisons called wings (*yi*), whose commanders (*yüan-shuai*) exercised both civil and military authority.[42]

During the rest of 1356 and most of 1357 Ming and Wu fought over the disposition of the densely populated region between Nanking and Soochow. Although Wu retained enough territory to ensure its numerical preponderance over Ming, the latter was more energetic and more successful in the actual military contest. In a series of campaigns of which the more important were led by Hsü Ta, Ming armies captured Chenchiang, Ch'angshu, Ch'anghsing, Chiangyin, Ch'angchou and finally Yangchow. The capture of Yangchow ended the process. For the next decade Ming and Wu faced one another across a frontier marked by well-fortified and strongly garrisoned walled cities. Neither succeeded in expanding at the other's expense through siege operations, though Wu made some valiant attempts.[43]

It was still possible for Ming to expand to the south. Chu Yüanchang took Ningkuo on 12 May 1357, allegedly capturing a hundred thousand men, and his old comrade Hu Ta-hai took Huichou three months later. On 13 November Ch'ang Yü-ch'un, who had not joined the Ming until shortly before the river crossing but in the end would rank second only to Hsü Ta in the order of Ming generals, took Ch'ihchou, thus inaugurating the conflict with Chao P'u-sheng that led to the Ming-Han war. Meanwhile a special army was formed under Hu Ta-hai to conquer Chekiang. On 26 April 1358 Teng Yü took Yenchou, and in November Hu Ta-hai laid siege to Chinhua, the chief inland city, which did not fall until January 1359 after Chu Yüan-chang had come down from Nanking with the main Ming army. On 3 December 1359 Hu took Ch'uchou from the Yüan commander Shih-mo Yi-sun, thus completing the partition of Chekiang among Ming, Wu, and Fang Kuo-chen's pirate empire.[44]

The Ming regime of Chu Yüan-chang now controlled part of Kiangsu and all of Anhwei south of the Yangtze, plus the four inland prefectures of Chekiang, areas with an aggregate population of about 7.8 million in 1393. Of the remaining prefectures of

Chekiang, the four in the north were under Chang Shih-ch'eng and the three on the east coast under Fang Kuo-chen. Ming conquests to date had been at the expense of Yüan militia and other local forces that in general did not cooperate with each other and so fell one by one. As 1360 opened, however, no regime in South China could expand further in this manner. The three great powers of Han, Ming, and Wu had divided up the Yangtze valley. Most of the rest of South China was under the control of five lesser regionalists: the already discussed Fang Kuo-chen, Ming Yü-chen, and Ch'en Yu-ting, plus Ho Chen in Canton and the prince of Liang, Basalawarmi, in Yünnan, both of whom were Yüan loyalists. These five were too weak to attempt expansion beyond their regions, but they were also too strong to be displaced save by a major effort by one of the great powers, which the other great powers could not be expected to permit. One of the great powers would have to destroy the other two before it could annex the smaller warlords, but the population balance among them made this unlikely. As of 1360, China appeared to be in for a replay of the Five Dynasties and Ten Kingdoms period—warlord conflict in the north and stable regional regimes in the south.[45]

The Lungwan and P'oyang Campaigns, 1360-1363

The emerging balance of power collapsed as a result of Chu Yüan-chang's complete victory over Ch'en Yu-liang, which led to the annexation of Han. Ming now had the sheer numbers needed to overwhelm Wu, and this in turn permitted Ming to conquer most of China rapidly in 1368. In its consequences, the Ming-Han war was thus a decisive event in Chinese history. Its importance is matched by its military interest. Both leaders led armies whose divisions were held together by personal ties; divisional commanders were thus quite capable of taking their men with them when they switched sides, as they occasionally did. Many division commanders in turn had succeeded in creating local power for themselves by repairing the fortifications of the cities where they were garrison commanders. Such commanders might interpret an order to move from their city as a sign of lack of confidence and be prompted to revolt. Even though the city commanders in Ming and Han were often old associates of Chu or

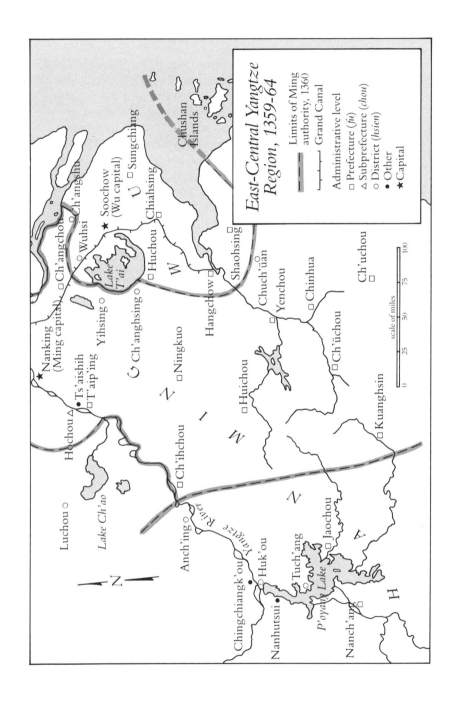

East-Central Yangtze
Region, 1359-64

Limits of Ming
authority, 1360
Grand Canal
Administrative level
□ Prefecture (fu)
△ Subprefecture (chou)
○ District (hsien)
● Other
★ Capital

scale of miles
0   25   50   75   100

Chushan
Islands

Sungchiang

Ch'angshu

Soochow
(Wu capital)

Ch'angchou

Wuhsi

Chiahsing

Huchou

Chuch'üan

Shaohsing

Ch'uchou

Yenchou

Chinhua

Hangchow

Lake
T'ai

Nanking
(Ming capital)

Yihsing

Ch'anghsing

Ningkuo

Ch'iihchou

Ch'üchou

Ts'aishih

T'aip'ing

Huichou

Kuanghsin

Hochou

Luchou

Lake Ch'ao

Anch'ing

Ch'ihchou

Chingchiangk'ou

Huk'ou

Tuch'ang

Jaochou

P'oyang Lake

Nanhutsui

Nanch'ang

N

Ch'en, both rulers had to deal with them carefully. Although both tried to enhance their effective power by employing relatives, by adopting children, by recruiting civil officials, and by other integrating devices, it was not possible for either to transcend the organizational limits imposed by the personalistic loyalty structure as long as his rivals were still in the field. Awareness of this fact emphasizes the importance of the purely military side of Chu Yüan-chang's victory and accounts for some of his subsequent paranoia about his generals.[46]

Organizationally the armies of 1360–64 were still the peasant armies of the earlier roving-bandit period, but operationally they had advanced to a much higher level. In contrast to the Chinese civil war of 1927–49, in this period city-based forces succeeded in destroying all country-based rebels. Each walled city dominated its surrounding agricultural region, and political power flowed downward from city to village. The cities were thus the principal military objectives, and their capture now required systematic, and often protracted, sieges. In the Yangtze valley, supplies for the besieging armies could only be brought up by boat, and this led to the creation of fleets, first for transport and later for fighting inland naval campaigns for the control of the Yangtze and its tributary lakes and rivers. It was against this background that the Ming-Han war played itself out (see the map on p. 38).[47]

When he murdered Chao P'u-sheng, Ch'en Yu-liang inherited his problems as well as his troops. The Ming reconquest of Ch'ihchou provoked him to retaliate in a way that led to all-out war. In 1360 Chu Yüan-chang was informed of Ch'en Yu-liang's intentions. He ordered Hsü Ta to Ch'ihchou and sent Ch'ang Yü-ch'un, who had been besieging Hangchow unsuccessfully for three months, to join him. Leading fifteen thousand men, the two generals ambushed a Han invading force and took three thousand prisoners. Ch'ang Yü-ch'un killed most of these, sending only a few back to Ch'en Yu-liang to tell the tale.[48]

The slaughter provoked Ch'en to immediate action. Placing his one hundred thousand men aboard ship, he came downstream and reached T'aip'ing on 11 June. T'aip'ing was commanded by Hua Yün, one of Chu Yüan-chang's original followers, who led a garrison of three thousand including one of Chu's adopted sons. For three days the Han soldiers assaulted the landward walls of the city unsuccessfully, and then Ch'en had an inspiration: he brought his larger ships up against the riverine wall and had his soldiers mount the wall from the high sterns of the ships. One rush and the outnumbered garrison was overcome. Hua Yün refused to submit to Ch'en Yu-liang, thus earning a martyr's death and posthumous honors. Ch'en was elated by his victory. On 16 June he moored his fleet by the jetty at Ts'aishih where the Ming had crossed the river in 1355. There he had his nominal emperor Hsü Shou-hui beaten to death and proclaimed himself emperor of the Han dynasty. While he sat on his improvised throne with his newly elevated officials standing before him on the grass, a summer thunderstorm interrupted the ceremonies. Undeterred by this bad omen, Ch'en sent an envoy to Chang Shih-ch'eng to urge the latter to attack the Ming from the rear, and then prepared to sail to Nanking himself.[49]

Consternation struck the Ming leadership when they learned on 18 June of the swift fall of T'aip'ing. Although the Ming had about as many men as the Han, its fleet was only one-tenth as large. The Han could therefore sail at will on the river, and if the Ming army attempted to chase after them on land, the Han could either avoid action or strike when the Ming troops were exhausted. Failure to do anything would have left Ch'en Yu-liang free to take the other Ming cities as he had already taken T'aip'ing. In the ensuing debate, some Ming generals proposed marching to recapture T'aip'ing, while others wished simply to abandon Nanking and hold out on the Purple Mountain east of the city.

Chu Yüan-chang overruled these proposals and put into effect his own plan, which was based on the assumption that Ch'en Yu-liang would fall for a chance to capture Nanking at one stroke with the aid of treachery from within the city. He summoned K'ang Mao-ts'ai, who had served with Ch'en before surrendering to the Ming in 1356, and ordered him to send a servant, a known double agent, with a letter to Ch'en. In the letter K'ang offered to defect and to admit Han troops into the city by opening the wooden bridge at Chiangtung (see the Map on p. 41). But when the agent returned with the news that Ch'en had agreed, Chu ordered Li Shan-ch'ang to rebuild the bridge in stone, since by then he knew that Ch'en intended landing at Lungwan, and wished to ambush him there.[50]

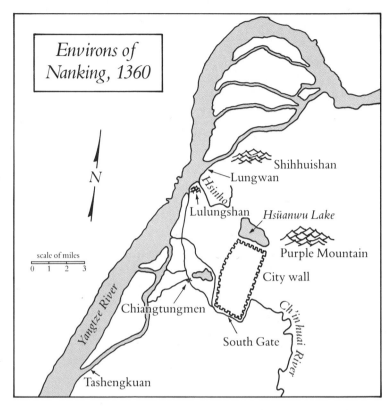

Environs of
Nanking, 1360

N

scale of miles
0 1 2 3

Shihhuishan
Lungwan
Hsinho
Lulungshan
Hsüanwu Lake
Purple Mountain
City wall
Yangtze River
Chiangtungmen
Ch'inhuai River
South Gate
Tashengkuan

Chu had sent Yang Ching to Tashengkuan, K'ang Mao-ts'ai to
the bridge, and Chao Te-sheng to the mouth of the Hsin River to
guard the water routes giving access to Nanking. Sharpened stakes
called "lotus flowers" had been driven into the river bank to
prevent ships from landing. While K'ang's servant was setting up
the original Ming ambush by the Chiangtung bridge, Ch'en's
younger brother Ch'en Yu-jen sailed downstream with ten
thousand men. He landed at Lungwan, captured a Ming force
under Shao Jung, and—probably on his own initiative—built
a stockade, thus inadvertently revealing his brother's previous
intention of attacking Nanking from that direction.

Lungwan was a better site for an ambush than the Chiangtung
bridge; Chu was gambling that, once in motion, Ch'en would

revert to his original plan if K'ang Mao-ts'ai's defection did not materialize. He sent thirty thousand men under Ch'ang Yü-ch'un and Feng Sheng to wait in ambush at Shihhuishan, while Hsü Ta was stationed outside the south gate of Nanking where he could support Yang Ching and K'ang Mao-ts'ai if necessary, and Chu stationed himself with the main body at Lulungshan. Chu directed that a red flag would signal the arrival of the enemy and a yellow flag would order the ambush forces to attack. The Ming fleet had been sent to safety downstream, and the Ming armies waited for dawn.[51]

On the morning of 23 June Ch'en Yu-liang took the Han fleet downstream and attacked Tashengkuan. Yang Ching put up a stiff resistance, and the harbor entrance was narrow, so Ch'en broke off the action and sailed to the Chiangtung bridge. When he saw that the bridge was made of stone, and when K'ang Mao-ts'ai failed to appear in response to his call, he realized that his plot had fallen through. Fearing ambush at the bridge, he sailed on to Lungwan, where the real ambush awaited him. Chu Yüan-chang, dressed in armor of purple horn, watched the Han soldiers leave their ships, and ordered his own men to eat and drink and rest in preparation for the battle. When the humid summer afternoon provided a convenient rainstorm, he had the red flag raised and ordered an advance on the Han stockade. Ch'en Yu-liang deployed his troops in the open field, eagerly grasping the opportunity to destroy what appeared to be another isolated division of the Ming army. When the rain stopped, Chu ordered the drums beaten to sound the attack, and had the yellow flag raised. As the Ming ambush forces of Ch'ang Yü-ch'un and Feng Sheng fell on the Han rear, the Han battle line disintegrated into a mob of soldiers struggling to escape. Many of those who reached the river found to their dismay that the tide had gone out and their ships were aground.

The Ming thus captured over one hundred large ships, including the *Hun-chiang-lung* ("River-muddying Dragon") and three others whose names are preserved, and several hundred smaller vessels, evidently more than half of the Han fleet. Ch'en Yu-liang and the majority of his men escaped by crowding on to the ships and boats that could be launched, and most of these reached Chiuchiang despite the Ming pursuit, which inflicted further losses. The Han left twenty thousand dead on the battlefield, and there were seven thousand prisoners, mostly Chao P'u-sheng's former men.[52] Anch'ing was captured by Hsü Ta in the course of the pursuit.[53] The Ming fleet, increased by the captured ships and the newly joined Lake Ch'ao sailors, was now strong enough to contest for naval superiority with the Han, and Ch'en Yu-liang's personal forces were no longer strong enough both to defend Kiangsi and to compel his local commanders to remain obedient. The initiative had passed to the Ming. Moreover, while the main Han army was suffering defeat at Lungwan, Hu Ta-hai led his army overland from Chekiang and took Kuanghsin in Kiangsi, thus opening that area to Ming intrigues.[54] Chang Shih-ch'eng did nothing throughout June, presmably hoping that Ch'en and Chu would destroy one another. He made a number of attacks on Ming cities later in the year, all of which were beaten off.

Upon returning to Chiuchiang, Ch'en Yu-liang faced a crisis of authority that he attempted to solve by further attacks on Ming possessions in 1361. Chu Yüan-chang's strategy at this time was to reserve his main forces for the struggle with Wu while at the same time sending armies overland into Kiangsi in the hope of exploiting the divisions in the Han political structure. These attempts were only partially successful. Hu Ta-hai and his adopted son Hu Te-chi, garrison commander at Kuanghsin, defeated a major Han attempt to recapture that city, but further north Teng Yü, after inducing the defection of the Han commander of Fouliang, was blocked in his attempts to reach P'oyang Lake and had to ask for reinforcements.[55] Clearly the important cities of Kiangsi would not defect unless the Ming armies appeared in force. But on 24 August 1361 Chang Ting-pien, the Han grand commandant (*t'ai-wei*), recaptured Anch'ing by surprise. The Ming commander Chao Chung-chung of the Lake Ch'ao group escaped and fled to Nanking, where Chu Yüan-chang angrily executed him, transferring his men to his younger brother Chao Yung.[56] Chu now decided that the threat posed by Ch'en Yu-liang was great enough to warrant a full-scale upstream expedition, despite the very real danger involved in reducing the strength of his garrison at Nanking.

The Ming fleet sailed on 11 September under Chu Yüan-chang's command. On the nineteenth they reached Anch'ing, where they destroyed eighty ships and captured twenty-seven but failed to take the city. Bypassing Anch'ing they continued upstream and reached Huk'ou on the twenty-third. In mid-voyage two Han commanders, Ting P'u-lang and Fu Yu-te, defected to the Ming with their squadrons. Off Huk'ou, Han patrol ships sighted the Ming fleet and sped off to Chiuchiang with the news, hotly pursued by the Ming squadrons. Ch'en Yu-liang, taken by surprise, nonetheless took his fleet out onto the river and offered battle. "[Chu Yüan-chang] divided his fleet into two wings and attacked [Ch'en] Yu-liang from both sides, defeating him severely. Over one hundred of his ships were captured." His weakness thus demonstrated, Ch'en withdrew the rest of his fleet into the natural harbor formed by the lake south of Chiuchiang. During the night he put most of his men aboard his remaining ships and fled upstream, somehow eluding the Ming fleet and ultimately arriving at Wuch'ang.[57]

The following morning the walls of Chiuchiang were stormed by the use of assault ramps, called "heavenly bridges" (*t'ien-ch'iao*), mounted on the sterns of the Ming ships. Chu Yüan-chang sent Hsü Ta with part of the fleet in pursuit. Hsü anchored off Hanyang, which he assaulted but failed to take, and blockaded Ch'en at Wuch'ang until April 1362.[58] Chu Yüan-chang kept the main body of the fleet with him at Chiuchiang. Thanks to the fleet's presence, the Han city commanders in Kiangsi began to see merit in the Ming cause. By 2 October Nank'ang, Jaochou, and Chiench'ang had accepted Ming authority, along with three cities in eastern Hupei. Chu Yüan-chang remained patiently at Chiuchiang, hoping to induce the surrender of Nanch'ang, the major city in the region, but by December the dangers of overextension were becoming obvious. Chu had to send Ch'ang Yü-ch'un to repel a Wu attack on Ch'anghsing. With Hsü Ta far away in Hupei and Chu himself several days voyage from Nanking, Chang Shih-ch'eng finally glimpsed an opportunity.[59]

On 9 December 1361 Teng Yü captured Fuchou in Kiangsi, and this prompted the Han commandant of Nanch'ang, Chancellor Hu Mei, to ask to surrender. His principal demand was that his men be kept together as a unit under him. Chu agreed to let him keep most of his men on the condition that he give up Nanch'ang and serve instead in the Ming reserve army. Hu agreed to these terms and later attained nobility as a Ming general. Chu Yüan-chang entered Nanch'ang on 10 February 1362 and remained there another month, during which time Yüanchou, Chian, and several smaller cities surrendered.[60] Except at Nanch'ang, the Han commandants who surrendered were left in control of their troops and cities, a dangerous policy of calculated mercy that was necessary to win further surrenders but that virtually guaranteed that the city commanders would sit on their hands in a crisis, as they had in 1361 and would again in 1363. Enforced troop reshuffling would have been necessary to bring Kiangsi under tight Ming control, but there was no time for that; Chu Yüan-chang had been away from his capital for too long already. On 11 March he set sail for Nanking.[61] While he was on the river, his authority very nearly disintegrated.

After breaking up the Wu general Li Po-sheng's siege of Ch'anghsing on 24 December 1361, Ch'ang Yü-ch'un had gone to Nanking. At this time Chekiang was held by the army of Hu Ta-hai, who was personally popular with his troops. However, the Miao soldiers in the army, formerly Yüan irregular troops under Yang Öljei, were extremely discontented. The reasons for this can no longer even be ascertained (one guess is that Hu, who was a strict disciplinarian, may have punished them for looting), but while Chu Yüan-chang was away upstream, the Miao contingents in the various Chekiang cities exchanged messengers and plotted an uprising. On 3 March 1362 the Miao troops at Chinhua rebelled and killed Hu Ta-hai, and four days later the Miao at Ch'uchou also rebelled, killing the city commandant, Keng Tsai-ch'eng, and capturing control of the city.[62]

On 16 March Chu Yüan-chang, now back in Nanking and cognizant of the situation, appointed his nephew Li Wen-chung, then in command at Yenchou, to be commander-in-chief in Chekiang. Moving swiftly, Li recaptured Chinhua, but the Miao rebels escaped and joined Chang Shih-ch'eng, who responded to the Ming troubles by sending his profligate brother, Chang Shih-hsin, to attack the outlying Ming city of Chuch'üan. Li was thus confronted by both invasion and rebellion, and on his own—Nanking had sent an expeditionary force under Shao Jung to reconquer Ch'uchou, but Li could expect no further assistance from outside his command. His response was first to spread the rumor that Shao Jung, reputed to be one of the three greatest Ming generals, was marching to the relief of Chuch'üan instead of Ch'uchou, and then he actually sent Hu Te-chi from Kuanghsin to Chuch'üan. The tactic succeeded. By the time Hu Te-chi reached Chuch'üan, conflicting reports had so confused the Wu army that a combined attack by Hu and the city garrison scattered it. Meanwhile Shao Jung recovered Ch'uchou.[63]

Chu Yüan-chang had left Teng Yü in command at Nanch'ang and had taken most of the former Han garrison to Nanking with him. However, he ordered two of Hu Mei's subordinates, Chu Tsung and K'ang T'ai, to sail upstream to reinforce Hsü Ta off Hanyang. Hu Mei told him too late that these two had opposed the surrender to the very end and had planned rebellion. Chu Tsung and K'ang T'ai turned around on the river and appeared before Nanch'ang with their fleet on the evening of 12 April. When they destroyed the Hsinch'eng gate with cannon fire and overran the city, Teng Yü escaped and rode alone to Nanking. Chu Yüan-chang now had to face the possibility that all of the Ming conquests of 1361 would have to be abandoned, and he ordered Ch'ang Yü-ch'un to repair the walls of Anch'ing against that eventuality. Hsü Ta was also ordered to abandon the blockade of Wuch'ang; he came downstream and recaptured Nanch'ang on 13 May.[64]

This ended the immediate crisis, but Kiangsi was clearly not yet secure. Chu made his other nephew, Chu Wen-cheng, commander-in-chief there, and Teng Yü his deputy. The garrison was increased, and during 1362–63 the walls were reconstructed at a certain distance from the river bank so that the city could not be taken by a ship-mounted assault as T'aip'ing had been in 1360. The main price paid for the reconquest of Nanch'ang, however, was the release of Ch'en Yu-liang, who now had all the resources of Hunan and Hupei at his disposal.[65]

In midsummer treason struck the Ming regime, already weakened by rebellion. Shao Jung, as we have seen, was described as one of the three leading Ming generals at this time, and in terms of formal rank he was higher than both Hsü Ta and Ch'ang Yü-ch'un. Yet he does not figure prominently in the campaigns as recorded, and his reconquest of Ch'uchou from the Miao in 1362 had been his first independent command in years. When he was not rewarded for this success, he could not stifle his expressions of resentment; then, fearing Chu Yüan-chang's wrath if his complaints should become known, he plotted rebellion along with another disaffected general. The plot was to arrange to have their own contingents at the head of the column when the Ming army reentered Nanking after a military review on 3 August, to shut and hold the gate as soon as their own men had followed in after Chu, and then to murder Chu during the confusion. But Chu changed his mind at the last minute because of an omen and entered the city by a different gate, and when an informant later revealed the conspiracy, Chu had Shao Jung and his collaborators arrested and sentenced to death. But he stayed his hand and consulted with his generals. Ch'ang Yü-ch'un, as spokesman for the generals, insisted that the conspirators be executed, and this was done. Chu had escaped from this affair largely by accident, and he was now dangerously dependent on his generals.[66]

The Ming regime thus entered the new year with its morale shaken by treason and rebellion, with its authority over Chekiang weakened by the loss of the Miao soldiers, and with its position in Kiangsi barely tenable. True, the murder of Chaghan Temür on 6 July 1362 had thrown North China into turmoil, thus ruling out the possibility of a Yüan loyalist combination against the Ming.[67] But there was no real respite. The new year opened with a surprise thrust· by Chang Shih-ch'eng against the symbolic center of the Red Turban movement. On 16 February 1363 the Wu general Lü Chen broke into Anfeng, killed its ruler, the once great warlord Liu Fu-t'ung, and captured the Sung emperor Han Lin-erh, Chu Yüan-chang's nominal sovereign. Outside of the Ming territories, the Sung empire by this time had been reduced to this one insignificant city in the midst of a largely depopulated area, yet Han Lin-erh was important because of the religious veneration still felt for him by significant segments of the Ming armies. This made a rescue mission imperative, and in March Chu Yüan-chang led the main army north. Ch'ang Yü-ch'un won the battle that led to the expulsion of Lü Chen from Anfeng and—by some miracle the sources do not record—to the recovery of Han Lin-erh alive. Chu Yüan-chang then returned to Nanking, while Anfeng, which had been abandoned, was recovered by the Yüan. Meanwhile Tso Chün-pi, the warlord of Luchou whose operations had initially driven the Lake Ch'ao group into Ming arms, had sent a force to aid Lü Chen's invasion. In retaliation, Hsü Ta and Ch'ang Yü-ch'un besieged Luchou unsuccessfully from April to August. This latter campaign was not strongly favored by Chu Yüan-chang; it tied up the largest Ming field army in a fruitless siege against a minor local warlord during a time of increasing danger in Kiangsi.[68]

Once free of Hsü Ta's blockade, Ch'en Yu-liang set about mobilizing all the able-bodied men of Hunan and Hupei and building a new fleet. The core of the fleet consisted of gigantic, red-painted, three-decked galleasses with iron-sheathed turrets for archers and sterns high enough to overtop any city's walls. One source claims that each ship could carry two to three thousand men. When Ch'en came downstream on the spring flood, these monsters were escorted by a fleet of boats and craft of every kind gleaned from the rivers and lakes of Hupei. He had perhaps three hundred thousand men in all. His intention was to repeat on a grander scale his 1360 capture of T'aip'ing, and to seize city after city by mounting their riverine walls directly from his ships. On 5 June 1363 he attacked Nanch'ang. Success there would have meant the recovery of Kiangsi, most of whose cities were under his former officers, and this in turn would have reestablished the favorable military situation enjoyed by Ch'en in late 1359.[69]

But the changes made in the walls of Nanch'ang in 1362 made it impossible to take the city by direct assault from aboard ship, and this upset Ch'en Yu-liang's timetable. For eighty-five days he blockaded Nanch'ang closely and subjected it to repeated assault. The Ming commanders, Chu Wen-cheng and Teng Yü, repelled all of his efforts and inflicted losses on the Han encampment through sorties. On one occasion, Han siege engines caused a large section of the wall to collapse, but Teng Yü's men held the attackers off with firearms (*huo-ch'ung*, probably gingals) while a crescent was built around the collapsed section. However, despite their successful resistance, attrition was taking its toll of the defenders. After 24 July the Ming obtained a truce by pretending to agree to surrender the city on a certain date. They also sent a messenger who was able to slip through the lines of the besiegers and reach Nanking on 4 August.[70]

This date is the first recorded notice that Chu Yüan-chang was aware of the siege of Nanch'ang, though he must have known something of it earlier, if only from interruption of communication. His hands were tied by the siege of Luchou, which stubbornly refused to fall, and by the rebellion on 8 June at Chuch'üan in Chekiang of the Ming commandant, who had been detected trafficking with Wu. The latter event led to Hu Te-chi's army being sent once again from Kuanghsin to Chuch'üan, which it failed to retake.[71] By 6 August, perhaps under the urging of Liu Chi, the eminent Chekiang Confucianist who had joined him in 1360, Chu Yüan-chang asserted himself against his generals: Hu Te-chi, now back at Kuanghsin, was ordered to march overland to relieve Nanch'ang, while Hsü Ta and Ch'ang Yü-ch'un were ordered to break off the siege of Luchou and reassemble their troops at Nanking.[72]

The Ming fleet left Nanking on 15 August. It was certainly not larger than the "one thousand ships and one hundred thousand men" recorded in the sources, so even after the losses sustained in the siege and the substantial detachments Ch'en Yu-liang had sent away to reestablish his power in central Kiangsi, the Han had a numerical margin that should have been decisive.[73] Also, the Ming had nothing to compare with the towering Han warships, which, even though designed for taking cities, would also hold the advantage in a naval battle fought largely by closing and boarding. Chu Yüan-chang was taking a desperate chance by embarking on an offensive against a superior enemy while still engaged in a two-front war. The only positive factor in the situation was that the water level of the rivers and lakes had dropped considerably since June, which was to the advantage of the smaller Ming warships. On 24 August the fleet reached Huk'ou and established fortified positions at Nanhutsui and Chingchiangk'ou to prevent the Han fleet from leaving P'oyang Lake or sailing downstream on the Yangtze. The relief of Nanch'ang was still the Ming objective, so they sailed into P'oyang Lake on the twenty-eighth. On the same day Ch'en Yu-liang raised the siege, put his troops aboard ship, and sailed into the lake. On the twenty-ninth, late in the day, the two fleets had their first encounter off the island of K'anglangshan.[74]

In the four-day naval battle that followed, the Ming inflicted heavy losses on the Han fleet, but they failed to destroy it and were themselves forced to retreat. On the morning of 30 August Chu Yüan-chang deployed his fleet in eleven squadrons, placing his heavier ships in the center, which he commanded himself with the aid of Hsü Ta and Ch'ang Yü-ch'un; he placed the lighter ships on the wings under the experienced Lake Ch'ao naval commanders Yü T'ung-hai and Liao Yung-chung. Then the Ming fleet advanced and attacked. Although Yü T'ung-hai gained the windward and used catapults to launch flaming projectiles that burned up over twenty Han warships, in the center the floating fortresses of the Han fleet drove the Ming line back. Hsü Ta's flagship was badly damaged, and Chu's was repeatedly attacked. Only by retreating into a shallow area were the Ming able to disengage, and then only at the cost of numerous grounding mishaps. The Ming were disheartened by the failure of the first day's battle, and during the night Chu sent Hsü Ta back to Nanking with the damaged warships, which would have been a hindrance had a fast retreat become necessary.[75]

When battle resumed on the following day, the great Han warships "seemed like mountains," and Chu Yüan-chang had to behead several subordinate commanders in order to get his fleet to advance. In the ensuing fight the Ming were driven back again, losing several of their prominent men. However, because of the success of Yü T'ung-hai's attack the day before, Chu Yüan-chang had ordered Ch'ang Yü-ch'un to prepare fireships, which he did by filling fishing boats with bundles of reeds stuffed with gunpowder. The Han fleet had achieved its successes by grouping its great warships closely together and driving the smaller Ming ships back by sheer mass. In the afternoon the wind shifted and blew from the direction of the Ming fleet. Seven fireships were ignited and drifted into the closely-packed Han formation with dreadful results. Several hundred warships were destroyed, and Han losses were reported to be sixty thousand against only seven thousand for the Ming. The best indication of the Han losses is the fact that two of Ch'en Yu-liang's brothers were killed in the battle. Both fleets were so battered by the 31 August battle that they spent the following day resting and making repairs.[76]

When fighting began again on the morning of 2 September, the Ming were able to engage the still superior Han fleet on much more favorable terms. On this occasion, the Han fleet was deployed in an open order because of their heavy losses on 31 August. Isolated Han warships were surrounded and destroyed, and at one point a squadron of six Ming warships penetrated the Han line and sailed completely around one end of it to rejoin the Ming fleet. Nevertheless, by about noon Chu Yüan-chang yielded to the pressure of his commanders led by Yü T'ung-hai and ordered disengagement and withdrawal from the lake. Yü had argued that the shallow water of the lake hindered their movements. Since the Han vessels were now fighting in a formation that ruled out fireship attacks on the scale of the 31 August operation, a prolonged battle of attrition with the superior Han fleet must have seemed a losing proposition to the Ming commanders. In addition, Chu had probably heard that Nanch'ang had been relieved by Hu Te-chi's army from Kuanghsin; if so, he knew the Ming fleet no longer needed to fight its way through the Han fleet but was free to adopt the defensive stance more suited to its inferior size and armament.[77]

On the night of 2 September each Ming ship mounted a lantern at its stern, and the fleet sailed away in single file to blockade the mouth of the lake. The Han fleet followed later. A dispute over whether to attempt a breakout or to abandon their ships and march overland to Wuch'ang caused two important Han commanders to defect to the Ming. Chu Yüan-chang then retired his fleet to Huk'ou and waited for Ch'en Yu-liang's food supplies to run out, meanwhile sending him insulting letters to provoke him into attacking. Some of the Ming commanders wished to return to Nanking at this time, but once again Ch'ang Yü-ch'un sustained Chu Yüan-chang's authority.[78] It was almost a month before the Han fleet attempted to break out. Finally they stormed Nanhutsui, arriving at Huk'ou on 3 October, and turned upstream into the Yangtze in an attempt to return to Wuch'ang. The Ming had prepared fireships, which were set adrift, and the Han ships promptly scattered downstream with the Ming in pursuit. By late afternoon clusters of ships locked in combat had drifted down to Chingchiangk'ou. At this juncture, Ch'en Yu-liang, who was crossing from ship to ship in a small boat, was struck in the eye by an arrow and killed. Their emperor's death destroyed the cohesion of the Han fleet. Chang Ting-pien escaped during the night with his contingent and returned to Wuch'ang, where he continued the Han empire in the name of a younger son of Ch'en Yu-liang. The rest of the Han fleet, fifty thousand men in all, surrendered the following morning. On 8 October Chu Yüan-chang took his fleet and his prisoners back to Nanking.[79]

The Ming-Han war, culminating in the P'oyang campaign, was the climax of the civil wars leading up to the founding of the Ming dynasty proper, and the death of Ch'en Yu-liang and the destruction of his armada gave Chu Yüan-chang the victory that had eluded him in 1361. Chu had been contending against superior numbers and the ever-present possibility that Chang Shih-ch'eng might attack from the rear; now the way was clear for the incorporation of Kiangsi, Hunan, and Hupei into his domains, thus tripling the Ming population and enabling Chu to raise twice as many soldiers as Wu, whose conquest was the next objective. Ming had thus emerged as the largest and strongest regional power, and her future conquests were to have a snowballing effect. Beyond that, the increase in prestige and territory gave Chu Yüan-chang enhanced authority within his own regime. Even though the scholar-gentry were still reluctant to serve him, his generals could now see him as a likely future emperor. The generals could no longer defy his orders openly, and his power to distribute captured troops among his commanders and to assign commands in the newly conquered territories gave him the means to assert collective discipline for the first time. The military victory in the P'oyang campaign is thus the critical event that made the founding of the Ming empire possible.[80]

The Ming March to Empire, 1364-1368

While the Ming state alternated between crisis and expansion between 1360 and 1363, Chang Shih-ch'eng remained consistently hostile to Ming aims, but his hostility was ineffectual. When the main Ming army and fleet were committed against Han in 1360, 1361, and 1363, he failed to exploit the situation by attacking Ming from the rear, and his brother Chang Shih-hsin and his general Lü Chen bungled the offensives they led against Ming in 1362 and early 1363. It is unclear precisely when he became aware of the extent of the Ming victory in the P'oyang campaign, but he surely realized that there would be no place for him in an expanding Ming empire. Chang's accommodation with the Yüan had apparently turned his regime into a fortress defending proper

Confucian government against Red Turban heterodoxy, and the wealthy scholar-gentry who had rallied to his support were terrified of the consequences of a Ming victory, even though Chu Yüan-chang, in contrast to the Red Turbans on the North China plain, maintained order and property rights wherever he conquered, and followed generally conservative social policies.[81] Chang now cut off his grain tribute shipments to the north on the grounds that they would be needed for his own defense, and on 5 November 1363 he declared himself prince of Wu, thus directly challenging the legitimacy of Chu Yüan-chang's claim to be duke of Wu.[82]

The other regional regimes reacted variously to the Ming success. Ch'en Yu-ting in Fukien became actively hostile and invaded Ming territory, but was contained by the Ming Chekiang army. Ming Yü-chen in Szechwan wrote proposing an alliance. Fang Kuo-chen, whose "loyalty" to the Yüan no longer brought him any advantage, offered tribute to the Ming late in 1364, and Chu Yüan-chang accepted on condition that Fang would surrender when the Ming captured Hangchow from Wu. In response to Chang Shih-ch'eng's challenge, Chu Yüan-chang proclaimed himself prince of Wu at the New Year (4 February 1364), a step that allowed him to award grander titles to his generals without disturbing Han Lin-erh's status as emperor.[83]

The systematic reduction of the territories formerly under Han took the Ming until 1365. The capture of Wuch'ang was the first step. Soon after the P'oyang campaign, on 23 October 1363, Chu Yüan-chang led the Ming army and fleet to Wuch'ang, which he besieged unsuccessfully for two months before turning over command to Ch'ang Yü-ch'un and returning to Nanking. Chu came back to Wuch'ang two days before the Han commander, Chang Ting-pien, surrendered the city on 22 March 1364. The fall of Wuch'ang brought formal declarations of surrender from the other major cities of Hunan and Hupei. Chu did not occupy them at this time, but instead brought his forces downstream, except for a garrison that he maintained at Wuch'ang under Yang Ching. On 15 May Hsü Ta and Ch'ang Yü-ch'un resumed their interrupted siege of Luchou, whose warlord Tso Chün-pi, on hearing that the Ming were coming to attack him again, fled to Anfeng and joined Chaghan Temür's successor, Kökö Temür. Under his subordinates Luchou held out for three months before falling on 15 August.[84] Wuch'ang and Luchou had been centers of outright defiance of Ming authority; their reduction was an essential prelude to the next stage of Ming conquest, the military occupation of the remaining cities of Hunan, Hupei, and Kiangsi.

Hsü Ta's army was sent to Hunan and Hupei. His task was to persuade city commanders who had already formally surrendered to admit Ming troops into their cities. Hsü owed his high position in Chu's esteem partly to his reputation for maintaining excellent military discipline, which was vital in this context: if Ming soldiers ran amok in any one city, the others could be expected to resist forcibly. Late in October Chiangling admitted Hsü's army, while detached forces from his command peacefully occupied Yiling and Ch'angsha. These successes were the prelude to the Ming takeover of the rest of Hunan. Though a few offered resistance, most Han commandants and aboriginal chiefs opened their gates without fighting. Hsü Ta was able to return to Nanking in April 1365 with his mission accomplished.[85]

Ch'ang Yü-ch'un's army went first to Nanch'ang, where Teng Yü joined him with part of the garrison. Despite his habit of murdering prisoners and sacking cities, Ch'ang was probably the ablest Ming field commander. His assignment was the conquest of central and southern Kiangsi, areas that either had never acknowledged Ming rule or had been reconquered by the Han in 1363—and in any case were under Han warlords who showed no inclination to surrender. Pushing up the Kan River, Ch'ang and Teng took Chian on 3 September 1364 and soon afterwards laid siege to Kanchou. The warlord of Kanchou, Hsiung T'ien-jui, had remained loyal to Han in 1361, using this as a pretext for attacking those Han commanders who surrendered to the Ming. During 1362 and 1363 he continued his empire building in Kiangsi and Kwangtung. Chu Yüan-chang was so fearful that Ch'ang Yü-ch'un would allow pillage and massacre when he captured Kanchou that he sent Wang Kuang-yang, a future chancellor, to restrain him. When Kanchou fell in February 1365, Ch'ang, contrary to expectation, occupied it without disorder or loss of life.[86]

While the larger Ming armies were thus occupied, a relative of an executed Han commander rebelled in Hsink'an. Chu Wen-cheng sent troops from nearby Nanch'ang to suppress it, but the campaign became the occasion for a major political incident. Chu Yüan-chang ordered T'ang Ho, whom he trusted implicitly and who had been in command at Ch'angchou since 1357, to take his troops to Kiangsi to suppress the rebels. On 16 February 1365, as T'ang Ho's army was approaching Nanch'ang, Chu Yüan-chang arrived there in person and deprived Chu Wen-cheng of both his actual command and his nominal position as commander-in-chief of all the Ming armies. Chu accused his nephew of kidnapping women for his personal pleasure, of usurping imperial prerogatives by decorating his bedchamber with dragons and phoenixes, and of plotting to surrender to Chang Shih-ch'eng. Chu Wen-cheng was popular in the army because of his successful defense of Nanch'ang in 1363, and many high-ranking officers interceded for him, so many that Chu Yüan-chang punished him merely with supervised exile. The accusation of treason against Chu Wen-cheng seems improbable, but Chu Yüan-chang may have felt that Chu Wen-cheng's high position threatened the future of his own children. Teng Yü, who was returning from the south, succeeded to the command of Nanch'ang.[87]

Chu conferred with Hsü Ta and Ch'ang Yü-ch'un at Nanking on 23 April. The only ex-Han territories still free from Ming control were the cities of the Han River valley, of which Hsiangyang and Anlu were the most important. Ch'ang Yü-ch'un captured these in mid-June. With the Han River valley under their control, the Ming could make either war or alliance with Kökö Temür's enemies in Shensi; and, as if in response to this fact, the Ming leadership temporarily gave credence to rumors that Kökö Temür was massing an army at Juning in Honan to invade them.[88] However, Kökö Temür was still frustrated by the opposition of the lesser northern warlords and did not interfere as the Ming turned to destroy Chang Shih-ch'eng.

By the late summer of 1365, some two years after the death of Ch'en Yu-liang, all of the territories formerly subject to him were tightly integrated into the Ming state; city garrisons of reliable Ming troops under commanders appointed by Chu Yüan-chang had replaced the old local warlords. Although the sources highlight the campaigns through which this integration was accomplished, an even more important process of reorganization was taking place as the ex-Han soldiers were amalgamated into the

Ming armies. Late in 1363 Chu had embarrassed his general Hua Yün-lung by discovering at a military review that Hua did not know how many troops he had under his command.[89] Early in 1364, soon after becoming prince of Wu, Chu undertook a comprehensive reorganization of his armies. The various wing commander's headquarters (*yi yüan-shuai fu*), whose establishment had marked the successive stages of Ming expansion, were redesignated guards (*wei*), and their troop strength was standardized for the first time at five thousand men; they were each divided into five battalions (*ch'ien-hu so*) of one thousand men, each of which were in turn divided into ten companies (*po-hu so*) of one hundred men. A new scale of military ranks was then introduced, and officers were assigned rank according to how many troops they actually had under their command.[90]

The significance of this reorganization was that it placed the Ming armies for the first time under bureaucratic regulation. The expansion of the Ming forces had been the result of surrenders that were often simply voluntary adherence. A leader would surrender in return for confirmation of whatever titles he had assumed plus continuance in control of his own troops and, often, of his own city. Such commanders would not permit interference or close inspection of their military units, which they regarded as personal property and which indeed were often inherited by a son or brother on the death of the original proprietor. The extent of Chu's 1363 victory removed the necessity for treating his commanders so tactfully. His own men were expecting promotions and the increase of their own commands with surrendered soldiers; the price he made them pay was the enumeration, inspection, and continued submission of their units to bureaucratic regulation. As for the ex-Han officers and men, they had surrendered under compulsion and could do no more than accept the relatively favorable treatment they received. Once he had achieved the desired degree of control over the internal administration of the military units, Chu did not attempt to abolish the proprietary system, but on the contrary affirmed it by making hereditary all military officers' positions from guard commander (*chih-hui shih*) down.

Reorganization was accompanied by redeployments designed to separate the less reliable soldiers from their native areas. The oldest Ming soldiers, the five wings of the Nanking reserve army that Chu had led in person in the 1360–63 campaigns, were divided into seventeen guards. The older soldiers of this group were permitted to retire completely, while the rest went into garrison duty cultivating the military colony lands around Nanking. Other soldiers, considered reliable but with shorter records in Ming service, were sent west to garrison the cities of Hunan, Hupei, and Kiangsi or to serve with the armies at Nanch'ang and Wuch'ang on which the control of those regions ultimately rested. The ex-Han troops, on the other hand, were brought down to the Nanking area and combined with the remainder of the Ming armies to form the expeditionary armies that Hsü Ta and Ch'ang Yü-ch'un led against Wu in 1366. While Chu, guarded by his old soldiers, adopted a less military and more truly imperial stance at Nanking, his old companions and other trusted generals now led armies in which the original soldiery was increasingly diluted with drafts of recently surrendered troops. In this manner the Ming military reorganized for the war with Wu.[91]

Chang Shih-ch'eng's only hope after the P'oyang campaign was an all-out offensive before the Ming could mobilize the military potential of the conquered Han lands. Their repeated failures in such offensives showed the degree to which the Wu armies had deteriorated in the long years of relative inaction. In November 1364 Chang Shih-hsin laid siege to Ch'anghsing but was driven away with heavy losses by a relief army from Ch'angchou led by T'ang Ho the following month.[92] In March 1365 Li Po-sheng, who had previously failed to take Ch'anghsing, led an army of two hundred thousand men to Chuch'üan, which had defected to Wu in 1363, and laid siege to Hsinch'eng, the new fortress that the Ming had built to mask Chuch'üan. Li Wen-chung went to break the siege with the main army of Chekiang. On the foggy morning of 12 March he broke the enemy line with a downhill cavalry charge; as the Wu army retreated in disorder past Hsinch'eng, the garrison sortied and turned the retreat into a rout. Before sunset, as Li Wen-chung surveyed a corpse-strewn battlefield, his troops captured the Wu camp intact. This was the last Wu attempt at an offensive. Lü Chen and Li Po-sheng had both been defeated, and Hsü Yi, the third of the once sharp "claws and teeth" of the Wu state, later refused to fight at all.[93]

The Ming offensive that developed late in 1365 aimed first at the Wu territories north of the Yangtze, conquest of which would reduce the likelihood of cooperation between Chang Shih-ch'eng and the northern warlords. In December Hsü Ta's army took T'aichou (Kiangsu), and then conquered several smaller cities near the Grand Canal, his campaign leading to the fall of Kaoyu on 24 April 1366. Hsü Ta next moved north on the canal and surprised and destroyed Hsü Yi's fleet, at which the Wu commandant of Huaian, Mei Szu-tsu, who later became a Ming noble, surrendered.[94] Haochou, Suchou, and Hsüchou surrendered in turn. Hsü then marched west along the Huai and captured Anfeng on 29 May.[95] Once again the conflict between the northern warlords prevented Kökö Temür from intervening.

The Ming armies were inactive in the summer, presumably engaged in farming. The surrendered Wu soldiers were incorporated into the Ming armies, some being sent, much against their will, to garrison cities in the wilder parts of southern Hunan.[96] In September the Ming army of two hundred thousand men invaded Wu. Chu Yüan-chang had insisted over Ch'ang Yü-ch'un's objections that the strategy of "clipping the wings" of Wu be continued, which meant taking Huchou and Hangchow first. The main Ming army attacked Huchou, which fell on 8 December, while Li Wen-chung and the Chekiang army laid siege to Hangchow. The Wu commandant of Hangchow, P'an Yüan-ming, surrendered on 15 December. This unexpectedly easy success permitted Hsü Ta and Ch'ang Yü-ch'un to proceed directly to Soochow, which was completely invested by 27 December.[97]

The ten-month siege that followed was the most spectacular of the many included in the accounts of these wars. Hsü Ta was in overall command of the besiegers, his deputy Ch'ang Yü-ch'un made camp on Tiger Hill overlooking the city, and eight other generals who later became dukes or marquises, plus one of Chu Yüan-chang's adopted sons, each blockaded a section of wall with his own division. Soochow was not famous as a fortress, but it was defended by Chang Shih-ch'eng's personal troops, whose elite regiment, the "Ten-tailed Dragons," always wore brocade robes and silver mail in battle. Chang refused all Ming exhortations to surrender, and after a decade of lethargy led his troops vigorously in person, attempting repeatedly to break up the siege by sorties from the city. Yü T'ung-hai, who had gained fame in the P'oyang campaign, died of wounds received during the siege. The Ming army surrounded Soochow with an unbroken wall of earthworks and built platforms, from which rotting heads and various other offal were thrown inside the walls. While flaming arrows and rockets damaged the buildings in the city, the walls shook to bombardment by the Ming siege artillery, one shot from which killed Chang Shih-hsin.[98]

The walls were finally breached on 1 October 1367. Chang Shih-ch'eng fell back fighting into the interior of the city, but the situation was hopeless. He retired to his palace and hanged himself, only to be cut down still living and made prisoner by the Ming, but he refused to take food and hanged himself again, this time successfully, after being taken to Nanking. The capture of Soochow, which in 1393 was the most populous and heavily taxed prefecture in the empire, ended Wu resistance and added 250,000 experienced soldiers to the already large Ming armies. Having conquered the entire Yangtze valley downstream from Szechwan, the Ming were now on the verge of taking the North China plain and the South China coast.[99]

As of 1367 the leading regional militarist in North China was Kökö Temür, originally named Wang Pao-pao, the nephew and adopted son and heir of Chaghan Temür. The latter had owed his rise to the brief florescence of the Red Turban Sung empire, which had shielded the rise of the Yangtze regimes and had thereby allowed the north and south to develop independently for over a decade. Chaghan Temür was from Honan and was descended from a *tamachi* soldier (a warrior in an army assigned to a fiefholder of early Yüan) who had participated in the conquest of that province in the time of Ögödei (r. 1229–41). He had passed the chü-jen examination before the outbreak of the rebellions, but despite this distinction the house of Confucian learning was not his favorite abode; he preferred to ride, shoot, and enjoy the company of his fellow landlords and locally powerful people. He became the leader of a group of similarly inclined braves, one of whom, a minor county official named Li Szu-ch'i, also became a prominent warlord. Socially and personally, Chaghan Temür resembled Kuo Tzu-hsing and, like Kuo, raised militia forces after the Red Turban rebellions. Though well rewarded for this, Chaghan and his militia lapsed into obscurity until 1355, when the rebellions spread after the dismissal of Toghtō. Until mid-1357 Chaghan Temür and Li Szu-ch'i cooperated with Dash Badulugh, who was then emerging as the semiautonomous military ruler of Honan.[100] The great Red Turban invasions of 1357 resulted in the fall of K'aifeng and the destruction of Dash Badulugh's power. When the rebels invaded Shensi as well, the Yüan authorities there invited Chaghan Temür and Li Szu-ch'i into Shensi with their armies. Rewarded by the court with high titles for driving the rebels out of the Wei River valley, Chaghan and Li then methodically suppressed the regular Yüan administration in Shensi, adding its troops to their own and appointing their own local officials. Campaigns to suppress rebels in the Fen River valley gave Chaghan a similar position in Shansi by the end of 1358. Hoping to retain some margin of control over him, the Yüan court acquiesced after the fact in Chaghan's territorial expansion, granting him title and authority in Honan and Shansi. In 1359 he held civil service examinations on his own authority in Honan, and in the summer of that year he dealt a deathblow to the Red Turban movement by capturing K'aifeng (see pp. 32–33).[101]

Soon after Chaghan's victory, the Yüan court, confronted once again by a great minister who had grown too powerful through fighting against rebels, attempted to curtail his authority. The instrument chosen for this task was Dash Badulugh's son, and his successor in the command of his armies, Bolod Temür, who had built up a power base of his own in Hopei and northern Shansi. When the court ordered Chaghan to transfer central Shansi, then a key agricultural area for military provisions, to Bolod's jurisdiction, Chaghan defied the imperial decree and resisted by force until both Bolod and the court backed down. Chaghan's successful resistance to the court's commands, contrasting so markedly with Toghtō's acquiescence in 1355, indicated the extent to which the Yüan imperial court had become a helpless observer of the process of territorial fragmentation even in North China.[102]

His power base secured, Chaghan turned against the remaining Red Turban strongholds in Shantung. His conquest of these was protracted compared to his swift takeover of Honan. While besieging Yitu, Chaghan was murdered on 7 July 1362 by two warlords, one of them an ex-Red Turban commander who had surrendered to him the previous year. The murderers justified themselves by accusing Chaghan Temür of not being a true loyalist.[103] Whatever their motives, the murder set back the political development of North China. Had Chaghan lived, it is very likely that he could have unified North China under his control by 1363 or 1364, in which case he would have been able to intervene decisively to prevent Chu Yüan-chang from fully exploiting his P'oyang victory. It would still have been difficult for the north to conquer the south, but it is not difficult to imagine Chaghan masterminding an extension of the North China political system to all of China, with all of the regional leaders pledging their nominal loyalty to the Yüan emperor while Chaghan played Ts'ao Ts'ao in the midst of it all. As it turned out, however, the Yüan court allowed Kökö Temür to succeed to his uncle's offices, and Kökö suppressed the murderers, conquered Shantung, and established his authority securely in Honan and Shansi. But Li Szuch'i and others of Chaghan's old henchmen refused to acknowledge Kökö's command over them, with the result that Kökö was still fighting for mastery in the north when the Ming northern expedition of 1368 swept over him like a tidal wave.[104]

The unsuccessful attempt of the Yüan crown prince, Ayushiridara, to impose his own rule over the contending armies in North China led to the seizure of the capital by Bolod Temür in May 1364. Ayushiridara fled to Kökö Temür's camp. Bolod proceeded to make himself intolerable, and in August 1365 he was assassinated on the emperor's orders. The court now gave Kökö military authority over all the North China armies and ordered him to suppress the rebels in the south. The result was that Bolod's former supporters in Shansi and Shensi joined forces with Li Szuch'i and company, and this combination waged civil war against Kökö. Faced with imperial orders intended to separate the combatants and direct all of them against the Ming, Kökö by his behavior showed himself a regionalist rather than a loyalist. Because he defied the imperial orders and carried on the civil war, Kökö was deprived of his offices, and finally, in February 1368, the emperor ordered the other northern warlords to destroy him. Kökö defeated this attempt on the battlefield, and his army remained the strongest military force in the disunited north.[105]

Immediately after the fall of Soochow, the Ming moved against

Fang Kuo-chen. Chu Liang-tsu took T'aichou (Chekiang) in October and Wenchou in November by land, while the Ming fleet under T'ang Ho simultaneously drove Fang himself from his capital at Ningpo, finally capturing him at sea in December.[106]

Meanwhile Chu Yüan-chang summoned his generals to Nanking to decide on plans for the conquest of the north. Ch'ang Yü-ch'un wished to march directly on Peking: for the battle-hardened Ming armies, conquering the north would be "as easy as splitting bamboo." Chu Yüan-chang disagreed and insisted on a four-stage plan of operations involving in succession the conquest of Shantung, the reduction of Honan as far west as the T'ungkuan pass, the conquest of the Peking area, and the conquest of Shansi and Shensi. Chu's insistence on the methodical annexation of territory meant that the Ming armies were to destroy Kökö Temür's rivals and drive the Yüan emperor into his hands. As a result, Kökö himself and his largely intact army survived to pose a severe threat to the Ming empire in the 1370's, consequences that were not foreseen when the formal orders for the Ming northern expedition were issued on 13 November 1367. The 250,000-man army for the conquest of the north was placed under Hsü Ta and Ch'ang Yü-ch'un. Hu Mei was to invade Fukien overland while the fleet under T'ang Ho and Liao Yung-chung was to sail down the coast to attack Fukien and Kwangtung from the sea.[107]

The southern campaigns quickly brought Fukien, Kwangtung, and Kwangsi under Ming rule. Hu Mei's army captured Shaowu on 28 December; the fleet arrived at Foochow on 18 January 1368 and captured it, and then sailed up the Min River to receive Ch'en Yu-ting's surrender of Yenp'ing on 17 February, which completed the conquest of the province. Liao Yung-chung and Chu Liang-tsu then took the fleet further south. When they reached Canton on 18 April, the Yüan governor, Ho Chen, promptly surrendered. The fleet then sailed up the West River and took Wuchou on 26 May; this was the key to the conquest of Kwangsi, though another two months of campaigning were necessary before the province was secured.[108]

The northern expedition also went according to schedule. Hsü Ta and Ch'ang Yü-ch'un took Tsinan on 28 December 1367 and spent the next two months in the conquest of Shantung, which they completed by taking Tungch'ang on 1 March 1368. Teng Yü then invaded Honan from the south, taking Nanyang while Hsü and Ch'ang marched in from the east. K'aifeng, surrounded, surrendered on 16 April. Nine days later the Yüan army suffered defeat near Loyang and that city fell. Feng Sheng's capture of T'ungkuan on 13 May concluded the second phase of the northern expedition according to plan.[109]

While the Ming troops rested or worked during the summer planting season, Chu Yüan-chang, now emperor, came north to K'aifeng to confer with his generals before launching the third phase of the campaign. No changes in plan were made, and after the harvest the Ming armies crossed the Yellow River in August. Peking fell on 14 September to Hsü Ta, who preserved it intact. The Yüan emperor, Toghon Temür, and the crown prince, Ayushiridara, escaped with some of the court barely in advance of the Ming armies and fled into Inner Mongolia. The name of the city was changed from Tatu ("Great Capital") to Peip'ing ("The North is Pacified") to symbolize the triumph of the south. Two weeks later the Ming armies marched into Shansi.[110]

Han Lin-erh died in 1366, drowned when his boat capsized crossing the Yangtze, an accident that according to one tradition was arranged on orders from Chu Yüan-chang.[111] Chu did not permit anyone to succeed the so-called Sung emperor. Instead, he designated the following year (1367) the first year of Wu and stopped using the Red Turban calendar.[112] Since calendrical usage was the clearest sign of political affiliation in traditional China, the effect of this step was to leave Chu's already nearly imperial apparatus in a kind of vacuum of legitimation that begged for the emergence of an emperor. On 23 January 1368, while his commanders were conquering both the North China plain and the South China coast, Chu Yüan-chang went through the formal rites of accession to the imperial throne. Although he did this at the prompting of his civil officials, he dispensed with the traditional hypocrisy of the "three refusals." The dynastic name Ming, employed anachronistically heretofore in our discussion (see pp. 33–36), was chosen, and 1368 was designated the first year of the period Hung-wu ("Overflowing Martial Accomplishment"), a term that celebrated the dynasty's founding by the success of its arms.[113] Chu Yüan-chang began the practice, followed later by the Ch'ing as well, of using a single calendrical designation (*nien-*

hao) throughout each reign, and he and his successors will henceforth be referred to by their reign names. The Ming empire was now in existence in name as well as in fact. Even though Szechwan was still unconquered, as were Yünnan in the south and Manchuria and Mongolia in the north, most of the Chinese cultural area acknowledged Ming rule. The era of rapid military unification was over, and while military problems remained, the new emperor now had to devote himself to the creation of the Confucian legitimacy that was needed to attract scholar-gentry officials to staff the government institutions that would rule the common people in peacetime.

THREE

Hung-wu: The Period of Consolidation, 1368–1380

Between 1368 and 1380 the new emperor attempted to establish his regime on a firm basis. Military affairs were less critical than during the preceding civil war period. Szechwan, the only Chinese-inhabited area not under Ming rule in 1368, was conquered and annexed, but on the northern frontier military defeat led the emperor to adopt a defensive posture. The economic and geographical base of Ming power continued to be the population and grain of the lower Yangtze region. In the military sphere the problem was to go from total to partial mobilization while still providing for those troops no longer required for active duty; the solution Hung-wu adopted was to extend the military colony system to all units, with the additional provision of rotating tours of active service, and the creation of a military high command of titled nobles.

Whatever his feelings about Confucians and Confucianism, Hung-wu knew that he had to identify himself with the tradition of legitimate Confucian political authority. He did this by cultivating the symbols—ceremony, language, dress—of Confucian rule and by suppressing the remnants of the heterodox origins of the Ming regime. However, in contrast to his military success, Hung-wu's choice of civil policies was marked by false starts. He first instituted and then abolished the civil service examinations, and encouraged and then prohibited contact with foreign countries. But despite his hesitations, he could not postpone the creation of a bureaucracy to administer the empire, and these years saw the steady growth of the civil administration and the elaboration of its functions.

Most of this growth occurred under the leadership of Chancellor Hu Wei-yung, who by 1380 was running the civil service as virtually his own political enterprise. In that year Hung-wu executed him on charges of treason and purged both the civil and the military elites. Fundamental changes in foreign and domestic policy followed.

The Emperor and the Nature of Imperial Authority

Discussion of the Hung-wu period should begin with the character of the emperor, but it is not possible to describe Hung-wu in a few words. Intelligence and compassion warred with fear and cruelty in his nature, the harsher elements eventually predominating, but the course of his life had given him reason for fears that make his cruelties in part understandable. His intelligence is evident in the generalship and statesmanship shown in his rise to power. His personal experience in the famines of 1344 and after made him aware of the political uses compassion could have, and his later career consistently showed solicitude for the common people, in his firm insistence on military discipline in the areas conquered by his troops, his prompt tax remissions and other relief measures in areas afflicted by natural disasters, and his creation of a military system that did not bear directly on the people at large. This was all good Confucian behavior, to be sure, but Hung-wu gave it considerably more emphasis than was strictly necessary, and generals who violated military discipline or civil officials who mismanaged relief operations quickly felt his wrath. However, as emperor his attitude toward the common people was thoroughly paternalistic. His compassion for them did not mean that he intended to be governed by their opinions. The people were expected to obey orders and work industriously in their proper occupations, the chief of which was agriculture.[1]

Certainly Hung-wu's behavior reflects a general sense of insecurity that limited him in the free exercise of his abilities and later led him to almost paranoid excesses of suspicion. This insecurity originally had a rational basis. Between 1352 and 1356 he had been involved at the ground level in the cutthroat world of Chinese warlord politics. His life was in danger on several occasions, and even though the sources have been prettified at this point, it is clear that his rapid rise was aided by his betrayal of the heirs of Kuo Tzu-hsing, behavior his own supporters might repay in kind. Any illusions that he had gained security by becoming duke of Wu were removed by the Shao Jung conspiracy of 1362. Even after he became emperor he could imagine his generals resenting the fact that he, once their childhood friend and equal, had been exalted so high above them. After 1380 he apparently could not escape these thoughts.

Hung-wu was physically ugly and had spent the years 1344–52 either as a novice in a Buddhist monastery or as a wandering monk. During his rise to power his ugly visage with its high forehead, thick nose, and protruding jaw fascinated his followers, and the Buddhist experience was responsible both for his physical survival and for whatever education he possessed. As he rose from prince to emperor, however, both his appearance and his background caused him pain. Scholars who were subservient in his presence made puns behind his back mocking his appearance. As his officials reworked his rough drafts of imperial decrees into suitably elegant Chinese prose, he felt their contempt.

The emperor could respond with denunciations of those whose experience was exclusively literary. "The 'outstanding' scholar-gentry sit in the market or village, pride themselves on their capability, and listen to people flatter and praise them. Yet all they know is writing on paper. They have never had any practical experience of affairs. They write books to establish doctrine, but all this amounts to is chewing on phrases and biting on words to the ruination of their students. When you examine what they do, it is nothing. They make grand discussions and thus consider themselves capable in affairs. They are of no benefit." He could respond more concretely by executing those guilty of real or fancied insults. But he could not execute the scholar-gentry as a class, or even refrain from attempts to attract them to his service.[2]

Behind his insecurity and suspicions, Hung-wu possessed a keen intelligence. He had definite opinions concerning the relationship between institutions and society, and believed that society could and should be reformed by changing institutions—a Legalist view contrary to fifteen centuries of Confucian orthodoxy that had emphasized the moral character of rulers and officials rather than their institutional relationships. In contrast to the shaky political superstructure, which collapsed soon after the emperor's death, the underlying foundation of administrative institutions created during the Hung-wu reign was solid. As reorganized and reconstituted by Hung-wu, the departments of the central government, the organization of local government, the provincial administration, and the fiscal and examination systems all proved their durability by lasting with only minor modifications until the end of the imperial state itself in the twentieth century. The census and land-survey systems and the military colony and *wei-so* systems created in his reign survived without formal modification until the end of the dynasty, though they admittedly were not punctiliously administered in the mature Ming period. In general, therefore, Hung-wu deserves his reputation as the creator of Ming institutions.

This does not prove, however, that the emperor wished to create the hyper-Confucian state and society characteristic of the mature Ming and Ch'ing periods. The early Ming period differed qualitatively from the following centuries. The Confucian scholar-gentry class played a secondary role, and the favored beneficiaries of the new empire were an aristocratic elite composed of a class of hereditary military officers headed by a small group of hereditary nobles and capped by the imperial family. The antecedent and model for this elite was the Mongol and so-called Se-mu aristocracy that had ruled the Yüan empire, whose institutions Hung-wu was thus attempting to translate into purely Chinese terms.* The scholar-gentry would play an important role in this conception of empire, but it would be as instruments of imperial rule. They would be valued for their administrative expertise, not for their function as ideal Confucian officials who should remonstrate with their emperor from a position of moral superiority

---

* Se-mu is a term meaning "colored eyes" that was used in the Yüan to designate peoples of Turkish and other Central Asian or western origin; the Se-mu ranked after the Mongols but before the Chinese in the Yüan system of ethnic stratification.

as authoritative expositors of the orthodox Confucian tradition. Hung-wu expected civil officials to be as obedient as military officers (though he did not reward them as well). Under these circumstances the elaborate Confucian trappings of government in the Hung-wu period appear to contain a large propagandistic element. The emperor wished to persuade the scholar-gentry of the legitimacy of his regime without according them the political role they had traditionally claimed.

In fact, the early Ming empire represented three distinct traditions. First, and best represented in the written sources, was its role as reincarnation of the proper Confucian empire of the Han, T'ang, and Sung dynasties. Hung-wu liked to compare himself to the Han founder. Barbarian names and barbarian styles of dress were banned, and court robes and court ceremony were modeled on those of the T'ang.[3] Much of this was ceremonial shadow; the institutional substance was provided by the second tradition, the recently departed Yüan dynasty, which served as the model not only for the military elite but for central and provincial government as well. Beyond that, the Yüan tradition haunted the early Ming empire, challenging it to conquer all the territories formerly under Yüan rule. The existence of active Yüan pretenders north of the Great Wall naturally added to this temptation. The third tradition was that of the Red Turban empire with its basis in Maitreya worship. After 1368 the emperor found his Red Turban antecedents embarrassing, and he attempted to wipe out the religion and eliminate its memory from the historical records.[4] Because of what the Ming empire later became, its embodiment of the traditional Chinese (as opposed to nomadic) ideal of empire was most easily remembered. It was to this ideal that the Chinese revolutionaries of 1926–28 appealed when they launched their own northern expedition against their enemies, made Nanking their capital, gave the name "Peip'ing" to their defeated rivals' headquarters, and buried their own founder near Hung-wu on the southern slope of the Purple Mountain at Nanking.[5]

However, in 1368 memories of the Yüan and the Red Turbans were still very vivid, as illustrated by the choice of the word *ming* ("bright") as the name of the dynasty. The practice of naming a dynasty after an abstract attribute had been introduced into the Chinese world by the Jurchen Chin, followed by the Mongol

Yüan, both dynasties of barbarian origin. Native Chinese dynasties had followed the practice of naming themselves after the state ruled by or the noble title borne by the dynastic founder. Hung-wu had been duke of Wu since 1356, had been prince of Wu since 1364, and had proclaimed 1367 the first year of Wu. This seemed to be pointing to the proclamation of a Wu dynasty. Instead, "Ming" was chosen.

The word had a twofold significance. First, it suggested the victory of the south over the north, of the rebels over the Yüan. Ming could stand for red or fire, the color and element of the south in the Five Elements classification, while Yüan punned on the word *hsüan* ("dark," "deep," as water); black and water were the color and element of the north. Second, and more important, Ming abbreviated Ming-chiao, the "Bright Religion," the name of the Manichaean cult whose doctrines had become jumbled with Maitreya worship in the general millenarian mixture that nourished the rebellions. The name of the dynasty was therefore both a consolation to the former religious rebels and a cudgel held over their heads. Han Lin-erh had been the Little King of Light (*hsiao Ming Wang*) whose arrival heralded the advent of Maitreya, the greater king. By calling his dynasty Ming, Hung-wu implicitly claimed Maitreya's part for himself and, within the context of White Lotus doctrine, justified his refusal to continue Han Lin-erh's line. The followers of the White Lotus and kindred faiths could now return to their lawful occupations, for the promises of their religion had been fulfilled; the new Ming empire was the promised Pure Land in this world, and Hung-wu was the long-awaited savior. Those who did not accept this interpretation suffered a fate similar to the Jews elsewhere as the newly imperial Ming government waged war on the remnants of the White Lotus sect and the other religious rebels, destroying their temples and exiling their adherents.[6]

Thus, of the three traditions existing in uneasy symbiosis in the China of 1368, Hung-wu had decisively rejected the Red Turban and had only partially accepted the Confucian. His main allegiance was to the kind of quasi-Legalistic managerial despotism exemplified in the Yüan empire as recently as the chancellorship of Toghtō. The emperor would now put this style of rule into Chinese dress.

The Frontier: Successes and Stalemates

Despite the symbolic importance of the capture of the Yüan capital, which had been a primary or secondary capital of barbarian dynasties since the tenth century, the military situation in the north was still not secure. Emperor Toghon Temür had come to rest at Yingch'ang in Inner Mongolia, where his court was the natural center of attraction for Mongol refugees and other pro-Yüan elements. Kökö Temür and the lesser Yüan regionalists, who were still squabbling among themselves, controlled all of Shansi and Shensi. They thus had a common frontier with Ming Sheng, son and successor of Ming Yü-chen, who continued his father's imperial pretensions in Szechwan. Although the Ming capture of the pass at T'ungkuan had locked the door on a Mongol invasion of the central plain, in certain other respects the military situation in the north was not favorable. Large areas were famine ravaged or depopulated, and supplies had to be brought overland from considerable distances. The terrain in the north enhanced the importance of cavalry, the arm in which the Ming was weakest. Both factors were even more pronounced north of the Great Wall. The interconnected wars in Szechwan and North China lasted four years (1368–72), only to end inconclusively in a series of defeats that led Hung-wu to abandon his desire to subjugate the remainder of the Yüan empire.

Hsü Ta's capture of Peking had followed a forced march that left many cities in his rear untaken. When Hung-wu on 27 September 1368 ordered the conquest of Shansi, it was necessary first to capture these. Ch'ang Yü-ch'un took Paoting and Chenting; Feng Sheng and T'ang Ho took Huaich'ing and then invaded Shansi from Honan. On 9 January 1369 the main invading army under Hsü Ta captured T'aiyüan. Kökö Temür retired west to Kansu, since he was still unable to gain the cooperation of the warlords of Shensi. Simultaneously Ch'ang Yü-ch'un invaded northern Shansi, taking Tat'ung on 3 March. During April Hsü and Ch'ang occupied the Wei River valley of Shensi with little resistance as the Yüan warlords withdrew to the northwest. Hsü Ta remained in Shensi long enough to supervise famine relief, and then in a series of marches captured Kungch'ang, Lint'ao, Hsining, P'ingliang and Yenan, thus leaving Kökö Temür as the sole surviving Yüan loyalist in the northwest.[7]

Ch'ang Yü-ch'un meanwhile had returned with his army to Peip'ing. In the summer he went north of the Great Wall and captured K'aip'ing, but on 9 August he died in camp after fourteen years of heroic violence in Ming service. The emperor ordered Li Wen-chung to assume command of his forces. The last military action of the year was Hsü Ta's conquest of Ch'ingyang on 22 September.[8]

During the autumn and winter the Mongols under Kökö Temür staged a series of attacks against Lanchow and other Ming border towns, while at the same time the Ming government was making diplomatic efforts to induce the Szechwan regime to surrender without fighting. If the Mongols could be severely defeated, this would both secure the border and deprive the Szechwan regime of any hope of assistance. These considerations led the Ming to launch a two-pronged offensive against the Mongols in 1370. While Li Wen-chung and Feng Sheng led the Peip'ing army through the pass at Chüyung to attack the Yüan emperor, Hsü Ta (assisted by Teng Yü and T'ang Ho) marched from Sian in search of Kökö Temür.[9]

Li Wen-chung's army took Hsingho and then marched to Chaghan Nor, where they captured an important Yüan general with his men. Meanwhile, on 23 May 1370 Emperor Toghon Temür died at Yingch'ang. The succession went to Ayushiridara, whose enmity to Kökö Temür was a bad omen for the Mongol cause. On 10 June Li Wen-chung's army arrived at Yingch'ang, took the defenders by surprise, and stormed the city. Ayushiridara escaped and fled across the Gobi to Outer Mongolia accompanied by only a few dozen horsemen. His young son Maidiribala was captured, and over fifty thousand Mongol warriors surrendered. Li Wen-chung had reason to be proud of his achievement, which ended the Mongol threat in the regions of Inner Mongolia bordering on Peip'ing and Shansi, but the language of his victory memorial was so extravagant that his uncle the emperor was displeased.[10]

On 3 May Hsü Ta's army made contact with Kökö Temür's forces near Tinghsi in Kansu. Evidently the Mongols had more men than expected, for the Ming army took a position where part of its front was covered by a stream and erected earthen ramparts to cover the rest. The Mongols attacked and outflanked the southeast wing of the Ming line, whose commander, Hu Te-chi, lost control of his men. With the Ming army on the verge of disaster, the furious Hsü Ta took personal command of that wing, executed several officers, and put Hu Te-chi in chains; he refrained from executing him only because of the memory of his adoptive father, Hu Ta-hai. The following day the Ming army counterattacked, and the apparently formidable Mongols collapsed. Kökö Temür fled across the Gobi to Qara Qorum with his family and immediate retainers, leaving over eighty-six thousand officers and men to fall into Ming hands. This victory broke Kökö Temür's hold on the northwest and achieved the purpose of the campaign; Hsü Ta spent the rest of the campaigning season reducing lesser cities in Shensi.[11]

The victories of 1370 lessened the threat from the Mongols and permitted the Ming to proceed to the conquest of Szechwan. Ming Yü-chen had sent envoys to Chu Yüan-chang in 1363 following the P'oyang victory, and the two regimes enjoyed cordial diplomatic contacts for the next several years, exchanging letters comparing themselves to Liu Pei and Sun Chien—and Kökö Temür, naturally, to Ts'ao Ts'ao. However, in 1366 Ming Yü-chen died, and his son Ming Sheng was too young to rule unaided. When the Ming state became imperially demanding, the leaders of Szechwan were not united on a policy either of resisting or of surrendering on favorable terms. The emperor sent Yang Ching, now his governor of Hukwang (Hunan and Hupei), to take Ming Sheng a decree exhorting him to surrender, but the Szechwan government did not reply.[12]

By early 1371 the Han River valley in southern Shensi was under Ming control, and the Ming armies were free for further conquests. The emperor ordered Hsü Ta to command at Peip'ing, sent Teng Yü to Hsiangyang to superintend the movement of military supplies up the Han River into Shensi, and sent Fu Yu-te to take field command there. Fu's mission was to invade Szechwan overland from the north, marching down the Chialing river toward Chengtu. Simultaneously, T'ang Ho and Liao Yung-chung were to take the Ming fleet up the Yangtze through the gorges. Ch'ü't'ang gorge had been strongly prepared for defense, with chain bridges suspended from the cliffsides across the river; catapults were mounted on wooden platforms hanging from the chains. T'ang Ho after one repulse refused to attack this position again. In the north Fu Yu-te was more successful, conquering Chiehchou and several other towns early in the summer. This reverse caused the Szechwan generals to transfer forces from Ch'üt'ang gorge to their northern front, where the reinforcements did not prevent the Ming from taking Hanchou on 13 July 1371. Meanwhile, by using cannon mounted on his ships to destroy the chain-suspended catapults of his enemy, Liao Yung-chung stormed the Ch'üt'ang position and sailed through the gorge to take K'ueichou. This roused T'ang Ho from his torpor, and he followed; the Ming fleets reached Chungking on 3 August and Ming Sheng surrendered. After a minor setback, Fu Yu-te completed the conquest of Szechwan by taking Ch'engtu a month later.[13]

The victories of 1370 and the capture of Maidiribala gave the Ming emperor an opportunity to attempt to settle the northern frontier by diplomatic means. He hoped for a formal acknowledgment of Ming supremacy from Ayushiridara and a renunciation of the latter's claim to the imperial throne; this would further fragment the Mongol tribes and help bring them under Ming control. Hung-wu hoped to achieve this goal by a combination of threats of force and favorable treatment for Maidiribala and the other high-ranking Mongols who had been captured. Twice in 1370 letters were sent to Ayushiridara (their contents also were circulated to other Mongol leaders) urging him to acknowledge the transfer of the Mandate of Heaven and threatening him with invasion if he did not. Ayushiridara made no reply. After the pacification of Szechwan, Hung-wu ordered the most far-reaching campaign the Ming armies had yet undertaken to crush the Mongols in 1372.[14]

Being advised that Kökö Temür's army was not over 100,000 strong, the emperor ordered Hsü Ta to march with 150,000 cavalry from Yenmen pass in Shansi across the Gobi to Qara Qorum, Feng Sheng with 50,000 cavalry to conquer the rest of the Kansu corridor, and Li Wen-chung with the same number to attack the Mongols of Inner Mongolia and Manchuria from Yingch'ang. Wu Chen, who had been a subordinate fleet commander in several previous campaigns, took charge of the movement of military provisions by sea to the Liaotung peninsula in support of the latter operation. Hsü Ta's army crossed the Gobi without any recorded difficulty. On 23 April 1372 Lan Yü, one of Hsu's subordinate generals, encountered part of Kökö Temür's army on the Tula River and inflicted a sharp reverse. Kökö avoided battle for over a month, apparently waiting for a time and situation of his own choosing. In any event, when the two armies met on 7 June in a decisive battle (concerning which no details are recorded) the result was a disaster for the Ming. Several myriads of troops were lost; faced with the prospect of losing his entire army, the once-invincible Hsü Ta had to retire in haste from Outer Mongolia. Li Wen-chung's army entered Outer Mongolia a month later. The Chinese encountered Manzi Qarajang's army by the Tula and pursued it to the Orkhon, where the Mongols counterattacked. The Ming soldiers defended themselves behind ramparts improvised from the carcasses of previously captured cattle, and after three days the Mongols, fearing a trap, withdrew. Li Wen-chung retired from Mongolia claiming a victory, but he had lost too many men and too many high-ranking officers to make his claim credible. Two weeks later (10 August) T'ang Ho likewise suffered defeat. Only in the west were the Ming success-ful. Feng Sheng's army marched as far as Tunhuang, defeating everyone they met and capturing droves of cattle.[15]

Despite Feng Sheng's feat, 1372 had been a year of disasters in the north, and the Mongols now defied Ming authority almost to within sight of the Great Wall. Hung-wu therefore abandoned his attempt to subjugate Outer Mongolia by direct force of arms. In addition to the loss of life caused by the defeats, there were other claims on Ming military resources. First, the growth of Japanese piracy to serious proportions required the diversion of troops to coastal defence. Second, conquests since 1367 had extended Ming authority over aboriginal peoples in Kwangsi, Hukwang, Szechwan, and Shensi who had felt much more at home under the multinational Yüan empire than they did under the new Ming regime, which was controlled by the same Chinese people who were encroaching on their lands. By 1372 this whole region was in rebellion, and major military operations were needed to pacify it.

The Ming government therefore adopted a defensive stance on the northern frontier that endured for the next fifteen years (until 1387). During this period the Ming armies held the defensive zone of the Great Wall against raids that were often of a scale large

gh to be called invasions, and Ming counterattacks did not
id farther than centers like Hsingho within a short distance of
wall. Hung-wu continued diplomatic exchanges with Ayu-
sin.idara, and in 1374 sent Maidiribala back to his father under
escort of two former Yüan eunuchs, but this attempt at conciliation
brought no lasting results. When Ayushiridara died in 1378, he
was succeeded by his younger brother Toghus Temür (r. 1378–
88), not by Maidiribala, who might have been responsive to
Chinese influence. However, as the Chinese imperial idea with-
ered on the Mongolian steppes, the Yüan pretenders' ability to
control the other princes of the house of Chinggis Qan correspondingly waned.[16]

The Transformation of the Military Establishment

By 1373 the new Ming empire was still a thin, hardly more than
rhetorical veneer giving a mere appearance of unity to a political
situation in which military force was still the predominant factor.
With territorial expansion temporarily halted, Hung-wu had to
fashion military institutions that would not strain a normal peacetime economy and yet would avert the catastrophic social consequences of a large-scale demobilization of troops. The generals
who had assisted in the founding of the dynasty had to be rewarded, but not on such a lavish scale that their power would become a
threat to dynastic stability. Hung-wu's attempts to solve these
problems—the *wei-so* system and the early Ming nobility—
crystallized in the 1370's. Both were extensions of the process by
which the original Ming armies had been formed.

In the mature Ming period the Ming armies (actually the pool of
men liable for active military service) consisted of those whose
military obligation was hereditary. They were for the most part
descendants of men who had entered the Ming armies in one of
three ways: as one of Chu Yüan-chang's early followers, as troops
of warlords who surrendered to Chu in the course of the civil wars,
or as the result of punishment for crime. The third group was not
numerically important during this period, and the only un-
qualified members of the first were Chu's original twenty-four
followers and the seven hundred men recruited in 1353, whose
survivors were at least middle-ranking officers by the 1370's. Thus

virtually all of the Ming soldiers were men who had surrendered to Chu at some stage in the civil wars in response to promises of favorable treatment usually coupled with force or the threat of force.[17]

The troops who surrendered had done so in organized bands usually recruited by a leader or leaders from a distinct area. The most important term in such a unit's surrender was Chu's promise to preserve the unit intact under its original leadership, well illustrated in his response to Hu Mei's offer to surrender Nan-ch'ang in 1362:

> You also fear that your troops will be scattered and divided up among the other commanders. In this you show excessive anxiety. It has been ten years since I first raised troops, and I have obtained rare talents and brave soldiers from the four quarters of the earth.... I have always promoted the sincere in heart and treated them well. I employ them in office according to their talents; if their troops are few, then I give them more; if their ranks are low, then I promote them; and if they lack riches, then I reward them. This is the spirit with which I treat my fighting men. How could I be willing to scatter their followers, thus punishing them for coming over to me?[18]

However, preserving the integrity of a unit under its own leadership meant that the leadership became a nontransferable corps of regimental officers whose rights of hereditary succession had in practice to be recognized. Hence, hereditary succession of military officers was a feature of the Ming military system from the beginning. Many famous commanders are examples: Liao Yung-chung inherited the naval command of his captured brother, Liao Yung-an; Feng Sheng that of his deceased brother, Feng Kuo-yung; and Chao Yung that of his executed brother, Chao Chung-chung.[19] During the critical phase of the civil war, Chu Yüan-chang could exert only a limited amount of control over the internal administration of such units.

The 1363 victories brought swarms of freshly surrendered troops into Chu's camp and, by eliminating his principal competitor, made it much more difficult for any single unit to contemplate defection. Chu took advantage of his increased power to impose on his armed forces a reorganization that placed the internal administration of military units under central control but compensated the regimental officers for their loss of autonomy by granting them enhanced prestige and formal hereditary status within the new system. In 1364, on Liu Chi's recommendation, the wei-so system was extended by decree throughout the Ming armed forces. The term derives from the words *wei* ("guard") and *ch'ien-hu so* ("battalion"; literally, "detachments of one thousand households") designating the principal units of the system. The military headquarters in the capital during the T'ang and Sung had been called wei, and the term conveniently translated the Mongolian *keshig* ("guard"), so wei became the designation in Chinese of the elite capital guards during the Yüan period as well. By contrast, *yi* ("wing"), the basic designation of Ming local military commands before 1364, had been applied to militia and other irregular forces during the Yüan. By redesignating the entire army as wei, Chu attempted to mollify all concerned by heightening their prestige. Of course, despite the theoretical equality thus imposed, the officers and men who had served the Ming before 1363, and particularly those who had joined before the 1355 Yangtze crossing, received favorable treatment.[20]

By the decrees of 1364 every wing became a guard, and each of the smaller independent commands (*tsung-kuan fu*) became an independent battalion (*shou-yü ch'ien-hu so*). The strength of each guard was fixed at 5,000 (later 5,600) men, and each was divided into five battalions of 1,000 (later 1,120), each of which was in turn subdivided into ten companies (*po-hu so*) of 100 (later 112). Officers' ranks and titles, which had previously been assumed unilaterally by the leaders of bands and then confirmed on the occasion of their surrender to the Ming, were now arranged in a uniform series and awarded, in the first instance, according to the number of troops under each officer's command. Each guard had the following officers: 1 guard commander (*chih-hui shih*, rank 3a); 2 deputy guard commanders (*chih-hui t'ung-chih*, 3b); 4 assistant guard commanders (*chih-hui ch'ien-shih*, 4a); 2 guard judges (*wei chen-fu*, 5b); 5 battalion commanders (*ch'ien-hu*, 5a); 10 battalion vice-commanders (*fu ch'ien-hu*, 5b); 50 company commanders (*po-hu*, 6a); and 10 battalion judges (*so chen-fu*, 6b). The enumeration of troops necessary for the assignment of these ranks meant increased central control over the internal administration of the military units. In return, however, the officers gained personal and hereditary title to ranks that were considerably higher than those of civil officials at corresponding degrees of responsibility.[21] From 1364 on the Ming established wei and so in new territories soon after they conquered them. By 1393 at least 326 guards and 65 independent battalions had been created. The status of units that had surrendered from 1364 on was not as sacrosanct as that of units that had joined the Ming earlier. Though the sources do not preserve much detail, it is apparent that batches of surrendered Han and Wu soldiers were assigned to already existing units that were under strength, that officers more senior in Ming service were placed in command of units composed primarily of newly surrendered troops, and that units were transferred or sent on campaign in a manner designed to separate surrendered troops from their native areas. Surrendered Han troops were thus pressed into the army that conquered Wu; some of the Wu soldiers captured during the campaign were sent west to garrison the former Han territories; and after the fall of Soochow, the ex-Han and ex-Wu troops served in the army that conquered the north and the fleet that conquered the south, while Chu Yüan-chang's original troops were concentrated in the garrisons of Nanking, which ultimately reached a strength of 49 guards.[22] By the end of the civil war period both Chu's original followers and the troops who had surrendered to him were uprooted from their native areas and so were dependent on the Ming military system for their continued existence and livelihood.

The armies could not be demobilized without great social disruption, but the cost of maintaining the armies as economic parasites was an unacceptable strain on the rest of society and might inhibit the restoration of a stable agricultural order. Even before the crisis phase of the civil wars, Chu had determined to solve this dilemma by making the armies self-sufficient through a massive extension of the military colony system. In 1358 he appointed K'ang Mao-ts'ai to be commissioner of agricultural colonies (*ying-t'ien shih*), an office that in Yüan times had been responsible for the leasing of government lands to tenants. K'ang's assignment, however, apparently involved using soldiers to cultivate the lands; by 1363 he had succeeded to the point of winning Chu's praise for producing 15,000 shih of grain, thus provisioning his own troops and leaving a surplus of 7,000 shih. This system provided an alternative to the direct requisition of grain from the civilian population, and Chu therefore ordered his other generals to follow K'ang's example. The brothers Wu Liang and Wu Chen, defenders of the isolated city of Chiangyin, which was almost surrounded by Wu territory, were nevertheless able to maintain their garrison through farming their military colonies while simultaneously repelling repeated Wu invasions; this demonstrated that the military colony principle was applicable even in an operational zone.[23]

As the Ming military system expanded after 1364, every newly created guard was assigned government land for its soldiers to farm, with the produce going first toward their own maintenance and any surplus toward general military provisioning. The military colony system that was thus established, though constructed of traditional elements, marked a new departure in emphasis. Originally essentially a frontier institution, as under the Han and T'ang, it was now empirewide; instead of being a system whereby the produce of specific lands farmed by civilians went to the support of specific military units, as under the Liao (907–1125), Chin (1125–1234), and Yüan, it now involved the soldiers' personally farming the lands of their own units. In principle, at least, in the interior large forces could be maintained on the produce of the military colonies without straining the civilian economy, while on the frontier or in non-Chinese areas a Chinese presence, agricultural development, and defense could be achieved all at once simply by creating a military unit.[24]

Under normal circumstances each military unit rotated its troops between farming and military duties. Later each unit was ordered to assign 70 percent of its men to farming, leaving the other 30 percent available for campaign or garrison duty. The amount of land assigned to each farming soldier varied according to the quality of the soil, generally being 50 *mou* in Nanking, central Anhwei, and other average areas, but going as low as 12–13 mou at T'aits'ang wei in the fertile Yangtze delta area, and as high as 100 mou in the more arid lands near the Great Wall.* In the mature Ming period military colonies made up a substantial

---

*One mou equaled approximately one-sixth of an acre in Ming times, but was subject to a great deal of local variation.

portion of the total arable land. Although figures are not provided for the military colonies in 1393, the total of 8,507,623 *ch'ing* of cultivated land recorded for that year gives a basis for comparison with later years.* In 1502 the military colonies cultivated 289,481 out of 6,228,058 ch'ing of arable land, and in 1578 they cultivated 635,343 out of 7,013,976 ch'ing.[25] The total strength of the army in 1392 was given as 2,747 officers in the capital and 13,742 in the provinces for a total of 16,489; 206,280 men in the capital and 992,154 in the provinces for a total of 1,198,434; and 4,751 horses in the capital and 40,329 in the provinces for a total of 45,080.[26]

On the basis of these figures (which incidentally reveal that the military units of that date were at only about five-eighths of their nominal strength), some 420,000 ch'ing, or 5 percent of the total cultivated land, would have been required to maintain the military colonies as envisioned by the emperor if we take 50 mou to be the average land allotment per farming soldier.

The military colonies fitted logically into the overall land and population policies of the emperor, who like Diocletian sought to restore order and prosperity by fixing everyone in a definite social and occupational station. Although the military colony system answered immediate needs, in the long run it interacted with the hereditary status of the soldier in a manner that destroyed the combat effectiveness of the Ming military. The families of soldiers were placed on a separate military population register (*chün-chi*), each family having the obligation to provide an able-bodied male for military service. If they committed offenses, they were tried by military judges, their appeals running up the same military chain of command that was responsible for the administration of the military colonies. The lower levels in this chain (guards, battalions, companies) were under hereditary officers who naturally came to regard these lands as patrimonial estates and the soldiers and their families as tenants, to the detriment of military training and readiness. During the mature Ming period, therefore, the military register carried only those unfortunates whom the civil officials could legally press into armies recruited for specific occasions.[27]

If the wei-so units be likened to the regiments of a Western army of the eighteenth or nineteenth century, then a corps of

* One ch'ing equals 100 mou.

general officers was necessary, a corps capable of commanding either the divisions of the main armies or forces operating independently, and of serving as the link between the regimental commanders and the emperor. This military high command existed under a variety of guises, and did not attain its final institutional form until after 1380. As we have seen, when Chu originally seized Nanking in 1356, he created a Branch Secretariat-Chancellery and a Branch Bureau of Military Affairs as his highest organs of civil and military authority, and these same agencies were established in the provincial governments created later as the Ming state expanded. However, as the higher command developed, it became standard practice for the lower-ranking generals to have titles in the Bureau of Military Affairs while the higher-ranking generals had titles in the nominally civilian Secretariat-Chancellery. The higher-ranking generals, if they were in the provincial governments, thus wielded both civil and military authority, and so did the lower-ranking officers who headed the wing commands, which then provided most of the civil administration at the local level. In 1362 the Bureau of Military Affairs was abolished and replaced by a Grand Chief Military Commission (*ta tu-tu fu*) headed by Chu's nephew Chu Wen-cheng, but this agency, like its predecessor (whose titles continued in use for several years more), was essentially a dummy organization for conferring formal rank on generals. Until his disgrace in 1364 Chu Wen-cheng was significant primarily as the theater commander in Kiangsi.[28]

The men who held the generals' positions in the Hung-wu reign divide naturally into three groups: the emperor's earliest followers, including his twenty-four original soldiers and a small member of others who joined before the 1355 Yangtze crossing; the leaders of the Lake Ch'ao pirate group who joined Hung-wu in 1355 and provided the naval means for the river crossing; and a few generals from other regimes who had surrendered to the Ming at critical junctures and had later won Hung-wu's confidence.[29]

In 1370, after the Ming victories over the Mongols, Hung-wu formalized the status of the military high command by granting five of its members the noble title of duke (*kung*) and twenty-eight others the title of marquis (*hou*). Li Shan-ch'ang was also made a duke, but only two officials whose background was entirely civil were ennobled, both with the lower title of earl (*po*). Later in 1370 another marquis was created, still another in 1377, and twelve more in 1379.[30] Like the military colonies, the military nobility that was thus created put traditional terminology to work in a novel institutional manner. During the T'ang and Sung dynasties dukes, marquises, and earls had held the second, third, and fourth ranks, respectively, in the nine-rank system, and the titles had been conferred on military and civil officials alike as mere (albeit lucrative) honors.[31] Under the Ming such nobles were officially designated as "above the ranks" (*ch'ao-p'in*), thus holding higher place than any officials, civil or military, held in the nine-rank system adopted by the Ming from its predecessors. Higher status corresponded to greater material rewards. The salary of the highest officials (rank 1a) in the nine-rank scale was only 1,044 shih of grain per year, but marquises usually received 1,500 to 2,500 shih plus the revenues of specially designated office lands, and dukes received even more.

Not only did generals hold a virtual monopoly of noble titles during the Ming; their noble titles were defined not as empty honors but as functioning military positions. Thereafter, when armies were formed for campaigns, a noble would be appointed grand general (*ta chiang-chün*) to exercise overall command, two or more others as lieutenant generals (*fu chiang-chün*) to assist him, and often another to superintend the movement of military supplies. When not actually on campaign, nobles might be assigned to command sections of the frontier defenses, to act as military advisers to princes, to train troops, to establish new military colonies, to supervise famine relief, or to be inspectors. After fulfilling any of these assignments, they had to return to Nanking to report to the emperor.[32]

The thirty-three military nobles created in 1370 and the twelve created in 1379 were arranged in a fixed order of precedence that determined their seniority for the purpose of exercising military command. The order illustrates the relative position of the three major groups within the Ming military leadership. The five dukes naturally came first, directly after Li Shan-ch'ang. All belonged to the pre-1355 northern Anhwei group that provided the greatest number of Ming officers, but their position at the head of the list was due to the special confidence the emperor had in them. Li

Shan-ch'ang, though usually considered a civil official, had commanded Nanking during Chu's absence on several occasions during the civil war, and he had created a secret police service and controlled the civil administration of the Ming state. Although he became more of an administrator than a soldier as the Ming state grew, he never entirely abandoned his military role, and his background as a local clerk and an expert in Legalism made it impossible to view him as an official of the Confucian ideal-type. Hsü Ta and Ch'ang Yü-ch'un (deceased but represented by his heir) had commanded the main Ming field army in Chu Yüan-chang's absence. Li Wen-chung and Teng Yü had been important theater commanders. Feng Sheng, the best educated of the senior commanders, had led the elite component of the main army, the imperial guards. Of the twenty-eight marquises created in 1370, the first fourteen had been among Chu's original twenty-four soldiers.[33]

Most of these men had commanded city garrisons or divisions of the main army during the civil wars, and they owed their high positions on the list more to their long service record than to their ability. Placed in independent field commands, they did not always do well. Thus T'ang Ho, who was instrumental in maintaining Chu's authority over the army at Hochou in 1355, exercised command over Ch'angchou during the civil wars. Afterwards he was successful in the naval campaigns of 1367–68, only to falter at the Ch'üt'ang gorge in 1371 and suffer defeat at Mongol hands in 1372. Yet he was not punished for his reverses, an immunity shared by Chu's other old comrades at this time.[34] Fei Chü and Lu Chung-heng, the two nobles most closely involved in the Hu Wei-yung affair of 1380, are described as "brave but stupid."[35] Keng Ping-wen, commandant at Ch'anghsing during the civil wars, survived the purges to preside in his old age over the first stage of Chien-wen's defeat in the civil war of 1399–1402.[36]

The next five marquises on the 1370 list were leaders of the Lake Ch'ao group: Chao Yung, Yü T'ung-hai's heir (Chao and Yü both had been important in the 1363 victory), Hua Kao (he was important in the 1360 victory), Yang Ching (he was important in 1360, had been governor of Hukwang since 1365, and also took part in the conquest of Kwangsi), and Liao Yung-chung (probably the real organizer of victory in the naval campaigns of 1367–68, and certainly the one who forced the Ch'üt'ang gorge in 1371 after T'ang Ho's failure). Yang's part in the 1360 campaign and Liao's in 1363 have already been recounted (see above, pp. 41–52), but despite their achievements they were placed twenty-fifth and twenty-second on the 1370 list, respectively, which suggests that length of service under Chu was the most important criterion. The nine generals who surrendered with their troops in 1356 or later brought up the bottom of the list of marquises.[37] Among them were K'ang Mao-ts'ai and Hu Mei, as well as Fu Yu-te, whose greatest achievements were yet to come. The twelve marquises created in 1379 were divided evenly between Chu's original followers and the Lake Ch'ao group.[38]

The creations of military nobles in 1370 and 1379 were both preceded by Hung-wu's sons' being created princes (*ch'in-wang*). The emperor's eldest son, Chu Piao, had been designated crown prince (*t'ai-tzu*) in 1368; the next nine were made princes in 1370, and the next five in 1378. In 1370 even Hung-wu's eldest sons were only in their teens. As they matured, however, they were sent out to princely palaces located in the regions indicated by their titles (prince of Ch'in to Shensi, prince of Chin to Shansi, and so forth), and each was assigned a noble as his military tutor (*wu-fu*). In the central government, one of Hung-wu's first acts as emperor had been to give the leading generals high concurrent positions in the household of the crown prince (*chan-shih fu*), traditionally the institutional means of educating emperors-to-be in Confucian values. So just as Hung-wu intended his nobles to be a hereditary class of generals, he also intended the princes of the ruling family to form the highest stratum of the military nobility and to assist in preserving the imperial authority of the Chu family by commanding armies and governing appanages. The near monopoly of provincial military command granted to the princes in the 1390's was merely a logical distortion of Hung-wu's original conception of their proper role.[39]

The creation of the chief military commissions of the Five Armies (*wu-chün tu-tu fu*) in 1380 following the Hu Wei-yung purges and the emergence of the regional military commissions (*tu chih-hui shih szu*) in the provinces completed the structure of military command above the guard level. Each chief commission was headed by varying numbers of chief commissioners (*tu-tu*, rank 1a), deputy chief commissioners (*tu-tu t'ung-chih*, 1b), and assistant chief commissioners (*tu-tu ch'ien-shih*, 2a). Usually there was one regional military commission per province; each was under a military commissioner (*tu chih-hui shih*, 2a) who was aided by two deputy military commissioners (*tu chih-hui t'ung-chih*, 2b) and four assistant military commissioners (*tu chih-hui ch'ien-shih*, 3a).

In addition to being links in the chain of command for military purposes, the chief military commissions and regional military commissions were steps on the ladder up and down which traveled orders relating to military personnel matters, military colony lands, administrative affairs, and military judicial appeals. These administrative duties came in the end to monopolize the work of the regional military commissions. At the central level, however, the civilian Ministry of War duplicated many of the administrative functions of the five chief commissions and was able to discharge them more effectively. The five chief commissions therefore soon became relatively unimportant as institutions, and survived chiefly as a means of assigning formal rank to unennobled generals who derived their real importance from the exercise of field command. The chief commissioners and their subordinates, and the regional military commissioners and their subordinates, were designated regularly appointed officers (*liu-kuan*) and promoted from among the lower-ranking hereditary officers (*shih-kuan*) of the guards. This did not mean, however, that wholly bureaucratic norms prevailed, even at the higher levels. Successful commissioners expected to become nobles, and the nobles as a class were to have another dozen years of power before the princes replaced them in control of the higher military command.[40]

The evolution of the various military institutions described above, like the dynastic name Ming, was justified by the appeal to unimpeachable Chinese precedents intended to conceal rather than to explain their actual significance. The wei-so units and military colonies, the hereditary officer class, and the military nobles and princes added up to more than an interrelated military system. The extremely preferential treatment given to the officers and nobles was nothing less than an attempt to impose a social order headed by an elite military aristocracy. Although elements of this system could be found in the Han and T'ang systems which

Hung-wu cited as precedents, the model in which they were all present was the Yüan empire in its glorious thirteenth-century heyday. As conceived by Hung-wu in the 1360's and 1370's, the Chu family would take the place of the house of Chinggis Qan at the peak of the social scale; the ennobled generals and their heirs would have a hereditary claim to the next level, as did the famous marshals and companions of Chinggis Qan; and the class of hereditary officers would rank next, as did the Mongol and Semu officers under the Yüan. The Confucian scholar-officials would stand below all of these—higher in status than under the early Yüan, but still confined to an instrumental role and valued more as bureaucrats who obeyed orders than as policymakers. They were to be contented with the revival of proper Confucian ritual while the material rewards went to the princes, nobles, and military officers. As originally conceived, the Ming empire was thus Mongol in form and structure; it was Chinese only in rhetoric and personnel.

The Evolution of Government

Just as the early Ming military system developed logically from its Yüan antecedents, so did the Ming system of administration and civil government evolve within a Yüan framework. And just as the circumstances of the Mongol conquest and the ideology of the Mongol rulers made it difficult for them to win the loyalty of the Confucian scholar-gentry class, so Hung-wu's Red Turban origins and particular values led to similar problems, despite his recognition of the importance of Confucian opinion and his attempts to win it over. The thoroughly Confucianized polity of the mature Ming period came into existence only after a long period of uncertainty and struggle.

The significance of Yüan governmental innovations may be seen in comparison with their Chinese antecedents. The system of bureaucratic, centrally directed local government (*chün-hsien*) was applied empirewide by the brief Ch'in dynasty (221–207 B.C.) at the very beginning of the imperial period, and was partially restored by the Han and extended by the T'ang and Sung. Under this system the empire was divided into commanderies (chün), each subdivided into districts (hsien). After the Han the commanderies were generally redesignated departments (*chou*), with those that contained capitals and other major metropolitan centers becoming prefectures (*fu*). Under the Northern Sung a maximum of 255 prefectures and departments controlled over a thousand districts. Despite increases in their number, prefectures and departments continued in most of their functions to report directly to the central government.

During the Han, regional inspectors (*pu tz'u-shih*) were appointed, each of whom performed his duties within a regional division (pu) composed of several adjoining commanderies. However, the inspectors were substantially lower in rank than the grand administrators (*t'ai-shou*) of the commanderies; their function was not to give orders to the grand administrators but rather to inspect their official conduct with a view to its conformity to law and regulation. By T'ang times the prefectures and departments were grouped in a number of circuits (*tao*), whose boundaries, corresponding in many cases to those of modern provinces, remained stable. In the Sung each circuit had several inspectors (fiscal, judicial, and the like), each in charge of a major functional division of administration. This was as far as the native Chinese dynasties were willing to go in the creation of provincial governments. For these dynasties checks and balances at the provincial level were signs of health, and concentration of power at the provincial level was a symptom of the warlordism that had in fact preceded the fall of both the Eastern Han and the T'ang.[41]

During the Mongol conquest, Chinggis Qan began the practice of granting quasi-sovereignty to his sons and trusted generals who acted in his absence. Much of the conquered territory in North China was granted in fiefs and appanages whose holders ruled with little supervision. The Yüan local government system, staffed at its higher levels with Mongols and Semu, reflected this tradition of substantial delegation of power. Hopei, Shantung, and Shansi were placed directly under the authority of the Secretariat-Chancellery, the core of the central government in the capital. Elsewhere in the empire governmental powers were delegated to agencies designated branch secretariat-chancelleries. Those for Shensi, Honan (including those parts of Kiangsu and Anhwei north of the Yangtze), Szechwan, Hukwang, Kiangsi (including Kwangtung), and Chiangche (comprising Fukien, Chekiang, and those parts of Kiangsu and Anhwei south of the Yangtze) covered the remaining Chinese-inhabited portions of the Yüan empire. Four others—Liaotung (Manchuria), Lingpei (Outer Mongolia), Kansu, and Yünnan (the southwest was still aboriginal)—covered the non-Chinese parts of the empire. The branch secretariat-chancelleries were the direct ancestors of the provinces (*sheng*) of Ming, Ch'ing, and modern times. Although the central Secretariat-Chancellery had empirewide jurisdiction, the highest officials in the branches had the same titles as their capital counterparts, and the same powers within their areas of jurisdiction.[42]

Between the secretariat-chancelleries (main or branch) and the districts the principal intermediate unit was the "route" (*lu*). In North China, demographically shattered by the Mongol conquests, a route frequently incorporated the territories of many departments, prefectures, or both, since they were too depopulated to require their previous degree of higher administration. In the Yangtze valley and in South China, Yüan authority had been established with much less disruption, and most prefectures and departments were simply redesignated as routes in the course of the conquest.[43]

During the civil war the Ming regime expanded by conquering or receiving the surrenders of the cities in its path. Route capitals played the decisive role; only if these fell would the surrounding district towns acknowledge Ming authority. Many cities surrendered in the hope that they could get away with merely recognizing Ming superiority, so effective Ming administration began only when Ming troops entered and occupied a city. This was always a delicate moment. Chinese soldiers then and later had a habit of sacking cities; the phrase "disorder caused by soldiers" (*ping-luan*) had become a cliché in the language, and the Red Turbans on the North China plain had fully lived up to their reputation. Since Chu Yüan-chang wished to annex the territories he conquered permanently, he made every effort to enforce strict military discipline and prevent looting. Hsü Ta was the model for the other generals; when he captured a city, the inhabitants "did not know there were soldiers present."[44]

If entry was accomplished without mishap, the Ming commander then had the responsibility of sealing up all granaries, treasuries, storehouses, and archives. Later he was required to send a report to Nanking stating the amount of grain stored in the city and the number of troops in the garrison. The troops were pressed into the Ming armies. Chu, if present, would address the elders of the city, attempting to reassure them that Ming rule promised stability. Typically he would promise an end to forced requisitions of grain for military supplies and urge the people to return to their occupations, thus implying that they would not all be forced into the army. During the civil war the Ming regime was naturally unable to dispense with forced requisitions of grain and soldiers, but from the beginning Chu attempted to fix people in their occupations and to prevent the military from being a burden on civil society. Cities that had been route capitals under the Yüan were frequently redesignated capitals of prefectures, and usually a wing headquarters would be established, primarily to exercise military command, but in this early period to take concurrent charge of civil administration. However, by 1360 many of the prefectures had prefects (*chih-fu*, rank 4a) in charge of civil administration, and the new military units (guards and independent battalions) created in and after 1364 were confined to military functions. At the local level, a degree of separation between civil and military functions had been achieved.[45]

Since many of the Yüan routes had been departments in Sung times, their conversion to prefectures meant that the prefectures became the main intermediate unit of local government. In the mature Ming period, most of the 1,172 district magistrates (*chih-hsien*, rank 7a) reported directly to one of the 140 prefects who in turn were directly under the provincial governments. However, many departments were carried over from the Yüan system, particularly in the north. The department magistrate (*chih-chou*, 5b) was intermediate in both rank and function between the prefect and the district magistrate. In the town that was his administrative seat and the area associated with it, he served as the primary imperial official and as the court of original jurisdiction in the manner of a district magistrate, but he might also have district magistrates under his authority in the manner of a prefect. Most of the 200-odd departments were classed as subordinate departments (*shu-chou*) and reported to a prefect, but there were about thirty independent departments (*chih-li chou*) that reported directly to the provinces and were in many respects treated as prefectures.[46]

The Ming central government that was created in 1355–56 had the character of a branch secretariat-chancellery or province of the rebel Red Turban Sung empire, but even while still confined to this status the Ming created its own new provincial governments to mark the successive stages of its territorial expansion. In two cases, T'aip'ing and Luchou, provinces created during the civil war failed to survive into the empire, but the rest did.

In 1359 a province was created at Chinhua to control the four inland prefectures of Chekiang; in 1366, as Wu collapsed, the provincial headquarters was moved from Chinhua to Hangchow, and the seven remaining Chekiang prefectures were added to it. The region acquired through Hu Mei's surrender in 1362 became the province of Kiangsi, and after the fall of Wuch'ang in 1364, the ex-Han area became the province of Hukwang (now Hunan and Hupei). In 1368, at the conclusion of the first phase of the northern expedition, the province of Shantung was created. The next year seven provinces were established to administer the recently conquered regions. In the south were Fukien (formerly under Chiangche), and Kwangtung and Kwangsi (under Kiangsi in the Yüan period); in the north were Honan and Shensi (provinces already established by the Yüan), and Shansi and Peip'ing (now Hopei), which along with Shantung had constituted the area under the direct authority of the central government in Yüan times. The creation in 1371 of Szechwan province following the conquest of Ming Yü-chen's successors completes the list, since the areas of the later Anhwei and Kiangsu provinces were directly subordinate (*chih-li*) to the capital at Nanking, the former Yüan provinces of Lingpei (Outer Mongolia) and Yünnan were still independent under princes of the house of Chinggis Qan, and in Kansu and Liaotung eventual Ming rule resulted in the creation of special military administrations rather than provinces.[47]

The creation of official positions by decree did not necessarily mean that they could be staffed. Illiterate military men frequently wielded concurrent civil authority on both the provincial and the prefectural level. This was partly due to the shortage of qualified administrative personnel. Under the Yüan the examination system had been revived late, and the number of men whose Confucian status was attested by an examination degree was much smaller than under the Sung. Most of these adopted a posture of loyalty to the Yüan. At the surrender of Nanch'ang in 1362 the Confucians expressed their happiness in poems, but despite such occasions, during the civil wars most of them avoided service with the Ming, preferring instead the Wu regime of Chang Shih-ch'eng, whose surrender to the Yüan gave him at least the appearance of legitimacy. Chu, unable to take the same step because of the religious devotion of his troops to the Red Turban emperor, Han Lin-erh, could only watch in frustrated resentment.[48]

However, even before crossing the Yangtze, Chu Yüan-chang had assembled a rudimentary civil service. When the Ming government was set up at Nanking, Li Shan-ch'ang and Sung Szu-yen headed it with the title of adviser (*ts'an-yi*). They controlled about a dozen other officials, including Luan Feng, Wang K'ai, Sun Yen, and Hsia Yü. Some of these men had held local secretarial positions under the Yüan, and they are described as having skill in planning and administration rather than as being scholars in the traditional Confucian sense. During the civil war, these officials served primarily as a military general staff, giving advice on operations and administering the distribution of grain and other supplies. Ming diplomatic missions were headed by officials drawn from this group, the repeated and fruitless embassies of Sun Yen and Hsia Yü to Fang Kuo-chen being examples. Provincial commanders also might receive officials from this group as staff officers, the function Sun Yen and Wang K'ai were performing when killed in the Chekiang rebellions of 1362. And when separate civil administrations were established, men from this group received appointments as prefects, the position held by Luan Feng when he was killed in the Chuch'üan rebellion of 1363. These officials obeyed Chu Yüan-chang's orders and did not voice moral objections to his policies; they kept the administrative machine running and were an integrating factor in the Ming state, but their constituting the highest layer of civil officials indicated that the vital Confucian scholar-gentry were not being attracted.[49]

In 1360 the Ming regime was joined by Liu Chi, Sung Lien, Chang Yi, and Yeh Ch'in, all natives of the Ming districts in Chekiang that bordered on Fang Kuo-chen's territories. Liu held the chin-shih degree from the Yüan, Sung had been a compiler in the Han-lin Academy, and the others were similarly distinguished. The defection of this group was due to Liu's revulsion at the spectacle of the Yüan court rewarding Fang Kuo-chen with higher titles every time he surrendered after one of his repeated rebellions. Acting on Li Shan-ch'ang's advice, Chu Yüan-chang summoned Liu and his colleagues to his service. Yeh Ch'in later became prefect of Nanch'ang, only to be killed in the rebellion there in 1362. Liu Chi had a part in the planning of the campaigns of 1360 and 1363, a role that was transformed and magnified in the later folklore of the founding of the Ming dynasty, in which he appears as a scholar-statesman and magician-strategist modeled on Chu-ko Liang of the Three Kingdoms period.[50]

The ensuing decade of cooperation between Liu Chi and Chu masked the fact that the two were pursuing different and incompatible goals. Liu's objective was the common Confucian goal of gaining influence over the emperor by becoming indispensable in practical matters and using it to promote good government in the traditional Confucian sense. Liu planned battles and interpreted portents, but his underlying aim was to fill officialdom with men like himself, who would restrain the emperor from tyranny and folly, and would exercise moral suasion to move him in preferred ideological directions. Chu, on the other hand, wished to use the defection of Liu Chi and his colleagues as a means of advertising the legitimacy of his regime. Chu needed more officials, which meant recruiting among the scholar-gentry, and he valued Confucian ideological exhortation as a means of rule, but he was not willing to admit the moral autonomy of the Confucian official or his right to sit in historical or moral judgment on the emperor. Wishing to be accepted as a legitimate Confucian monarch, Chu nevertheless would not tolerate principled opposition from Confucians or any other group.

The contradiction between these two viewpoints became evident after the proclamation of the Ming dynasty in 1368. Liu Chi and Chang Yi were both given the position of vice-president of the Censorate (*yü-shih chung-ch'eng*), a post of importance and honor to be sure, but scarcely at the apex of the policymaking hierarchy. The highest civil appointments in the 1370's were given to Yang Hsien, Wang Kuang-yang, and Hu Wei-yung, three men whose appointments Liu Chi had opposed and whom the emperor would later execute. In 1370 Liu Chi and the future chancellor Wang Kuang-yang were made earls with the derisory stipends of

240 and 360 shih, respectively. In 1371, after further disagreements with the emperor, Liu Chi retired. He died in 1375.[51]

Hung-wu's treatment of Liu Chi and others to whom Confucianism was a matter of principle indicated his preference for officials who were willing to act as mere instruments and agents of his will. But it was still necessary to recruit Confucians. Hung-wu dealt with this problem by appointing Confucians to literary and ritual positions, where they would be honored and highly visible in the performance of what were vital functions in the Confucian ideal order, yet not be directly involved in decision-making. Thus in 1368, directly after the fall of the Yüan capital, Sung Lien was made head of the commission to draft the official history of the Yüan dynasty. The work was rushed to completion in six months and presented to the throne, the unseemly haste being due to Hung-wu's desire to show by the issuance of an official history that the Yüan dynasty was defunct, even though the last Yüan emperor was alive and independent in Inner Mongolia. Mongol names and dress were forbidden, and court dress was standardized on the T'ang model. Other commissions were appointed to research the precedents of previous Chinese dynasties and to correct the regulations for ritual and sacrifice. Confucian officials with literary reputations were assigned to draft laws and decrees.[52]

When Chu Yüan-chang proclaimed himself prince of Wu in 1364, he gave his government a quasi-imperial form. Li Shan-ch'ang and Hsü Ta became chancellors (*ch'eng-hsiang*), and Ch'ang Yü-ch'un and Yü T'ung-hai, administrators (*p'ing-chang cheng-shih*). By 1368 the highest positions in the central government, following the Yüan model, were a left (senior, reverting to Chinese from Mongol practice) and a right chancellor, four administrators, a left and a right assistant (*ch'eng*) and four consultants (*ts'an-chih cheng-shih*). Yü T'ung-hai was dead by 1368, in which year Li Shan-ch'ang and Hsü Ta were still the senior and junior chancellors; Ch'ang Yü-ch'un, Liao Yung-chung, Hu Mei and Li Po-sheng were the four administrators; Chao Yung and Wang P'u were the two assistants; and Yang Hsien and Wang Kuang-yang were among the consultants.[53]

This composition of the Secretariat-Chancellery illustrated the balance among the military factions, the relation between central and provincial government, and the degree to which the central government had evolved by 1368. Li Shan-ch'ang was the effective head of the Secretariat-Chancellery; Hsü Ta's chancellorship was merely an additional honor, since he remained the senior Ming field general until his retirement and was usually away from the capital. The four administrators and two assistants also were generals whose status was enhanced by high, but essentially honorific, civil appointment. Ch'ang Yü-ch'un represented Chu's pre-1355 followers; his position as third after the emperor was underscored by his title of junior guardian (*shao-pao*) of the crown prince, compared to the higher titles of junior preceptor (*shao-shih*) of the crown prince and junior tutor (*shao-fu*) of the crown prince held by Li and Hsü, respectively. Liao Yung-chung and Chao Yung represented the Lake Ch'ao sailors, Hu Mei and Wang P'u the group of Ch'en Yu-liang's Kiangsi commanders who surrendered in 1361–62, and Li Po-sheng the surrendered troops of Chang Shih-ch'eng.

Under the Yüan (especially after 1355) chancellors had frequently been appointed to head provincial governments, giving these a status nearly equal to the central government. Under the Ming the provinces were intended to be subordinate from the start. Military men placed in control of provinces were given the title of administrator, which was held exclusively by generals until the abolition of the Secretariat-Chancellery in 1380. During the critical phase of the civil war, the highest-ranking Ming generals had held the titles of administrator, assistant, and consultant, and real civil officials had been confined to low-status secretarial positions. By 1368, however, all of the consultants were civil officials, and they constituted the highest functional level below Li Shan-ch'ang himself in the Secretariat-Chancellery. The years 1368–80 saw a progressive separation of civil administration from military command in terms of both form and practice, and a concomitant rise in the status of civil officials. After 1369, when Yang Hsien was promoted to assistant, civil officials monopolized that level also. In 1371 Wang Kuang-yang became chancellor, and until 1380 that position was held only by him and Hu Wei-yung. In the provinces the separation of military from civil began in 1369 with the creation of the chief guards (*tu-wei*), forerunners of the regional military commissions. Increasingly, even in those provinces that had a military man with the title of administrator in nominal authority, actual control passed into the hands of the senior civil official, who was usually a man sent to the province as a consultant after a period of service in the capital.[54]

Subordinate to the chief officials of the Secretariat-Chancellery were the Six Ministries (*liu-pu*), whose final organization dated from the Sui dynasty. In principle, the division of functions among them comprehended all government business and was paralleled by the organization of the clerks in local government offices. The Ministry of Personnel (*li-pu*) controlled the assignment of posts to civil officials, their merit ratings, promotions, and demotions, and the award of honors and noble titles. The Ministry of Revenue (*hu-pu*) was in charge of population registration and land survey, government accounts, tax collection, granaries, grain transport, and related matters. The Ministry of Rites (*li-pu*, written with a Chinese word different from the *li* of the Ministry of Personnel), had oversight of ritual and sacrificial duties, which were important components of the routine of Confucian government, and also managed the reception of tributary embassies from foreign nations and the education and civil service examination systems. The Ministry of War (*ping-pu*), staffed entirely by civilians, was charged with military personnel administration, plans of fortifications, arsenals, military granaries, the postal relay service, and related military-administrative functions. The Ministry of Justice (*hsing-pu*) controlled the judicial system and approved or disapproved the decisions in criminal cases reported by the provinces. The Ministry of Works (*kung-pu*) managed the construction of buildings and a host of other activities, including civilian state farms, water conservancy, and exploitation of natural resources.[55]

After some initial uncertainty, each ministry was divided into four bureaus, again on the T'ang model, and each ministry was headed by a minister (*shang-shu*, rank 3a), who was one grade lower than a consultant (2b).[56] The ministers, in other words, were responsible administrative officials rather than policymaking cabinet members. They were entirely civilian from the beginning, being appointed by recommendation from among those who had Yüan administrative experience, examination degrees, or established scholarly reputations.

TABLE I. *Turnover Among Ministers, 1368–1379*

Ministry	Total appointments	Transfers to provinces	
		Promotions	Demotions
Personnel	19	3	1
Revenue	29	14	2
Rites	14	2	2
War	17	3	1
Justice	34	11	3
Works	16	6	
	129	39	9

SOURCE: The data in this table are extracted from the lists of ministers appended to T'an Ch'ien, *Kuo-ch'üeh*.

In the 1368–79 period the turnover among the ministers was very high. This was due partly to the death in office or early retirement of ministers who were elderly when appointed, and in a few cases to the dismissal or execution of ministers who fell afoul of the emperor's notoriously short temper. The greatest single cause of turnover, however, was transfer to the provinces, as shown in Table 1. During the civil war the Nanking Secretariat-Chancellery had served as a training school for prefects; now it was performing the same function at a higher level. After a period of service in the capital, many ministers (especially those of revenue or justice) were sent out to the provinces; they were either promoted to the rank of consultant or higher and thus in fact sent to govern the province or, less often, demoted to the position of prefect. The provinces were thus progressively shifted to administration by civil officials and removed from military jurisdiction. In 1376 the official designation of the provincial governments was changed from branch secretariat-chancellery to provincial administration office (*ch'eng-hsüan pu-cheng szu*). The position of administrator, which had been held exclusively by generals, was abolished, and the consultants who had been running the civil government were formally placed in charge of the new offices, with the title of administration commissioner (*pu-cheng shih*, 2a), each of whom had two deputy commissioners (*ts'an-cheng*) under him.[57]

Since the territorial expansion of the Ming empire and the growth of the civil administrative apparatus within it were occurring simultaneously, the need for civil officials was enormous and could be met only by recommendation. On 6 November 1368, after the capture of the Yüan capital had provided the symbol of the transfer of power, the new emperor ordered his government to search for able officials. "Now that the empire has just been secured, we wish to discuss the way of enlightened government with the Confucian scholars. Those who are able will help us to aid the people. The competent offices are to search for them with ceremony." Pursuant to this, on 12 December officials were sent throughout the empire to search for the worthy and talented. In 1370 the emperor issued three further decrees, one ordering a search for men capable of being employed in the Six Ministries, one desiring merely the well educated and diligent, and the third seeking men proficient in the classics and in good government. On 19 November 1369 the prefectures and departments were ordered to establish schools.[58]

Hung-wu was sincere in recruiting from the Confucian class and promoting Confucian education, but his commitment to the Confucian political order was more rhetorical than real. The prompt revival of the civil service examination system in 1368 would have symbolized the restoration of the orthodox Confucian state as no other measure could, and it also would have facilitated appointment through recommendation by making the scholar-gentry more willing to serve the Ming regime. Yet Hung-wu did not commit himself to the examination system until 1384 and only experimented with it reluctantly in the 1370's. As usual, the main reason was his desire to be in complete command. Under the examination system, as it had existed and would develop again, the examinations were read and graded by officials who were themselves products of the system, and the type of post obtained by a successful candidate depended largely on how high he passed. Civil personnel administration thus became largely self-regulating, and the emperor, despite his grand ceremonial role within the system, actually lost control over the composition of the civil service. Hung-wu was more concerned to be autocratic than to appear orthodox, and he naturally preferred to appoint his officials directly.

The earliest steps in reinstituting the examination system were thus affected by the tension between Hung-wu and his civil officials as their role expanded. On 5 June 1370 a decree ordered that examinations be held. By this time Li Shan-ch'ang was chancellor, and Yang Hsien and Wang Kuang-yang were assistants. These three were the leading civil officials; Hu Wei-yung was one of the consultants. Li was ill and losing favor with the emperor, and Yang appeared likely to be his successor, but on 21 August he was suddenly executed. This left Wang as the probable next chancellor. He became an earl later in the year, along with Liu Chi, and when Li was summarily dismissed on 18 January 1371, Wang succeeded him. Wang moved at once to carry out the June decree. On 8 February it was decreed that both examinations and routine promotions and transfers of officials were to be held triennially.

On 18 March the successful candidates of the first capital examinations were presented at court and received their chin-shih degrees. This should have inaugurated the regular triennial sequence of examinations, but before the second could be held, Wang Kuang-yang was dismissed on 4 February 1373 and sent to be consultant of Kwangtung province. Soon afterwards Hung-wu ordered the examination system suspended (17 March). He was so annoyed with Wang because of this and other issues that he considered leaving the chancellorship vacant, but relented later in the year and appointed Hu Wei-yung. Hu, who was from Tingyüan and a relative by marriage of Li Shan-ch'ang, served as chancellor until his execution in 1380. He made no attempt to revive the examinations, and recommendation became the rule, though Hu practiced recommendation in such a manner that his residence was constantly surrounded by swarms of job seekers holding out bribes. Wang's political comeback (1377–80) did not alter this situation.[59]

Despite the uncertainties in the personnel selection system, a distinct civil service emerged during the 1370's, a development symbolized by the elevation of Wang Kuang-yang to the chancellorship and by the creation of the provincial administration offices. During the mature Ming period, the highest civil and military agencies in both the capital and the provinces were associated with an independent organ charged with surveillance and remonstrance. In the capital the Censorate (originally designated *yü-shih t'ai*) remained an agency of limited importance during the Hung-wu reign, with its highest positions frequently either left vacant or assigned as honorifics.[60]

In the provinces the situation was different. Surveillance commissioners' offices (*t'i-hsing an-ch'a shih szu*) were created, one for each province, in 1367. Their fundamental duties were to review and inspect the conduct of officials, and to impeach any suspected of misconduct. In principle they were the ruler's eyes and ears, but during the civil war the shortage of civil officials and lack of real central authority over many of the walled cities meant that occasional surveillance was often the only form of civil administration Chu Yüan-chang could enforce. Only during the 1360's and 1370's, as officials were more regularly appointed to local government offices, were the surveillance offices gradually restricted to their specialized function.[61]

The splitting up of the highest civil and military agencies in 1380, in the wake of the Hu Wei-yung purge, facilitated direct control of the government by the emperor. The trifurcation of provincial authority among the administrative, military, and surveillance commissioners is usually related to the same objective, yet this pattern had taken form in the provinces by 1376 and was not affected by the 1380 reorganizations. Civil and military institutions evolved in a complementary fashion during the 1370's, with the military withdrawing into its own fiscally, administratively, and judicially autonomous realm. This left most of the empire to the civil service, whose growth had to be forced in order to enable it to meet its increased responsibilities. Though apparently directed largely against the military, the 1380 purge actually had a much more disruptive effect on the evolution of the civil service, and it should be viewed against the background of the continuous expansion of the scope of civil government in the 1370's.

The Purges of 1380

Hu Wei-yung's actions in office led to the purges. He had headed the government as sole chancellor until 1377, when Wang Kuang-yang, restored to favor, became his junior colleague as chancellor of the right. Wang's subsequent banishment and forced suicide preceded by a few weeks the execution of Hu, which marked the commencement of the purges.

The position of chancellor, though created by the Ch'in, had been continued by the Han dynasty, under which the civil bureaucracy came to exemplify the Confucianism that had come to dominate Chinese society as a whole. As the highest office of the bureaucracy, the chancellorship gained a prestige that endured through successive dynasties. In the Confucian view, which prevailed under the Sung, the role of the emperor was merely to approve proposals initiated by the chancellor, who was to supervise the conduct of government business by subordinate officials. As an intimate of the Legalist-inclined Li Shan-ch'ang, who had recommended him for office, Hu Wei-yung was not a deeply principled Confucian, and it is ironic that the moral mantle of the chancellorship should have fallen on him. Nevertheless, Hu fully exploited the traditional authority and autonomy of the office; he was a man whose decisive and autocratic personality was a match for the emperor's, and under him the civil bureaucracy grew strong enough to wrest control of provincial and local government from the military. The interconnected questions of tax assessment and collection, land survey, population registration, and the settlement of displaced persons on vacant lands were being dealt with successfully, but despite these achievements, during Hu's administration severe tensions developed on both the civil and the military sides of the Ming state.[62]

The morale of the civil service was damaged by the humiliating and savage punishments the emperor somewhat capriciously inflicted. The suspension of the civil service examinations in 1373 naturally made the recruitment of officials difficult, and Hu Wei-yung had to make appointments on the basis of recommendations. He naturally preferred relatives, friends, and followers, and those who were appointed tended to repay their gratitude with personal loyalty to him. Hung-wu had suspended the examinations in order to maintain control over civil appointments, but by 1380 he found the bureaucracy behaving increasingly as the chancellor's personal tool. This contradiction led to the reestablishment of the examinations, but only after the emperor had decided to be his own chancellor. The charges of cronyism that formed a substantial part of the case against Hu were certainly justified, but it is not clear how else he could have acted in the absence of an examination system.[63]

Conspiratorial dealings with foreigners were also among the

charges lodged against Hu. In foreign affairs, Ming relations with Japan and the maritime countries of Southeast Asia had gone sour in the 1370's after a promising beginning. The underlying cause of the trouble was Hung-wu's attempt to suppress private Chinese trade while simultaneously refusing to permit an equivalent volume of trade within the framework of the tribute system. Hu was trapped between the emperor's unreasonable expectations and the fact that satisfactory relations with the maritime countries depended on meeting their requirements for trade.[64]

Hu's case was also shaped by tensions in the military establishment that were due both to military failures and to increasing restrictions being placed on the authority of the generals. The elements were interconnected, since large-scale campaigns might have succeeded militarily and also restored the position of the generals within the Ming state. In fact, however, the defensive strategy adopted in 1372 made permanent a low-level military threat on both the northern and the southwestern borders. In the north the death of Kökö Temür ended any immediate threat that the Mongols would unite their forces and seriously attempt a Yüan restoration, but lesser Mongol leaders emerged, Naghachu in southern Manchuria chief among them, who maintained their leadership by raids and small-scale invasions of Chinese territory. The Ming response, limited retaliatory expeditions followed by the strengthening of border defenses, was not usually effective.

But larger offensive efforts in the north were ruled out by the need to employ so many Ming troops in the south and west to repress the disaffected tribal peoples. The generals ennobled in 1379 won their honors chiefly in these campaigns.

The main factor in the situation in the south and west was the continued existence of the loyalist regime in Yünnan headed by the Yüan prince of Liang, which encouraged tribal rebellions and on occasion invaded Ming territory. The post-1372 defensive stance implied a reluctance to annex non-Chinese territory. However, in the southwest, where areas of Chinese settlement were expanding at the expense of the lands of the tribal peoples, the Yünnan regime was a focus around which opposition to the Chinese could unite. Soon after the execution of Hu Wei-yung, Hung-wu ordered the conquest of Yünnan.[65]

Many of the generals who had conquered and ruled entire

provinces during the civil war were now confined to routine duties. Compared to civil officials, they had been treated generously in the distribution of honors and rewards, but it is unlikely that they perceived their treatment as generous; Liu Pang's generals, after all, had been made kings and had actually ruled kingdoms. Furthermore, the mass creations of nobles in 1370 and 1379 were both preceded by the creation of groups of the emperor's sons as princes. In the late 1370's the princes of Ch'in, Chin, and Yen (the second, third, and fourth sons of Hung-wu) were in their teens, and their palaces at Sian, T'aiyüan, and Peip'ing were becoming involved in the administration of the northern frontier armies. Since 1368 Hung-wu had required a military education for his younger sons, a development suggesting that the already diminished sphere of the military nobility would contract still further in the future. Hung-wu had to establish a state of peace and to subject the generals to the dynastic principle or the civil war would have been fought in vain. He realized that these policies were bound to discontent the generals, and so he watched carefully for signs of disaffection. As it turned out, conspiracy with rebellious generals was the gravest of the charges against Hu Wei-yung.[66]

Late in 1379 a tribute mission from Champa arrived in Nanking. Hu Wei-yung did not report this to the emperor, who found out about it through a eunuch informant. Hung-wu ordered an investigation and although Hu and Wang Kuang-yang accepted responsibility, they claimed that the whole matter was nothing more than a procedural error by the Ministry of Rites. But Hung-wu's temper was up; he exiled Wang Kuang-yang and ordered him to commit suicide. Frightened by this, T'u Ch'ieh, vice-president of the Censorate, memorialized accusing Hu Wei-yung of plotting to murder the emperor at the annual sacrifice to Heaven and Earth scheduled for 17 February 1380. After interrogation, Hu was executed on 12 February along with the president of the Censorate, Ch'en Ning, and the unfortunate T'u Chieh, who in Hung-wu's judgment had reported the conspiracy only to cover up his own part in it.[67]

The official account of the Hu conspiracy as later published contained the following additional charges: (1) Hu had written to the Yüan ruler (presumably Toghus Temür) calling himself "subject" and asking for the assistance of Mongol troops; (2) Hu had conspired with the Ningpo guard commander, Lin Hsien, who had gone overseas to try to win Japanese support for the plot; (3) two marquises, Lu Chung-heng, whom the emperor had rebuked for making personal use of the military post system, and Fei Chü, who had been reprimanded despite his victories, had lent their military authority to the plot (both were among Hung-wu's twenty-four original companions); and (4) Hu and Ch'en Ning had arrogated to themselves authority to examine the troop registers and had ordered the military commanders to mobilize their forces, presumably to support the rebellion.[68]

The charges were supported with detailed accounts of Hu's organization of the conspiracy that add to the impression of inconsistency made by the charges themselves. For Hu to have been guilty of everything charged, he must frequently have been in two or more places at once. Like the victims of Stalin's purges, Hu had become the scapegoat for everything that had gone wrong since his appointment as chancellor. Unconquered Mongols, unsatisfactory foreign relations, rebellious generals, and corrupt officials all could be blamed more conveniently on Hu's villainies rather than on more basic political and structural problems. Furthermore, the charges against Hu were so constructed that their possible ramifications were unlimited. Any official could be accused of having belonged to Hu's faction, any officer could be accused of having failed to report Hu's plot to rebel, and no conceivable evidence could rebut the charges. Official life had been uncertain enough before 1380, and it became worse afterwards, as a tragic drama was played out that climaxed in the massive purges of the 1390's. Before Hung-wu's death most of the military nobility had been executed or posthumously involved in either the Hu conspiracy or the later Lan Yü case, and the Hu case alone had claimed over 30,000 lower-ranking victims.[69]

If the charges against Hu are unsatisfactory from a western legal viewpoint, they are nevertheless of historical importance for the light they shed on the emperor's fears and concerns at this time. His fear of the two remaining Mongol regimes and of his own military aristocrats goes far toward explaining his actions during the remainder of his reign, but of more immediate importance was his apparently sincere belief that, as in 1362, he had narrowly escaped assassination. If a reigning emperor was in fact to be assassinated by a cabal of civil officials led by the chancellor, then the annual sacrifice to Heaven and Earth was the appropriate occasion. The emperor's physical presence away from most of his palace attendants and guards was required, and his movements were controlled by agencies under the chancellor's control. And Hung-wu in all of his long reign only rarely and irregularly left the palace on other occasions.

The source of this danger was the authority and autonomy of the chancellor, which extended to military administration as well. On 17 February 1380, after performing the sacrifice to Heaven and Earth, Hung-wu abolished the chancellorship and other offices down to consultant in the Secretariat-Chancellery, and raised the rank of the six ministers from 3a to 2a, ordering them henceforth to report to him personally. The Censorate, whose highest officials had been directly implicated, was abolished, but it soon reappeared under a new Chinese title (*tu-ch'a yüan*) that lacked the historical connotations of the previous term. On the military side, the Grand Chief Military Commission, now under Li Wen-chung, was replaced by five chief military commissions (*tu-tu fu*) designated as of the left, right, center, van, and rear armies, respectively. Each of these exercised command over some of the troops in the capital and over the regional military commissions in the geographical area corresponding to its designation. Twelve guards in the capital were designated imperial guards (*ch'in-chün*), taken out of the command structure entirely, and placed directly under the emperor. The chief of these was the Chin-yi (Brocade Uniform) Guard, which specialized in secret police work and became the cutting edge of imperial terror. In the provinces the threefold authority structure of provincial administration commissioner, provincial surveillance commissioner (abolished in 1380 but restored in 1381), and regional military commissioner, which had emerged in the 1370's, was not affected by the reorganization.[70]

The Ming government after 1380 was thus characterized by fragmentation of authority at both the central and provincial levels, but more extremely at the center, where the five chief military commissions, the twelve guards, the Six Ministries, the Censorate, and a swarm of lesser agencies competed for the emperor's attention. In order to preserve the security of his position, the emperor determined to act as his own chancellor, and he spent the rest of his reign reading official documents. In 1395, as his reign was drawing to a close, he enjoined the same system on his successors in the following decree:

Since antiquity the three dukes have recommended the proper path and the six ministers have divided the duties of government. Ch'in first instituted [the office of] chancellor, but [their empire] promptly collapsed. Han, T'ang, and Sung continued [the office] and, though there have been worthy chancellors, the majority of those employed during these dynasties were petty men who usurped authority and wrought disorder in the government. Our dynasty has abolished the chancellorship and has established the five chief military commissions, the Six Ministries, the Censorate (*tu-ch'a yüan*), the Office of Transmission (*t'ung-cheng szu*), the Grand Court of Revision (*ta-li szu*), and other offices that separately manage the affairs of the empire, all going about their business without daring to interfere with one another. Problems [of jurisdiction] are decided by the imperial court, and thus [the system] is stable. The monarchs who succeed me are not permitted to appoint chancellors, and if officials dare to memorialize proposing the [re]establishment of [the chancellorship, the other] civil and military officials are to impeach them forthwith, and they are to be sentenced to the heaviest penalty.[71]

By blaming Ch'in for first instituting the chancellorship, Hung-wu could implicitly claim to be restoring a more proper ancient state of affairs, but here again Confucian rhetoric masked an anti-Confucian purpose. Even under a chancellor as dubiously Confucian as Hu Wei-yung, the bureaucracy had gotten dangerously out of control, so Hung-wu effectively decapitated it by abolishing the chancellorship. When the principled Confucians ultimately did win control of the bureaucracy, there was no representative of the civil service who had the necessary stature to stand up to the emperors. Despite their insignificant personalities, the later Ming emperors were able to continue the despotic style of rule established by Hung-wu, a style that the great Manchu emperors also found congenial. The balance between imperial and ministerial authority, which had given Sung politics their quasi-constitutional appearance and which had been revived in the late Yüan, was now tipped permanently in favor of the emperors.

FOUR

Hung-wu: The Period of Direct Rule, 1380–1398

After 1380 Hung-wu ruled directly and personally, intensifying the terror directed against the official classes. He resumed the initiative in government and moved decisively to settle several of the issues that had gone unresolved in the 1370's. He stopped trying to win peace with the Mongols by diplomatic means, and ordered the annexation of Yünnan and the resumption of large-scale military expeditions in the north. He attempted to suppress private overseas trade, and thus drove the merchants of Japan and Southeast Asia and the natives of South China into smuggling and piracy, the latter reaching crisis proportions by 1387. In 1384 he restored the civil service examinations, this time permanently, frightened into it, perhaps, by Hu Wei-yung's bureaucratic empire building. He completed the land policies inaugurated in the 1370's by ordering the census and land survey of 1393.

But the emperor maintained his personal control by inhibiting the development of the stable institutions needed to manage civil politics and military command. Administrators and generals alike were tied to the throne through intermediaries whose loyalty was to the person of Hung-wu rather than to the office of the emperor, and when Hung-wu's death dissolved the bonds that held his personal apparatus together, the result was a succession crisis of ungovernable proportions.

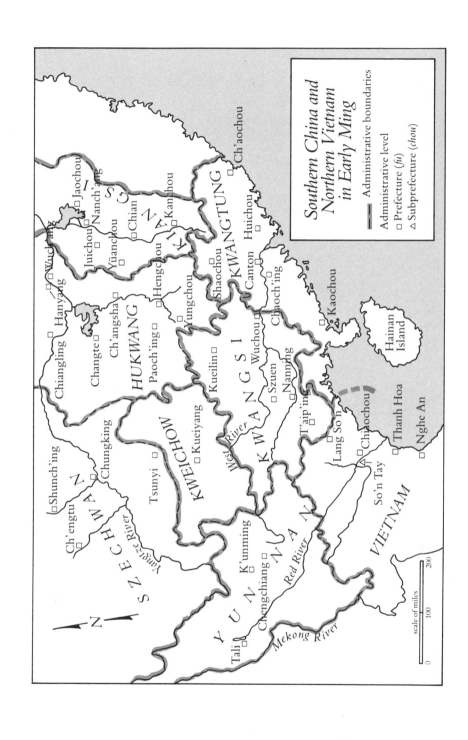

Southern China and
Northern Vietnam
in Early Ming

Administrative boundaries
Administrative level
□ Prefecture (fu)
△ Subprefecture (chou)

Ch'aochou

KWANGTUNG
Shaochou
Huichou
Canton
Chaoch'ing

KIANGSI
Kanchou
Chian
Yüanchou
Hengchou
Yungchou
Kueilin
Nanning
Szuen
Wuchou

Kaochou

Hainan
Island

Juichou
Nanch'ang
Jaochou

Wuch'ang
Hanyang
Chiangling
Changte
Ch'angsha
Paoch'ing
HUKWANG

KWANGSI
West River
T'aip'ing
Lang So'n

Chiaochou
Thanh Hoa
Nghe An

So'n Tay
VIETNAM

Shunch'ing
Chungking
KWEICHOW
Tsunyi
Kueiyang
K'unming
Chengchiang
Red River
Tali
Mekong River

Ch'engtu
SZECHWAN
Yangtze River

N

YUNNAN

scale of miles
0   100   200

The Frontier: Yünnan and the Non-Chinese Peoples

Yüan authority in Yünnan had been maintained without interruption since the mid-1360's by the prince of Liang, Basalawarmi, a descendant of Qubilai's fifth son. When Ming Yü-chen tried to add Yünnan to his domains after proclaiming himself emperor in Szechwan, the prince of Liang rallied the Pai people of the formerly independent kingdom of Tali and defeated him. This victory established a pattern of relationships in the southwest. The Yüan provincial regime in Yünnan, whose population was largely non-Chinese, provided a rallying point for the aboriginal peoples of the southwest to resist Chinese encroachment, maintaining its ties to the Yüan emperors in Mongolia by sending envoys every year to affirm their loyalty. Ming problems of border defense in the north and in the southwest were thus connected, and it was very difficult to maintain a defensive stance in the southwest, since tribes included in the Chinese provinces were encouraged to rebel by the example of related tribes living free from Chinese influence under the Yünnan regime. Nevertheless, after 1368 Hung-wu considered Yünnan too difficult to conquer; he attempted to secure its submission by diplomatic means instead.[1]

In 1372, before the Ming defeats at the hands of the Mongols, the Ming government sent Wang Wei as envoy to the prince of Liang. Wang was accompanied by a Yünnan envoy to the Mongol imperial court whom the Ming armies had captured en route. When the prince of Liang received Wang in audience, the Mongol envoy to Yünnan accused him of plotting to surrender, and the prince had to prove his loyalty by executing Wang Wei. Another Ming embassy in 1375 also resulted in failure. The deputy commissioner of Hukwang, Wu Yün, was sent to Yünnan bearing an imperial decree and escorting yet another captured Yünnan envoy. The envoy gained control of the embassy party after it had entered Yünnan territory, tried to persuade Wu Yün to alter the text of the imperial decree, and killed him when he refused. The prince of Liang returned Wu's body to the Ming, but Hung-wu made no further diplomatic overtures.[2]

Possibly this was because in 1375 the overall military situation in the southwest seemed satisfactory. In the winter of 1372 Wu Liang and Chou Te-hsing had spent several months suppressing tribal rebellions in southern Hunan, the area of the later province of Kweichow.[3] In the summer of 1374 further campaigns were necessary in the region of Yungchou and Taochou.[4] After that there were no major outbreaks for over three years. When large-scale fighting resumed in 1377, it was the result of the Ming government's decision to chastise the Tibetan tribesmen who were raiding the western regions of Shensi and Szechwan. Teng Yü was made general—and the emperor's young adopted son Mu Ying, lieutenant-general—of an army that marched into Tibet as far as the K'unlun mountains. Mu Ying was created marquis for this campaign, and when Teng Yü died the following year, Mu succeeded him in command in the west; Chief Commissioner Lan Yü was his deputy. In 1378 their armies captured tens of thousands of rebellious tribesmen and extended Ming authority in the Tibetan-inhabited regions of Shensi and Szechwan. The Ming generals were nearing the Tatu River, the difficult but passable route down which Qubilai had marched to conquer Yünnan in the preparatory stages of the conquest of the Southern Sung, and along which now rode the envoys between the Yünnan regime and the Yüan court.[5]

While these campaigns were in progress, aboriginal revolts in other parts of South China reached serious proportions. They were caused by the strengthening of Ming civil administration in the 1370's, which led to official support for Chinese encroachment on tribal lands. In the winter of 1377 the Ch'iang tribes along the Min River in Szechwan rebelled, and it took four months to suppress them.[6] In the summer of 1378 the Kweichow natives rebelled again, killing the Chingchou guard commander, and it took five months to suppress them.[7] The following year rebellions in the mountainous regions of southwest Shensi required the attention of Mu Ying's army, while another Ming army first suppressed the Tibetans in the Sungp'an region of northwest Szechwan and then marched south to suppress "bandits" in the region of Mount Omei.[8] Officially these campaigns were successful and provided the occasion for the creation of twelve new marquises (Lan Yü was one of them) when Mu Ying brought his army back in 1379. However, most of the new nobles were deserving generals of the civil war who had been passed over in 1370.[9] The situation in the south and west was still very unsettled, but Sung Lien, the chief compiler of the official history of the Yüan, was nevertheless exiled to Maochou in 1380.[10]

The summer and fall of 1381 were devoted to Hsü Ta's campaign against the Mongols (below, pp. 140–41). By late autumn this campaign had been concluded, and the temperature in the south had cooled sufficiently to permit military operations. Fu Yu-te, one of Hsü's two deputies in the campaign just ended, was commissioned general and ordered to subdue Yünnan. His two lieutenant generals were the rising stars Lan Yü and Mu Ying; Lu Chung-heng coordinated the movement of supplies from Ch'engtu. The Yünnan regime was in a precarious situation, as the prince of Liang had first distrusted and then executed Tuan Te-kung, the head of the family that had ruled Tali since before the Mongol conquest. On 14 January 1382 Fu Yu-te caught the chief remaining Yüan army at the Paishih River near Ch'üching and destroyed it, reportedly killing or capturing one hundred thousand men. Deprived at one stroke of his military power, the prince of Liang killed his wife and children and hanged himself.[11]

This marked the end of the Yüan regime in Yünnan, and the emperor issued the appropriate victory proclamation. However, the small tribes and states that had been subordinate to the Yüan empire and had then remained loyal to the Yünnan regime had to be subdued individually. Lan Yü and Mu Ying marched west and entered Tali on 9 April. Minor expeditions and the sending of envoys took up the rest of the year, as the local chieftains formally surrendered and received new seals of authority from the Ming. By the late spring of 1383 this process had gone so far that the emperor ordered most of the army to return. Mu Ying remained behind as military commander in Yünnan, a special position he and his descendants were to hold throughout the Ming dynasty.[12]

The destruction of the prince of Liang's regime eliminated the specter of a rebellion of all the non-Chinese peoples of the southwest united around a Yüan restoration movement. Ming authority in the southwest was not seriously shaken for nearly two and one-half centuries—until the great aboriginal rebellion of 1621. However, rebellion on a lesser scale, though often serious enough to require sending an army commanded by a noble, became even more common after the conquest of Yünnan. The basic cause of the rebellions—encroachment by Chinese settlers on native lands, a development that was actively abetted by Chinese local officials—was if anything aggravated by the conquest of Yünnan, which opened up the entire province to the Chinese.

Kweichow, where Chou Te-hsing was busy suppressing a rebellion even while the army for the conquest of Yünnan was being assembled, gave the Ming armies more trouble in the Hung-wu reign than did any other region in the southwest. In the summer of 1385 the natives of Szuchou rebelled. The emperor, experimenting with the system that would become standard in the 1390's, named his son Chu Chen, prince of Ch'u, to command the army sent to suppress them and assigned T'ang Ho and Chou Te-hsing to assist him.[13] The rebellion of the chieftain A-tzu in 1388 had to be suppressed the following year by Fu Yu-te, and minor rebellions continued for the next two years. In 1391 A-tzu rebelled again, but he was quickly captured and allowed to surrender. However, in 1394 he rebelled still again, and Mu Ch'un (heir of Mu Ying, d. 1392) had to march against him; Mu beheaded him the following year.[14] Rebellions continued to break out throughout the Hung-wu reign and afterwards, usually being dealt with by troops sent from Yünnan. In 1413 Kweichow became a separate province, and remained so from that time.[15]

The tribes in Yünnan were larger and better integrated than those in Kweichow, and some were on the frontier with Burma, a kingdom powerful enough to challenge the Ming empire itself in the southwestern region. At the time of the Ming conquest the tribal chieftains had reluctantly accepted Ming supremacy. Late in 1385 Szu Lun-fa, ruler of Luch'uan, west of the Salween River on the Burmese frontier, launched a carefully prepared rebellion. Szu had earlier been granted the Ming title of pacification commissioner (*hsüan-wei shih*). Defeating the local Ming commander, Chief Commissioner Feng Ch'eng, he maintained his independence and crossed the Salween to invade Ming territory in 1388. Then, defeated and fearing invasion of his own territory, he surrendered voluntarily in 1389. By 1397 he was apparently considered too pro-Chinese by his subjects, for his expulsion by a subordinate signaled the beginning of the next anti-Chinese revolt. However, the Szu family retained its influence until the Cheng-t'ung reign, when the partition of Luch'uan stabilized the western frontier of Yünnan to a degree.[16]

The first Ming census of Yünnan and Kweichow showed a population of only one-quarter million out of an empirewide total of over 60 million. This indicates the overwhelmingly non-Chinese character of Yünnan and Kweichow at this time, since aboriginal peoples were excluded from the Yellow Registers. They were governed under the system the British would later designate "indirect rule." Native chieftains were granted official seals as symbols of their authority and bore Chinese-style official titles that were hereditary, although succession to the title was subject to imperial approval. The chieftains thus became "native officials" (*t'u-kuan*). The individual forms of this institution varied from province to province, often being constrained by specific Yüan or earlier precedents. In Kwangsi, where there had been substantial Chinese settlement since Han times, the sophisticated and largely sinicized Chuang people were organized into departments under hereditary native department magistrates (*t'u chih-chou*).[17] In Kweichow the warlike Miao and other tribes were mostly divided into seventy-six chieftainships (*chang-kuan szu*) under hereditary chiefs (*chang-kuan*, rank 6a), each of whom in turn was under one of the ten prefectures in the province. The prefecture thus became the lowest rung of the bureaucratic ladder in Kweichow, and its role in controlling the tribes was more important than its normal function of supervising the districts, of which only fourteen had been established by 1644.[18]

Larger tribal units such as those of the Yi and the Shan in Yünnan were under rulers who either were given one of a variety of titles that are translated as pacification commissioner (*hsüan-wei shih*, rank 3b; *hsüan-fu shih*, 4b; *an-fu shih* or *chao-t'ao chih*, 5b), or, less often, were made prefects of specially designated military prefectures (*chün-min fu*). Representatives of most of these types, including the chieftainships, were found in Yünnan as well as in the tribal areas of western Hukwang and southern Szechwan (the latter were largely annexed to Yünnan and Kweichow under the Ch'ing). The higher-ranking native officials (prefects and pacification commissioners) were usually directly subordinate to the provincial governments, or else to still higher-ranking native authorities. The tribes were thus generally subject to Chinese civil authority, whether provincial or prefectural, but there were many exceptions to this rule, especially in Hukwang and Szechwan, where the tribal officials were usually subordinate to the nearest military unit (guard or battalion).[19] Chinese imperial residents (*liu-kuan*), usually with the title of deputy (or assistant) pacification commissioner, were appointed to watch over the courts of the more important tribal states.[20]

The policy of "converting aboriginal to regular" (*kai-t'u kuei-liu*)—that is, of depriving the tribal peoples of their hereditary chiefs and placing them under appointed Chinese magistrates of the usual sort—seemed to follow logically on increased Chinese settlement, and it was vigorously pursued under the Ch'ing and the Republic. Under the Ming, in contrast, Yünnan and Kweichow retained their basically non-Chinese tribal character throughout the dynasty. The rate of Chinese immigration into the malarial and unattractive southwest was too small to shift the demographic balance in favor of the Chinese, though it was large enough to disrupt the economy and society of the tribal peoples.

By the end of the Hung-wu reign Chinese rule had been established along lines that survived until the fall of the Ming in Yünnan, Kweichow, and the other non-Chinese areas in the southwest. Recurrent native rebellions had failed to pose a serious threat to the basis of that rule. Thus, by the end of the Hung-wu reign, a precedent had been established that argued persuasively, despite the emperor's deathbed injunction against foreign conquest, that expansion and annexation of non-Chinese territories might in the long run be the cheapest way to deal with a threatening frontier situation.

Foreign Relations During the Hung-wu Era

The early Ming period coincided with major changes of regime in several of the countries traditionally engaged in relations with China. In Korea revolution and civil war terminated the Wang (Koryŏ) dynasty in its fourth century of rule, and the successful general Yi Sŏnggye founded a new royal house.[21] Similar convulsions in Vietnam led to the displacement of the Tran by the Le.[22] In Japan the period of division between rival northern and southern imperial lines (Namboku-chō) came to an end and the Ashikaga shogunate entered its period of greatest power.[23] Even under normal circumstances these events would have strained the smooth conduct of foreign relations under the tributary system and would have required the making of such important foreign policy decisions as whether and under what terms to recognize the new governments.

Under the special circumstances of the early Ming period, successful foreign relations were even more important because of the significance of the tribute system in certifying imperial legitimacy. The new Ming empire represented both the transfer of the Mandate of Heaven to a new ruling house and the replacement of putatively unorthodox barbarian habits with acceptably orthodox Chinese customs. Foreign rulers were naturally expected to send tributary missions to Nanking, thereby repudiating the Yüan and recognizing the Ming. But this was not enough. The tributary system had to be restored to its orthodox form in order to demonstrate the legitimacy of Ming rule, and this required that its moral and ideological aspects (the spectacle of foreign rulers being attracted from afar by the power of imperial virtue) receive primacy over its economic side (the simple desire of foreign rulers to trade with China). The conduct of foreign relations thus became intertwined with the components of the emperor's ideologically determined policy toward foreign trade: first, to bring it under government control within the tribute system; second, to diminish its volume drastically.

These objectives were consistent with the emperor's belief that he could restore order and security only by subjecting the economy, and society in general, to government control; but in this area he was challenging an established pattern of overseas trade. Trade had been profitable to both the merchants of South China and the nations of Southeast Asia, and it had enjoyed government support under the Yüan, who had inherited its customary practices from the Southern Sung. Hung-wu was trying to suppress this trade without providing satisfactory economic alternatives for those who had come to depend on it. Naturally those involved in the trade, both Chinese and foreign, attempted to maintain it illegally through smuggling and piracy. Hung-wu in response ordered naval expeditions against the pirates' lairs in the islands off the South China coast and also created numerous coastal garrisons. His attempt to solve the problem by force was in vain, and Yung-lo subsequently was led to expand the volume of trade permitted within the tribute system. However, in the long run the policies of the Hung-wu period set the precedent for the exclusionary policies of the rest of the dynasty.[24]

It was late in 1368 that Hung-wu formally inaugurated the tribute system by sending envoys to Korea, Vietnam, Champa, and Japan to announce the founding of the Ming dynasty. In 1369 Korea, Vietnam, and Champa sent tribute missions in response. In 1370 a mission arrived from the great Majapahit kingdom of Java. In 1371 Japan, Siam, Cambodia, and "Shrivijaya" (actually the Malayu-Jambi kingdom on Sumatra) sent their first tribute missions. In 1372 the first mission from the island kingdom of Liuch'iu (Ryūkyū) arrived. In the twenty-nine years of the Hung-wu reign in which tribute missions were received (1369–97), the five countries that sent them most often were Liuch'iu and Korea (each twenty missions), Champa (nineteen), Siam (eighteen), and Vietnam (fourteen).[25]

Each of these kingdoms had its own reason for desiring peaceful and regular relationships with the Ming, and in each case political and cultural factors outweighed economic ones. This was true even in the case of Liuch'iu, despite the importance of the tributary trade in the economy of that small kingdom, and after the islands split into three kingdoms late in the Hung-wu reign, the role of the Chinese emperor as the dispenser of legitimacy in the non-Chinese Confucian world became even more marked than before.[26] For Korea the political factor in its relations with China was more important than ritual legitimation. Korea had accepted Ming overlordship promptly in 1369 in the hope, largely fulfilled, that Ming demands would be less harsh than those of the Mongols and that the Ming would provide military assistance against Mongol attacks. Korea sent tribute missions on almost an annual basis until 1379, when the Ming court rejected the Korean tribute as inadequate. The ruptured relations were restored in 1385 and continued amicably from then on. In 1389 Yi Sŏnggye deposed two successive kings whom he stigmatized as usurpers, and then placed a collateral prince of the Wang dynasty on the throne. The Ming court acquiesced in this, and, when Yi Sŏnggye himself usurped the throne in 1392, was even willing to recognize the change of dynasty, insisting only on such formal details as a change in the name of the kingdom from Koryŏ to Chosŏn.[27]

Vietnam was the only sinicized state in the generally Hindu and

Buddhist world of Southeast Asia, but despite this the Chinese treated it with markedly less respect than either Korea or Liuch'iu. During the fourteenth century continuous warfare had led to the expansion of Vietnam at the expense of Champa, which adjoined it to the south, and Champa had sent tribute embassies to the Ming court in the hope of assistance against Vietnam. Hung-wu was firmly opposed to military adventures in Southeast Asia and declined to intervene, except by reproving the Vietnamese for fighting. The Vietnamese general Le Qui Ly, who rose to prominence in these wars, in 1388 and 1389 murdered two Tran monarchs in succession. The situation was strikingly parallel to that in Korea, but when Le Qui Ly usurped the throne after the death of Hung-wu the result was Chinese intervention.[28]

In Siam during the fourteenth century, the kingdom of Ayut'ia was still in the process of asserting its paramountcy over the other Thai kingdoms while at the same time warring with Cambodia, which itself sent eight tribute missions during the Hung-wu reign.[29]

To facilitate the reception of tributary missions, five foreign trade superintendencies (*shih-po szu*) were established in 1367 and afterwards. Two of these were abolished in 1370, leaving only those at Ningpo in Chekiang, Ch'üanchou in Fukien, and Canton. Each country that sent missions by sea was assigned to one of these offices, and among his other duties the Chinese official serving as superintendent had to regulate the sale of private trade goods brought in by the individual members of the tribute missions. Surviving examples from later in the reign show that the total volume of trade brought in by the tribute missions was quite large: in 1392 a Siamese mission carried 170,000 catties (over 38 tons) of aromatics, while in 1382 a Javanese mission had brought 75,000 catties of pepper. In the early years of the system, when the embassies' trade seemed to have at least the tacit consent of the Ming government, the amounts must have been even larger. In 1374, on the grounds that cunning merchants were abusing the excessive freedom of trade, the emperor ordered that the three remaining superintendencies be abolished.[30]

By creating the trading superintendencies in the first place, Hung-wu had aroused hopes in the maritime Malay world that the old Shrivijaya-China relationship of the T'ang and Sung periods would be restored. This relationship rested upon both Chinese acceptance of a large volume of trade within the tributary system and the maintenance of a regular tributary relationship between Shrivijaya and the empire, a combination of factors that enabled Palembang, the capital of Shrivijaya on Sumatra, to develop a trading monopoly as entrepôt for goods destined for transshipment to China. The wealth generated by this trade enabled the Maharaja of Shrivijaya to maintain hegemony over the maritime Malay world through the lavishness of his largesse. The countries of continental Southeast Asia were happy to profit incidentally from a tribute system whose main significance for them was political. The maritime Malays, on the other hand, depended for both political unity and independence on the maintenance of the tribute system in its mid-T'ang form. The development of a private overseas trade carried in Chinese bottoms sailing directly to the areas where desired cargoes were produced ended the monopoly once enjoyed by Palembang. The resulting decline in the Maharajas' wealth weakened their hold over their vassals, and by the mid-thirteenth century both the lesser Malay principalities, on Borneo and the islands, and the greater centers, at Palembang and Jambi on Sumatra, had been forced to acknowledge the supremacy of the empire of Majapahit centered in inland Java. But in the 1370's the Ming ban on private overseas trade and the revival of the trading superintendencies seemed to reestablish the preconditions of the Palembang system.[31]

The maritime Malay states responded quickly to the new situation, word of which reached them from the Chinese envoy Chao Shu, who was sent to Southeast Asia in 1370. In 1371 Brunei renounced its allegiance to Majapahit and sent a tribute mission. Between 1371 and 1378 eight tribute missions came from rulers in southern Sumatra, including no less than six from "Shrivijaya" (apparently Malayu, whose capital was Jambi). According to Hung-wu, who was determined to maintain the priorities of the tribute system, embassies could be accepted only from independent rulers. Sumatra's princes, more vulnerable to Javanese retaliation than Brunei, realized that their independence was contingent on the revival of the tributary trade. They claimed independence in their dealings with China and hoped that the Javanese would not find out. In 1377 a Malayu mission was in Nanking requesting imperial investiture for their ruler. Javanese envoys, also in Nanking at this time, reported this to their king, Hayam Wuruk (r. 1350–89), who responded by capturing the Chinese envoys en route to Malayu and murdering them. Sometime later he invaded southern Sumatra and forced the rulers of Palembang and Malayu to acknowledge their continued vassal status.[32]

Embassies from the maritime Malay princes thereupon ceased, and the same Javanese dynasty that had tricked and defeated the Mongol expeditionary force in the thirteenth century continued to maintain its power over the archipelago. Even though embassies from the continental states kept the tribute system functioning, the lack of missions from the maritime princes was embarrassing. By 1397 Hung-wu was blaming the whole problem on Hu Wei-yung, whom he accused of suppressing the fact that the Sumatran princes were vassals of Java in order to profit personally from their trade.[33]

Relations with Japan followed a similar pattern: promising beginnings followed by complete rupture. There were false starts; the Chinese envoy sent in 1368 never reached Japan, and attacks by Japanese pirates continued. In 1369 a second Chinese envoy was sent bearing a decree reproving the Japanese for their piracy and threatening force if they did not mend their ways. This embassy landed at Dazaifu in Kyushu, where Prince Kanenaga ruled as the representative of his father, Emperor Godaigo of the Southern Court. Annoyed by the tone of the Chinese decree, Kanenaga imprisoned the Chinese envoys and executed some of their staff. Hung-wu, who still faced military problems on his northern and western frontiers, could not contemplate military action against Japan at that time, and in 1370 he sent another envoy with a more conciliatory message. When Kanenaga responded favorably the following year and sent a mission headed by the Buddhist monk Sorai, Emperor Hung-wu honored the Japanese envoys with a massive ceremony at the T'ien-chieh-szu in Nanking attended by over a thousand monks; it was the largest Buddhist gathering in the Hung-wu period.[34]

The success of this affair led the emperor to appoint two monks, Tsu-shan and K'o-chin, to lead the next embassy to Japan in 1372. Unfortunately, this embassy coincided with the conquest of Dazaifu by Imagawa Ryōshun, deputy in Kyushu of the Ashikaga shogun. Discovering the true political situation in Japan, the Chinese envoys made their way to Kyoto, where as Buddhists they made a favorable impression on the Ashikaga authorities. Tsushan and K'o-chin arrived back in Nanking in 1374 in the company of an Ashikaga embassy headed by three Japanese monks.[35]

The way this embassy was received raised the confusion to new heights. The emperor conferred with Tsu-shan and K'o-chin before receiving the Japanese monks, but apparently he could not disabuse himself of the notion that Prince Kanenaga was the legitimate "king" of Japan, from which perspective the Ashikaga could only be rebels. He therefore refused to accept their tribute and exhorted them to return to submission. The Ashikaga sent no further embassies until 1380, while the Southern Court continued to correspond with China in the name of Prince Kanenaga, a convention that often obscures the identity of the true Japanese party. However, the tone of all exchanges became increasingly bellicose after 1374, coincidentally the year in which the three trading superintendencies were abolished. The Chinese wanted the Japanese to end their piracy, but since piracy was the substitute for legal foreign trade, naturally no Japanese overlord was eager to suppress it as long as the Chinese also refused to permit trade.[36]

In letters sent in 1374, 1376, 1380, and 1381 Hung-wu tried to force the Japanese into compliance with his will by threatening to invade them. The Japanese response was negative and nationalistic, referring repeatedly to the Yüan failure to conquer Japan. A Japanese letter sent in 1382 escalated the war of words by explicitly denying the unique and universal authority of the Chinese emperor: "Heaven and earth are vast; they are not monopolized by one ruler. The universe is great and wide, and the various countries are created each to have a share in its rule. Now the world is the world's world; it does not belong to a single person." Although the Japanese of both courts made several attempts, even after this, to reopen relations with China, Hung-wu consistently refused to receive them, and relations between the two countries remained suspended until after his death.[37]

Hung-wu had ruled against military conquest of Japan or Southeast Asia, being aware of the unpropitious Yüan precedent, and his attempts to cow the Japanese by threats had failed. The only remaining alternative was total severance of relations coupled with military defense against the Japanese pirates. Between 1383 and 1387 Hung-wu decided on the latter course, and by 1387 he had added the breakdown in Sino-Japanese relations to the long list of problems for which he blamed Hu Wei-yung's conspiracies.[38]

Coast defense measures expanded as foreign relations and legal foreign trade contracted. In 1371 Wu Chen had resettled Fang Kuo-chen's former followers. The next year, four guards were assigned to provide crews for the fleets Wu led every year to patrol the sea lanes during the sailing season. This system proved adequate protection against piracy for a dozen years, but the severance of relations between China and Japan and China and Southeast Asia, together with the virtual elimination of legal overseas trade, made different and stronger measures necessary. In 1384 T'ang Ho was placed in command of coastal defenses, and during the next several years, especially 1387–88, numerous new garrisons were created along the coasts of Shantung, Chekiang, Fukien, and Kwangtung. In the four coastal prefectures of Fukien, one-third of the adult male population was conscripted into the coast defense forces; this provided 15,000 men who were divided among five newly established guards and twelve independent battalions. Coast defense developed similarly in the other provinces. In 1390 Shantung constructed a large number of small forts and stockades on offshore islands and other exposed places. In the same year, every company headquarters and police station (*hsün-chien szu*) was ordered to maintain two seagoing ships. The coastal garrisons were assigned a full quota of military colony lands in the manner of the rest of the military system.[39]

By shifting over to a defensive system that emphasized coastal garrisons at a time when the Ming fleets were just at the height of their effectiveness, the emperor revealed to history the extent of the dislocation his foreign policies had caused among the trade-dependent people of the South China coast. Given his premise that foreign trade was useless and pernicious, his solution to the problem was clever: the men he conscripted into the coastal garrisons were those who might have joined the pirates and smugglers; furthermore, through the military colonies, he gave them a new means of livelihood to replace the one he had destroyed. He had returned them to the "fundamental occupation" of agriculture, subjected them to government control, and turned them into soldiers all at one stroke.

Early in his reign, and again at the close of his life, Hung-wu included Japan and the Southeast Asian countries in the list of distant and hard to reach countries that his successors were enjoined from attacking.[40] During his reign he faithfully observed this injunction, which was based on the precedent of the disastrous failures of the Yüan expeditions to these areas. However, by refusing to trade with them as well, he was attempting to reduce foreign relations under the tribute system to an entirely political level. Those foreign states that participated in the tribute system for economic advantage, as well as those Chinese who had come to depend on overseas trade, were naturally resentful, and their resentment was one of the factors that led Hung-wu's son Yung-lo to attempt a radically different approach to foreign affairs.

Resettlement and Registration: The Land and Tax Systems

For Hung-wu the maintenance of lasting peace and the orthodox Confucian order entailed the establishment of the greatest possible measure of government control over society and the economy. In practical terms this meant that displaced and vagrant persons, who were without livelihood or made their living by antisocial means, had to be settled in regular occupations and connected to officialdom by means of deliberately created institutions, a step that usually required joining a mutual responsibility group and registering in a hereditary occupational class. This concern appeared early in the course of military registration and of establishing the military colonies; it was urgent because of the importance of stabilizing the status of the large number of soldiers mobilized in the course of the civil war.

In the civilian agricultural sector, as well, the restoration of peacetime conditions and the resettlement of vacant lands went hand in hand with the imposition of government controls. The land and tax systems, whose evolution was essentially complete by 1393, rested on four major institutions: (1) the Yellow Registers (*huang-ts'e*) promulgated in 1381, which recorded the population by family membership, place of residence, and labor services owed; (2) the Fish-scale Charts and Registers (*yü-lin t'u-ts'e*), which in principle showed every parcel of cultivated land in the empire, graded as to quality, with its tax quota and ownership; (3) the tax-captain (*liang-chang*) system whereby the wealthier land-owning families were made liable for the collection of grain taxes in their districts; and (4) the *li-chia* system whereby peasant households were organized into groups that were mutually responsible for the payment of taxes.[41] The two systems of registers overlapped in their contents, thus permitting government officials to check one against the other; the two systems of collection guarded against malfeasance in either one. The completion of this complex system of interlocking controls required many years of adaptation, and was carried to completion only because of Hung-wu's persistence.

Hung-wu originally ordered that the registers were to be revised annually. This requirement ran counter to both the desire of the wealthy to conceal any increase in the value of their holdings and the desire of Confucian administrators to show benevolence to the populations under their charge by refusing to raise tax quotas, so almost from the date of the emperor's death the local magistrates began to treat this requirement as a dead letter. However, this was due to the failure of Hung-wu's successors to emulate the dynastic founder's administrative standards, and it should not obscure the extent of his achievement: land registration on such a scale had not been attained since the seventh century, and population registration of such completeness is equaled only by part of the Ch'ing period (specifically 1776–1850) and by the census of 1953.

During the civil war military requirements determined land and tax policy. Grain was collected for military consumption, or to prevent its use by enemy forces, by local commanders who were not bound by fixed rates. The sources frequently record Chu Yüan-chang as ordering his commanders to be lenient in requisitioning grain, but the very frequency of the repetitions indicates that his exhortations were not effective; military needs actually were pressing, and the Ming central government at this time was in no position to enforce stringent restrictions on its local commanders. Instead, the Ming central administration attempted to lighten the burden of its armies on the population by making the armies self-sufficient through the military colonies and by establishing in 1362 a system of government-licensed salt distribution, the revenue from which was specifically earmarked for military purposes.[42]

The creation of the central army at Nanking (which was composed primarily of men from Anhwei), the relocation of surrendered Han and Wu troops in areas far from their place of origin, and the creation of a line of defense on the northern frontier together added up to the resettlement of several hundred thousand men with their families, even though resettlement was incidental to the military purpose of these transfers. The regime also instituted a long-range program of transfer and resettlement among the civilian population. The combined effect of the famines preceding the outbreak of the rebellions and of Chu Yüan-chang's evacuation of the area in 1355 had been to leave central Anhwei considerably depopulated. When the emperor redesignated Haochou as Fengyang prefecture and located the central metropolis (Chungtu) there, this became a logical place to send settlers.

After the fall of Chang Shih-ch'eng, the estates of his more ardent supporters among the landowning gentry of the Soochow area were confiscated, and the families were sent to Fengyang.[43] This weakened a concentration of landed power that had been strong enough to defy the Yüan and whose support of Hung-wu's archrival had earned his hatred; the resurgence of this class was inhibited by the imposition of especially high land-tax rates on the Soochow area.[44] It is true that the rates were occasionally modified, but the disproportion remained throughout the dynasty.* Peasants from this overcrowded region were also sent to colonize Fengyang, as later were peasants displaced by famine in Peip'ing province, Shansi, and other places. In the Peip'ing area itself, civilian colonization supplemented the military in repopulating the region. In the third lunar month of 1371 over 17,000 households "from behind the mountains" were resettled in Peip'ing province, followed in the sixth month by 32,000 households "abandoned in the desert", households presumably captured when Li Wen-chung took Yingch'ang the previous year. Also in the

---

* In March 1400 the Soochow-Sungkiang tax rates were reduced (see below; pp. 164 and 279, n. 17), but this measure was later revoked; in 1502 Soochow's quota was 2.0 million shih out of an empirewide total of 22.2 million, and was still essentially unchanged seventy years later.

sixth month, 35,000 other households were resettled in various places in the interior. These three instances add up to perhaps 450,000 people resettled in 1371 alone.[45]

Beginning in 1369 the government took steps to enumerate the population, and in 1370 the Ministry of Revenue was ordered to carry out a comprehensive census of the country. Because the armies were temporarily between campaigns, the troops were ordered to assist the civil officials in conducting the census. Every household was given half of a certificate, on both halves of which family name, place of residence, occupational classification, and the names, ages, and relationship of all family members, including minor children, were recorded. Each household was to preserve its half of the certificate carefully, and the registrations were to be revised annually, at which time the certificates retained by the individual households were to be compared with those held by the district government. If they tallied, the household was to be treated as being in good standing, but if they did not, the household was to be punished. Significantly, the punishment specified was transfer to the military register maintained by the Ministry of War, which made the household liable for military duty and subject to the military judicial system.[46]

When Hung-wu took personal charge of the administration after the fall of Hu Wei-yung, he was dissatisfied with the laxness of the population registration system and soon issued decrees to tighten it. In the first month of 1381 the same decree that established the li-chia system also revised the population registration system into the form of the Yellow Registers. Every 110 households, in principle, were organized in a li—called *fang* ("lane") within the walled cities and *hsiang* ("village") in the suburbs. The heads of the ten households having the greatest number of adult males or paying the highest amount of taxes were made headmen (*li-cheng*), and the remaining households were grouped in ten chia. Every year one headman and his chia would be responsible for the performance of labor services by the li. Widowed people and orphans, who were not responsible for labor services, were nevertheless included on the register as "odds and ends." Classifications were reduced to commoner status (*min-chi*, mostly peasants), artisan status (*chiang-chi*), and military status (*chün-chi*, recorded separately and not included in the Yellow Registers); medical doctors and Confucian scholars, previously registered separately, were now assigned to the commoner classification. Since the labor service liability would rotate throughout each li once every ten years, it was ordered that the registers be revised decennially. In 1391 the officials were ordered to concentrate on changes in the number of adult males and on tax payment when revising the registers, thus opening the door to the regular underregistration that prevailed after the death of Hung-wu. The registers were to be made out in four copies, of which the district, prefecture, and province each would retain one; the fourth copy, bound in yellow covers, was to go to the Ministry of Revenue, there to be stored in specially constructed brick archives on the island in Lake Hsüanwu north of the city wall of Nanking.[47]

The purpose of creating the li-chia system had been to ensure the fulfillment of labor service, but the headmen also were responsible for the compilation of the registers of property values and tax assessments as well, besides which the labor services themselves might be converted to money payments. Consequently, it was natural for the li-chia to develop into a mechanism for the general collection of taxes. However, beginning in 1371 the responsibility for the collection of land taxes proper was placed on tax captains appointed by the district magistrates, one for each subdivision of the district with a tax liability of at least 10,000 shih. The tax captains collected the tax grain and issued receipts, and were themselves financially liable for any failure to meet their quotas. Because of this liability, it was ordered that the tax captains be chosen from among the wealthiest households in each district. Although the tax captain system functioned effectively during the 1370's, it seems to have been conceived from the beginning as a temporary measure, and in 1382 the tax captains were abolished, their functions being transferred to the li-chia. In effect, mutual responsibility had replaced individual responsibility. Three years later, in 1385, the tax captains were reestablished with their original duties.[48]

Interpretation of tax captains as a system has been controversial. The authority granted to the tax captains has been used to argue that Hung-wu sold out the peasants to the landlords after becoming emperor. Since there is a sense in which he had betrayed the peasants, by suppressing the Red Turban movement, it is at least arguable that he betrayed them in the economic realm as well. However, there is very little in the sources to suggest that Hung-wu or his contemporaries viewed issues in economic class terms, in contrast to their clear perception of such dichotomies as Chinese versus barbarian, Confucian versus heterodox, and scholar versus non-scholar. Hung-wu's vision of the ideal social order required the harmonious cooperation of families of different degrees of wealth and the freezing of the population into essentially hereditary occupational strata, all maintained and enforced by a powerful and paternalistic state. The emperor saw himself as regulating the whole order, not as representing any segment of it. His view of the tax captain system, or any other institutional arrangement, was therefore largely functional, and was subject to change as Ming fiscal administration grew more sophisticated.

When the tax captain system was first instituted, the country was recovering from a long period of civil war, with all of its attendant devastation and administrative confusion, and an individual's designation as tax captain had frequently meant paying a large portion of his assigned quota from his own income. Once cultivation and recordkeeping were restored, the tax captain could collect more, which gave him the opportunity to keep the amount over quota, and also to commit other abuses. The compilation of the registers allowed the government to revise tax quotas on the basis of more detailed and accurate knowledge of population distribution and landholdings, so the li-chia may have seemed less subject to abuse as a tax-collecting system than were the tax captains. Yet abolishing the personal responsibility of the tax captains meant that the richer households no longer had a specific interest in seeing that the quotas for their districts were met; they could use their local influence to shift part of their tax burden to less prosperous households within the li-chia framework. Ending this abuse required reviving the tax captains, this time as a complement to the li-chia system. This reasoning stresses the role of the tax captain as guarantor of the state's tax revenues and suggests that the authority he enjoyed did not compensate for the burden of paperwork and the prospective financial loss he had to face.[49]

The effective functioning of the li-chia system quickly exposed the gaps in the government's detailed knowledge of land tenure and productivity. Following the reestablishment of the tax captains in 1385, they and the li-chia headmen were given the main responsibility for the compilation of new registers that would give a record of the ownership, physical description, and productivity of the cultivated land of the empire. The compilation of these registers was ordered in 1387 and was based on Hung-wu's awareness of the deficiencies in the previous registration procedures that had permitted rich landowners in the Soochow and Ch'angchou area to evade taxes by putting their lands in the names of kinsmen and tenants:

> Upon hearing of this, the emperor despatched the student of the imperial academy (*chien-sheng*) Wu Ch'un and a number of his colleagues to go to these areas, which were to be subdivided for the purposes of land-tax payment. For each such land-tax subdivision four headmen were appointed who were to assemble the *li-chia* personnel and elders to carry out a land survey. The areas of the holdings were computed and given registered numbers with the owners' names attached. All of these were written at the four corners of the registers, which were officially coded. They were called Fish-scale Charts and Registers (*yü-lin t'u-ts'e*) because the charts [of the various parcels of cultivated land] looked like fish-scales.[50]

The land was assessed for productivity according to three grades (upper, middle, and lower), each of which was in turn divided into three subgrades. In the resulting classification the tax rate per mou would vary according to the grade, but the number of mou recorded would, in principle, represent the actual total area under cultivation. However, it became common in the Hung-wu reign, and standard from Yung-lo on, to convert several mou of inferior land into one mou representing a standardized amount of tax liability. Totals of mou then came to represent land tax quotas, rather than total land under cultivation. This change in emphasis in land registration parallels the development whereby population registration came to concentrate on taxpaying adult males (*ting*) rather than the whole population. After 1398 the civil bureaucracy viewed the land and population registration systems merely as the means of maintaining an existing fiscal system whose quotas of both land taxes and labor services were essentially fixed.[51] Hung-wu, on the contrary, had viewed the two registration systems as the statistical means of ensuring governmental control over both land and people, and thus of permitting land taxes and labor services to rise as more land came under cultivation and the population rose.

In the light of this objective, the involvement of the larger landowners (tax captains) in the survey process appears as another attempt to make them assume direct responsibility for tax payments, an interpretation that is consistent with the fact that the compilation of the Fish-scale Charts and Registers began in the landlord-dominated Yangtze delta and Chekiang areas, and was most meticulously carried out there. It is not clear exactly when the land registration was completed empirewide, but by 1393 both land and population had been registered to an extent sufficient to permit the publication of statistical summaries that became the basis for the later tax quotas. The population that year was 10,652,789 households and 60,545,812 individuals, and the total area of land under cultivation was 8,507,623 ch'ing.[52] The population figures are slightly higher—and the land figures substantially higher—than those reported during the rest of the dynasty.

The land taxes were collected on the schedule of the two-tax system (*liang-shui fa*) inaugurated by Yang Yen in 780, and the 1393 quotas for the summer tax (*hsia-shui*, due in the seventh lunar month) totaled 5,041,187 shih while the autumn grain tax (*ch'iu-liang*, due in the eleventh month) totaled 24,735,239 shih, for a grand total of 29,776,426 shih of land-tax revenue.[53] The size of this figure, well over twice the grain revenues of the Yüan dynasty (eventually fixed at 12,114,708 shih), coupled with the fact that the army, always a major consumer of tax revenues, provided much of its own support through the military colonies meant that the new dynasty rested on an extremely solid fiscal basis. A substantial surplus of revenue over expenditure came to be regarded as the norm, and this surplus could be used to finance tax remission and disaster relief, as Confucian officials preferred, or to finance military campaigns and palace construction, as Yung-lo and his successors insisted. Not only did the empire enjoy financial abundance for the first time since the seventh century, but the abundance had been achieved by means of the land tax. The regime was thus freed from dependence on monopoly and commercial taxes, and later generations of officials were in a position to put into practice ultra-Confucian policies unfavorable to trade and other economic activities regarded as "nonfundamental" from a strict Confucian viewpoint.

However, revenue from other sources was not entirely abandoned; during the Hung-wu reign the regime derived substantial revenues from salt and from commercial taxes. In 1361, at the peak of the civil war, the Nanking government began to sell licences permitting merchants to distribute salt imported from the producing regions on the Chekiang coast, then under the control of Fang Kuo-chen. It established tax-collection stations at which a duty of one-twentieth (later raised to one-tenth) was collected on salt, and one-fifteenth on other goods.[54] In a period when most of the land taxes were under local control, the salt and commercial taxes were a welcome addition to the central government's disposable revenue. Later, as the Ming regime expanded, the originally unified system of salt and commercial taxation was divided. The commercial tax stations, which came to number over four hundred, were placed under the control of prefectural governments and their revenues applied to local uses.[55]

As the Ming's territorial expansion brought the major salt-producing areas of China under its control, the salt system changed from one of private production whose sale was licensed and subject to tax to one of government-controlled production that was coupled with a distribution system partly in state and partly in private hands, and in which taxation no longer played a part. By the middle of the Hung-wu reign the final system of six salt commissions (*tu chuan-yün yen shih szu*) and seven salt superintendencies (*yen-k'o t'i-chü szu*) had emerged to control hundreds of branch offices, salt wells, salt pans, and other facilities. Each salt worker was expected to turn in 3,200 catties of salt to his commission or superintendency each year, receiving as compensation one shih of grain per 400 catties. Each commission and superintendency had its own annual quota, and these added up to a national total of 459,316,400 catties, whose theoretical cost to the government was thus 1,148,293 shih. Some of the salt was sold directly by the government at fixed prices, with the purchase compulsory, but most was sold at higher prices to salt merchants who passed their costs on to the consumers. Salt producers also sold their over-quota production outside the system; this was necessary since their compensation for quota salt added up to only about two-thirds of the amount considered necessary to maintain a household at sub-sistence level.[56]

There were vast profits to be made in salt, but the system suffered from corruption and mismanagement from the begin-ning, so most of this income was never seen by the government. The quota salt alone should have brought a price of about 7.5 million taels of silver on the open market, and perhaps twice as much non-quota salt was being produced and sold, illegally or otherwise; yet before the seventeenth century government in-come from the salt system averaged only 1.2 million taels annually. Since grain prices in the late fourteenth century averaged one tael per shih, the income from salt revenue was minor compared to the nearly 30 million taels collected (largely in kind, to be sure) through the land tax. This is in contrast to the situation under the Yüan dynasty, when over half of the government's revenues were provided by the salt monopoly. Commercial taxes and other nonagricultural sources of revenue were even less important, both individually and cumulatively.[57]

Examinations and Bureaucracy

The government structure established in the wake of the Hu Wei-yung purge remained substantially unchanged for the rest of the Hung-wu reign. The Censorate in fact suffered little more than a change of name, though it remained headless until 1384. The threefold division of authority in the provinces was a result of evolutionary modifications, made during the 1370's, that it suited Hung-wu's purposes to retain. And the creation of the five chief military commissions did not in practice alter the way in which military command was exercised by the military nobility, nor did it provide any institutional safeguard against the emergence of a man on horseback, as was shown by the Lan Yü affair.

The aspect of government most affected by the 1380 reorgani-zation was the relationship between the emperor and the highest agencies of civil administration in the capital. The abolition of the Secretariat-Chancellery and the office of chancellor itself, insti-tutions that for centuries had represented the corporate Confucian civil service vis-à-vis the emperors, now made the emperor for the first time the immediate superior of the Six Ministries. The ministers and vice-ministers now became by default the most important civil officials in the empire. This did not mean that they were expected or permitted to assume the leadership in the central government formerly exercised by the chancellors. On the contrary, Hung-wu, having for two decades seen officials as sources of threats and insults, now determined to subject them to the closest possible personal supervision. He personally read and routed all incoming documents and decided the responses to them, in effect combining the policy-determining functions of the chancellors and the routine administrative functions of the Secretariat-Chancellery. This meant an enormous workload: in one eight-day period in which the details were recorded, he read and ruled upon 1,660 documents dealing with 3,391 different matters.[58]

Since the ministers now outranked the provincial administrative commissioners, they were no longer as a rule transferred out to head provincial governments. Although a minister's position was by no means easy, and he still ran considerable risk of leaving office by execution, the rate of turnover among the ministers decreased markedly after 1380, especially after 1385. Between 1380 and 1398 Hung-wu appointed ten ministers of personnel, twelve ministers of revenue (one twice), eleven ministers of rites, nine ministers of war (one twice), eleven ministers of justice, and nine ministers of works (one twice), which totals sixty-five appointments to the six positions in eighteen years; but from 1384 to 1398 only ten men held the two presidencies of the Censorate.[59]

In 1384 the civil service examinations were revived, with the first metropolitan examinations in the new sequence being held in 1385; thereafter they were held regularly at three-year intervals. Including 1371, there were six chin-shih examinations in the Hung-wu period, the last being in 1397. In the broader historical context the Hung-wu reign saw the finalization of the narrowly classicist eight-legged essay (*pa-ku wen*), which lasted unchanged as the examination format until 1905. Despite their allegedly stultifying effect on original thought, these examinations played a major role in establishing the moral authority, and hence the political power, of the scholar-gentry over the alternative elites. The revival of the examination system, this time permanently, was thus a major step in solidifying the domination of Chinese society by civilian gentry that marked the last two dynasties of Chinese

schools and their students. The triennial provincial examinations conferred a permanent degree status on successful candidates (*chü-jen*), who in the early Ming period had a good chance of winning official appointment and making a successful career with the provincial degree alone. Throughout the dynasty the instructorships in the local schools continued to be reserved for chü-jen.[65]

Every three years the metropolitan examinations were held in Nanking after the provincial examinations. Successful candidates were then subjected to the palace examination, the papers from which were theoretically read and placed in final rank order by the emperor himself. As the climax of the examination ritual, usually on the first day of the third lunar month, the successful candidates were presented to the emperor in order of highest ranking and granted the appropriate rewards and honors; hence their title "presented scholar" (*chin-shih*). In the examination of 1371 some 120 chin-shih degrees had been granted; in 1385, 472 were awarded, a figure never surpassed in the Ming and equalled only in 1404. The remaining Hung-wu examinations produced far fewer degrees. Ninety-seven were granted in 1388, only 31 in 1391, exactly 100 in 1394, and 51 in 1397—for a total of 871 during the entire Hung-wu reign.[66]

At its full development the Ming civil bureaucracy contained perhaps fifteen thousand officials, of whom at least five thousand were instructors in the government schools and at least four thousand others were petty district officials (ranks 8 or 9) holding positions too unimportant to be filled by chin-shih, who normally began their careers as at least district magistrates (7a).[67] Even excluding these lower positions, it is clear that not enough chin-shih had been produced by 1398 for them to hold a majority of even the official positions that were later largely reserved for chin-shih. However, to state the situation in that way is to miss the real significance of the revival of the examinations. They in fact opened the door to the thoroughgoing Confucianization of the civil service, and therefore they led to the revival of the traditional emperor-minister tension after Hung-wu's death, even though Hung-wu's reforms left his successors in a better position to play the despot than emperors of previous dynasties. The chin-shih were the normative ideal. Both the examinations and the state school system were created and geared to turn them out, and they naturally set the tone for civil officialdom as a whole. The chin-shih also were highly competent as individuals, and the members of each triennial class had a strong sense of group feeling. For chü-jen who did not succeed in obtaining the chin-shih, becoming a student of the national university (*kuo-tzu chien*, also called the imperial academy) offered an alternative route to office, one that was open to other students as well. After a period of satisfactory matriculation at the university, where he could be observed by the capital officials, any chien-sheng could be recommended for official appointment. In 1368 over 1,000 entered official life in this way, and 639 were given office as late as 1391. In other words, appointment following a term in the national university continued to be an important route of entry into the bureaucracy even after the examination system was fully functioning; before then, it had been the route that conferred the most prestige. Hung-wu also frequently ordered serving officials to recommend worthy men, who were then immediately appointed to office. In 1380 some 860 men became officials in this manner.[68]

The 1380 reorganizations fixed the ranks of Ming civil and military positions at relative levels that lasted until 1644. Basically, a civil officialdom recruited through examinations confronted a hereditary military officer class. The latter were led by a small group of nobles and an increasing number of imperial clansmen, who were given military titles and in the Hung-wu period were also expected to perform military duties. In time the civil officials came to dominate all governmental functions; this development reduced the complex of military officers, nobles, and imperial clansmen to sinecurists, or to ciphers who exercised merely instrumental executive functions. In Hung-wu's political order as originally conceived, however, the civil officials were to do the work of administering a system whose beneficiaries were to be the military officers, nobles, and imperial clansmen. These, all of whom held hereditary positions of some sort, were his own descendants, or the descendants of those who had helped him gain the throne and thus had a special claim upon his favor. The gentry scholars, in contrast, had joined him belatedly and reluctantly. Hung-wu had concluded from history that the scholars had to be employed as civil officials if his dynasty was to be regarded as legitimate, but he felt little reason to be grateful to them or to extend them more than minimum favor. Furthermore, Hung-wu was influenced by the example of the living Yüan empire in which he had grown up; Yüan imperial princes and great noble houses maintained their military traditions, and their military officers formed a distinct hereditary caste. Each of these had its corresponding element in the early Ming system of hereditary positions.[69]

Ming civil officials held one of nine ranks, each of which was divided into two grades, giving a total of eighteen grades, from 1a (*cheng yi-p'in*) to 9b (*tsung chiu-p'in*), plus a supernumerary unclassed grade (*wei ju liu*) at the very bottom. Military officers' ranks ranged only from 1a to 6b. Civil and military officers of the same rank received the same salary, calculated in shih of grain paid annually. Table 2 shows the salary in each grade and lists the civil and military positions with the largest number of incumbents. The number of deputy and assistant prefects and departmental and district magistrates cannot be determined, but there is reason to believe that they were fewer than the corresponding prefects and magistrates. The only civil positions in rank 1 were honorific and were not regularly filled. Most of the existing military positions are actually listed in the right-hand column (the numbers are based on the assumption that each guard had its full complement of officers, which was not always the case). In contrast, many civil positions are excluded from the left-hand column. Nonetheless, this comparison shows the essential relationship between civil and military; there were many more military officers than civil officials, and they enjoyed significantly higher rank and pay.

A new chin-shih would usually begin as a district magistrate or, less often, in a central government position of higher prestige but similar rank; in such positions he ranked below all military officers. After a long career he could hope to end as a minister of a provincial administration commissioner, where he would be at the apex of the civil service but still inferior to several score chief commissioners and deputy chief commissioners. A military officer, however, might inherit a position as high as guard commander, from which, were he lucky and successful, he could reach rank 1a in a couple of promotions—and nobility after that.

Military officers had a near monopoly of entry into the nobility, who outranked everyone in the nine-rank system. Only two

TABLE 2. *Official Grades, Positions, and Salaries*

Grade	Salary (*shih*)	Civil positions Title	Civil positions Number	Military positions Title	Military positions Number
1a	1,044			Chief commissioner	
1b	888			Deputy chief commissioner	
2a	732	Minister[a]		Regional military commissioner	
2b	576	Provincial administration commissioner		Deputy regional military commissioner	
3a	420	Provincial surveillance commissioner		Guard commander	325[b]
3b	312	Deputy provincial administration commissioner		Deputy guard commander	650
4a	288	Prefect	140	Assistant guard commander	1,300
4b	252	Assistant provincial administration commissioner			
5a	192	Deputy prefect		Battalion commander	1,700
5b	168	Department magistrate	200	Deputy battalion commander	3,400
6a	120	Assistant prefect		Company commander	17,000
6b	96	Deputy department magistrate		Battalion judge	3,400
7a	90	District magistrate	1,200		
7b	84	Assistant department magistrate			
8a	78	Deputy district magistrate			
8b	72				
9a	66	Assistant district magistrate			
9b	60	Prefectural instructor			
Unclassed	36	All other instructors			

SOURCES: For positions, MS, 72–76; for salaries, MS, 72: 13a.
[a] Titles closely follow Hucker, "Chinese Government."
[b] Calculations are the author's.

civilians became nobles in the Hung-wu reign, both being made earls, one with a stipend of 360 shih, and the other of 240. A successful general, on the other hand, could reasonably hope to join the ranks of the marquises, whose stipends were raised to 2,500 shih in the 1370's; and the relatively few who attained the status of duke received a minimum of 3,000 shih. In addition, during the period of greatest noble influence in the 1370's and 1380's, members of the nobility each received 100 ch'ing of office lands, the yield from which should have been several times their stipends.[70]

Alongside the military nobility were the imperial clansmen, represented in the Hung-wu reign chiefly by the emperor's sons and grandsons. The sons received the title prince of the blood (*ch'in-wang*) with a stipend of 10,000 shih and 1,000 ch'ing of office lands, all of which were inherited by their eldest sons; their younger sons were created hereditary commandery princes (*chün-wang*) with stipends of 2,000 shih, and successively more distant generations of clansmen received military titles and stipends ranging from 1,000 down to 200 shih.[71] By the 1380's the princes were commanding armies, and by the 1390's they had become the principal bearers of military command authority.

Hung-wu's attempt to create a Yüan-style empire using only Chinese components was of course a failure, and Chinese society in the mature Ming period operated on lines very different from those he envisaged. In part this was inevitable; the hereditary officers, nobles, and imperial clansmen were not culturally different from the rest of the Chinese population, and when the second generation of hereditary placeholders failed to maintain martial attributes and values, they were submerged in the essentially civilian Chinese society. Previous Chinese military aristocracies had been maintained by a situation of more or less continuous warfare. However, even before natural decay took place, Hung-wu lost faith in the efficacy of hereditary privilege as a support to the throne; after years of bearing down harshly on the civil service, he turned against the military nobility in the 1390's and nearly wiped it out. As a consequence of his own rise to power, Yung-lo naturally terminated the special military position of the other princes. Both emperors were profoundly hostile to the Confucian ideal of the monarch in their style of rule and their policy goals, yet both emperors recruited large numbers of officials by examination and entrusted them with both the civil administration and the education of their heirs. The civil officials could bide their time and wait for a sympathetic emperor to ascend the throne, one with whose blessing they could run the state in a completely Confucian manner. This happened ephemerally in 1398 and permanently in 1424. In retrospect, therefore, the major institutional development of the 1380's was the revival of regular civil service examinations.

Lan Yü, the Mongols, and the Revival of the Purges

The Hu Wei-yung purge and Hung-wu's assumption of personal rule were accompanied by renewed hostility toward the Mongols, whom he accused of complicity in the conspiracy. The conquest of Yünnan was the first result of this new aggressiveness, and was followed by the campaigns of the 1380's that destroyed the unity of the Yüan empire in exile. These campaigns brought to prominence a new group of military nobles headed by Lan Yü and gave the military nobility its Indian summer of glory and power. Hung-wu had turned against them by 1390. He implicated many of them in the Hu Wei-yung conspiracy and placed his own sons in command in the provinces. In 1393 he executed Lan Yü on a trumped-up charge, and the resulting purge was even more extensive than the Hu affair, finally including all but a few of the military nobility, a large proportion of the commoner military officers, and thousands of their families and subordinates.

The Ming armies had conducted punitive expeditions against the Mongol tribes in 1380, and in 1381 Hsü Ta had led an army against the Mongol chief Nayur Buqa; Hsü reached the Ordos region, captured four Mongol tribes, and returned.[72] However, the conquest of Yünnan absorbed most available Ming military resources in 1381, and even after the defeat of the prince of Liang, strong armies were required in the southwest to pacify the tribal peoples. Further, the deterioration of relations with the Japanese was causing the diversion of resources to coastal defense. These factors forced continuation of a defensive posture on the northern frontier for several years after Hung-wu had decided on a more aggressive strategy.

The stalemate permitted the formation of relatively strong

Mongol tribal groupings in Inner Mongolia. Following the campaigns of the 1370's, the Yüan imperial court itself had remained beyond the Gobi in Outer Mongolia, where Ayushiridara died in 1378 and was succeeded by his brother Toghus Temür.[73] Chieftains in Inner Mongolia raided the Ming frontiers in the name of the Yüan empire, but their actual tribal following depended on their personal military skill and success. By the mid-1380's a leader named Naghachu had won hegemony over the Mongol tribes in a wide area including much of Jehol and Liaoning. His forces were large enough to threaten invasion as well as small raids, and late in 1386 Hung-wu ordered him destroyed. Early in 1387 Feng Sheng, duke of Sung, was commissioned grand general, assigned Fu Yu-te and Lan Yü to assist him, and ordered to raise an army to conquer Naghachu. The peasants of four provinces (Peip'ing, Shantung, Shansi, and Honan) were mobilized to transport grain to the north.[74]

Campaigns against the Mongols had traditionally been led by Hsü Ta, but Hsü had died in 1385, one year after Li Wen-chung. Ch'ang Yü-ch'un and Teng Yü were long dead; the only surviving dukes among the 1370 nobles were Li Shan-ch'ang, who had never held a field command; T'ang Ho (marquis 1370, duke 1378), now busy constructing coastal defenses against the Japanese; and Feng Sheng. Feng therefore was the senior noble available; his most recent field command had been the Kansu campaign of 1372.[75] Lan Yü and Fu Yu-te, on the other hand, had both risen to noble rank as a result of more recent victories, Fu having become a duke as a result of his leadership in the conquest of Yünnan.[76]

On 20 March 1387 Feng Sheng led the army north through the Great Wall. In Southern Jehol they constructed four fortresses, at Taning, Fuyü, Huichou, and K'uanho. These were finished at the end of the summer, and a regional military commission was created at Taning to command them.[77] Hung-wu's son Chu Ch'üan, prince of Ning, was later stationed at Taning in overall command of these fortresses.[78] While the fortresses were under construction, Feng Sheng and his main army marched eastward. On 7 July Ch'en Yung, marquis of Linchiang, whose division had become separated from the main army, was ambushed and Ch'en himself killed. Nevertheless, seven days later Naghachu surrendered and accompanied the army on its return march. Many of the lesser Mongol chieftains were unwilling to go along with Naghachu and regarded his easy surrender as a defection. Before the Ming army reached the safety of the Great Wall, its rear guard was ambushed, with heavy losses, and its commander, the chief commissioner P'u Ying, was killed. Despite these setbacks, Feng Sheng had scored a substantial success: his army of two hundred thousand, of which fifty thousand had to be left behind to garrison the four fortresses, had procured the surrender of Naghachu's still larger horde, including families and domestic animals. This was the first real triumph over the Mongols in the north since the generally disastrous year 1372, in which Feng Sheng had also been victorious.[79]

Hung-wu was pleased by the first report of the victory, but he soon allowed himself to be persuaded by the slanders of Feng Sheng's son-in-law Ch'ang Mao (heir of Ch'ang Yü-ch'un), who accused Feng of appropriating the best captured horses for himself and of mishandling the army in the debacle that had led to the death of P'u Ying. On 8 September Feng Sheng was relieved of his command. He avoided execution for five more years and later performed military duties of a routine sort, but never again did he exercise operational command. Before the end of the year Ch'ang Mao also was exiled in disgrace.[80]

Lan Yü succeeded to the command of the army. On 11 November he was formally commissioned grand general, with two marquises, T'ang Sheng-tsung and Kuo Ying, as his lieutenant generals. Encouraged by the surrender of Naghachu, the emperor ordered Lan to take his 150,000 men across the Gobi to crush the Mongol emperor, Toghus Temür, the focal point of Mongol loyalties.[81] The following year, 1388, the Ming army went out through the wall, marching first to Taning and then north to Ch'ingchou, where they learned from spies that the Mongol emperor and his horde were encamped near Buyur Lake in northwestern Manchuria. The Ming army pressed northward by forced marches. Coming to within 40 li of Buyur Lake without sighting the Mongols, Lan almost lost heart; his subordinate general Wang Pi, marquis of Tingyüan, reminded him how foolish it would look to bring such a large army back without first accomplishing something. Discovering that the Mongols were northeast of the lake, the Ming troops marched under cover of darkness. Aided by a convenient sandstorm at the last minute, they took the Mongol camp completely by surprise on the morning of 18 May 1388. The Mongol crown prince, his younger brother, and some 3,000 other Mongol notables were captured, along with 70,000 ordinary Mongols and the usual myriads of domestic animals.[82] Toghus Temür himself, the successor of Chinggis Qan and Qubilai, happened to be mounted at the time of the attack. He escaped and fled into Outer Mongolia, only to be assassinated within a year. His death disrupted the always fragile succession practices of the house of Chinggis Qan, and the Mongols were fragmented and without effective leadership for over a generation thereafter.[83] Before the end of the month Lan Yü captured another large Mongol horde.[84]

Lan Yü's army returned on 26 September. The emperor greeted them with a victory proclamation comparing Lan to the famous Han general Wei Ch'ing, scourge of the Hsiung-nu during the reign of Wu-ti (140–87 B.C.). Later he created Lan duke of Liang with a stipend of 3,000 shih (later raised to 3,500) and the honorific title grand tutor (*t'ai-fu*). Only Hsü Ta had received greater rewards for military success, only the retired Li Shan-ch'ang had a higher stipend, and only the title grand preceptor had more prestige than the one granted Lan. Six of Lan's subordinates were created marquises on this or other occasions, and the other officers and men of the army that had won the Buyur Lake victory were also generously rewarded. In addition to its significance in the history of Ming relations with the Mongols, Lan's victory marks the high point of the power and prestige of the early Ming military nobility as an institution.[85]

After about a year, Hung-wu's suspicions that many more of his generals were involved in the Hu Wei-yung conspiracy revived, for reasons partly connected with Lan's victory. He had been suspicious ever since 1380, for obvious reasons: Hu was from Tingyüan in the same central Anhwei area that had produced most of the top stratum of the early Ming leadership, Li Shan-ch'ang had recommended him for repeated promotions, the Hus and the Lis had close marriage connections, and during his long tenure as chancellor Hu had had the opportunity to come into contact with every other high official of the empire. Guilt by association was a respectable standard of judgment in Chinese society, and by that standard the entire leadership group was suspect. Beyond that, among the prisoners captured by Lan at Buyur Lake were the envoys Hu Wei-yung had sent to the Mongols in the course of his conspiracy.[86]

Li Shan-ch'ang pulled strings from his retirement, trying to keep the news of the envoys' recapture from reaching the emperor, but the latter found out despite Li's precautions when a censor impeached Li's son and nephew for their connections with Hu. The result was an explosive reopening of the whole conspiracy case. In midsummer of 1390 Li Shan-ch'ang was allowed to commit suicide as a mark of special imperial favor. The nobles (all marquises) executed at this time included Lu Chung-heng, T'ang Sheng-tsung, Fei Chü, and Cheng Yü-ch'un, all of whom had belonged to Hung-wu's twenty-four original companions, plus Chao Yung of the Lake Ch'ao group, Huang Pin, and Lu Chü. Other nobles, among them Yang Ching, Yü T'ung-yüan of the Lake Ch'ao group, and Ku Shih, an original companion, were posthumously convicted; their heirs were executed and their titles suppressed. As usual the purge extended to lesser figures, and family members of the victims were executed as well. These events left only five survivors of the thirty-four military nobles created in 1370: Feng Sheng, T'ang Ho, Chou Te-hsing, Keng Ping-wen, and Fu Yu-te. Although a few of the deceased nobles were survived by successors to their titles, that was true of none of those who had been purged; consequently, most of the remaining active military nobles were of the 1379 and 1384 creations, which meant they were beholden to Lan Yü or Fu Yu-te for their titles.[87]

Along with the new purges came measures directed specifically against the military nobility as a class. In 1385 Hung-wu had experimentally placed one of his sons in nominal command over T'ang Ho in a campaign against the Miao in the southwest.[88] In 1390 his third son, Chu Kang, prince of Chin, and his fourth son, Chu Ti, prince of Yen, were placed in command over Fu Yu-te in a campaign against the Mongols. The prince of Yen led another expedition the following year.[89] Thereafter the princes increasingly concerned themselves with military affairs; in addition to exercising field command, they served as administrative supervisors of the troops stationed in the regions of their fiefs, coming to court at regular intervals to report. In 1391 the emperor's ten youngest sons were equipped with princely titles and fiefs, and in 1392 three princes were transferred from the interior of the empire to the border regions, the better to fit into the emerging princely military command system.[90] These were also the years in which the census and land registration of the empire (above, pp. 122–29) were being completed, and the military establishment was intimately involved. In 1392, as part of the land settlement, the nobles were deprived of their office lands and made to live solely on their stipends.[91]

Meanwhile, in the summer of 1392 Lan Yü conducted his last campaign against rebellious tribesmen in Hantung (near Tunhuang in western Kansu). Lan reached Hantung on 22 May and spent the summer and autumn chasing the rebels, finally killing the leader of the rebellion on 26 December. He was then summoned back. While he was away, two more marquises, Chou Te-hsing (28 August) and Yeh Sheng (14 September) had been executed for alleged complicity in the Hu Wei-yung affair. Far from slowing down, the purge was turning into a deliberate extermination of the military leadership group. Of the nobles created after 1370, Yeh Sheng was the first to fall. Lan's preeminence within this group was so evident that his survival obviously depended on circumspect behavior.[92]

Lan Yü had been away from the court for a long time and may not have realized the gravity of the situation on his return. The emperor was trying to force the nobles to relinquish their commands voluntarily and retire. To Lan this seemed like shabby treatment after years of successful service, and he voiced his resentment on social occasions. When Feng Sheng and Fu Yü-te were given additional honorific titles early in 1393, Lan began complaining that he had not been given the highest title of grand preceptor, vacant since the death of Li Shan-ch'ang.[93]

Word of Lan's indiscretions reached the emperor's ear through the commander of his principal secret police agancy, the Chin-yi Guard. It amounted to no more than talk on Lan's part, but even so it was too much for the suspicious emperor. Lan was arrested immediately, and on 22 March he was executed along with four marquises, an earl, and the minister of personnel, Chan Hui. More executions followed, ultimately involving ten other nobles, sixteen chief commissioners, and many lower-ranking officers, together with all their families. The total number of victims came to over fifteen thousand. The official account of Lan's alleged plot was published on 26 March, and on 16 October 1393 the remaining members of the Hu Wei-yung and Lan Yü factions were officially pardoned.[94] Despite this, the executions continued; Fu Yu-te fell in late 1394, Wang Pi and Feng Sheng, early the following year.[95] The military nobility was now represented by three dukes—Hsü Hui-tsu, Ch'ang Sheng, and Li Ching-lung—all of whom had inherited the title; by Keng Ping-wen, sole survivor of the 1370 nobles; by Mu Ch'un, heir to Mu Ying's essentially viceregal position in Yünnan; and by a handful of lesser marquises. Furthermore, they were no longer in control of the armies, but had been replaced by the emperor's sons serving as his direct agents. The appointment in April 1393 of the princes of Chin and Yen to command all the troops in Shansi and Peip'ing, respectively, symbolized this fact.[96] It took place a scant month after the execution of Lan Yü.

The two purges have been a subject of continuous controversy. Many of the victims were rehabilitated later in the Ming dynasty, and the final verdict of traditional Chinese historiography was expressed by the Ch'ing compilers of the Ming official history, who placed Hu Wei-yung's biography in a special section reserved for traitorous ministers and placed Lan Yü and the other executed generals at the front of the biographical section along with the other heroes who had aided in the founding of the dynasty. In other words, Hu was guilty and Lan was innocent, as were most of those executed for complicity with either. More recently Hung-wu's modern biographer Wu Han, himself to be the victim of a political purge, argued convincingly that Hu could not have been guilty of everything charged against him; but then he concluded that he was therefore guilty of nothing. Recent historians have generally followed Wu Han in attributing both of the purges and the many lesser applications of terror to Hung-wu's homicidal paranoia, which admittedly worsened as he aged.[97]

On reflection it seems that the judgment of the traditional historians is closer to the truth. The key is the fact that a great many—probably the majority—of the people executed for alleged involvement with Hu were actually killed in 1390 and later, after Li Shan-ch'ang's connection with the affair came to light.

Viewed chronologically, the two cases therefore reduce themselves to the execution of Hu and his closest associates, the reorganization of the government in 1380, and a protracted reign of terror, lasting from 1390 to 1395, during which most of the victims of the Hu purge and all of the victims of the Lan purge perished. Hung-wu was genuinely frightened by what he thought his chancellor was up to in 1380, but his primary response was personally to take over the routine of running the administration and developing the civil service, which he had previously left to Hu. Both before and after 1380 Hung-wu was quite capable of having individuals executed for capricious and arbitrary reasons, but it was only in 1390 that a real Stalin-type purge developed. People were incriminated solely because of their association with previous victims, and the circle of victims therefore expanded to include, potentially, the whole of the most important class within the ruling elite. The circumstances suggest that, whether correct or not, Hung-wu's 1390 judgment that so many of his old comrades-in-arms had been involved with Hu Wei-yung led him to lose faith in the idea that a military nobility in the Mongol manner could serve safely as the leading class in the state. Yet the military nobility did not cease to be powerful merely because the emperor ceased to trust it. He had to decimate it physically, or it would have remained a threat.

While the 1380 and 1390–95 purges differed in their consequences, they resemble one another in that both were harsh and decisive responses by Hung-wu to perceived threats to his control. The desire to seize, wield, and defend power occurs again and again as the primary explanation of Hung-wu's policies, and it is the most consistent factor in both his character and his reign. Such an autocrat could never consider ruling in the approved Confucian manner, as the mouthpiece for civil officials drawn from the scholar-gentry class, but the 1390–95 purges had badly crippled the alternative institutional basis of rule that he had carefully nurtured ever since the days of the civil war. With the nobility purged and the scholar-gentry prevented from taking their place, the political vacuum was filled by the emperor's sons and by others whom Hung-wu trusted because of their relation to him as a person rather than to the office of emperor. The lack of a stable institutional basis for politics compounded the uncertainties about the succession after the death of the crown prince, Chu Piao, in 1392.[98] The last years of the Hung-wu reign therefore saw the development of an explosive political crisis.

The Border Princes and the Legacy of Hung-wu

Hung-wu had twenty-six sons, of whom the eldest, Chu Piao, became crown prince (*huang t'ai-tzu*), and the youngest died in infancy; the remaining two dozen became princes, the first nine in 1370, the next five in 1378, and the last ten in 1391. When each prince reached about twenty, he was sent away from the capital to a fief located in the area indicated by his title. Thus in 1378 the prince of Ch'in took up residence at Sian and the prince of Chin at T'aiyüan, and in 1380 the prince of Yen went to his fief at Peip'ing; by 1395 a total of seventeen of the emperor's sons had gone to the provinces.[99]

Once established on his fief, each prince received both a grain stipend and a grant of land, ideally ten thousand shih and one thousand ch'ing, though the amounts varied according to imperial favor. The prince was aided and assisted, and his finances managed, by a princely establishment (*ch'in-wang fu*) with a large staff of officials headed by a chief secretary (*chang-shih*). In the mature Ming period these establishments concerned themselves solely with the management of the princely households, since members of the imperial clan were then excluded from any governmental role.[100] This was not the case in the Hung-wu period. In 1370 he appointed members of the military nobility to tutor the nine recently created princes in the military skills and Confucian scholars to tutor the crown prince in the civil and literary skills.[101] Hung-wu here evoked traditions as old as the Chou dynasty, which had established the practice of making the eldest son the heir to a royal authority conceived primarily in civil terms, while enfeoffing the younger sons to act as military protectors of the throne. In the 1370's the princely establishments of Ch'in and Chin managed the logistics of the armies engaged in the anti-Mongol campaigns.[102]

The potential importance of the princes increased from 1378 on, as they grew up and went to their fiefs. There they each exercised direct command of several princely guards (*hu-wei*), usually three,

TABLE 3. *Hung-wu's Sons*

Order	Name	Title	Dates			Location	Number of princely guards
			Title	*Residence*	*Death*		
2	Shuang	Ch'in	1370	1378	1395	Sian	3
3	Kang	Chin	1370	1378	1398	T'aiyüan	3
4	Ti	Yen	1370	1380	1424	Peip'ing	3
5	Su	Chou	1378	1381	1425	Kaifeng	3
6	Chen	Ch'u	1370	1381	1424	Wuch'ang	3
7	Fu	Ch'i	1370	1382	1428	Ch'ingchou	2
8	Tzu	T'an	1370	1385	1390	Ch'angsha	1
10	T'an	Lu	1370	1385	1389	Yenchou	2
11	Ch'un	Shu	1378	1385	1423	Chengtu	3
12	Po	Hsiang	1378	1385	1399	Chingchou	2
13	Kuei	Tai	1392	1392	1446	Tat'ung	
14	Ying	Su	1392	1392	1419	Kanchou	1
15	Chih	Liao	1393	1393	1404	Kuangning	1
16	Chan	Ch'ing	1391	1393	1401	Ninghsia	1
17	Ch'üan	Ning	1391	1393	1403	Taning	2
							30

SOURCES: Farmer, p. 77; number of princely guards from MS, 90.4a–7b.

but sometimes only one or two.[103] From 1390 on, the prince of Yen in particular, and to a lesser extent the princes of Ch'in, Chin, and Ch'i, commanded the armies sent north of the Great Wall against the Mongols.[104] In 1392–93 three more princes were transferred from fiefs in the interior of the country to locations on the northern border.[105] As Hung-wu came to trust the military nobles less, he made the exercise of military command by the princes more systematized. Like the nobles in the 1370's and 1380's, the princes in the 1390's alternated periods of military command in the field with regular visits to Nanking for audience with the emperor. The position of the princes now was such that they bypassed the regular military high command, but as the emperor's own sons they did not appear to be any threat to the stability of the throne as long as Hung-wu lived.

By 1393 the principalities listed in Table 3 had been created and were still exercising military functions. The emperor's ninth son, Chu Ch'i, had died without heirs in 1371, so his fief lapsed; the principalities of T'an and Lu were represented in 1393 by the heirs of the original princes; and the princes of Chou, Tai, Su, and Liao

TABLE 4. *Ming Military Units, 1393*

RMC[a]	Guards			Total guards	Independent battalions
	Nanking	RMC HQ	Elsewhere		
Personal (*ch'in*)	12			12	
Left (*tso*)	8			8	
Chekiang		2	14	16	4
Liaotung		6	14(1)[b]	20(1)	
Shantung		1	10(4)	11(4)	4
Right (*yu*)	5			5	
Yünnan		3	12	15	1
Kweichow		1	17	18	1
Szechwan		8(3)	9	17(3)	3
Shensi		6(3)	21(2)	27(5)	2
Kwangsi		3	3	6	1
Center (*chung*)	5		18	23	2
Chungtu		6	2	8	1
Honan		3(3)	16	19(3)	1
Van (*ch'ien*)	5		1	6	
Hukwang		5(3)	28(3)	33(6)	14
Fukien		3	8	11	
Fukien Branch		3	3	6	1
Kiangsi		2	3	5	9
Kwangtung		4	7	11	13
Rear (*hou*)	6			6	
Peip'ing		6(3)	13	19(3)	1
Peip'ing Branch		5(2)	2	7(2)	
Shansi		6(3)	4	10(3)	5
Shansi Branch		3	2	5	
	41	76(20)	207(10)	324(30)	63

SOURCE: Data from wei-so lists, MS, 90.4a–7b.

[a] Regional military commission.

[b] Number of princely guards included in total.

had been transferred from their original fiefs. The prince of Tai, though without a princely guard of his own, was nonetheless militarily important, since his fief was located at the headquarters of the Shansi Branch Regional Military Commission, whose operations he supervised.[106]

The thirty princely guards made up slightly less than 10 percent of the total number of guards reported in the general enumeration of 1393, but their strategic location at the headquarters of the regional military commissions gave them a leverage greater than their numbers would indicate. Table 4 shows the distribution of

Ming military units in that year. The listing of independent battalions is incomplete since many of the coastal defense battalions in Shantung, Chekiang, Fukien, and Kwangtung were in fact created before 1393 but not included in the 1393 lists from which the table is drawn. However, for the guards the table accurately reflects the late Hung-wu situation, since the later changes in the distribution of guards came about as a result of Yung-lo's accession to power.

Hung-wu's treatment of the princes meant that at his death seven of the regional military commissions (Peip'ing, Peip'ing Branch, Shansi, Shensi, Szechwan, Honan, and Hukwang), aggregating 132 guards, were commanded from headquarters dominated by princely guards, with the princes themselves in formal command in most cases. Three other regional military commissions (Liaotung, Shantung, and Shansi Branch) aggregating 36 guards were under very strong influence from princes within their borders and adjoining princely provinces. The ten commands together covered all of the northern border and much of the central plain and western China as well. In contrast, the emperor could rely on 41 guards in Nanking and 27 more in the metropolitan area (including the Chungtu defense command). The remaining 88 guards would probably also be loyal, but many of them were in distant Yünnan and Kweichow. Of course there was no certainty that the princes would unite against the throne, but consciously or not, Hung-wu had written a scenario that made it likely his successor's first order of business would be to reduce the power of the princes, and that the latter would react as a class to such a threat to their position.

When Chu Piao died, Hung-wu designated Piao's son Yün-wen (1377–1402) crown prince (in this case *huang t'ai-sun*, "grandson heir apparent"). Suggestions that Hung-wu considered designating one of his younger sons instead of his grandson are all from sources that favor Yung-lo and so are most suspect.[107] The last few years of the reign were generally peaceful, so much so that in 1394 surplus arms and armor were collected throughout the empire and put in storage.[108] Sporadic minor housekeeping expeditions against Mongols, Japanese pirates, and domestic rebels continued under the princes and the few remaining nobles. In 1396 the prince of Yen won a victory while on a patrol north of the

Great Wall, and in 1397 branches of the imperial stud (*hsing t'ai-p'u szu*) were established for Liaotung, Peip'ing, Shansi, Shensi, and Kansu to coordinate the raising and pasturing of horses for the military units in the north.[109] Hung-wu died on 24 June 1398 after a month's illness. He was buried six days later in a tomb on the southern slope of the Purple Mountain east of Nanking.[110]

Interpretations of Hung-wu have clustered around two poles. Traditional Chinese historians have viewed him as an archetypal dynastic founder whose laws, institutions, policies, and example were the basis on which the continued rule of his successors rested. When his ministers canonized him as T'ai-tsu ("Grand Progenitor"), they invited stereotyped comparisons with the founders of other dynasties; and when the Ming dynasty fell, historians naturally attributed its collapse in part to the departure of its later emperors from the practices of the dynastic founder. This opinion was finally codified in the Ch'ing-compiled official history of the Ming dynasty. On the other hand, modern historians, both Chinese and non-Chinese, who have written in the shadow of twentieth-century dictators and under the influence of current antimonarchical ideology and psychohistorical theory have tended to view Hung-wu as a tyrant and dwell on the capricious executions and recurrent terror of his reign—and the mental imbalance that these apparently reflect.[111] The traditional historians had to acknowledge Hung-wu's despotism, and the others have had to admit his achievements; both schools reflect the truth, but only as shaped by the concerns of later times. This account has attempted to view Hung-wu in the immediate political and military context of late fourteenth-century China, from which the man drew his experiences and concerning which the emperor formulated his policies. Seen in this light, a number of consistent themes run through Hung-wu's life and career and help to illuminate both what he was trying to do and the extent of his achievement.

First of all, Hung-wu spent most of his adult life attempting to restore and preserve a stable social and economic order centered on agriculture. The death of most of his family in the famines of the 1340's was the central event in the formation of his character, and his subsequent expressions of concern for the peasantry were not mere Confucian charades but the reflection of convictions based on bitter personal experience. In his rise to power he regularly took measures to prevent the farming population from being harmed by military operations, and as emperor he frequently remitted taxes in areas hit by disaster. Beyond that, he believed that the agricultural order could be maintained only by constant government intervention and supervision. Irrigation and famine relief systems had to be kept up, and displaced persons had to be settled on uncultivated lands discovered for that purpose. Effective execution of these policies made it necessary for the government to collect information about the agricultural sector on a scale unprecedented since T'ang times; the result was the census and land survey completed in his reign. Increased control over agriculture led to a corresponding increase in tax revenues from that sector, which in turn permitted the government to be financed largely from the land tax.

As a result of Hung-wu's background, and of his success in restoring agriculture and its relation to the economy, his concern for agriculture was matched by an indifference to other sectors of the economy that bordered on hostility. Here Confucian prejudice coincided fortuitously with the emperor's personal experiences and views. He grew up in a rural backwater of central Anhwei and had traveled only there and in southern Honan before the start of his military career in 1352. When he appeared as a conqueror in the Yangtze valley, which with the South China coast had been the main area of the phenomenal urban growth of the Sung and Yüan periods, his chief interest in the commercial economy of the region was to tax it to support military operations while trying to reduce land taxes elsewhere. So it is not surprising that as emperor he was indifferent to any adverse effect his policies might have on commerce or industry. His curtailment of trade with Japan and Southeast Asia seriously harmed the economies of the coastal cities, but he never relaxed the policy; people displaced from commercial occupations could, after all, be resettled in the more proper occupation of agriculture.

All of these policies were made possible only by Hung-wu's military success in unifying China within defensible frontiers. Military necessity had led the Sung to rely on commercial and monopoly taxes, and thus to promote trade and industry despite Confucian ideology. The same necessity would have been present if China had remained disunited after the midcentury rebellions, with several different states each raising armies to the limit of its strength; or if China had been only partially reunified, with the Mongols still existing in force south of the Great Wall. Both of these were likely outcomes of the situation as it existed around 1360. However, Hung-wu destroyed his rivals and expelled the Mongols, a degree of success that drastically reduced the pressure of military spending on government income and permitted the government to follow policies based on ideological preference even when these reversed previous economic trends. Emphasis on agriculture and indifference to commerce fit logically with the repopulation of the North China plain and the corresponding weakening of the dominant position in China's economy and society that had been held for so long by the Yangtze delta area. It was this shift in the regional balance that made Yung-lo's later transfer of the capital possible, if ill advised. The Hung-wu reign thus begins the period of transition in which the trend toward a "modern" commercial economy was reversed and its "traditional" agricultural economy recovered unchallengeable dominance. The reversal was not the result of long-term economic trends but of deliberate policy decisions made possible by military success.

It must be kept constantly in mind that Hung-wu's emotional makeup shaped his responses and policies. Both his rise to power and his later policies aroused opposition, and not only from landowners who objected to having their holdings accurately registered. His response to opposition was to extend the machinery of control, and his mania for control swiftly grew from a means to an end in itself. As the state assumed an ever-increasing degree of control over society, the emperor became more and more concerned lest the machinery of state slip from his hands.

He also became more and more isolated from the world he was intent on changing. Though he came to power in the field, he never led a campaign after 1364 and never left Nanking after 1370. Most of his reign was spent in the palace reading reports. Such isolation adversely affected his ability to comprehend the society he was trying to control and aggravated his tendency to regard any minor infraction he discovered as a sign of hidden conspiracy. These problems resulted from the excessive strain the emperor placed on himself in trying to run everything personally, but his response was to extend the apparatus of control through spies and personal imperial agents until in the end it seriously undermined the political structure he was attempting to build.

And Hung-wu was a man of the Yüan dynasty. Despite Ming propagandists and their search for Han and T'ang precedents, it was the Yüan empire that provided the model for the institutions created by Hung-wu. His departures from the Yüan example usually stemmed either from a desire for empirical rationalization or from a wish to increase or defend his personal power. This is most apparent in the formal structure of governmental institutions, where Hung-wu began by imitating the Yüan almost exactly. Here his later piecemeal modifications were made strictly to suit his needs and preferences, not to further adherence to Confucian forms. Still more important is Hung-wu's acceptance of basic Yüan assumptions of how society should be organized and of how the elite groups within society should relate to one another. Following the Yüan model in all cases, the emperor made his army into a distinct occupational caste within the population, created a hereditary officer class to govern it, gave the military officers a clearly superior status compared to their civil counterparts, created a nobility with a defined military function to head the officer class, and then assigned military roles and titles to his own descendants, placing them at the apex of the pyramid of military status. In other words, far from betraying his peasant followers in the interests of the landlords, as is sometimes alleged, Hung-wu attempted to keep his troops and their families permanently distinguished from the rest of Chinese society—a new conquering horde, but this time Chinese in origin—while creating from within the army a new stratified elite group with the imperial clan at the top. The emperor would determine the goals of the state, the military elite would receive the rewards of society, and the civil officials (drawn from the gentry scholars, who represent the much-maligned landlord class if any identifiable social group does) would collect the taxes and file the papers needed to make the whole system function.

The only important Yüan institution missing from the picture is the elite drawn from the merchant corporation (*ortaq*), and from

among the tax farmers and government financial experts who had
been so important under Qubilai; they had disappeared from the
Yüan regime before the birth of Hung-wu, and in any case they
would not have been compatible with his consistently proagricul-
tural and anticommercial policies. Even so, the traditional Chinese
elite of scholar-gentry and civil officials remained at the bottom of
the social and political elite, very distant indeed from the highest
position under the sovereign that their self-image demanded, and
which they were to attain by 1435. Despite the large-scale executions of nobles and officers from 1390 on, Hung-wu found no
happy replacement for this vision of the ideal social order and his
concessions to the civil officials and the social class they represented
were belated and grudging.

Finally, Hung-wu was pursuing policy goals that were in many
respects incompatible with both the ideological norms of Chinese
Confucian society and with tendencies that had been dominant in
that society for several hundred years. The tensions this created,
along with the emperor's sensitivity about his background and
appearance, account for the atmosphere of terror that is such a
prominent feature of his reign. The emperor was in no way
hesitant to execute those he considered disloyal or disrespectful, or
their families; and as he aged he grew both increasingly suspicious
and increasingly willing to condemn on mere suspicion.
However, the executions were confined to the elite; the common
people continued to be the objects of imperial benevolence.

Militarily, Hung-wu reunified the empire and held it together
securely. Administratively, he had carried out a comprehensive
census and land survey that restored the land tax to primacy in
government finance. These were long-term accomplishments of
great importance, but at his death he left behind immediate problems. These included a politico-military structure excessively dependent on personal ties with the deceased emperor, and a class
structure too much at odds with the natural social order to be
stable. The resolution of these problems and the emergence of the
mature Ming order took four more reigns.

FIVE

Chien-wen: Civil War,
1398–1402

The twenty-one-year-old grandson of Hung-wu who succeeded
to the Ming throne in the summer of 1398 chose Chien-wen
("Establishment of Civil Merit") as his regnal title. The term
contrasted sharply with Hung-wu ("Overflowing Martial
Accomplishment") and foretold the new emperor's attempt to
reverse certain of his predecessor's policies. Chien-wen's reign
foreshadows that of his cousin Hung-hsi (r. 1424–25), who also
chose a reign title ("Overflowing Splendor") that was meant to
evoke comparisons with his grandfather Hung-wu. Both cousins
came to the throne under the influence of Confucian officials and
pursued policies aimed at giving civil officials the preeminence in
government that Confucian ideology required. Hung-hsi basically succeeded, but Chien-wen provoked a civil war that cost him
his throne and his life. His failure led later historians to label him
impractical and idealistic, but under the circumstances it is difficult
to see what else he could have done. His own security required him
to dismantle the structure undergirding the special military position of his princely uncles, and they naturally resisted to protect
themselves; both he and his uncles were victims of the situation left
behind by Hung-wu.[1]

In the autumn of 1398 Chien-wen promoted Ch'i T'ai from
vice-minister to minister of war, transferred Huang Tzu-ch'eng to

be president of the Court of Imperial Sacrifices, and appointed the prefectural instructor of Hanchung, Fang Hsiao-ju, to a post in the Han-lin Academy. These three became Chien-wen's closest advisers. Huang had placed first in the chin-shih examination of 1385, in which Ch'i also received his degree; Ch'i had been first in the Nanking chü-jen examinations in 1384. Fang was a brilliant scholar who had twice been recommended for high office and had won the respect of both the future Chien-wen and his father, Crown Prince Chu Piao; however, Hung-wu could not stomach him and so sent him to languish in obscurity in Hanchung. Ch'i T'ai was the leading political figure of the group. He had spent most of his career in the Ministry of War, becoming vice-minister in 1395, and had consistently impressed Hung-wu by his detailed and ready grasp of military administrative questions.[2]

The biggest problem in the sphere of military administration was how to reduce the power of the princes. Hung-wu had belatedly realized that the princes would pose a problem for his successor, and he had left a will containing the provision that they not come to the capital for his funeral, among others designed to keep them on their fiefs and prevent them from conspiring with one another.[3] The princes resented their exclusion from the center of power, and the court assumed collusion among them from the start. The prince of Chin had died in 1398, leaving the prince of Yen as the oldest surviving son of Hung-wu. By an unlucky coincidence, he was the most able of them militarily, and he commanded one of the largest field armies from his headquarters in Peip'ing, which was both the main supply point for the Ming armies in the northeast and the former capital of the Yüan emperors, in whose palace the prince resided. The court had two options. It could strike directly against the prince—who until then had committed no offense and was popular with his troops—in the hope of removing him at one blow and depriving the remaining princes of their natural leader. Or it could move against the lesser princes one by one, in the hope that by the time the prince of Yen was finally provoked into rebellion much of his potential support would have vanished and the act of rebellion itself would put him clearly in the wrong as far as elite opinion was concerned.

The court adopted the latter strategy. Soon after Ch'i T'ai and his colleagues took office, the prince of Chou was convicted of a

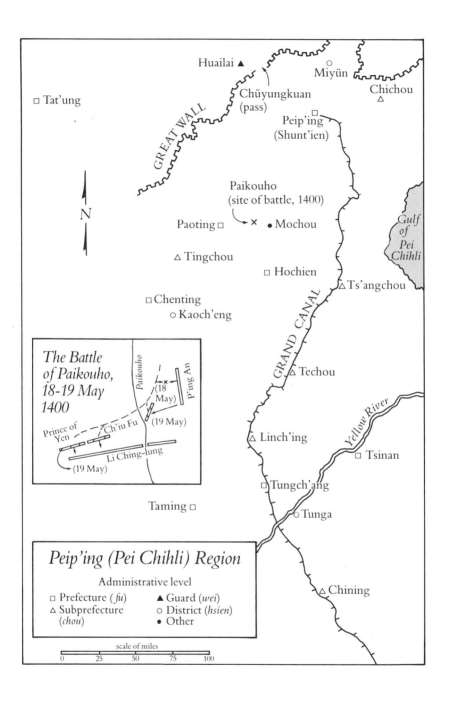

Huailai ▲

Miyün ○

Chichou △

□ Tat'ung

Chüyungkuan
(pass)

Peip'ing □
(Shunt'ien)

GREAT WALL

N

Paikouho
(site of battle, 1400)

Paoting □ × ● Mochou

△ Tingchou

□ Hochien

△ Ts'angchou

Gulf
of
Pei
Chihli

□ Chenting

○ Kaoch'eng

*The Battle
of Paikouho,
18-19 May
1400*

Paikouho

P'ing An

×
(18
May)

(19 May)

Prince of
Yen

Ch'iu Fu

Li Ching-lung

(19 May)

GRAND CANAL

△ Techou

Yellow River

△ Linch'ing

□ Tsinan

Taming □

□ Tungch'ang

○ Tunga

Peip'ing (Pei Chihli) Region

Administrative level

□ Prefecture (*fu*)   ▲ Guard (*wei*)
△ Subprefecture   ○ District (*hsien*)
(*chou*)   ● Other

△ Chining

scale of miles

0   25   50   75   100

crime, deprived of all his titles, and exiled to Yünnan.[4] Late in 1398 the vice-minister of works, Chang Ping, was appointed administration commissioner of Peip'ing, while Hsieh Kuei and Chang Hsin took over the regional military commission.[5] These appointments were attempts by the court to bring the bureaucratic and military offices of Peip'ing province under its own control. In the summer of 1399 the prince of Hsiang burned himself to death while under investigation, and soon afterwards the princes of Ch'i and Tai were reduced to commoner status for alleged crimes. Both were near neighbors of Yen, and to allay the suspicions of the prince, his three sons Kao-chih (the future Emperor Hung-hsi), Kao-hsü, and Kao-sui were sent back to Peip'ing. A month later the prince of Min was convicted of a crime and exiled to Changchou in Fukien as a commoner.[6]

With five of his brothers deposed from their positions of authority, the prince of Yen could have no doubts about the objective of the emperor and his advisers. The prince realized that he would have to rebel in self-defense, but the carefully orchestrated attack on his brothers, each of whom was charged with some isolated individual offense, gave him no real pretext or occasion. In the time-honored manner of Chinese princes faced with similar threats, he feigned madness and dissipation while actually taking increasingly desperate counsel with his supporters and advisers. Chief of these was the Buddhist monk Tao-yen (Yao Kuang-hsiao), who advised patience: when the prince's whiskers grew down to his waist, he said, it would be time to rebel. During the first half of 1399 the prince watched his whiskers grow and his authority shrink as the court's appointees took over command in Peip'ing province. However, the prince still retained the personal loyalty of the regimental officers who had served under him, and he secretly maintained his contacts with them. Also within the confines of his princely palace at Peip'ing he instructed two trusted officers, the guard commanders Chang Yü and Chu Neng, to train a bodyguard of 800 men to protect him from any attempt at arrest.[7]

By the late summer of 1399, Chien-wen, emboldened by the successful deposition of five of his uncles, accepted the advice of Huang Tzu-ch'eng that the court was strong enough to deal with the prince of Yen even if he rebelled. On 13 July Ni Liang, a company commander in one of the princely guards of the Yen fief, reported to the throne that the prince of Yen was plotting to rebel. Given the efficiency of the secret police agencies and the nature of the political maneuvers afoot, Ni's report cannot have been news to the emperor, but Chien-wen nevertheless made it the pretext for decrees ordering the Peip'ing provincial administration office and the regional military commission to place the prince of Yen under arrest. On 6 August 1399, when Chang Ping and Hsieh Kuei attempted to enter Peip'ing to enforce this decree, they were ambushed and killed at the Tuan-li gate by the prince of Yen's bodyguards, who then seized all nine gates of the city. The other regional military commissioner, Chang Hsin, already had defected to Yen. T'ungchou, Tsunhua, and Miyün (all near Peip'ing) sur-rendered soon afterwards.[8]

The prince of Yen then issued a manifesto that designated Ch'i T'ai and Huang Tzu-ch'eng as evil ministers who were deluding the emperor. For good measure he accused Chien-wen of listening to monks and eunuchs (as he did himself), and declared that he was making war only to rid the throne of these noxious influences. He called his forces the Ching-nan (Trouble-suppressing) Army, and exercised the traditional right of a prince to grant ranks and titles to his followers. His old comrades among the northern military commanders defected, and within twenty days several myriads of the perhaps one hundred thousand troops (nineteen guards and one independent battalion) of Peip'ing had gone over to him. The Yen forces took Chichou, east of Peip'ing, on 9 August; three days later the strategic pass of Chüyungkuan fell; and five days after that the Yen forces took Huailai by storm, killing Chief Commissioner Sung Chung, the last of the senior officers whom Chien-wen had inserted into the Peip'ing command structure.[9]

The carefully planned strategy of gradually isolating the prince of Yen had come very near to destroying him without provoking a major rebellion. However, as a result of the events of 6 August and immediately after, the prince had gained a position from which he could be dislodged only by a full-scale campaign. On 25 August the court, long mindful of this possibility, appointed as its commander-in-chief Keng Ping-wen, one of Hung-wu's original followers, who had been made marquis of Ch'anghsing in 1370 in memory of his defense of that city during the civil wars. Keng assembled the main body of his army at Chenting prefecture, 150 miles southwest of Peip'ing, where a special administration office had been set up under the former minister of justice Pao Chao to manage logistics for the army. Two other marquises and nine generals led separate contingents northward; the total strength of the imperial army was reportedly three hundred thousand men.[10]

The appointment of Keng Ping-wen illustrated a fundamental problem facing the court. The executions of Lan Yü, Fu Yu-te, and their protégés meant that most of the younger generals nurtured in the campaigns since 1372 had been eliminated. The chief commissioners, regional military commissioners, and lesser commanders who were active in 1399 were comparatively recent appointees; they were of unproven quality, and inexperienced in the command of large bodies of troops. For such experience the court could turn only to a few survivors among Hung-wu's followers, men like Keng himself, who were then in their sixties and seventies.

Keng Ping-wen had assembled 130,000 men at Chenting, with other forces in readiness at Hochien, Mochou, and Hunghsien. On 14 September, at night, the prince of Yen took Hunghsien by surprise. He then marched southwest and on the twenty-fourth fell upon both flanks of Keng Ping-wen's army, then encamped in the countryside north of the Hut'o River near Chenting. The Yen army won a great victory, capturing Keng Ping-wen's three principal subordinates and taking 30,000 severed heads. Keng himself retired with what was left of his army into Chenting city, which the Yen troops surrounded for two days before withdrawing.[11]

The Yen failure to take Chenting argued that their rebellion could still be contained. Imperial forces under Wu Kao, marquis of Chiangyin, had marched overland from Liaotung and were besieging Yungp'ing prefecture. The emperor had ordered the princes of Liao and Ning back to the capital, and while the prince of Ning had not obeyed, neither had he joined up with Yen.[12] The territories under Yen control were still confined to the northern part of Peip'ing province, surrounded on all sides by hostile or potentially hostile armies. However, Keng Ping-wen's defeat indicated that he was not equal to the task of orchestrating a multipronged operation against the agile prince of Yen. He was therefore dismissed and replaced by the emperor's second cousin, Li Ching-lung, successor to the great Li Wen-chung as duke of Ts'ao, a man who had inherited his father's arrogance, but unfortunately not his ability. Li was authorized to raise five hundred thousand men, and by 10 October he had assembled a large fraction of this number at Hochien.[13]

Instead of merely waiting for Li Ching-lung (whose character he affected to despise) to launch an offensive, the prince of Yen marched to the relief of Yungp'ing, causing Wu Kao to retire to the strategic pass of Shanhaikuan. Leaving his heir apparent to hold Peip'ing, the prince hurried north to Taning, which he took by surprise on 3 November, capturing the prince of Ning and adding both the Chinese regulars and the Mongol auxiliaries there to his own forces, which he then divided into five armies, each under a general and two lieutenant generals.[14] He then marched back to Peip'ing, which Li Ching-lung had besieged. On 1 December the Yen cavalry crossed the frozen Pai River and the next day attacked the camps of the besieging army. The imperial troops were thrown into confusion and scattered. Li Ching-lung fled all the way south to Techou, where he busied himself reassembling his army; he announced more or less publicly that he would not resume the offensive until the spring.[15]

Despite their second major defeat, the imperial armies still retained a preponderance of force over the Yen rebels, although the latter contained a higher proportion of cavalry, and all of the Yen troops were accustomed to northern conditions and the northern winter. In contrast, the imperial armies included large contingents from Nanking and other southern regions, who suffered and sickened in the northern cold. Hearing of Li Ching-lung's plan to spend the winter at Techou, where he could be comfortably supplied by the Grand Canal, the prince of Yen led his own armies into the Tat'ung area of northern Shansi in January 1400, when the winter was at its worst; there he received the surrender of two of the smaller garrisons. Since Tat'ung itself was too important to be allowed to fall without a fight, Li Ching-lung was obliged to march his troops from Techou via the Tzuching pass into northern Shansi, a route difficult for the transport of supplies even under conditions of good weather and peace. When the imperial army finally arrived at the scene in March, the Yen forces had retired to Chüyungkuan without threatening Tat'ung. Li Ching-lung had already lost many men through cold and hunger, and the survivors had to march all the way back to Techou.[16] The imperial army thus began its planned campaigning season in 1400 in a state of exhaustion.

After his December victory the prince of Yen sent another letter to the court denouncing Ch'i T'ai and Huang Tzu-ch'eng; Chien-wen dismissed them from their official positions but kept them at court and continued to rely on their advice. The worsening military situation led Chien-wen to undertake activities designed to display himself as an ideal Confucian monarch. Officials who came to court were ordered not to present gifts, and official titles were changed in an attempt to bring government institutions into harmony with the ideal prescriptions of the *Rituals of Chou*. On 24 March 1400 the punitively high tax rates imposed in 1367 on the Soochow-Hangchow region were ordered reduced to the levels current elsewhere, and two days later Chien-wen received the successful candidates of the 1400 chin-shih examination, who were headed by Hu Kuang, later to be a principal minister under Yung-lo.[17]

No matter how much posturing went on in Nanking, Chien-wen's continuance in office depended on Li Ching-lung's offensive. At the beginning of summer, Li advanced to Hochien and ordered the forces led by his subordinates Kuo Ying, Wu Chieh, and P'ing An to rendezvous with him at Paikouho, further north on the march to Peip'ing.[18] Unbeknownst to the imperial generals, the prince of Yen had already left the city in order to frustrate their plans. On 18 May 1400 he attacked P'ing An's corps, defeated it, and drove it back, and then he fell on the right wing of Li Ching-lung's force (see the map on p. 159). The tired Yen troops were defeated this time, but the prince was able to disengage and reassemble his army that night. Under cover of darkness the Yen army crossed the river, which separated Li Ching-lung's main body into two parts. On the next day the Yen rearguard was attacked and defeated, presumably while still crossing, but the prince of Yen, undeterred, ordered the subordinate general Ch'iu Fu to attack the imperial center, and he himself fell on their left. The resulting battle raged indecisively most of the day.

Although Li Ching-lung's leadership was unimaginative, his army was deployed in a line stretching "several tens of li" (perhaps ten miles) from east to west and was simply too large to be demolished quickly. Ch'iu Fu failed to break the imperial center, and the prince, after initial successes on the imperial left, found himself the object of an intense counterattack. Extricating himself with some difficulty, he rode to the top of an embankment and gestured with his whip as though summoning reinforcements. Eventually his son Kao-hsü came up with the reserves, at which Li Ching-lung broke off the action and retired within his lines, which were partly covered with a wooden palisade.

The Yen troops were discouraged, but the prince roused them to make one more attack, himself leading a force to strike at the imperial rear. Suddenly there arose a wind from the north, of such force that it snapped the pole holding Li Ching-lung's general's flag. While the imperial troops were still demoralized by the apparent loss of their leader, the Yen army took advantage of the direction of the wind to discharge flame weapons that set fire to the enemy palisades. Smoke filled the skies, and the imperial army broke and ran. Kuo Ying's troops scattered to the west, while Li Ching-lung burned his commission and insignia of authority and led the flight to Techou. Several myriads of corpses were left on the battlefield, and over 100,000 drowned crossing rivers while fleeing.[19] On 1 June the Yen army reached Techou, which Li made no attempt to defend, instead fleeing to Tsinan. On 8 June the Yen forces drove Li's field army away from Tsinan and laid siege to that city. As usual, the Yen army, strong in cavalry and weak in engineers, was unsuccessful in the siege, and on 4 September they broke camp and returned to Peip'ing.[20]

Sheng Yung, the commander who had successfully defended Tsinan, reoccupied Techou as the Yen army withdrew. He was made marquis of Lich'eng (Tsinan) and imperial commander-in-chief, in place of Li Ching-lung; his civil collaborator, T'ieh Hsüan, became administration commissioner of Shantung and later minister of war. P'ing An and Wu Chieh had established themselves at Tingchou, and Hsü K'ai was at Ts'angchou; despite the Paikouho debacle, the imperial armies were once again poised to march on Peip'ing. However, on 24 October the prince of Yen surprised and captured Hsü K'ai, and in the next two months the

Yen armies marched down the Grand Canal past Linch'ing toward Tungch'ang.[21]

On 9 January 1401 the prince rashly attacked Sheng Yung's positions there, and the Yen troops were decimated by cannon and crossbow fire. P'ing An's corps, which had marched down from Tingchou parallel to their route, then attacked them in the rear. The Yen forces were heavily defeated, losing several myriads of captives, and had to fight two more battles with P'ing An and Wu Chieh during their retreat to Peip'ing.[22] The emperor celebrated the victory by reappointing Ch'i T'ai and Huang Tzu-ch'eng to office (31 January).[23] His optimism was premature, however; the prince of Yen was able to resume the offensive on 28 February, less than six weeks after returning to Peip'ing.[24]

On 5–6 April the two armies clashed at Chiaho near Techou. On the first day the imperial forces were victorious and succeeded in placing the prince of Yen in jeopardy. On the following day the Yen army, again aided by a favorable wind, inflicted a severe defeat on Sheng Yung, who withdrew his army in an orderly manner into Techou. The Yen forces once again failed to take the city, and they withdrew northwestwards when an imperial relief army under Ho Fu arrived on the eleventh. P'ing An and Wu Chieh had once again marched eastward to cooperate with Sheng Yung, but they failed to arrive in time for the Chiaho battle; on the twenty-seventh the prince of Yen defeated them at Kaoch'eng and drove them back within the walls of Chenting.[25]

Though much less dramatic than the Paikouho battle, these defeats marked the actual turning point in the civil war. Thereafter the fortunes of the emperor gradually but steadily deteriorated. He fired Ch'i T'ai and Huang Tzu-ch'eng once again and sent an envoy to command Yen to disband its armies; the prince countered with the demand that the imperial armies now immured in Chenting and Techou be withdrawn from his territory. There was no future in these negotiations, and they ceased in July when Chien-wen imprisoned the prince's envoy.[26]

Throughout the summer the prince of Yen followed the strategy of sending looting expeditions southward in the hope that his interdiction of the supply routes to Techou and Chenting would force the armies of Sheng Yung and P'ing An to withdraw. He marched from Chenting via Shunte and Kuangp'ing and arrived at

Taming on 10 May. In July his general Li Yüan looted P'eihsien and burned the rice barges that had been destined for Techou; in August Changte was looted. Despite these operations, the imperial generals remained firmly in their bases. Sheng Yung tried unsuccessfully to cut off supplies to the Yen army; P'ing An marched on Peip'ing itself; and the commandant of Tat'ung, Fang Chao, brought his troops over Tzuching pass and laid siege to Paoting. These threats finally caused the prince to return. His general Liu Chiang turned back P'ing An's attack on Peip'ing, and on 7 November the prince forced Fang Chao's withdrawal by destroying a column sent to reinforce him.[27]

Except for minor skirmishes, this concluded the campaigns for the year, and on 29 November the prince of Yen and his army entered Peip'ing for a brief winter rest. The prince was discouraged. After three years of fighting and four major victories in the open field, he still controlled only the three prefectures of Shunt'ien (the administration seat of Peip'ing), Yungp'ing, and Paoting. Despite his success in battle, no end to the war was in sight.[28] In fact, the prince's pessimism was unwarranted. The loss of the supply barges at P'eihsien had undermined Sheng Yung's position at Techou, and the entire imperial presence in Peip'ing province, so imposing in appearance, was ready to collapse at a touch.

On 15 January 1402 the prince of Yen led his army from Peip'ing. Marching swiftly, without any regard for lines of communication, he bypassed Techou, crossed the Yellow River, and within a month took Tunga, Tungp'ing, Wenshang, Yenchou, and Chiyang. P'eihsien fell on 12 February, and the Yen army reached Hsüchou on 3 March and placed it under siege. Their supply lines totally disrupted, the imperial armies were forced to evacuate Peip'ing province and defend the Nanking metropolitan area against Yen attack. Sheng Yung withdrew from Techou and marched all the way to the Huai River. Ho Fu, Ch'en Hui, and P'ing An assembled their armies at Chining, which, along with Tsinan and most of Shantung east of the Grand Canal, was still held by imperial troops. On the day that P'eihsien fell, Chien-wen ordered Hsü Ta's son, Hsü Hui-tsu, duke of Wei, to lead an army to relieve Shantung.[29]

In April the prince of Yen sent a force to take Suchou in

northern Anhwei. P'ing An was harassing the Yen army with his cavalry corps, which reportedly numbered 40,000 men, and he engaged and defeated this force, killing its commander. P'ing An himself then fell into an ambush set by the prince of Yen near the Fei River and was defeated badly, after which Suchou fell. Two weeks later the same pattern repeated itself: a Yen force sent to cut the supply lines to Hsüchou was hard pressed by an imperial force, which in turn was mauled by the main Yen army.[30]

As a result of these operations, by May the main Yen army was south of Lingpi masked by the armies of Ho Fu and P'ing An, while the newly mobilized army of Hsü Hui-tsu marched to join them. On 16 May P'ing An inflicted a sharp reverse on the Yen army, killing a general. The following morning Hsü Hui-tsu arrived, and on the twenty-third the combined imperial armies fought and defeated the Yen troops, killing a number of generals. The Yen officers were disheartened by these reverses, and the men were uncomfortable in the steamy lowlands of South China, which were growing hotter as the summer progressed. They wished to call off the campaign and return to the north. The prince argued that if they could hold out longer, the imperial armies would begin to suffer from inadequate supplies. Meanwhile Chien-wen persuaded himself that the Yen forces had already withdrawn to the north as a result of P'ing An's victory on the sixteenth, so he recalled Hsü Hui-tsu, who must have withdrawn shortly after the fight on the twenty-third and left Ho Fu and P'ing An without support against the prince of Yen.[31]

The latter then moved his main body to the rear of the imperial forces in order to cut their supply routes entirely. At this P'ing An took 60,000 men to defend them. On the twenty-ninth the prince attacked the flank of P'ing An's army, cutting it in two. When Ho Fu heard of this, he abandoned his prepared positions and marched to P'ing An's assistance. At this point, the troops the prince of Yen had placed in ambush under his son Kao-hsü rose up and struck the imperial army in the rear. Ho Fu fled, and P'ing An and many other important commanders were captured. As it turned out, the last imperial army able to stand up to the Yen forces had been smashed beyond repair. After taking Szuchou, the Yen armies crossed the Huai River and defeated Sheng Yung on 9 June.[32]

Either Fengyang or Huaian would have been a logical next

objective, but the prince feared that he could not take them by assault. He determined instead to march directly to Yangchow in order to threaten the capital. He surrounded Yangchow on 17 June, and on 1 July the assistant chief commissioner Ch'en Hsüan, commanding the river fleet, surrendered to him, thus giving him the means to cross the Yangtze.[33] This defection was not the first. For obvious reasons Chien-wen was losing the confidence of his nobles and generals. As his situation worsened, he fell back on his civil officials, restoring Ch'i T'ai and Huang Tzu-ch'eng to office once again and sending other officials out to raise troops. Twice he proposed a division of the empire to the prince of Yen but was ignored.[34]

The Yen army crossed the Yangtze on 3 July, brushing aside the feeble resistance of Sheng Yung, who had hastily converted the remnants of his army into a river flotilla. The commandant of Chenchiang surrendered to Yen. In the next ten days Chien-wen sent his former commander-in-chief, Li Ching-lung, and the princes of Ku and An as envoys in his final desperate attempts to talk the prince of Yen into returning to the north. Nanking was divided into wards for its defense, each under one of the princes still in the capital. However, when the Yen army appeared before the walls on 13 July, Li Ching-lung and the prince of Ku betrayed the emperor, opened the Chinch'uan gate, and admitted the Yen soldiers. In the confusion that occurred as the latter took control of the city, the imperial palace caught fire, and the emperor and empress burned to death.[35]

The death of Chien-wen concluded the civil war. The prince of Yen at once launched a vendetta against the civil officials (some fifty men headed by Ch'i T'ai, Huang Tzu-ch'eng, and Fang Hsiao-ju) whom he had identified as evil ministers in his propaganda letters during the civil war; they were rounded up and executed. But otherwise the prince attempted to inaugurate his rule on a note of conciliation. Princes and officials who had been deprived of their titles and positions by Chien-wen were reinstated. On 17 July the prince responded to the predictable spontaneous demands of the Nanking notables and ascended the imperial throne. Three days later a charred corpse purported to be that of Emperor Chien-wen was buried, but rumors persisted that he had escaped and survived.[36]

*

The Chien-wen reign, far from witnessing the establishment of civil virtue, had been taken up almost entirely with civil war, which had ended by destroying the emperor. Four points of analysis suggest themselves.

First, by granting so much regional military authority to the princes, Hung-wu had made a conflict between them and his successor inevitable. In the Ottoman Empire, where the custom was to make the ruler's sons provincial governors with military authority, the death of the ruler regularly led to civil war among his sons, the succession going to the victor. This was formally sanctioned by Hung-wu's contemporary among the Ottomans, Sultan Bayazid I "the Thunderer" (r. 1389–1402), who issued a testamentary edict ordering each new Ottoman sultan to begin his reign by executing his brothers. Similar, if less explicit, customs had been practiced by the Seljuks and would be practiced by the Mughals, so settling the succession through civil war was a regular practice in the highly militarized Turkish empires.[37] Such occurrences were of course highly irregular in China, and it was not Hung-wu's intention to have his successors chosen by civil war. He had placed his sons in military command positions in the belief that he could rely on them to be personally loyal to himself, other instruments having failed. He justified this by appealing to historical precedents wherein military feudatories were to shield (*fan*) and support an essentially civil throne. Successive generations of emperors and princes were intended to play complementary, not conflicting, roles, and the authority of the princes was hedged with various legal restrictions aimed at preventing rebellion.

But Hung-wu was evoking historical precedents whose failure to work in practice was widely understood. From the beginning of his reign, Chien-wen acted on the assumption that the personal loyalty that his uncles had given their father would not be extended to him. Since the prince of Yen was the most famous general, held the most important command, and was the senior survivor among the sons of Hung-wu, it was also to be expected that the general conflict between emperor and princes would turn into a specific conflict with the prince of Yen.

Second, even though the struggle with the princes was inevitable, the Yen victory was a military upset. This is apparent from the preceding narrative of the civil war. The imperial armies were much larger in the beginning; the great majority of Chinese officials—military as well as civil—had accepted Chien-wen's legitimacy as emperor, and his control over the state machinery enabled him repeatedly to raise fresh armies even after the most terrible defeats. Although the imperial armies did suffer from a lack of truly inspired generals, both P'ing An and Sheng Yung were certainly competent. The imperial armies suffered from the disadvantage of being underfed and underclad, since they were southern troops fighting in the north. Even more, it was difficult for the imperial commanders to coordinate the movements of their armies, which usually had to maneuver separately because of their size and the difficulty of supplying them. Significantly, the greatest victory of the imperial troops, that of Sheng Yung and P'ing An in January 1401, was won by Moltke's formula of rendezvous on the battlefield. Despite defeats and difficulties, by the end of 1401, after three years of civil war, the imperial armies had succeeded in confining the Yen rebellion to three prefectures of Peip'ing. In their successful 1402 campaign, the Yen armies were much aided by Chien-wen's premature recall of Hsü Hui-tsu. Yet as they approached Nanking in July, they left strong imperial armies behind them, across their path of retreat. Virtually to the end of the civil war, the Yen armies entered every battle facing the serious possibility that their entire rebel movement might collapse at one defeat; the imperial forces in contrast revived again and again after catastrophic reverses. Like his father, the prince of Yen attained supreme power abnormally and unexpectedly, by winning an upset military victory against long odds.

Third, the Yen rebellion was a rebellion of the army and society of the northern frontier against the center of power in South China. The prince of Yen and his generals and officers were bound together by their long common service, since 1378, on the northern frontier. The Yen army was composed mainly of cavalry, who were able to forage for themselves, in contrast to the imperial armies, which contained a higher proportion of infantry and were more dependent on their supply trains. This is apparent from the Yen troops' ability to move with ease through regions where the imperial armies suffered from shortages of supplies, from their ability to march across the front of the imperial host (as happened to Li Ching-lung in May 1400), from their practice of bypassing uncaptured imperial cities, and even from their general ineffectiveness in conducting sieges. As had happened previously in Chinese history, the armies created to man the Great Wall against nomadic invasion had themselves assimilated certain characteristics from the nomads that differentiated them from the rest of Chinese society.

Fourth, the prince of Yen found it difficult to separate himself from this frontier milieu. He spent most of his reign in the north, ultimately moving the capital to Peip'ing (Peking). In the long run, this seriously undermined the dynasty's strength and increased its vulnerability to foreign invasion. However, in the more limited context of the Yung-lo reign itself, it certainly made sense for the sometime prince of Yen, feeling morally and politically insecure in his new position as emperor, to remain physically and socially as close as possible to the army that had won him the throne.

Chien-wen had failed, but he had failed by such a narrow margin as to suggest that his major political goal—centralizing civil and military authority in the emperor and delegating both to the civil officials in the approved Confucian manner—was fully practicable. His cousin Hung-hsi ultimately achieved this goal, but only after another generation of rule by a monarch whose purposes were often distinctly un-Confucian, and whose policies markedly affected the shape of the mature Ming system.

SIX

Yung-lo: Emperor on
Horseback, 1402–1424

The new emperor redesignated the rest of 1402 as the thirty-fifth year of Hung-wu, making the following year the first year of Yung-lo ("Perpetual Happiness").[1] Emperor Yung-lo's previous experience had been as a soldier, and this was the life he preferred, but political considerations kept him in Nanking for several years. As ruler, Yung-lo dealt both ruthlessly and subtly with individuals he considered enemies, but he tried to conciliate the classes they represented. Although the individual ministers and generals who had supported Chien-wen mostly either suffered execution or committed suicide while facing criminal charges, civil officials and military officers as classes benefited from his continuation of the examinations and revival of the military nobility. The princes lost their troop commands, but they regained their titles and properties.

Yung-lo attempted to live up to both the Chinese and the Mongol versions of the imperial ideal. The former involved the enhancement of the Confucian ideal through government-sponsored literary projects and the conscientious administration of famine relief and the criminal law. The latter required the military conquest of adjoining countries and the opening of diplomatic and commercial relationships with other lands. Yung-lo's reign recalls Qubilai's in its outstanding events: the conquest of the south, the establishment of the capital at Peking, the opening of relations with Japan (peaceful, this time), an ultimately abortive attempt to conquer Vietnam, and naval expeditions to Southeast Asia and the Indian Ocean. But in contrast to the repeated fiascos of Qubilai's reign (the failure to crush Qaidu and the botched invasions of Japan, Vietnam, and Java), Yung-lo was everywhere successful in his projects—or so it seemed when he died (1424), since the collapse of the Chinese position in Vietnam was then still three years in the future.

Nevertheless, Yung-lo was the heir of the native Chinese imperial tradition, and his attempts to follow two paths at the same time resulted in hopeless contradictions. As a model Confucian emperor, Yung-lo enhanced the position of the civil officials, restoring them to a place in the central government comparable, if not quite equal, to that which they had enjoyed prior to 1380. Moreover, many of the officials whom he favored were distinguished by both scholarship and principle. Naturally they opposed all of his military, diplomatic, and commercial ventures. He tolerated their criticisms as his father never would have done, occasionally jailing some of them but usually afterwards relenting. Meanwhile, he allowed them to run the government with little imperial supervision, turning the projects connected with his plans of aggrandizement over to eunuchs and generals whom he could trust to carry out his orders. Yung-lo's contradictory objectives thus led to the division of the Ming state into two different sets of institutions: a civil bureaucracy that opposed the emperor's policies and looked to the crown prince to reverse them, and an establishment of eunuchs and military officers that carried out the emperor's policies and was sustained in power only by the emperor's favor. The spectacular achievements of his reign were in conflict with the line of institutional development that he himself promoted, but for the most part his successor was able to reverse the policies the civil officials opposed and embrace without reservation the ideology of the Confucian state.

Yung-lo as a Soldier: The Mongolian Campaigns

Yung-lo had come to power as the leader of a northern frontier army, and even as emperor his main ambition was to return to the north and lead his army beyond the Great Wall. He was thus personally concerned with military and Mongolian affairs, a characteristic of his outlook that grew more pronounced as his reign progressed. However, for several years he had to suppress these inclinations and remain in Nanking.

In September 1402 he awarded noble titles to his generals. Ch'iu Fu and Chu Neng became dukes, thirteen others became marquises, and eleven became earls. In addition, one marquisate and three earldoms were awarded to men who had joined him after the fall of Nanking.[2] By these steps Yung-lo revived the military nobility, in which his creations now constituted a majority, and the nobles resumed their commanding role in the armies free of competition from the princes, who were now systematically excluded from any military role. In appearance these steps restored the command structure of the early Hung-wu period, but in fact there were important differences. Hung-wu's nobles had begun as social equals of the emperor, but by the 1370's Hung-wu had come to view the personal connection of the nobles with their troops as a threat, since he himself had become increasingly isolated from his armies.

Yung-lo's nobles, in contrast, began in 1399 as the clear inferiors of the prince of Yen. As nobles they were placed in command of groups of units led by generals of comparable seniority who had been on the wrong side in the civil war and thus had no opportunity to acquire noble titles. In consequence, the position of the new nobles was that of appointed deputies of Yung-lo, and they had less opportunity to build up the kind of loyalty within their commands that might have constituted a threat to the throne. Finally, in contrast to his father, Yung-lo never gave up the exercise of direct military command and thus never became isolated from the soldiers. The new military nobles thus were more dependent on the emperor as an institution than had been the Hung-wu nobility, who owed their position to the emperor as a man. Their generally lower stipends and the preponderance of earls among them (fourteen out of thirty new titles) indicated their lower status. In the summer of 1403 three more marquises and six more earls were created.[3]

In the Eurasian steppe north and west of China, the effective pretensions of the House of Chinggis Qan to the Mongol imperial throne had largely dissipated with the murder of Toghus Temür. Subsequent *qaghans* (emperors) were ephemeral puppets manipulated by tribal leaders whose lack of descent from Chinggis Qan prevented them from ruling in name as well as in fact. Under these circumstances the Mongol nation fragmented still further. The Uriyangqad Mongols of the Taning region north of Peip'ing had fought in the Yen armies during the civil war. Presuming them loyal, Yung-lo in the spring of 1403 withdrew the Peip'ing branch regional military commission from Taning to Paoting, south of the Great Wall.[4] This left the Uriyangqad in control of a large portion of the Inner Mongolian steppe. Except in Manchuria, no regular Chinese garrisons would thereafter be placed beyond the Great Wall.

In Manchuria substantial Chinese settlement took place under the military colony system, and was accompanied by an extension of Chinese influence among the Jurchen descendants of the former ruling nation of the Chin dynasty. Jurchen chieftains were given titles (hereditary subject to the emperor's confirmation) in the Ming military hierarchy, was severing their connection with the former Yüan ruling house and making them subject to some degree of Ming control.

In the west the rulers of the oasis states of Sinkiang had been awed by the campaigns conducted by Lan Yü in the year before his execution. Their caravan trade depended on regular relations with China, which Yung-lo was more willing to allow than his father. In 1404 Engke Temür, ruler of Hami (Qomul), accepted the title prince (*wang*) from the Ming, and embassies from the small states of this area afterwards increased steadily in numbers and importance. The Oirats (Western Mongols) were also under Ming influence at this time, and in 1409, on the eve of Yung-lo's first campaign as emperor against the Eastern Mongols, their three principal chieftains—Mahmud, T'ai-p'ing, and Batu Bolod—accepted the title prince from the Ming.[5]

Still further west loomed Tamerlane, undefeated in his campaigns in Russia, India, and the Near East, in which he had inflicted slaughter and destruction on a scale surpassed only by Chinggis Qan himself. He had executed one group of Chinese envoys sent by Hung-wu and another sent to announce Yung-lo's accession; the unique authority claimed by the Chinese emperors conflicted with the similarly grand pretensions advanced by Tamerlane on behalf of his nominal emperor, a prince of the Chaghatai branch of the house of Chinggis Qan. In 1405, having laid waste the land in all other directions, Tamerlane marched eastward to conquer China. This campaign is one of the great might-have-beens of military history. Yung-lo was no more than a competent general; though ultimately victorious, he had been defeated on several occasions during the civil war. Tamerlane, in contrast, was an inspired genius, an artist who used the battlefield as his canvas. But Tamerlane was old, and he died on the march, hundreds of miles from the nearest Chinese outpost. His body was entombed in Samarkand, and his successor Shāhrūkh (r. 1405–47) attempted only to hold the core of his father's empire together. Eventually Yung-lo was able to conclude amicable relations with the Samarkand regime as well.[6]

Within the whole northern steppe area, it was thus only the Mongols of eastern Outer Mongolia who consistently refused to acknowledge Ming imperial authority, killing the Ming envoys sent to proclaim it. In 1408 the Mongol qaghan was murdered and another puppet, Bunyashiri, installed in his place. The following year, with the Vietnam war having come to an apparently successful conclusion (see pp. 206–10) and with construction underway at Peip'ing, which had been renamed Peking, Yung-lo undertook a northern tour. Transferring the government to his son Kao-chih, he left Nanking on 23 February 1409 and went by way of Feng-yang to Peking.[7]

This should have been a mere imperial progress; military operations in Vietnam were continuing, the Japanese raiders were active, and Yung-lo's presence in Nanking was desirable to concert countermeasures. However, events intervened. In the summer it was learned that Kuo Chi, sent as Chinese envoy to Bunyashiri, had been killed by the Mongols. Yung-lo ordered a punitive expedition in retaliation, and in the autumn commanded Ch'iu Fu, duke of Ch'i and one of the outstanding Yen generals of the civil war, to take an army north of the Gobi. Four marquises assisted him. On 23 September the Ming army did battle with the Mongols by the Kerülen River and was wiped out. Ch'iu Fu and the four other nobles were killed. The disaster was worse than Hsü Ta's defeat in 1372; it was also unexpected, as the Mongols were visibly weaker than in Hsü Ta's time. On 14 October Yung-lo awarded posthumous dukedoms to two of the fallen marquises and determined to lead the next expedition personally. After initial hesitation he made his old friend Ch'iu Fu the scapegoat for the disaster, stripping him posthumously of his titles and exiling his family.[8]

For his own expedition Yung-lo summoned Ch'en Mou, marquis of Ningyang, to be his deputy, and placed his young grandson Chan-chi (the future Emperor Hsüan-te) in command at Peking with the experienced minister of finance, Hsia Yüan-chi, to advise him. Yung-lo left Peking on 15 March 1410 and completed the organization of his army on 4 April. Accompanying him were two earls and four marquises, including Ho Fu, who had been one of the leading imperial generals in the civil war.[9]

In the ensuing campaign, the imperial army crossed the Kerülen, caught up with Bunyashiri's horde, and scattered it on 15 June. Then Yung-lo turned his attention to Arughtai, the chieftain who had originally made Bunyashiri qaghan and who had masterminded the defeat of Ch'iu Fu the previous year. Arughtai pretended to surrender, but on 10 July his horde attacked the Ming army. Yung-lo had been expecting this, and in the four-day running battle that followed, the Chinese army drove the Mongols back over 100 li. Yung-lo then disengaged and withdrew, mindful that Ch'iu Fu had met disaster by pursuing the retiring Mongols too far and too rashly. He had in fact achieved little, but on returning to Peking he treated the campaign as a victory, raised Liu Sheng from earl to marquis, and granted other rewards. Chien-wen's former general Ho Fu, who had displeased Yung-lo during the campaign, committed suicide. Yung-lo returned to Nanking in the winter of 1410, and before the end of the year Arughtai sent a tribute of horses in an attempt to mend relations with the Ming court.[10]

Arughtai's submission was only partly due to Yung-lo's military power; Outer Mongolia was passing into the hands of the Oirats. Bunyashiri in his flight from the Ming armies had ended up in the hands of Mahmud, one of the three Oirat chieftains given princely titles by the Ming in 1409. In 1413 Mahmud killed Bunyashiri and installed a puppet qaghan of his own, thus serving notice that he was reaching for hegemony over the Mongols. In the autumn Arughtai accepted the title of prince of Honing from

Yung-lo, who had arrived in Peking on 30 April. On 27 November Mahmud crossed the Kerülen and marched east. When Arughtai warned the emperor of the Oirat invasion, Yung-lo ordered the border garrisons to be vigilant and also ordered the troops of Liaotung, Honan, and other provinces to assemble in Peking.[11]

On 25 February 1414 Yung-lo went to war against the Oirats with five marquises and an army of five hundred thousand men. Over a month was spent organizing this host, which did not leave Peking until 6 April. At Hsingho the emperor drilled his troops during the first month of summer, issued general orders, and appointed civil officials to each division of the army to check on observance of orders and to record deeds deserving of reward. The army then crossed the Gobi, receiving on the way the surrenders of Eastern Mongol chieftains hoping for protection against the Oirats.[12] On 23 June Mahmud attacked the Ming army at Qulan Qushwan in Outer Mongolia, but was defeated and pursued to the Tula River, where he finally succeeded in disengaging his army and escaping. Yung-lo once again did not pursue further. He sent an edict announcing his victory to Arughtai, who in return sent an envoy to the court. The Ming army withdrew from Mongolia and arrived on 15 August in Peking, where Yung-lo basked in the congratulations of his court and celebrated his victory by promoting junior officers and remitting the land taxes of Peking for two years. Though not decisively crushed, Mahmud had been frightened, and early in 1415 he offered to submit formally and send tribute, which Yung-lo allowed.[13]

There were no further imperially led military expeditions until 1421, but during the intervening years Yung-lo spent most of his time in the north devoting his attention to turning Peking into a lavish imperial capital. In 1415 the chin-shih examinations were held in Peking for the first time. In 1416 Arughtai, having defeated the Oirats, came in person to present his captives. With the war chiefs of both the Eastern and Western Mongols dancing attendance, the Ming emperor could feel that his influence extended throughout Mongolia. In the winter of 1416 Yung-lo returned to Nanking for a brief visit, but he returned to Peking in the summer of the following year. He spent the next three years in peaceful pursuits in and about his newly constructed palaces in Peking. In

1420 he announced his formal decision that Peking was to become the principal capital of the empire.[14]

By 1421 disputes with Arughtai over the reception of his tributary envoys and the value of Chinese gifts to him had gone beyond control, and Arughtai was raiding the frontiers. The grant of titles to his mother and wife did not make him more submissive. Two of the principal Oirat leaders, Batu Bolod and T'ai-p'ing, had come to court, which suggested that Arughtai would receive no support from that quarter. So in the autumn of 1421 Yung-lo announced a campaign to chastise Arughtai and began to organize his army. The civil service, angered and frustrated after years of famine in the north while the new palaces were under construction, protested vehemently against the proposed campaign. This angered Yung-lo, who imprisoned the minister of revenue, Hsia Yüan-chi, and the minister of justice, Wu Chung. Minister of War Fang Pin killed himself while facing investigation. Eight days later, on 19 December, the emperor ordered the populations of Pei Chihli (formerly Peip'ing province), Shansi, Shantung, Honan, and several prefectures and departments in Nan Chihli to deliver grain to Hsüanfu by the end of the second lunar month of 1422. In that month Chang Hsin, marquis of Lungp'ing, and the new minister of war, Li Ch'ing, were placed in charge of the porters for the expedition, who ultimately numbered 235,000 men transporting 370,000 shih of grain.[15]

The following month Arughtai invaded Hsingho and killed the Ming regional military commissioner. On 17 April the Ming army left Peking. It was divided into a vanguard, three cavalry divisions led by a marquis and two earls, and five infantry divisions led by four marquises and Chang Fu, duke of Ying, the chief luminary of the Vietnam war. Marching slowly and drilling along the way, the host took two months to get to K'aip'ing, which it reached on 18 June; from there it moved in square array out onto the steppe. Arughtai had succeeded in adding the Uriyangqad Mongols to his horde. These Mongols had supported Yung-lo during the civil war, and to reward them he had moved the Chinese garrison away from Taning in the heart of their grazing lands. The Uriyangqad had also scouted for the Ming armies in the previous campaigns, and without them the Chinese leadership was partially blinded.

Arughtai's first move was to mount a diversionary assault on Wanch'üan in order to keep the Ming army in the vicinity of the Great Wall.[16] Yung-lo, not deceived, advanced in the direction of Arughtai's principal encampment, near Dalai Nor. He detached twenty thousand men to attack the Uriyangqad, who were defeated in a series of battles; the remnants of the tribe came in and surrendered on 6 July. Meanwhile Arughtai had abandoned his main camp hurriedly, and Yung-lo sent his vanguard to burn it and seize the livestock. Arughtai then retired into Outer Mongolia, but Yung-lo again declined to be drawn into an extended pursuit. The Ming army therefore retired from Mongolia and arrived back in Peking on 23 September. The two generals who had commanded the vanguard, Chief Commissioner Chu Yung and Assistant Chief Commissioner Hsüeh Kuei, were both made earls for their part in the campaign.[17]

The expedition had failed to crush Arughtai, and it ended, as it had begun, on a note of disharmony between the emperor and his civil officials, the latter working through the crown prince. While the emperor was away, the crown prince had seized on the pretext of flood damage to remit over 610,000 shih of grain and fodder taxes in precisely those four provinces from which the supplies for the campaign in progress had come. This step increased the already formidable logistical problems involved in maintaining a large Chinese army in the Mongolian grasslands. The emperor returned to the capital in a rage; he reprimanded the crown prince severely and imprisoned his chief adviser, Grand Secretary Yang Shih-ch'i. However, in the summer of the following year Yung-lo himself had to order tax remissions for flood-damaged areas along the Yellow River.[18]

Another expedition against Arughtai was undertaken in 1423. This time no less than eleven nobles commanded the divisions of the army, which left Peking on 29 August. The crown prince was again left in charge of the government, and again he promptly began granting tax remissions. After two months of fruitless marching in Inner Mongolia, Yung-lo heard a rumor that Arughtai had been defeated by the Oirats and his horde scattered. On the strength of this he returned to Peking with his army and disbanded it.[19]

Arughtai reassembled his horde over the winter and celebrated the new year with an invasion of the K'aip'ing and Tat'ung areas. The sixty-five-year-old emperor called for advice from his ministers, and on 9 February 1424 ordered troops to be mobilized from Liaotung, Shantung, Honan, Shansi, and Shensi to gather at Peking and Hsüanfu in three months. On 1 April the emperor reviewed the army and named as divisional commanders twelve nobles including the Mongol prince Esentü Qan, who had come in to surrender the previous winter. On 2 May the army left the capital to begin three months of fruitless wandering in search of the elusive Arughtai. The latter was not where reported, and the emperor ordered Chang Fu to search thoroughly for 300 li, to no avail. When the Ming vanguard returned because its provisions were exhausted, the emperor ordered the army to withdraw from Mongolia. On 12 August, before the army reached the Great Wall, Yung-lo died in camp. The eunuchs in attendance concealed his death until the army reached Peking.[20]

The history of these campaigns reveals that sclerosis had begun developing in the Ming military establishment even during the Yung-lo reign. In the 1370's and 1380's Ming generals had led cavalry armies that could overtake and engage the nomadic Mongol hordes. Even in the civil war of 1399–1402, Yung-lo's army, because of its superior mobility, was able to escape annihilation by larger forces and ultimately to defeat them in detail. In contrast, the armies in Yung-lo's Mongolian campaigns became increasingly bound to their supply trains as the reign progressed, and their complexity of organization grew correspondingly. The ineffectiveness of the Ming armies reduced the ability of the government to intervene in the politics of the steppe, so Arughtai remained uncrushed and unrepentant to the end of the Yung-lo reign; he simply eluded the Ming armies and refused to do battle with them. After this the Ming could still influence Mongol chieftains by granting them rewards and titles, but a credible threat of force was lacking. In this respect the early Ming period ended even before 1424.

The New Capital and the Military System

In 1403 Yung-lo ordered Peip'ing renamed Peking (Northern capital), and he established there a Branch Ministry (*hsing-pu*) to manage the affairs of the Six Ministries, a National University, and a Branch Chief Military Commission of the Rear Army (*hsing hou-chün tu-tu fu*). Peking had become an embryonic imperial capital. And since Yung-lo spent most of his time in the north in the latter half of his reign, Peking had also become the effective center of decisionmaking. As of 1421 it became the formal capital as well. Nanking then became in practice merely the administrative center for those fourteen prefectures and four independent departments that were not subordinated to provinces. This area (Nan Chihli) was later divided into Anhwei and Kiangsu provinces by the Ch'ing. Skeletal versions of the major imperial administrative departments remained at Nanking.[21]

Just as Hung-wu reconstructed Nanking, so Yung-lo built walls and palaces at Peking, establishing the form and style the city was to retain down to the present. He accompanied his construction with measures to establish a sound social and economic infrastructure for the new capital. Displaced persons were settled in the capital and surrounding areas. After years of attempting to supply the capital by shipping grain by sea from the Yangtze delta area, the regime finally settled on transport via the Grand Canal, a step that fostered the development of the regions traversed by the canal.[22]

Attending the transfer of the capital were transfers of troops and their families that added up to a fundamental change in the basis of the Chu family's imperial rule. Not wishing to see his successors deposed by a future edition of himself, Yung-lo systematically stripped the princes of their princely guards and all related military functions. Their troops were usually transferred, often to Peking. At Peking, Yung-lo raised the best of his veterans from the civil war to the status of imperial guards and transferred all but cadre elements of the Nanking capital guards (*ching-wei*) to the new capital. Peking became the military center of the reconstituted Ming empire without any princely provincial armies to exert centrifugal force. Moreover, Yung-lo made the rotation of the wei-so soldiers between agriculture and military duties the basis for the recruitment of even the largest armies. This led to the creation of three great camps (*ying*) in Peking where the troops recruited from the provincial military establishment were drilled, trained, and transformed into effective combat units. It led also to the emergence of a distinct operational (as opposed to administrative) hierarchy in the chain of command. Garrison positions along the Great Wall and elsewhere were commanded by officers, seconded for fixed tours of duty, who retained their hereditary ranks in the wei-so system.[23]

For several years (1402–8) Yung-lo remained at Nanking, and the Vietnam war and other matters kept his attention away from the north. During these years there was a steady stream of rescripts announcing tax remissions, famine relief, and attempts at resettlement in the north, perhaps because of a series of bad harvests. Presumably the lands still vacant in the north after a generation of government-promoted resettlement during the Hung-wu reign were of marginal quality. So in 1405 when the emperor sent his third son, Kao-sui, prince of Chao, to assume military command at Peking, he also ordered a two-year tax remission for Shunt'ien, Paoting, and Yungp'ing, the three prefectures that had supported Yen throughout the civil war. In 1406 over 120,000 landless households from the Yangtze delta area were resettled in the north. In 1407 relief grain had to be distributed at the beginning of the summer to three Peking area prefectures (Shunt'ien, Paoting, and Hochien), and in 1408 government operations in Peking and the purchase of grain there for government use were both ordered reduced in order to relieve the burden on the population. The Peking area could scarcely support its existing population, so its growth into a true imperial capital required grain transported from the south.[24]

Yung-lo's arrival at Peking in 1409, on the eve of his expedition against the Mongols, called his attention to this problem. Afterwards he ordered the minister of works, Sung Li, to dredge and repair the Grand Canal, using as laborers men assigned to the army as punishment for crimes. In 1411 Sung Li finished the Shantung section of the canal. After that, although sea transport of grain to the north, particularly to Liaotung, continued, Peking itself came to rely on the Grand Canal, which permitted the capital to survive even if agricultural conditions in the north were adverse. Until the end of the dynasty, the boat crews on the Grand Canal were organized under military command as an integral part of the army.[25]

Under these conditions, both the building of the capital and the military campaigns in the north could continue, southern grain supplying the decisive margin of support. Northern agriculture itself remained precarious. In 1412 flood-damaged areas in Peking had to be forgiven their taxes. Despite this, the next year farming families were ordered to raise horses for the army. In 1414 the land taxes of the Peking prefectures were remitted for two years. In 1415 emergency grain relief had to be distributed in Peking, Shantung, and Honan, which was suffering from floods, and in 1416 actual famine in those three provinces required the distribution of 1,370,000 shih of relief grain shortly after the new year. When the summer came, a plague of locusts disrupted agriculture in all three provinces. Conditions were better the two following years, but in 1419 flood damage in Shunt'ien prefecture again led the government to remit taxes.[26]

During these same years Yung-lo gave further signs of his intention to remain in the north. In 1415 he had the metropolitan examinations held in Peking. The opening of the locks at Ch'ingchiangp'u in the same year removed the last obstacle to grain transport by canal to Peking. However, 1416 was the year of no return: Yung-lo ordered the construction of a new imperial palace at Peking, only afterwards consulting with the civil officials.[27]

While Yung-lo returned to Nanking for a brief visit, the construction of the Peking palaces commenced. Ch'en Hsüan, earl of P'ingchiang, took charge of the transport of lumber to Peking via the Grand Canal early in 1417. On 3 March Ch'en Kuei, marquis of T'aining, took command of the actual construction project, assisted by two other nobles, Liu Sheng and Wang T'ung. The construction gangs consisted of men drawn from the wei-so units. On 27 March the emperor ordered that criminals sentenced to less than death be transported to Peking to serve as palace construction laborers. On 12 April Yung-lo once again turned over the administration to the crown prince and set out for the north, while at Peking the nobles in charge of construction urged their men on; the new palace was completed on 13 May, three days before the emperor's arrival.[28]

Yung-lo remained in Peking from this time on, though the crown prince continued to govern from Nanking for three more years. But when Yung-lo ordered in late autumn of 1420 that

Peking be designated the primary capital from 1421 on, he also ordered the crown prince to come north. The crown prince and his eldest son arrived in Peking late in the winter, shortly before the completion of the Temples of Heaven and Earth and the other government buildings required for the full exercise of ceremonial imperial functions. On New Year's Day in 1421 the Chu family ancestral tablets were installed in the new ancestral temple. The emperor then received the not entirely sincere congratulations of his officials, many of whom had opposed the move and would later try to reverse it, and celebrated the occasion with a grand banquet. Ten days later, on 12 February, he performed the suspended annual sacrifices to Heaven and Earth for the first time since 1417—and for the first time in Peking in the Ming dynasty. Peking thereby became the symbolic center of the Confucian world order as well as the actual center of power.[29]

The years 1420–21 also marked the completion of the military transfers and reorganizations of the Yung-lo reign. This restructuring of the armed forces involved four major changes from the Hung-wu system: virtual elimination of the princely guards; transfer of most of the Nanking guards to the north and promotion of certain northern units to the status of imperial guards (after this the capital guards located at Peking were the largest body of troops in the empire); creation of the capital training camps for managing and drilling the men regularly rotated to active duty from the provincial wei-so units; and the creation of border defense commands along the Great Wall.

The princely guards. Twenty of the thirty princely guards in existence in 1398 had been located at the headquarters of regional military commissions, which had given the princes a dangerous influence within the military establishment and had provided Yung-lo with the opportunity to rebel successfully. This experience led him to repudiate his father's policy of involving the emperor's sons in military command. He had only four sons of his own, of whom the eldest defended the Yen capital during the civil war and later served as regent during the Yung-lo reign when the emperor was absent. A younger son, Kao-hsü, prince of Han, accompanied Yung-lo in the field during the civil war and was his favorite. His arrival with the reserve on the first day of the

Paikouho battle in 1400 prevented a major catastrophe for the Yen rebels, and Kao-hsü spent the next two decades intriguing against his elder brother the crown prince. The latter, though estranged from his father, nevertheless had the solid support of Confucian officialdom both because he was the eldest son and because he shared their ideological biases. In 1417 Yung-lo reluctantly resolved the issue in favor of his eldest son, banishing Kao-hsü to his fief at Loan in Shantung.[30]

Yung-lo also severely curtailed the influence of the princes who were his brothers. Many were convicted of crimes on various occasions after 1402, and the sentences always included being deprived of their princely guards. By the end of the reign only four princely guards remained out of the 30 that had existed in 1398. The three Yenshan guards, formerly of the Yen fief, had of course been promoted into the group of guards (expanded by Yung-lo from 12 to 22) constituting the emperor's personal army (*ch'in-chün*). Of the remaining 23, some were redesignated ordinary guards, usually with a change of location as well, and the rest were disbanded outright, their troops being reassembled to form new guards at Peking. Fiefs created later for new imperial princes rarely included princely guards, and never more than one; by the late sixteenth century there were less than a dozen princely guards in a military establishment that had grown to 493 guards and 359 independent battalions.[31]

The Peking capital guards. As of 1398 the military establishment at Nanking consisted of twelve guards of the emperor's personal army and twenty-nine other guards directly subordinate to the five chief military commissions. These forty-one guards, collectively known as capital guards, consisted of Hung-wu's first soldiers and their descendants, presumed more loyal than those who had surrendered later. Their concentration at Nanking gave the emperor a reliable ready reserve large enough to crush a rebellion by the troops of any single regional military commission or smaller unit. Nevertheless, this reserve had not been effectively employed by Hung-wu's successor, and Yung-lo had come to the throne at the head of just such a provincial rebellion.

As emperor, Yung-lo had to reshape this central military reserve into an army loyal to himself. Had the capital remained at Nanking, it would have been necessary to transfer his northern troops there permanently. Instead, the relocation of the capital became the occasion for substantial shifts of troops to the north, a process that was completed in 1420–21. The capital guards in Peking consisted from then on of three major elements: guards formerly under the Peip'ing regional military commission, since promoted to the status of capital guards; former Nanking capital guards, which were transferred to Peking except for cadre battalions left behind at the former capital; and troops from princely guards and a few other demobilized units, which were moved to Peking and organized into new guards there.[32]

When the three Yen-shan princely guards and seven of the sixteen guards formerly under the Peip'ing regional military commission received imperial guard status and moved to Peking, they sent battalion-sized cadres to Nanking. By 1420 most of the troops of the twelve original guards of the personal army had been transferred from Nanking, leaving cadres behind. These units together were called the twenty-two superior guards and were under the direct command of the emperor. In Peking this personal army or imperial guard aggregated 159 battalions: 17 in the Chin-yi Guard, whose status as the principal secret-police agency continued under Yung-lo; 5 in the Ch'i-shou Guard, whose members specialized as artisans, making weapons and other military equipment; 25 in the Fu-chün Vanguard (*ch'ien-wei*), whose battalions had the task of training the young men born into the capital guards; and 112 in the nineteen other guards. Not included in the personal army, but still directly under the emperor, were six more guards, three transferred from the former Peip'ing regional military commission and three others newly formed from the troops of demobilized units elsewhere; men from these guards were regularly employed as construction gangs. In 1433 four more guards aggregating 32 battalions were organized from military families engaged in raising horses in the north. In 1424 a new guard was assigned to Yung-lo's tomb following the precedent of Hung-wu's tomb at Nanking, and at the death of every emperor thereafter a guard was transferred from the group of guards under the Chief Military Commission of the Rear and assigned to guard his tomb. All of these guards were in principle also under the emperor.[33]

In addition to the personal army, the group of guards at Nanking had contained twenty-nine other guards, each under the command authority of one of the five chief military commissions in the capital. By 1420 most of nineteen of these had been transferred to Peking and placed under the corresponding chief military commissions there. The guards left behind were primarily those that specialized in naval affairs, for which the new capital did not provide a convenient base. After further reorganizations the Nanking guards stabilized at seventeen guards of the personal army and thirty-two guards under the five Nanking chief military commissions, aggregating 118 battalions plus 2 independent battalions. At most, the ten guards not transferred to Peking, the guard at Hung-wu's tomb, and four other guards (including one in the personal army) that were either newly created or newly transferred to Nanking would have had their full complement of battalions; the other thirty-four were represented by skeletal establishments of one or two battalions each. The guards in the outlying cities of Nan Chihli, subordinate in Hung-wu's time to the Nanking Chief Military Commission of the Center, were now made subordinate to the same chief military commission at Peking, an organizational anomaly that underscores the vestigial nature of the Nanking governmental organs after Yung-lo.[34]

As Peip'ing province was being transformed into the northern metropolitan area, the Peking Chief Military Commission of the Rear took on the corresponding local command function for that area. When the Peip'ing regional military commission was abolished, those guards formerly under it that were not transferred to Peking as imperial guards remained in their original garrison cities, but were made subordinate to the Chief Military Commission of the Rear. When Yung-lo dispossessed his brother the prince of Ning, he transferred the headquarters of the Taning regional military commission to Paoting to take command of a new group of guards there; however, the guards formerly under Taning were mostly brought to Peking and also placed under the Chief Military Commission of the Rear. In the end the Army of the Rear included sixteen new guards made up of troops from former princely guards and other demobilized units who had been transferred to Peking; fully eleven of these later became mausoleum guards.[35]

The transferred and newly created capital guards did not account for all of the troops moved to the north as a result of Yung-lo's policies. Under the new Taning regional military commission at Paoting were five guards created in 1403 and six other guards created later, all including troops transferred from the interior of the country. In 1429 another regional military commission was created at Wanch'üan commanding fifteen guards; many of these troops were originally from the north, but further transfers from the south were needed to bring the units up to strength.[36]

As a result of the reorganizations during and immediately after the Yung-lo reign, the capital guards at Peking came to number seventy-four, whose distribution in 1435 was as follows: directly under the emperor were twenty-two guards (159 battalions) of the personal army, four guards (32 battalions) engaged in raising horses, six guards employed chiefly as construction workers, and two guards stationed at the tombs of Yung-lo and Hung-hsi; under the command of the five chief military commissions were nineteen guards transferred from Nanking; and under the command of the Chief Military Commission of the Rear were six guards transferred to Peking from other areas in the north, chiefly Taning, and fifteen new guards formed of troops from demobilized units.[37]

The extent of the population movement involved in these troop transfers can be roughly estimated. The first twenty-six of the guards listed above aggregated 191 battalions, and there were four additional independent battalions. No other discrete figures for the total number of battalions in the Peking capital guards are given, but the fact that there were so few battalions left in Nanking after the transfers suggests that the units came north with a full or nearly full complement of battalions. Furthermore, there is no evidence to suggest that the new units were created with less than the normal number of battalions. These circumstances permit an estimate of 240 battalions for the remaining forty-eight capital guards, making a grand total of 435. About 100 of these represent units already stationed in the north whose relocation in the city of Peking did not add to the population. Statistics previously cited (see pp. 80–81) suggest that Ming military units averaged some five-eighths of their nominal strength in the 1390's. If so, there were about 700 men per battalion, and so the approximately 335 battalions transferred (or formed out of transferred troops) brought at least 235,000 men, many with families, to the north and to Peking. However, the true figure was probably higher, since the new battalions probably began their existence at something like full nominal strength.[38]

All of Peip'ing province had a population of 1,926,595 in 1393. The Hung-chih period population figure for Shunt'ien prefecture alone is 669,033; due to the underreporting that was common by then, that figure should be taken as a lower limit for the Yung-lo period. It of course includes a large area surrounding the capital, but in any event, in the Ming from Yung-lo on, as under the Manchus, the troops stationed permanently in Peking formed a substantial portion both of the population of the capital and of the empire's total military establishment.[39]

The Peking capital training camps. The troops in the capital guards never constituted the whole of the garrison of Peking at any given time. In Yung-lo's reign the rotation of the wei-so troops between farming in their regular units and active duty on a detached basis, an irregular practice in the Hung-wu period, was made formal and routine. The result was to create a permanent split between the old wei-so units, thereafter confined to administrative functions connected with the registration of the military population and the management of the military colony lands, and the new organizations that controlled military training and operations, of which the most important were the capital training camps (*ching-ying*) and the nine border-defense commands (*chiu-pien*). All military formations were officered and manned by hereditary personnel from the wei-so units.

Yung-lo's failure to win decisive success in his earlier Mongolian campaigns led him to increase the scale of the later campaigns. In 1415, following the second campaign, the emperor ordered all the guards in the northern provinces and the southern metropolitan area to send contingents to Peking for training. The three principal capital training camps, called the Three Great Camps (*san ta ying*), were formed to organize these troops into combat units and give them combat training. Each camp was under the joint supervision of a eunuch and, usually, two nobles or other high-ranking generals, who were assisted by additional military officers in charge of the divisions and sections of the camp. Eunuch control of the camps lasted the rest of the Ming dynasty and provided the basis for the cooperation between eunuchs and nobles that often came to be directed against the civil service.[40]

The Three Great Camps were the Wu-chün (Five armies) Camp, the San-ch'ien (Three thousand) Camp, and the Shen-chi (Divine mechanisms) Camp. Though organized in a similar fashion, they performed different specialized tasks. When the prince of Yen rebelled in 1399, he organized his army into five divisions named the Chung-chün (Central army), Tso-yi and Yu-yi (Left and Right supports), Tso-shao and Yu-shao (Left and Right patrols), each under a general and two lieutenant generals, most of whom later became nobles. The much larger armies that Yung-lo later led into Mongolia were also organized in a more elaborate version of the same five-division pattern. The term *wu-chün* "five armies," which strictly speaking applied in Ming only to the five chief military commissions, came to be applied to the five divisions of the imperial expeditionary armies as well. The Wu-chün Camp thus had the primary task of organizing the inexperienced levies coming in from the provincial guards into an effective field army. This meant first assigning the men to the five divisions and their subunits, and then training these units in battlefield maneuvers. Organizing and training for combat, functions originally performed by the wei-so units themselves, were thus transferred in the Yung-lo reign to the first of the Three Great Camps.[41]

The other two camps supplemented the Wu-chün Camp. Three thousand Mongol horsemen who had defected were transferred to Peking and became the nucleus of the San-ch'ien Camp, which had responsibility for cavalry training, including such specialties as scouting and patrolling, and flag and drum signals.[42] Firearms had been important to a degree since the wars of the 1350's, but the Vietnam campaigns in the Yung-lo reign raised firearms technology to a new level of importance, due to Vietnamese proficiency in that branch of weaponry. Organized originally around captured and defected Vietnamese, the Shen-chi Camp had the primary task of training the troops in the use of firearms.[43] Since each of the five main divisions of an imperial expeditionary army included both mounted troops and troops armed with firearms, the internal organization of both the San-ch'ien Camp and the

Shen-chi Camp was generally parallel to that of the Wu-chün Camp.

One other capital training camp deserves brief mention. This was the Szu-wei (Four guards) Camp, staffed by troops drawn from the four guards that specialized in raising horses for the army.[44]

The nine border defense commands. Hung-wu's approach to the problem of frontier defense in the north had been to establish guards in strategic locations beyond the Great Wall in the hope that, with Chinese garrisons in their midst, Mongol tribes would be less likely to form hostile coalitions. Although Yung-lo at his accession pulled back most of these garrisons, the imperial expeditions on which he relied to keep the Mongols disunited grew increasingly expensive in proportion to the results achieved, and his successors did not continue them. Subsequent Mongol disunity was more a function of social disorganization than of positive Ming policy, and in exceptional cases Mongol coalitions controlling Inner Mongolia posed a significant threat to North China. Ming defenses after Yung-lo depended on the Great Wall.

Although the wall itself was scarcely intact throughout its fifteen-hundred-mile length, and the tribes in the vicinity were quite familiar with the places where it could easily be crossed, strong points along the wall were difficult to capture, and the beacon towers could usually be relied upon to give warning of invasion. Of course, the continued efficacy of the wall as a defense system depended on its being adequately manned by a well-organized force. The soldiers in the wall garrison were originally drawn exclusively from the nearby wei-so units, but in the Yung-lo reign the practice was introduced of having men first train in the capital training camps and then complete their tour of duty in the wall garrisons. As the wei-so soldiers gradually sank to the level of a class of peasants who were merely liable (not already trained) to serve in the military, those actually conscripted served longer and longer terms until they in effect constituted a long-service professional army.

The officers who commanded the border garrisons were also selected from among the regular military officers. The original Ming practice had been to give the commander of an offensive expeditionary army a general's commission descriptive of his assignment ("General Who Conquers the West" is an example).

Commanders of the border defense regions continued to receive such commissions even while performing entirely defensive roles, but they came to be known commonly by their more specific territorial designations as officers commanding troops (*tsung-ping kuan*). Each was assisted by one or more deputies (*fu tsung-ping kuan*) and by lesser officers bearing such titles as assistant commander (*ts'an-chiang*), patrol general (*yu-chi chiang-chün*), and so forth. These designations, originally conferred for a single campaign on officers whose rank and pay were determined by their place in their wei-so units or the regional or chief military commissions, eventually hardened into a fixed hierarchy of tactical commands. By the end of the dynasty the tactical commands, which then existed in every province, were the only military positions of consequence, and they rather than the wei-so units were the basis on which the Manchus organized their Chinese Green Standard Army.[45]

By 1435 the nine border commands (*chiu-pien*) that lasted the rest of the dynasty were in existence. From east to west they were: (1) Liaotung, corresponding to the Liaotung regional military commission's area of jurisdiction; (2) Chichou, east of Peking; (3) Hsüanfu, corresponding roughly to the area of the Wanch'üan regional military commission created in the Hsüan-te reign; (4) Tat'ung, corresponding to the Shansi branch regional military commission; (5) Shansi itself, at the provincial capital; (6) Yensui, located at Yülin and defending the area of Shensi immediately south of the Ordos; (7) Shensi itself, located at Kuyüan; (8) Ninghsia; and (9) Kansu, corresponding to the Shensi branch regional military commission.[46] Chichou, Yensui, and Ninghsia were created to command specific sectors of the wall; the other six did the same, but they also assumed the operational functions of the regional military commissions in their areas.

Eunuch Admirals and the Tributary Trade

Yung-lo's military expeditions and his attempt to conquer Vietnam both showed a conception of foreign relations radically different from Hung-wu's. Instead of attempting to preserve

Chinese society by sealing it off from both foreign invasion and foreign trade, Yung-lo followed a policy of active counteroffensive. As applied to Southeast Asia, where expectations of a revival of commerce with China had been dashed by Hung-wu in the 1370's, Yung-lo's active policy took the form of naval expeditions led by the eunuch admiral Cheng Ho. On seven occasions between 1405 and 1433 Chinese fleets visited the countries of East and Southeast Asia, and crossed the Indian Ocean to reach Ceylon, the Persian Gulf, and the East Coast of Africa. Although they resorted to force to gain their ends on a few occasions, the Chinese expeditions in general were peaceful, unlike the later Portuguese depredations. The Ming emperor was not interested in conquering or looting the countries reached by his fleet, but rather in exploring and expanding commerce and diplomatic relations within the tribute system. Rumors that Emperor Chien-wen had escaped and fled to Southeast Asia played a part in Yung-lo's decision to launch the expeditions.[47] The geographical knowledge derived from these expeditions was the basis of Chinese understanding of the maritime world until the nineteenth century (see the map on p. 196). The naval expeditions formed the main channel for the promotion of trade with the countries of the south, and tributary trade with Japan also was resumed—at Japanese initiative. For a while the diplomatic and commercial policies forbidden by Hung-wu were revived.

The first of the naval expeditions (1405–7) involved 27,800 men sailing in sixty-two great "treasure ships" (*pao-ch'uan*) of which the largest carried nine masts and were 440 feet in length and 180 feet in the beam. Sailing down the South China Sea, this fleet visited Champa and then Java before going on to Sumatra. There they found that the court and dynasty of Shrivijaya had deserted the harbor of Palembang, partly in response to the difficulties in the Malay world wrought by Hung-wu's policies. The harbor had been taken over by a Chinese pirate leader, Ch'en Tsu-yi, who made a surprise attack on Cheng Ho's ships but was himself captured and later sent to Nanking and executed. The fleet went on to visit Ceylon and Calicut on the western coast of India. The second expedition (1407–9) visited the same places and also Thailand and Cochin in India.[48]

By the time of the third expedition (1409–11) a regular pattern

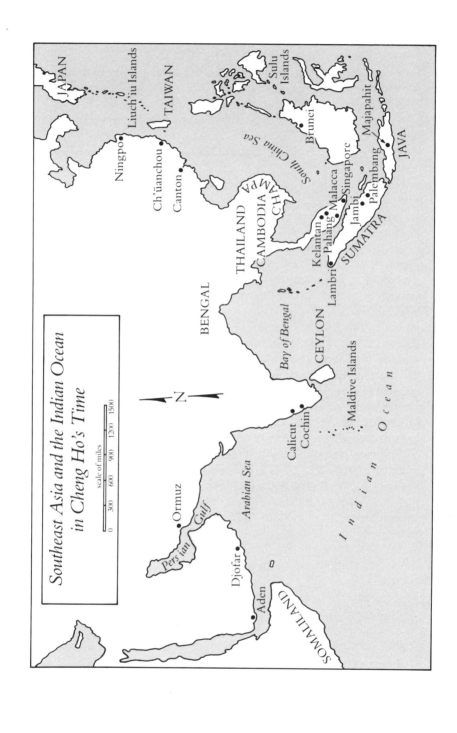

Southeast Asia and the Indian Ocean
in Cheng Ho's Time

scale of miles

0   300   600   900   1200   1500

JAPAN

Liuch'iu Islands

TAIWAN

Sulu
Islands

Brunei

Majapahit

JAVA

South China Sea

Ningpo

Ch'üanchou

Canton

Palembang

CHAMPA

Singapore

Malacca

Pahang

Jambi

SUMATRA

THAILAND

CAMBODIA

Kelantan

Lambri

BENGAL

Bay of Bengal

CEYLON

Maldive Islands

Calicut

Cochin

N

Arabian Sea

Indian   Ocean

Ormuz

Persian   Gulf

Djofar

Aden

SOMALILAND

of visits had been established, with the fleets using Malacca as their base and dividing into squadrons assigned to particular missions. This expedition visited the same places as the previous two, plus Quilon in southwestern India. In Ceylon in 1410, the main body of the expedition ran into trouble. Cheng Ho and his guards were lured into the interior by the Sinhalese king, who demanded exorbitant presents and sent troops to attack the Chinese ships. Undaunted, Cheng Ho pushed on and took the capital, captured the offending monarch, and defeated his army. The king was taken to Nanking and treated kindly there, though the Chinese insisted on his being replaced as ruler by his cousin.[49]

The fourth expedition (1413–15) made stops at the Southeast Asian countries visited previously. At Lambri in northwestern Sumatra, Cheng Ho's troops fought and captured Sekandar, a pretender to the local throne who was dissatisfied with his share of the Chinese gifts. He was sent to Nanking and ultimately executed; this was the last incident involving the use of force in the history of the Ming naval expeditions. However, the main objective of the fourth expedition was the further exploration of the Indian Ocean. The main fleet based itself on Ceylon, and squadrons were sent to Bengal, the Maldives, and throughout the Arabian Sea as far as the sultanate of Ormuz on the Persian Gulf. The prosperity of the many city-states of the Arabian peninsula and the east coast of Africa depended on maritime trade, which in turn depended on normal patterns of West Asian commerce that had not yet recovered from the disruptions caused by the career of Tamerlane. The news of the Chinese armada in Indian waters caused the rulers of these city-states to apprehend danger even as they hoped for an expansion of trade. Their response was to send ambassadors, who converged upon Nanking in a swarm in 1416.[50]

Returning these ambassadors to their homes provided the occasion for a fifth expedition (1417–19), whose ships visited the Liuch'ius, Brunei, and the usual Southeast Asian countries before sailing into the Indian Ocean and exploring the Arabian coast from Ormuz to Aden and the African coast from Somaliland to Zanzibar. It was on this voyage that giraffes were brought back for the emperor's zoo; they were identified with the mythical *ch'i-lin* beast, whose appearance was a sign of good government.[51] The sixth expedition (1421–22) also concentrated its attentions on the

Arabian and African coasts.[52] Thus, by the death of Yung-lo in 1424 the naval voyages based on Nanking under eunuch leadership had developed into an ongoing enterprise, as had the military expeditions from Peking into Mongolia. Yung-lo's successor, Hung-hsi, reversed both programs, cancelling the voyage scheduled for 1424, but his successor Hsüan-te allowed Cheng Ho to lead a seventh and final voyage (1431–33) before retiring honorably as military commandant (*shou-pei*) of Nanking.

Chinese naval capabilities had been highly developed for three centuries preceding the Yung-lo reign, ever since the great Southern Sung emperor Kao-tsung (r. 1126–62)—intent on patching together a regime from the debris left behind by the Jurchen invasions—removed himself to Hangchow, resolved to make the taxation of maritime trade one of the pillars of his empire, and so created a navy. This navy grew to control the East China Sea, and its ability to defend the Yangtze River and assure communications with Korea was a major factor in the successful resistance of the Southern Sung to Jurchen attack. The Yüan emperor Qubilai inherited this naval capability when he conquered the Southern Sung, and he employed it to launch expeditions aimed at the conquest of Japan (1274 and 1281), Champa (1282), the Liuch'ius (1291), and Java (1292). These expeditions were consistent failures, but they were several times more numerous in ships and men than any of Cheng Ho's voyages.[53] Although they had possessed the organizational and technical abilities for a long time, it was nevertheless only in the Yung-lo reign that the Chinese were motivated to launch Cheng Ho's powerful but peaceful naval expeditions.

Yung-lo's motivations in launching the voyages were twofold. First, he was never certain that the charred corpse found among the ruins of the Nanking imperial palace in 1402 really was that of Emperor Chien-wen. Rumors that Chien-wen had escaped grew quickly into folk legends, and as late as 1440 a man was executed and his accomplices exiled because he claimed to be Chien-wen. The most persistent rumor had Chien-wen escaping Nanking in the guise of an itinerant Buddhist monk and fleeing to Southeast Asia, so Cheng Ho was ordered to search there for news of him. This was not the sole motive for the expeditions, but it explains the timing of the first one. After about two years on the throne, whose

seizure even his most ingenious advisers could not justify ideologically, Yung-lo faced up to the fact that legends concerning Chien-
wen's escape were spreading among the population and sent
Cheng Ho to find out the truth.[54]

Second, Yung-lo was motivated by diplomatic, commercial,
and explorational interests that were never clearly differentiated,
but that became dominant as the expeditions progressed. Yung-lo,
born in 1360, went to his northern fief only in 1380; before then he
was in Nanking, a witness to the heyday of early Ming trade with
Southeast Asia. Naturally no record of his personal impressions
survives, but the sight of foreign ambassadors bringing exotic
wares as tribute evidently made a deep impression on him, and to
the end of his life he was always pleased to receive strange things
from distant lands. Beyond that, Yung-lo's intentional reversal of
the generally passive and isolationist foreign policies of his father's
later years implied an active search for diplomatic relationships as
well. The show of submission required of countries desiring to
enter into diplomatic relations quite frankly dramatized the superior majesty and power of the Chinese emperor, but many foreign
countries were happy to accept this precondition in order to
increase their trade.

In Southeast Asia the Ming expeditions visited the mainland
countries and Majapahit on Java, all of which had for political
reasons sent tribute more or less regularly during the Hung-wu
period. By demonstrating the scale of Chinese naval power and
securing new statements of submission from these kingdoms,
Cheng Ho's armada laid the foundations for a revival of the China
trade carried on by the maritime Malay principalities within the
tributary system. Majapahit and Thailand were ordered not to
interfere, and states such as Sulu and Brunei, Pahang and Kelantan
on the Malay Peninsula, and Jambi and Lambri on Sumatra now
sent envoys directly to the Ming court. But the most important
state in this category was Malacca, where the former dynasty of
Shrivijaya had removed itself in 1401 (turning Moslem in the
process), after a stay at Singapore. A Chinese diplomatic mission
headed by the eunuch Yin Ch'ing in 1403 led to Malaccan friendship throughout the period of the naval voyages. The Ming fleets
based themselves on Malacca, and in 1411 the ruler of Malacca
came to Nanking in person. Under the Chinese umbrella, Malac-

can sea power grew, and after the cessation of the Chinese voyages, Malacca maintained control of the straits, naval hegemony in the South China Sea, and a predominant position in the trade with China. The peace provided by Malaccan hegemony in turn provided an opportunity for Chinese merchants to trade throughout Southeast Asia—and for Chinese emigrants to settle—even after the Ming government withdrew from the naval scene.[55]

As the attention of Cheng Ho's expeditions shifted westward into Indian and then African waters, exploration instead of commerce or diplomacy became the driving force. Here the Chinese, like the Europeans later in the century, entered areas about which nothing was known and of which anything could be believed. Medical doctors accompanied the voyages and, especially in Africa, compiled catalogues and collected examples of plants and animals and gems and minerals, some for use as medicines, others merely as objects of wonder. Yung-lo's infatuation with this aspect of the voyages roused the stuffy Confucian intellectuals into paroxysms of peevishness. Reciting the same arguments used by Han Yü in the ninth century, they held that the emperor's quest for strange and useless foreign things portended the collapse of the Ming empire. In view of the seemingly clear precedent afforded by the T'ang, the Confucian position was bitter and nonnegotiable; hostility toward the eunuch establishment that was managing the voyages merely intensified their already hard ideological stance. The voyages were doomed the moment the Confucians gained a clear ascendancy in the state.[56]

Confucian hostility later resulted in the deliberate destruction of the plans for Cheng Ho's treasure ships. The official Ming history gives the dimensions of the largest, the nine-masted "treasure ships," as 440 feet long and 180 feet in the beam; the second largest, the eight-masted "horse ships" (*ma-ch'uan*), are described in another source as 370 feet long and 150 feet in the beam. The accuracy of these figures was confirmed in 1962 when the excavation of the Lung-chiang shipyard at Nanking turned up the rudderpost of one of the treasure ships; calculations based on its measurements yielded even larger dimensions for the ships than those given in the sources. They suggest shallow draft vessels with flat bottoms and watertight bulkheads, and without the keel-and-frame construction that imposed smaller size limits on western wooden ships. A displacement of 3,100 tons has been suggested for the treasure ships, which are said to have carried between 450 and 500 men, not an excessive complement for such a large ship; if the number refers to the military personnel manning the ship, there would have been much additional space for passengers and cargo. The 27,800 men of the first expedition, when divided among its sixty-two ships, yields almost exactly 450 men per ship, so the treasure ships and other large classes may have predominated in the Cheng Ho fleets. The treasure ships were three decks high at the stern, which calls to mind Ch'en Yu-liang's river warships of 1363, but the Chinese had been sailing the seas in great ships capable of carrying several hundred men since the days of Marco Polo and before.[57]

The ships employed in the Cheng Ho voyages were built in the Lung-chiang shipyard in Nanking, were manned by troops from the Nanking guards, and sailed under the direction of the court eunuchs. The voyages are the most spectacular example of Yung-lo's use of eunuchs to supervise and military personnel to carry out large-scale activities, particularly of the sort disapproved of by Confucian opinion. Other examples include the refurbishing of Peking and the management of the timber-cutting operations in the southwest that provided lumber for both palaces and fleets.[58]

The site of the Lung-chiang shipyard, hard by the wall of Nanking on the Ch'inhuai River, had been the headquarters of Ming naval activities since the capture of Nanking in 1356 and the creation of the Ch'inhuai wing soon afterwards. From 1403 on shipbuilding was a high priority matter and between then and 1419 the Lung-chiang shipyard, aided by other yards in Chekiang, Fukien, and Kwangtung, built a total of 2,149 seagoing vessels of all types, including 94 treasure ships of the large type described above; it also converted 381 freighters of the oceangoing grain-transport service for service in Indian and African waters. At the peak of this activity, Taoists were ordered to select auspicious days for beginning new construction, and the best artisans were posted to the shipyards from all other projects. In 1420 the shipyards were placed under a new administrative agency called the Ta-t'ung-kuan superintendency (*t'i-chü-szu*).[59]

After 1419 very few seagoing ships were constructed, and the subsequent expeditions were carried out by already existing vessels. Having laid firm foundations for high-seas naval power, Yung-lo spent the last several years of his reign undermining them. In 1411 Sung Li finished the section of the Grand Canal from the Yellow River to Peking, and until 1415 canal and oceangoing transport of grain to the north coexisted. However, in 1415 ocean transport was suspended, and Ch'en Hsüan, earl of P'ingchiang, was ordered to build three thousand grain transports for use on the Grand Canal. The regime no longer had an economic need to maintain a deep-water fleet, a need that the oceangoing grain-transport system had provided. The connection between that system and the revival of naval expeditions was not lost on the civil officials, who thereafter consistently opposed the revival of oceangoing grain transport.[60]

The Ming navy was not sharply distinguished institutionally from the army; ships were assigned as part of the regular military equipment of guards and battalions located along coasts or rivers. As of 1420 an estimated 1,350 small patrol craft and an equal number of large warships were distributed among the appropriate provincial garrisons. These were backed up by a main fleet, based in the Nanking area, composed of about four hundred large warships and four hundred grain freighters plus two hundred fifty treasure ships and other large vessels used in Cheng Ho's voyages. Presumably many of these were laid up at any given time, but the ships in commission were manned largely by troops from the Nanking garrison. Of the ten guards under the chief military commissions at Nanking that were not transferred to Peking, four bear names that show that they specialized in naval affairs.* Virtually all of the Nanking guards were still operating at least a few ships even as late as the sixteenth century, and the men in the Nanking garrison who were not skilled as sailors would nevertheless have been useful as marines. Even after the 1420 troop transfers the strength of the Nanking garrison was eighty thousand men or more, easily sufficient to provide the personnel for the Cheng Ho voyages, though levies from the provincial garrisons probably participated as well.[61]

Cheng Ho's fleets were of a size that would have required a

---

* The four were the Right and Left Shui-chün ("Marine Forces") Guards, the Kuang-yang ("Ocean-covering") Guard, and the Heng-hai ("Sea-spanning") Guard.

noble as commander during the Hung-wu period. Although Hung-wu was willing to use eunuchs in confidential assignments, and Yung-lo had begun the practice of assigning eunuchs to some of the military command positions usually reserved for nobles, even in this respect the fleets were exceptional. In the great camps and the regional defense commands the eunuchs shared control with nobles, and in the field armies the nobles predominated, but in the fleets eunuchs' control was not qualified by the presence of nobles or military officers higher in rank than regional military commissioner. Both the main fleet and its squadrons were led by eunuchs, and in addition to Cheng Ho, who was accredited as the emperor's envoy to the various countries he visited, numerous lesser eunuch envoys led diplomatic missions to the other states in the region. These eunuchs were always grand directors (*t'ai-chien*) in the twenty-four offices into which the eunuch establishment had been organized during the Yung-lo reign. Eunuch control over the fleets was paralleled by eunuch control over the Nanking garrison. The absence of the emperor on his Mongolian campaigns and the withdrawal of his eldest son and eldest grandson to Peking in 1420 had left the Nanking chief military commissions and the guards of the emperor's personal army, all nominally directly under the emperor, in fact without any common superior in the city. The gap was filled by creating the position of military commandant to take charge of the forces at Nanking in lieu of the emperor. Though often held by a noble, the position was also often held by a eunuch, especially in the early period. The naval voyages and the Nanking establishment that supported them were eunuch-managed to an extent that was unusual even in the Yung-lo reign.[62]

The voyages were only one instance of Yung-lo's generally positive approach to foreign contacts and foreign trade. Outside the framework of the voyages, relations with Japan were resumed and a degree of friendship established with Tamerlane's successor Shāhrukh, while tributary missions from Korea and the Liuch'ius continued to be received.[63]

Despite Hung-wu's severance of diplomatic relations with Japan, both the Ashikaga and the Southern Court continued to send envoys to Ming China. In 1399 Yoshimitsu, the third Ashikaga shogun, established his authority firmly over western

Japan by conquering the Ōuchi clan, so that henceforth a single authority spoke for Japan. The shogun also was much less concerned than Prince Kanenaga had been to uphold the dignity of the Japanese imperial house. A Japanese mission bearing a suitably respectful letter arrived at the court of Chien-wen in 1401 and ended the coldness hitherto prevailing in Ming-Japanese relations. A Chinese mission in response reached Japan in 1402. The following year Yoshimitsu sent a large embassy of over three hundred persons bearing a letter in which the shogun described himself as "your subject, the King of Japan."[64]

When the embassy arrived at Nanking, Yung-lo was already established as emperor. One of his first acts had been to reopen the maritime trading superintendencies (*shih-po t'i-chü szu*) at Ningpo, Ch'üanchou, and Canton. Approving the contents of the Japanese letter, Yung-lo ordered Chao Chü-jen to go to Japan to negotiate a commercial treaty. His objectives were to end Japanese piracy by suppressing the long-illegal private trade from which it sprang, while at the same time providing for the expansion of trade through official diplomatic channels. These goals were accomplished by permitting trade only to Japanese missions carrying specially prepared tallies that matched stubs kept by the Chinese authorities. Under the resulting tally (*k'an-ho*, Japanese *kangō*) system, Japanese missions were to land at Ningpo, were to consist of not more than two ships and two hundred persons, were not to carry weapons, and were to be sent only once every ten years. However, the last provision was ignored completely in the next several years.[65]

Between 1404 and 1410 missions went between China and Japan on approximately an annual basis. Japanese tribute was matched by lavish Chinese gifts, and repeated edicts from Yung-lo praised Yoshimitsu for his loyalty. Keeping their side of the bargain, the Ashikaga authorities arrested Japanese pirates and presented them to the Chinese court. This was the central problem from the Chinese point of view; after all, the Japanese were scarcely as exotic as either the Southeast Asians or the recently discovered African countries. When Yoshimitsu died in 1408, Yung-lo first sent letters containing elaborate eulogies of his accomplishments, and then sent an injunction to the succeeding shogun, Yoshimochi, to continue to suppress piracy. For the next two years Yoshimochi continued to send and receive missions in conformity with the pattern set by his father.[66]

However, when Yoshimochi refused even to receive the Chinese mission of 1411, it was evident that Japanese policy had been reversed. For the next six years Japan sent no tribute missions, and the Chinese for their part declined to risk a further rebuff. In Yoshimochi's later decree breaking off relations completely, he blamed Kenchū Keimei, the leader of several of the Japanese missions, for misrepresenting the Japanese position. Kenchū, abbot of Tenryūji and a fervent admirer of Chinese culture, either died or lost his influence with the shogun about this time. For the next six years there were no official relations between China and Japan.[67]

When Chinese troops captured a few score Japanese pirates in 1417, Yung-lo used this as a pretext to attempt a reopening of relations. He sent the prisoners back to Japan under the custody of a junior official of the Ministry of Justice, Lü Yüan, who bore a letter referring to Yoshimochi as "King of Japan" that reprimanded him for failure to control the pirates. Lü Yüan's mission was a failure, which he attempted to disguise by bringing back an embassy from Shimazu Hisatoyo, grandson of the Shimazu daimyo of western Japan who had tried to deal directly with Hung-wu four decades previously. This mission was an expression of the long-standing Shimazu interest in trade with China (whether legal or piratical), but Yung-lo accepted the pretense that it came from the Ashikaga, and late the following year he sent Lü Yüan on a return mission to Japan. Lü Yüan succeeded in presenting his emperor's letter to Yoshimochi in 1419, but the shogun's response was uncompromising: relations with foreign countries were prohibited by the gods of Japan, Yoshimitsu had been misled by his advisers, and the shogun was not responsible for the activities of Japanese pirates. There were no more official contacts between China and Japan in the Yung-lo reign.[68]

Relations with other countries presented fewer problems and less Chinese effort, unless war actually broke out. The Liuch'ius had broken up into three kingdoms, all of which vied with one another in sending envoys to the Chinese court throughout the Yung-lo reign, but Yung-lo was not moved to intervene militarily or diplomatically in favor of any of them.[69]

Tamerlane's son Shāhrūkh did not continue his father's invasion of Ming China, but on the contrary was preoccupied with maintaining the core of the Timūrid empire in Transoxiana. Yung-lo, similarly preoccupied with the Eastern Mongols, had no desire for conflict with Shāhrūkh. After an exchange of letters in which the Ming emperor addressed the Timūrid sultan on nearly equal terms, peaceful relations between the two monarchs were uninterrupted. The Ming sources for the Yung-lo reign record a steady sequence of tribute missions from Samarkand (that is, from Shāhrūkh), from Herat and other cities in Khūrasan, and from Khotan, Khoja, Hami, and the other Central Asian oasis cities traditionally involved in trading patterns along the Silk Road. In fact, the Ming military presence did not reach that far west, and these tribute missions somewhat transparently disguised the fact that the traditional caravan trade was coming more and more under Chinese government supervision as it grew in volume.[70]

In 1406 Yung-lo ordered the establishment of additional horse markets on the northern frontier in order to revive the tea and horse trade, which Hung-wu had first established but had allowed to fall into decay. Under this system Chinese tea was exchanged for barbarian horses at stations controlled by Chinese officials; the profits went, in theory, to the Ming regime.[71]

Vietnam

Yung-lo's attempt to emulate his father by annexing further territory in the southwest led the Ming empire into an overly ambitious attempt to assimilate the Vietnamese nation, which resulted in the worst political and military disaster of the early Ming period. An intervention based on false premises led to a massive commitment of resources, which then turned into a vested interest in maintaining the Chinese presence. Only after twenty expensive years did the Ming government write off the Vietnam adventure.

The Vietnam imbroglio was rooted in the ambiguous cultural relationship between Vietnam and China, wherein Vietnam borrowed her culture from China but, in contrast to Korea and the Liuch'ius, merely feigned acceptance of the Chinese political supremacy that act implied.[72] Vietnamese leaders believed that they could manipulate Chinese policy for their own purposes, and the

Vietnamese fourteenth-century dynastic crisis unfortunately came to a head just as there came to the Ming throne an emperor disposed by temperament to intervene.

A Vietnamese state had come into existence in the Red River valley as part of the wreckage of the T'ang empire in the tenth century. When the other South China kingdoms were absorbed by the Sung, Vietnam remained independent. Chinese institutions superimposed on the native language and culture gave Vietnam the cohesion and strength necessary for expansion to the south at the expense of backward tribal peoples and the Hinduized kingdom of Champa, while ritual observance of the tribute system generally preserved Vietnam from Chinese invasion. The Tran dynasty had ruled since 1225. Repeated Mongol invasions between 1257 and 1287 under the Yüan emperor Qubilai were repelled by the Tran rulers, but at heavy cost. Consequently, unlike the peoples of southwestern China, the Tran welcomed the rise of the Ming empire, entered into relations with it in 1369, and received the title of king of Annam from Hung-wu. By the death of Hung-wu the Tran were firmly implanted in the Chinese official mind and in the tribute lists as the legitimate rulers of Vietnam.[73]

The passing away of Mongol military activism allowed the Tran to resume their wars with Champa after 1312, wars that continued after the founding of the Ming dynasty despite Cham diplomatic attempts to secure Ming intervention. They were accompanied by intrigues and usurpations within the Tran royal family that ended only in 1388 when Le Qui Ly, a leading general and minister, murdered the king and seized authority. To facilitate relations with China, Le Qui Ly ruled through a succession of puppet Tran monarchs. However, in 1400, while all China was distracted by the civil war, Le Qui Ly deposed the Tran ruler, proclaimed himself king, and then abdicated in favor of his son. In 1403 he sent envoys to the new Ming emperor Yung-lo asking for formal recognition of his son as king; the request was duly investigated and granted that winter.[74]

In 1404 a refugee claiming to be a prince of the Tran family arrived in China and persuaded the Ming government of his claim to Vietnam's throne. The following year Yung-lo sent an edict reprimanding Le Qui Ly. The latter, having spent nearly two decades exterminating the Tran family, had reason to doubt the pretender's claim, but he sent back a letter confessing his crimes and agreeing to receive the pretender as king. In the spring of 1406 the pretender, bearing Ming documents appointing him king of Annam and Le Qui Ly's son a duke, entered Vietnam with a Chinese military escort of five thousand men. Their hand forced, Le Qui Ly's partisans ambushed and defeated the Chinese force and killed the pretender.[75]

The action of the Le rulers was motivated by desperation, but since Ming troops had been attacked and his own orders flouted, there was no chance that Yung-lo would ignore the affront. He at once went into consultation with his military chiefs, and in the autumn he appointed Chu Neng, duke of Ch'eng, as general in command of an expedition against Vietnam. Chang Fu and Mu Sheng were the lieutenant generals; Chang was the son of the civil war general Chang Yü, and Mu represented the tradition of expertise in southwestern military affairs begun by his father Mu Ying. Two other nobles were assigned to the army, and three high-ranking civil officials took charge of provisions and other administrative matters. Chu Neng died before the start of the campaign, and the emperor assigned the supreme command to Chang Fu.[76]

In the winter Chang Fu's army invaded Vietnam, joined forces with Mu Sheng's troops from Yünnan, and in the subsequent campaign demonstrated that the Chinese had not forgotten the techniques of siege and river warfare that had been so instrumental in the founding of the Ming dynasty. In eight days the two Vietnamese capitals and the other major towns of the Red River delta were captured, and the Le leaders fled by sea to raise new armies in the southern provinces. Chang Fu spent the next six months hunting them down. He defeated them in three pitched battles, in the last of which Le Qui Ly and his son were captured and sent to Nanking. It seemed that Vietnam had been conquered easily, and that the Chinese armies had shown themselves superior to the Vietnamese not merely in numbers but also in their mastery of advanced military techniques.[77]

In the sixth lunar month of 1407 Yung-lo proclaimed the conquest of Vietnam and ordered it annexed as a new province, for which he revived the Han dynasty designation, Chiaochih. He was so confident that Chiaochih was pacified that he ordered Chang Fu's army to Kwangsi to assist in quelling a disturbance there. The new regional military commission in Chiaochih was placed under an assistant chief commissioner; he and his second in command had been the leaders of the Chinese force escorting the Tran pretender at the time of his death. The provincial administration commissionerships went to a former minister of works and a former deputy administration commissioner of Fukien, while a former surveillance commissioner of Honan was appointed surveillance commissioner. Huang Fu, one of the ministers who had accompanied the expeditionary army, was left in Chiaochih with supervisory authority over the administration and surveillance commissioners. The existing local units were reorganized into 15 prefectures, 5 independent departments, and 36 departments controlling a total of 210 districts. The first census (1408) showed a total pacified population of about 3,120,000 together with an unsinicized tribal population of 2,087,500. Chiaochih, in other words, seemed to resemble provinces like Kwangsi and Yünnan, where the non-Chinese population tended to be rebellious to the degree that it was unsinicized. In the autumn of 1408 Chang Fu and Mu Sheng traveled to the capital and were created dukes.[78]

Establishment of the province of Chiaochih implied that Chinese would be the language of administration and that the law of avoidance, under which officials could not serve in the province of their birth, would apply as elsewhere in the empire. Educated Vietnamese might in principle take the examinations and serve in other provinces; here the parallel was the relatively successful assimilation of Yünnan, which had coincidently (1408) developed to the point that provincial examinations were ordered held there.

But the idea that the sinicized Vietnamese would welcome incorporation in the only civilized empire—no matter how reasonable from the perspective of Nanking—ignored the strength of the historical traditions of Vietnamese independence and their hostility toward Chinese overlordship. Although Korea might view China as a mentor in civilization and as an ally against a common nomadic peril, Vietnam could handle her other neighbors by herself, if only China would leave her alone. More immediately, the native mandarin class resented their confinement to the lower levels of office and power.

In 1408 Tran Nguy, a former Tran official, raised the flag of rebellion, proclaimed the kingdom of Dai Viet, and captured the prefectural city of Nghe An and other places. One month after being created duke of Ch'ien, Mu Sheng was ordered south with an army of 40,000 men to suppress him. On 9 January 1409 Mu Sheng did battle with Tran Nguy and was completely routed. Mu escaped with his life, but the minister Liu Chun, who was accompanying the army to handle supply and administrative matters, was killed, as were the regional military commissioner and others. This news did not delay the emperor's northern tour, and on the day of his departure (23 February) he ordered Chang Fu and Wang Yu (created marquis in 1408) to raise 47,000 men from the southern coastal provinces to crush Tran Nguy.[79]

Chang Fu held that Tran Nguy's successes to date had been due to his skillful use of seapower, which the Chinese could match. He prepared carefully, building ships and making deals with coastal pirates, before moving. In the autumn the Chinese fleet moved south, taking Thanh Hoa, Nghe An, and the lesser coastal cities, and twice defeated Tran Nguy's forces. To gain popular support, Tran Nguy proclaimed as emperor of Vietnam his own Tran pretender, Tran Qui Khoang, taking for himself the title of abdicated emperor. However, on 16 December Chang Fu defeated and captured Tran Nguy and sent him to China for execution. Tran Qui Khoang was still free, so Chang Fu proposed that Mu Sheng be left in command with a strengthened garrison to deal with him.[80]

Mu Sheng's operations led Tran Qui Khoang's supporters to ask to surrender. Yung-lo offered Tran the title of administration commissioner of Chiaochih, but the Vietnamese wanted Tran recognized as king of Annam, so they rejected the emperor's offer, and the war continued. Once again reinforcement became necessary. Early in 1411 Chang Fu was sent back with 24,000 men, this time to serve as Mu Sheng's deputy. Chang Fu's basic approach was to use a strong fleet to move his troops down the coast, trapping the Vietnamese rebels in the rivermouth harbor towns that served them as bases. Mu Sheng cooperated by marching on land in parallel with Chang's fleet. In the autumn and winter of 1411 Chang Fu won two victories: he captured important prisoners and retook Nghe An. Still the rebellion continued. More Chinese troops were sent, this time from Kwangsi. In the autumn of 1412 Chang Fu won another battle, but it required a final battle on 29 December 1413 to break the back of the rebellion. Mopping-up operations took three more months, but on 30 March 1414 Tran Qui Khoang was finally captured and Chiaochih once again seemed pacified. Most of the Chinese troops were withdrawn the following year. Chang Fu remained in command, but in 1416 he too was summoned back.[81]

Chang's successor Li Pin, marquis of Fengch'eng, was appointed on 26 February 1417. Soon afterwards Chiaochih sent its first contingent of students to the national university at the capital. However, Vietnamese acceptance of assimilation was only superficial. At the time, palace construction in Peking and shipbuilding in the navy yards at Nanking and elsewhere had created a tremendous demand for timber. Timber-cutting operations were under the control of the palace eunuchs, despite the protests of the civil officials, and because of the deforestation of the long-settled Chinese provinces, a disproportionate share of the burden of providing timber fell on the provinces with large non-Chinese populations. The eunuch Ma Ch'i was in charge of timber cutting in Vietnam, and his exactions apparently alienated most of the educated Vietnamese holding minor local office.[82] This class, which already resented their exclusion from major offices and honors and had provided the leadership for the previous rebellions, was an indispensable intermediary between the Chinese officials and the Vietnamese common people.

The Peking palaces were finished in April 1417, but in the next six months Li Pin had to deal with two local rebellions, both of which he crushed, beheading the leaders. Two more rebellions broke out at the beginning of 1418, and this time their leaders remained at large, even though the Chinese commanders claimed victories. Le Lo'i of the coastal city of Thanh Hoa was the most important rebel leader to emerge at this time. In the summer of 1419 he was defeated again, this time by the chief commissioner, Fang Cheng, but he still survived. The Ming government did not suspect that these outbreaks were more significant than the sporadic battles that were common in the southwest. In the autumn Ma Ch'i went to Chiaochih to speed up timber deliveries, and at that point the Vietnamese prefect of Nghe An rebelled.[83]

The entire coastal region south of the Red River delta was ablaze, and the Vietnamese officials who had surrendered and received local positions as part of the settlement of the Tran Qui Khoang rebellion were now leading the new rebellions. Chang Fu, the one Ming general who had been consistently successful fighting the Vietnamese, was now wasting his time accompanying Yung-lo on his northern promenades. Li Pin defeated Le Lo'i at the beginning of 1420, but again Le Lo'i escaped. Later in the year the rebels won a victory, and then Le Lo'i was defeated once again by Fang Cheng. By now a classic guerrilla warfare situation had developed. The Chinese armies could beat Le Lo'i whenever they could catch him, but Le Lo'i increasingly won the support of the Vietnamese countryside.[84]

Yung-lo, by now largely preoccupied with the north, gave only marginal attention to Vietnam. In 1421 he ordered the establishment of military colonies there. In 1422 Li Pin died. His successor was Ch'en Chih, earl of Yungch'ang, who inflicted another defeat on Le Lo'i at the beginning of 1423. Le Lo'i once again escaped, and his power base was intact when Yung-lo died.[85]

The Grand Secretariat: Confucians on the Rise

In contrast to the rapid official turnover and institutional fluctuations of the Hung-wu period, the higher levels of the civil administration under Yung-lo were dominated by a comparatively small number of officials who served long terms. Yung-lo trusted his ministers and the civil service, and although he occasionally removed and imprisoned individual officials for showing opposition, there was none of the purge atmosphere that had been common under Hung-wu. Instead of trying to force his officials to perform tasks distasteful to Confucian ideology, Yung-lo entrusted such assignments to eunuchs and military officers, leaving the civil officials undisturbed in their management of the financial, judicial, and other routine aspects of administration. As a result, the atomization of the civil service that had prevailed under Hung-wu ended, and the burden of administrative detail bore less heavily on the emperor. However, this also meant that the civil service coalesced into a political body that was animated by a stronger sense of continuity and purpose than any other elite group in the

Ming empire, and that was able to oppose Yung-lo and to over-awe his successors.

The rise of the Grand Secretariat (*nei-ko*) was the most important sign of these changes. The ministers heading the Six Ministries aided the grand secretaries in the capital, and the provincial governorships that emerged out of the Censorate performed a similar function in the provinces. The cohesion of the civil service around Confucian principles was further advanced by the examination system, which every three years produced a new crop of classically indoctrinated chin-shih ready to begin service as officials.

The Grand Secretariat originated in 1382 when several officials entitled grand secretary (*ta hsüeh-shih*, rank 5a) were added to the Han-lin Academy. Their Chinese title indicated literary and educational functions, but Hung-wu, overburdened with detail since 1380, began to use the grand secretaries to help him in drafting documents. Each was assigned to one of the halls (*tien* or *ko*) within the palace compound, and from this position of privileged access to the emperor the grand secretaries rose from clerks into great ministers of state as the Han masters of writing (*shang-shu*) had risen to preside over the Six Ministries centuries before.[86] Of course, under Hung-wu the role of the Grand Secretariat remained purely instrumental.

When Yung-lo seized the throne in 1402 he appointed seven new grand secretaries, but no more until 1425. He gave his grand secretaries concurrent appointments in the household of the crown prince, and when he set out for the north in 1409, he left the crown prince in control of the government, designating as his advisers Grand Secretaries Huang Huai (chin-shih 1397) and Yang Shih-ch'i, Minister of Personnel Chien Yi, and Minister of War Chin Chung. This pattern of imperial absence coupled with government by the crown prince in council became normal in the later Yung-lo years, so that by Yung-lo's death the Grand Secretariat had evolved into a governing cabinet. The new emperor, Hung-hsi, recognized this situation by granting the grand secretaries honorific titles higher in rank than the ministers of the Six Ministries. The crown prince also developed close personal relationships and a community of viewpoint with the grand secretaries, becoming in effect a spokesman for the Confucian position within the imperial family. This had direct political consequences, both before and after 1424.[87]

Four of the seven grand secretaries appointed in 1402 served continuously until their deaths. They were Hu Kuang (d. 1418), Chin Yu-tzu (chin-shih 1400, d. 1431), Yang Jung (chin-shih 1400, d. 1440) and Yang Shih-ch'i (d. 1444). During the first years of the Yung-lo period the leading personality in the Grand Secretariat was Hsieh Chin (chin-shih 1388). At this time Yung-lo cared more for his younger son Kao-hsü, prince of Han, who had accompanied him and commanded troops successfully during the civil war, than for his eldest son, the crown prince. Hsieh Chin argued successfully against making Kao-hsü crown prince, thus alienating Kao-hsü completely and somewhat estranging himself from the emperor. When he later opposed the Vietnam war, this estrangement became complete, and in 1407 Yung-lo in effect banished him by appointing him assistant administration commissioner of Kwangsi (technically a promotion from rank 5a to 4b) and later transferring him to Chiaochih. However, Kao-hsü accused him of intriguing with the crown prince. As a result, Hsieh Chin was imprisoned in 1411 and then murdered in 1415 at the orders of Chi Kang, commander of the Chin-yi Guard. Rivalries among Yung-lo's sons were also responsible for the downfall of Grand Secretary Huang Huai. When Yung-lo returned from his second northern expedition in 1414, Kao-hsü used a minor protocol error to denounce the crown prince's conduct of the government. Yung-lo then imprisoned Huang Huai along with Yang Shih-ch'i and the future grand secretary Yang P'u (chin-shih 1400, d. 1446). Yang Shih-ch'i was released almost at once, but the others languished in prison until 1424. In 1417 Kao-hsü was exiled to his fief in Shantung, and his henchman Chi Kang was executed; both measures enhanced the security of the crown prince and the stability of the Grand Secretariat. The last of the 1402 grand secretaries, Hu Yen, left the Grand Secretariat in 1404 to head the Imperial University.[88]

The fall of Hsieh Chin left Hu Kuang as senior grand secretary (*shou-fu*), the post that was the nearest equivalent of the chancellorship of the mature Ming period. When Hu died in 1418, Yang Jung succeeded to that position. Hu, Yang, and Chin Yu-tzu accompanied Yung-lo on his first northern expedition, and one or more of the three went along with the emperor on each successive Mongolian campaign. Yang Shih-ch'i, in contrast, remained with the crown prince and was duly rewarded in 1424 with the senior grand secretaryship, which he held until his death in 1444. By then the Grand Secretariat had a long history of functioning as an institution; before 1424, on the contrary, the grand secretaries had only a low formal rank and an uncertain standing vis-à-vis other officials, and their influence depended much more on their personal connections with the emperor and the crown prince.[89]

The routinizing of administrative patterns in the Yung-lo period also owed much to the relatively small group of men who headed the ministries for long periods. Left generally undisturbed in their work despite flashes of imperial anger, they developed expertise in their respective areas and transmitted a smoothly functioning bureaucratic machine to the emperors Hung-hsi and Hsüan-te.

Chien Yi (b. 1363), who served with one brief interruption as minister of personnel from 1402 until his death in 1435, was the outstanding example of long tenure in office. His ministry controlled appointments, postings, merit ratings, promotions, and demotions in the civil service, so he was well placed to influence the composition of the bureaucracy, which he did by consulting the preferences of his friend Yang Shih-ch'i. At the Ministry of Rites, after a sequence of ministers who lasted only a year or two, another friend of Yang's, Lü Chen, was appointed minister in 1408 and held the office, also with only one brief interruption, until his death in 1426. In addition to its ceremonial functions, the Ministry of Rites administered the civil service examinations, so Lü also was well placed to bring Yang's influence to bear upon the composition of the civil service.[90]

The Ministry of Revenue was controlled by Hsia Yüan-chi (1366–1430) from 1402 until his imprisonment in 1421. Hsia's standardization of his ministry's procedures entailed what was virtually the total abandonment of Hung-wu's administrative goals; the annual population census in effect ceased, and the system of using the old population figures year after year as mere tax quotas became firmly entrenched. Hsia was adept, however, at getting the grain collected and delivered at the right place to support military operations, a task that depended upon close cooperation with the minister of war.

The Ministry of War was headed from 1402 to 1406 by Liu Chun, who was then sent to Vietnam, where he was killed in 1408. Chin Chung, appointed as a joint minister in 1404, succeeded Liu as senior minister and served until his own death in 1415.* He was one of the four persons designated as advisers to the crown prince at the time of Yung-lo's first Mongolian campaign. In 1409 Fang Pin was appointed to serve as a joint minister of war; he served as senior minister from Chin's death until 1421. In that year, just after the transfer of the capital had been completed, Yung-lo announced his intention of launching a third Mongolian campaign. Fang Pin, Hsia Yüan-chi, and Wu Chung, who had been minister of justice since 1416, protested strongly that the proposed campaign would impose excessive additional burdens on the people. Yung-lo, infuriated, ordered Hsia and Wu thrown into prison, where they languished until 1424. Fang Pin was so frightened that he killed himself. Chao Hung, who had been joint minister of rites from 1407 to 1411 and had been appointed minister of war in 1417, had charge of the Ministry of War from 1421 until 1424.[91]

The Ministry of Works was also closely involved in the transfer of the capital. Its first minister under Yung-lo, Huang Fu (served 1402–5) was in fact sent north to assist Kuo Tzu (minister of revenue, 1402–3) at the head of the auxiliary ministry set up to oversee the transformation of Peking into the main capital. This left Sung Li, first appointed joint minister in 1404, in charge of the Ministry of Works until his death in 1422. Sung Li's major accomplishment was the repair and reconstruction of the section of the Grand Canal running to Peking, a project that was completed in 1411. Once it became possible to transport grain by canal from the southeast all the way to Peking, the capital could be transferred there and Chinese maritime activities could be allowed to deteriorate. Wu Chung served as a joint minister of works from 1407

---

* I use the term "joint minister" arbitrarily for cases in which more than one minister serves concurrently; it does not have a Chinese equivalent, and precedence among joint ministers seems to have been determined by general rather than institutional criteria. In some instances "junior minister" or "cominister" (which I have used elsewhere) seem more appropriate. I use "senior minister" for the main incumbent where seniority is clear.

to 1416, and when he was released from prison after the death of Yung-lo, he served again for a long term (1424–42), but between the death of Sung Li in 1422 and the reappointment of Wu Chung in 1424 actual control of the Ministry of Works was exercised by Li Ch'ing, who had become a joint minister in 1420.[92]

In the legal offices—the Ministry of Justice and the Censorate (the chief censors were equivalent to ministers)—the choice of ministers was unfortunate. After a career in the Censorate, Ch'en Ying was appointed chief censor at the beginning of 1403. Wu Chung was his colleague from 1404 to 1407 before going to the Ministry of Works. Ch'en remained chief censor until 1411, when he was executed for abusing his powers. The office was then vacant for over four years. In 1415 Liu Kuan left the Ministry of Justice to become chief censor. Wang Chang also served as chief censor from 1420 until his death in 1427. In the 1420's Liu Kuan came to symbolize official corruption. In 1428 he and his collaborator Chin Ch'un (joint minister of rites, 1416–24; minister of justice, 1424–28) were forced from office in the major political scandal of the Hsüan-te era. Despite this, Liu Kuan had gained a reputation as an effective administrator during his term as minister of justice (1408–15), a post he took over after several ministers had served in rapid succession. In 1402 Cheng Tz'u had become minister of justice, but in 1405 had gone to the Ministry of Rites, where he died in 1408. Lü Chen succeeded Cheng Tz'u as minister of justice in 1405 and then as minister of rites in 1408. Liu Kuan's successor at the Ministry of Justice was Wu Chung (1416–21), but after Wu's imprisonment in the 1421 affair, the Ministry of Justice remained without a minister until Yung-lo's death.[93]

To summarize the administrative continuity under Yung-lo, four of the Six Ministries (Personnel, Revenue, Rites, and Works) were controlled during most or all of the reign by the same minister (Chien Yi, Hsia Yüan-chi, Lü Chen, and Sung Li, respectively) while perhaps a dozen other men also exercised significant power at the ministerial level. This reversed the Hung-wu pattern of fragmented authority and short official terms.

In provincial administration, too, the Yung-lo period started a trend toward greater concentration of authority. An official of ministerial or vice-ministerial rank would be sent to a province beset by crisis to "tour and soothe" (*hsün-fu*) or in one case to "generally superintend" (*tsung-tu*) the province or region involved, with authority to control the three regular provincial authorities. (These terms later became the official titles of governors and governors-general, respectively.) Although the practice became stable in the Hsüan-te and early Cheng-t'ung reigns, it was under the direction of Yung-lo's surviving grand secretaries that the system became regular and empirewide.

Before 1424 the sending of capital officials to special assignments in the provinces was exceptional, though there were many examples. For instance, those ministers sent from 1403 on to the branch ministries (*hsing-pu*) at Peking were clearly the nucleus of a future central government; similarly, the ministers at Nanking after 1420 were in principle cosmopolitan rather than provincial officials.[94] As another instance, when the province of Chiaochih was set up, the former minister of works Huang Fu went there with authority to direct the administration and surveillance commissioners, a precedent that anticipated the powers later granted to provincial governors. It was also customary in Chiaochih to appoint at least one minister to assist the commanding general in both strategic and administrative affairs. The title of this office, "consultant for important matters" (*ts'an-tsan chi-wu*), was held by Liu Chun when he was killed in 1408. Ch'en Ch'ia received it in 1415 and held it until he was killed in action in 1426; and the same title was regularly held by the Nanking minister of war after 1420, since his position vis-à-vis the Nanking military commandant (*shou-pei*) was theoretically analogous.[95] Finally, Sung Li, while serving as minister of works, was sent north in 1411 to supervise the opening of the Grand Canal, and on other occasions he went into the interior to supervise timber-cutting operations.[96]

In addition to the influence of the grand secretaries and ministers, the regular sequence of civil service examinations advanced Confucian attitudes by adding increased numbers of educated and indoctrinated chin-shih to the bureaucracy. The examination that should have been held in 1403 was postponed until 1404 due to the civil war, but the 1406 examination was on schedule. In 1409 Yung-lo was away, and the candidates of that year had to wait until 1411, but from 1412 on the examinations were held at regular three-year intervals. A total of 1,833 chin-shih degrees were granted in the course of the reign. The examinations of 1404 (472 degrees) and 1415 (351) saw the highest number of successful candidates, those of 1411 (84) and 1412 (106) the lowest, with the other years falling in between (219 in 1406, 250 in 1418, 201 in 1421, and 150 in 1424). By 1424 there were enough chin-shih to staff most of the responsible posts in the civil service from district magistrate up, and the examination route had become the normal means of selecting officials. These trends continued after 1424 under the influence of Yang Shih-ch'i and his cohorts in the Grand Secretariat. Compared to previous Chinese dynasties, the Ming was anomalous in the high degree of reliance it placed on the examinations in choosing civil officials; the proportion of its officials recruited by heredity, guaranteed recommendation, or any other system was very low. However, since the Ming system was continued by the Ch'ing, the Europeans of the Enlightenment who idealized the Chinese system took it to be the norm.[97]

The Yüan refusal to hold examinations until late in their regime was a measure of the Mongol rejection of Confucian political ideology, and the eagerness of early Ming civil officials to restore the examinations was partly in reaction to Mongol repudiation. The leaders of the civil service in the Yung-lo period who furthered the domination of the bureaucracy by examination-recruited officials were themselves mostly holders of examination degrees. Four of the seven grand secretaries appointed in 1402, plus Yang P'u (appointed 1424), had received chin-shih degrees between 1388 and 1400. Chien Yi, who was minister of personnel for three reigns and was therefore to some extent responsible for the composition of the bureaucracy as of 1435, was a 1385 chin-shih, as were Cheng Tz'u, Kuo Tzu, and Fang Pin.[98] Even the officials and ministers who did not have chin-shih degrees tended to have had Confucian educations or to have entered the civil service under programs considered exceptional (such as direct recruitment of imperial university students); they therefore tended to share the values of officials who had been recruited by examination.

Chien Yi's longevity was exceptional. Midway in the Yung-lo reign the large chin-shih class of 1385 began to retire in significant numbers, and after that time the successive chin-shih examinations were held to fill vacancies caused by the death or retirement of active chin-shih rather than to add to the number of chin-shih in the civil service. However, the fast civil service expansion that caused such a shortage of officials in the Hung-wu reign had slowed markedly by 1424. As the number of chin-shih within the civil service stabilized, so did the size of the civil service as a whole. With sufficient chin-shih to fill the responsible positions, and with chü-jen filling most of the remainder, nonexamination routes into the bureaucracy ceased to be of significance after 1435.

Hung-wu had attempted to make every sector of Ming society and state respond to his will. Yung-lo was more modest. He insisted on having his own way only in areas that interested him personally. The spectacular activities of his reign were undertaken on his personal initiative by eunuchs and soldiers, often over the protests of the civil service, which cooperated only grudgingly. By the end of his reign the civil service was under the control of a small clique of officials united by a common ideological perspective and sense of purpose, and opposed to Yung-lo's personal projects. Hung-wu would never have allowed such a development; that it occurred under his successors was more significant for later Ming history than the voyages and campaigns willed by Emperor Yung-lo. As the army returned to Peking bearing the body of the emperor in the autumn of 1424, it was an open question whether the imperial court, the army, or the eunuch establishment could sustain a sense of continuity and purpose comparable to that animating the civil service.

SEVEN

Hung-hsi and Hsüan-te:
Normal Confucian
Government, 1424–1435

The new emperor, Hung-hsi (Chu Kao-chih, b. 1378), was a contemporary of Chien-wen, who was his cousin. He grew up skilled in archery but he also loved the Confucian classics, and, like Chien-wen, he became the hope of the Confucian element in the regime. During the Yen rebellion he won his father's admiration for skillfully defending Peking with a garrison of only 10,000 men against the imperial general Li Ching-lung; that success reminds us that through his mother he was a grandson of Hsü Ta. Yung-lo, however, had more affection for his younger sons Kao-hsü and Kao-sui, who accompanied the field army, and he delayed until 1404 before formally investing Hung-hsi as crown prince. But afterwards the crown prince regularly administered the empire while the emperor was absent from the capital. Separated from his father, he was also alienated from his father's policies, a situation not improved by the 1414 affair in which Yung-lo, returning from a campaign, was swayed by Kao-hsü's slanders to reprimand the crown prince and imprison his closest collaborators. The Kao-hsü cabal ceased to be a threat after Kao-hsü's exile in 1417, but by then the relationship between Yung-lo and his eldest son was hopelessly poisoned.[1]

Yung-lo died on 12 August 1424. Immediately upon receipt of the news the crown prince ordered the release of Hsia Yüan-chi and the other victims of the 1414 affair. On 7 September he formally ascended the throne, designated 1425 as the first year of the Hung-hsi period, and issued a general pardon. On the same day he issued decrees canceling the Cheng Ho voyage scheduled for that year and abolishing the tea and horse trade on the frontier and the lumber-cutting expeditions in Yünnan and Chiaochih, acts that suggested that although Yung-lo was not yet buried, his policies were about to be laid to rest with him. On the next day Hsia Yüan-chi and Wu Chung, imprisoned since 1421, were restored to ministerial rank, Hsia to his former place as minister of revenue and Wu as minister of works.[2]

On 9 September Hung-hsi reorganized the Grand Secretariat. Huang Huai, dismissed from the Grand Secretariat in 1414, and Yang P'u, imprisoned on the same occasion, were both appointed grand secretaries; Yang Shih-ch'i, the new emperor's mentor and closest collaborator, became senior grand secretary; and Yang Jung and Chin Yu-tzu were continued as grand secretaries. At the same time Hung-hsi gave the grand secretaries concurrent appointments in vice-ministerial or other posts of comparable degree; though still lower than that of the ministers, the formal rank of the grand secretaries was rising to correspond more nearly with their real political importance. Hung-hsi thus restored to power those officials who had taken his side in his disagreements with his father. He did so without actually purging any official for supporting Yung-lo, but it was by then clear that the new reign portended a full-scale reversal of Yung-lo's programs.[3]

Hung-hsi spent the rest of 1424 making administrative reforms and issuing the pardons that had been deferred during Yung-lo's lifetime. Excess officials were dismissed, and serving officials were ordered to retire at seventy. The practices of requisitioning materials and obtaining gold and silver from the populace, condemned by Confucian opinion, were ordered abolished. When the Yellow River overflowed, Chief Censor Wang Chang was sent to supervise relief measures, and the emperor later scolded the Office of Transmissions for lack of care in keeping rainfall records. Officials with exemplary service records were appointed as local officials, and the emperor ordered that worthy, talented, and strict officials be appointed to positions having jurdisdiction over law cases. Despite the imperial concern, the corrupt Liu Kuan continued as chief censor, and he was not the only corrupt official to stay in office. On 18 October Hung-hsi presented the grand secretaries Yang Shih-ch'i, Yang Jung, and Chin Yu-tzu, and the minister of personnel, Chien Yi, with specially engraved silver seals and ordered them to report to him in secret when they discovered failings in other officials. The same privilege was awarded to Hsia Yüan-chi before the end of the year. It was normal for a new emperor to celebrate his accession by issuing pardons, but before the end of 1424 Hung-hsi had gone well beyond routine clemency; he had freed from slavery or other legal disabilities and had pardoned the families of ministers and officials executed in 1402 for their loyalty to Emperor Chien-wen. By thus implying that they had some excuse for their obstinacy, the emperor cast doubt on the propriety of his own father's seizure of the throne.[4]

Other ceremonial duties also claimed the emperor's attention. On 29 October he promoted his wife to the status of empress. (This lady, who died in 1442 as the grand dowager empress Chang, acted as regent during the minority of her grandson Emperor Cheng-t'ung and, by her close cooperation with the surviving grand secretaries, ensured the survival for a while of the political system established by her husband and maintained by her son.) Three days later Hung-hsi made his eldest son Chan-chi crown prince and his eight younger sons princes of the blood. Hung-hsi had more children than Yung-lo, and he was more concerned about the position of the imperial clansmen; he ordered their stipends increased but continued to exclude them from political or military roles.[5]

During the rest of his short reign Hung-hsi ruled in an exemplary Confucian manner and exhorted his officials to do the same. Local grain shortages were endemic in China, even in this period of general prosperity, and on some highly publicized occasions Hung-hsi intervened personally to speed up the administration of famine relief. In one case he ordered that relief grain be distributed free, rather than lent at a low rate of interest as had been customary; in another he angrily overruled the grand secretaries and ordered that the distribution of relief grain be begun and the summer tax remitted in certain areas, a suspension of the usual procedures of the Ministries of Revenue and Works. He then observed that "saving the people from famine is like rescuing them from fire or drowning; one may not hesitate." Hung-hsi consistently saw himself as representing the welfare of the people as opposed to the profit or advantage of the state, a standard conservative Confucian position going back to the opponents of Han Wu-ti's introduction of the salt and iron monopolies. His desire to moderate the severity of criminal punishments reflects the same concern.[6]

When making official appointments the emperor was equally Confucian in his stress on exemplary personal conduct and character. This was the basis of his admiration for Yang P'u. Early in 1425 he appointed Ch'üan Chin, a minor official of the Court of Official Entertainments, to the Grand Secretariat because of his extraordinary filial piety; Ch'üan's appointment was honorific rather than functional, and he retired from official life later in the year. However, officials who failed to meet all of the Confucian stereotypes were not necessarily excluded from the imperial favor, or at least from its outward marks. Though prevented from carrying out further exploratory voyages, Cheng Ho was consoled by being named commandant of Nanking on 25 February.[7] Despite his frequent outbursts of anger, Hung-hsi ruled by example rather than punishments and was apparently sincere in his repeated calls for fearless remonstrance.

On 16 April, intending to transfer the capital back to Nanking as the final step in his reversal of Yung-lo's policies, Hung-hsi ordered all of the Peking agencies redesignated "auxiliary" (*hsing-tsai*), as they had been in the 1403–20 period. On 30 April he sent his crown prince to visit the tomb of Hung-wu and remain in charge of Nanking. Despite reports of earthquakes in the Nanking area, the return of the emperor and the main capital seemed imminent. Then, on 27 May, two minor officials of the Han-lin Academy submitted a memorial fearlessly remonstrating with the emperor for, among other weighty matters, having sexual relations with his concubines during the period of mourning for Yung-lo. This was too much even for Hung-hsi; the monarch temporarily overwhelmed the Confucian in the emperor's character, and he lost his temper and sent the offending remonstrators to prison. But the next day the emperor himself fell ill. He dispatched a messenger to recall the crown prince, but on the following day he died. He was in his forty-eighth year.[8]

Hung-hsi's father and grandfather had died in their sixty-fifth and seventy-first years, respectively, and compared to them Hung-hsi had died prematurely. He had the same degree of determination as his two famous predecessors, and his main goal as emperor was to terminate the specific policies of his father that he regarded as heterodox and to establish what he believed to be proper Confucian government, in which a morally worthy emperor ruled by the advice of wise and upright ministers. In addition to returning the capital to Nanking, this implied discontinuing the military and explorational expeditions favored by Yung-lo and sustaining the civil officials against the other Ming elites. Despite his short reign, he came very near to attaining his goals. Empress Chang and the grand secretaries Yang Shih-ch'i, Yang Jung, and Yang P'u all survived into the 1440's, so the Confucian group that had gained control of the state in 1424 retained its control without challenge throughout the reign of Hsüan-te and the minority of Cheng-t'ung. Thereafter, Confucian officials routinely dominated the political process, despite intermittent challenges from the palace eunuchs. Notwithstanding occasional longings to emulate his grandfather, Yung-lo, Emperor Hsüan-te was basically under the influence of his father, Hung-hsi, articulately represented by Empress Chang and the grand secretaries. He vacillated, but in the end he terminated the Vietnam war, allowed the naval expeditions to end after one last voyage, and confined his own military ambitions to harmless promenades in the vicinity of the Great Wall.

However, Hung-hsi's premature death in 1425 imposed permanent limits on the extent of the Confucian victory of 1424. The civil officials never were able to abolish all of the special economic enterprises run by the palace eunuchs, nor did they ever succeed in controlling the size or organization of the eunuch establishment, which grew larger under Hsüan-te and remained a permanent threat to the civil officials. And none of Hung-hsi's successors shared his conviction that the capital should go back to Nanking; that policy formally lapsed in 1441.[9]

*

The crown prince, Chu Chan-chi (b. 1398), who was summoned back to Peking at the onset of Hung-hsi's illness, took the throne on 27 June, issued the customary general amnesty, and designated 1426 as the first year of the Hsüan-te period.[10] A talented artist and poet, he was somewhat more interested in these and other private pleasures than in governing. He ruled conscientiously and attempted to deal equitably with the several components of the Ming ruling elite, but he lacked the definite political program and the desire to impose his will on the officialdom that his predecessors had all manifested. The new emperor was capable of being decisive when the occasion demanded, but usually he followed the advice of others, chiefly the grand secretaries and other high officials inherited from his father.

There were two major issues left over from the Hung-hsi reign. One, the return of the capital to Nanking, was tacitly abandoned by the new emperor, who preferred the north. He shared Yung-lo's liking for hunting and riding, and from 1411 on he had accompanied Yung-lo on the Mongolian campaigns.[11]

The second issue was the worsening military situation in Vietnam. Yung-lo's efforts to coax Le Lo'i into surrendering had failed, and the Vietnamese rebel celebrated the accession of Hung-hsi by inflicting a sharp defeat on the regional military commissioner, Fang Cheng, at the departmental town of Tra Long.[12] Hung-hsi recalled his minister Huang Fu from Chiaochih. Then, on the advice of his eunuch general Shan Shou, who had known Le Lo'i before his rebellion, the emperor tried again to induce Le Lo'i to surrender by sending Shan Shou with credentials appointing Le Lo'i prefect of Thanh Hoa. Le Lo'i retaliated by raiding Thanh Hoa and killing its commander on 7 October 1424. Tra Long remained under siege, but despite his failure to relieve it, Fang Cheng in December was promoted to chief military commissioner. In April 1425 Li An, earl of Anp'ing, was sent to share the supreme command in Chiaochih with Ch'en Chih, earl of Yungch'ang.[13] These changes did not include reinforcements; for no good reason, Hung-hsi apparently hoped that Chiaochih could be pacified without additional troop commitments. Soon afterwards, Hung-hsi died.

Tra Long fell shortly afterwards, and early in 1426 Ch'en Chih and Fang Cheng led their army to recapture it. In April Le Lo'i attacked them and defeated them heavily. The prefect of Nghe An was killed in the battle. This defeat led to another shake-up in the Chinese command structure in Chiaochih. On 8 May Wang T'ung, marquis of Ch'engshan, became the new commander-in-chief, with the minister Ch'en Ch'ia, who had been in Chiaochih since 1415, as his civil assistant. Chen Chih and Fang Cheng were stripped of their ranks and ordered to accompany the army to redeem themselves. Mu Sheng was ordered to raise fifteen thousand troops and three thousand crossbowmen from the guards in the southwest, and additional reinforcements were sent. Finally, Hsüan-te issued yet another decree offering Le Lo'i pardon and official position if he would surrender.[14]

Le Lo'i's victory of April 1426 had demonstrated that he could defend territory against large-scale Chinese attack, and so had converted him from a mere guerrilla into a credible regional ruler. He now based himself on Thanh Hoa, and all of Chiaochih from that prefecture south was from then on lost to the Ming. Previously, Chang Fu had destroyed fixed centers of rebellion by attacking them from the sea, but Chang Fu was now cooling his heels in Peking while Wang T'ung, a man of no military ability who owed his noble title to his father's death in action, commanded in Chiaochih. Wang blundered overland in the direction of Thanh Hoa, but before he arrived Le Lo'i destroyed most of his army in a series of battles that came to a climax on 4 December, when the minister Ch'en Ch'ia was killed.[15]

This led to the final showdown in Vietnam. In January 1427 the emperor ordered Mu Sheng, duke of Ch'ien, with two earls under him, to lead an army from Yünnan, and Liu Sheng, marquis of Anyüan, with an earl and a chief military commissioner under his command, to lead a second army from Kwangsi. The minister of war, Li Ch'ing, was to handle the administrative side. Despite the reputation that generals from the Mu family had earned in Yünnan and Kweichow, Mu Sheng had not particularly distinguished himself in the previous Vietnam campaigns. Furthermore, the division in the Chinese leadership paralleled a fundamental uncertainty of purpose at the Ming court. Even worse, Le Lo'i, riding a nationalist tide, had extended his zone of operations to the Red River valley, thus endangering the provincial capital held for the Ming by the ill-starred Wang T'ung.[16]

Wang T'ung repelled Le Lo'i's first assault (4 March 1427) on the city of Chiaochou (Hanoi), collecting ten thousand severed heads in the process, but he did not pursue the retreating Vietnamese despite the urgings of his officers. Le Lo'i regrouped his forces and on 28 April captured Xu'ong Giang, located northeast of Chiaochou on the route by which he expected Liu Sheng's army to come. Le Lo'i continued to be aided by defections of Vietnamese personnel in the Chiaochih government, and he was vigorously arguing in letters to the Ming court and to Wang T'ung's command that his only motive in rebelling was to restore the legitimate Tran royal house. Nine days after the fall of Xu'ong Giang and the death of its Chinese officers and garrison, Wang T'ung concluded a formal truce with the rebels. Later, on 6 August, the rebels seized the major pass leading into Kwangsi.[17]

Against this background, Liu Sheng's army, racked by fever, marched into Vietnam. On 30 September it fell into a trap near Lang So'n. Liu Sheng was killed and one of his deputy commanders died of illness. The next day the other deputy commander was killed and the minister Li Ch'ing died of illness. Without leaders the army was cut to pieces and destroyed. News of this debacle reinforced Wang T'ung's desire to save his own skin, and on 12 November he agreed to a military convention under which he evacuated Chiaochou and recognized Le Lo'i's master, the pretender Tran Cao, as king; in return he was promised safe-conduct to Kwangsi for himself and his men. Le Lo'i kept the bargain and delivered eighty-six thousand soldiers from the Chinese army to the frontier. Mu Sheng had reached the upper affluents of the Red River and was building boats preparatory to coming downstream. When he heard of the evacuation, he pulled back his army and awaited further orders.[18]

Deciding what orders to give had been a problem. During his short reign, Hung-hsi had considered abandoning Vietnam, a course urged by the grand secretaries Yang Shih-ch'i and Yang Jung but strongly opposed by the minister of personnel, Chien Yi, and the minister of revenue, Hsia Yüan-chi. With his civilian ministers divided, Hung-hsi took the easy way out and opted to maintain the status quo, as did Hsüan-te during 1425–26. When the same issue was raised in late 1427, however, Le Lo'i controlled or threatened all of Chiaochih and was besieging its capital. Under these circumstances the choices were abandonment or reconquest, and even though Chang Fu was there to argue for reconquest, the emperor adopted the view of the grand secretaries. On 19 November he appointed commissioners to pardon Le Lo'i and confer the title of king on Tran Cao. The emperor did not know that Wang T'ung had abandoned Chiaochou seven days before.[19]

This unhappy coincidence gave the impression that China had abandoned Vietnam solely because of its military defeat. Le Lo'i's political position was now unassailable. When the Chinese envoys arrived, he claimed that Tran Cao had died and that there were no Trans left, demanded Chinese recognition for himself, and refused to repatriate any more Chinese. The emperor tried to keep to the original terms, and in 1428 and again in 1429 he sent envoys to Vietnam to demand the restoration of the Trans. Le Lo'i refused, and Hsüan-te eventually gave up. In 1431, after receipt of a suitably obsequious letter from Le Lo'i, the emperor granted him a commission and seal conferring authority "to administer the affairs of the state of Annam," thus reviving the title he had used under the Trans but refusing to call him king. Le Lo'i sent a tribute of gold and silver utensils and local products, which the Ming accepted in 1433.[20] Le Lo'i meanwhile had proclaimed himself emperor and was busily constructing his government as a replica in miniature of the Ming imperial system, complete with thirteen provinces and suitably official titles for his followers. When he died in 1434, the Ming court recognized his son as his successor, granting him the formal title "King of Annam" two years later. However, for domestic consumption the Le monarchs continued to call themselves emperors. Of course the Tran were never restored, but the Tran policy of ingesting Champa continued, that kingdom being totally absorbed in 1471 during the reign of Le Lo'i's greatest successor, Le Thanh Tong (r. 1460–97).[21]

Though the decision to abandon Vietnam had not been taken on strict civil-versus-military lines, its effect was to heighten the developing ascendancy of civil officials over military officers within the Ming political system. From 1427 until 1449 military operations were largely confined to police actions, minor campaigns on the northern frontier or in the southwest that gave little scope for the emergence of generals of political significance. A few new nobles were created, but most were earls, and the men who inherited the higher titles lacked both the will and the ability to maintain the position of the nobility vis-à-vis the civil service. The abortive rebellion of the emperor's uncle (see pp. 231–32) confirmed the wisdom of excluding the princes from military command. The failure of the Vietnam adventure gave the civil service a rhetorical weapon against future large-scale military undertakings, a weapon that was strengthened by the T'umu disaster of 1449.*

As the military nobility and the officer corps came more and more to consist of men who had inherited their positions and had known only peace during their adult lives, they predictably turned to the exploitation of military personnel and military colony lands for personal gain. In 1427, coincidentally, censors and supervising secretaries were for the first time given special commissions to investigate and rectify abuses in military administration.† Local defense organizations fell under the control of civilian military defense intendants drawn from the ranks of the deputy and assistant surveillance commissioners. However, increased civilian supervision did not discernibly arrest the decay of the Ming military establishment. The officers continued to appropriate military lands for their own use and encourage their soldiers to desert in order to pocket the funds designated for their support, and the imposing wei-so system turned more and more into an empty shell.²²

Military considerations were also among the reasons for the institution of quasi-formal provincial governors in the Hsüan-te period. The official Ming history dates this development to September 1425, when two officials were ordered to "tour and soothe" (*hsün-fu*) Nan Chihli and Chekiang. As noted earlier, the term was used in the Yung-lo reign, and Hung-hsi, Hsüan-te, and the father of Chien-wen, while they were still crown princes, had carried out similar assignments. Officers called hsün-fu were ap-

---

* In 1449 the Ming emperor, Cheng-t'ung, at the urging of his eunuch confidant Wang Chen, led an expedition against Mongol invaders. This was the first large-scale Ming military undertaking since 1427. The Mongol leader Esen Tayisi surrounded and destroyed the Ming army at the village of T'umu, capturing the emperor. See Frederick W. Mote, "The T'u-mu Incident of 1449," in John K. Fairbank and Frank A. Kierman, eds., *Chinese Ways in Warfare* (Cambridge, Mass., 1974).

† Supervising secretaries were officials of the offices of scrutiny, of which there was one to each of the Six Ministries; they exercised a censorlike supervisory power over the work of the ministries.

pointed on a continuing basis in 1430 for Honan, Shansi, and Szechwan, in 1439 for Hukwang, and in 1440 for Shantung. Such officials had existed in Chekiang since early in the Yung-lo period, in Kiangsi and Shensi since about 1426, and intermittently in Kwangtung and Kwangsi. Huang Fu had exercised similar powers in Chiaochih. The office became a regular one in Yünnan in 1444 and in Kweichow in 1449. Only in Fukien was the appointment of a hsün-fu postponed until the end of the sixteenth century. So during the Hsüan-te reign and immediately afterwards, the hsün-fu metamorphosed from occasional imperial delegates sent to remedy abuses in specific provinces into de facto provincial governors, a status the succeeding Ch'ing dynasty formalized.

The governors received concurrent appointments as vice-ministers, usually of war, and later as chief censors or deputy chief censors (to inhibit impeachment by touring censorial personnel); they were formally empowered to control the three provincial commissioners (administrative, surveillance, and military); and they were additionally designated "coregulator of military affairs" (*tsan-li chün-wu*), a term adapted from the similar title *ts'an-tsan chi-wu*, which first had been borne by the ministers who had participated in the Vietnam war and later was retained by the Nanking minister of war.[23] In other words, despite its long-run administrative significance, the immediate purpose of the radical extension of the hsün-fu system—which took place mostly in the 1430's, the period of peace between the end of the Vietnam war and the T'umu incident—was the transfer of command in the field from military to civilian hands. Shortly after the death of Hsüan-te, while the new emperor, Cheng-t'ung, was still a minor, the grand secretaries carried this trend still further by appointing civilian governors to control six of the nine defense commands on the northern border: such appointments were made for Yensui and Kansu in 1435 and for Liaotung, Ninghsia, and Hsüanfu (the latter controlling Tat'ung) in 1436.[24]

Compared to the Vietnam war and the subsequent civilian takeover of field command, Emperor Hsüan-te's personal exercise of military command had trivial consequences; however, at that time it maintained the impression that the imperial style of the Yung-lo era was continuing. The first such occasion was the rebellion of the emperor's uncle Kao-hsü, prince of Han, in

August 1426. Kao-hsü, who had intrigued for the succession until his exile in 1417, now hoped to repeat his father's successful usurpation of the throne from a young and presumably inexperienced nephew. He rebelled on 28 August 1426. Seven days later the emperor, having ordered two of his younger brothers to take command of the capital, mobilized the capital garrison. On 6 September the army set out for Loan in Shantung, where Kao-hsü's fief was located. Instead of assaulting the town, Hsüan-te ordered arrows with messages warning of the consequences of rebellion shot over the walls. Kao-hsü had been taken by surprise, and his supporters abandoned him; he surrendered on 17 September and spent the rest of his life under house arrest. Subsequent investigation revealed that Kao-hsü's brother Kao-sui, prince of Chao, and another prince were also involved in the plot; Hsüan-te ordered no prosecutions but later deprived the other prince of his title.[25] The 1399 rebellion of the prince of Yen had been a tragedy for the reigning emperor, but the 1426 affair of the prince of Han was mere farce. The emperors in question both had attempted to respond appropriately to the threats; the outcome in 1426 reflected the disappearance of princely power as a result of Yung-lo's policies.

Otherwise, accounts of military activity in the Hsüan-te period make tame reading. Touring the border in 1428, the emperor heard of a minor raid by the Uriyangqad Mongols, and he personally apprehended the raiders at the head of three thousand cavalry soldiers. The emperor's other occasional excursions from the capital were for hunting. In 1424, soon after Yung-lo's death, Arughtai had presented a tribute of horses, and the Eastern Mongols at least remained quiescent after that, while the Oirats went so far as to present tribute almost every year. Military operations were fairly regular only in the southwest, where campaigns against tribal peoples took place nearly every year. However, these campaigns were not on a scale large enough either to endanger the empire or to engage a major part of its armies.[26]

In his relations with countries other than Mongolia, Hsüan-te struck a middle course between the seclusion favored by Hung-wu and the activism of Yung-lo. After the cancellation of the naval voyages in 1424, ambassadors from the Southeast Asian kingdoms, especially the rising trading sultanate of Malacca, continued to come to court, as did envoys from the small Moslem oasis states of Sinkiang—but envoys from most of the states bordering on the Indian Ocean, those that were discovered for the Chinese by Cheng Ho, had ceased to come. The leading civil officials consistently opposed the resumption of the voyages, and as late as 1429 Hsüan-te yielded to them and ordered the abolition of one of the few remaining eunuch-directed shipbuilding programs. But in 1431 he was persuaded to change his mind and again send Cheng Ho to sail the South China Sea and the Indian Ocean. Cheng's ships were as large, numerous, and well manned as ever, and when he returned in 1433, he brought with him ambassadors from Ceylon, Cochin and Calicut in India, Ormuz on the Persian Gulf, Aden on the Arabian Peninsula, Djofar in Africa, and other places.[27] Hsüan-te was pleased by these results, and at his untimely death in 1435 Chinese seapower seemed as firmly established as ever.

In fact, the end of the early Ming period also marks the end of the three centuries during which Chinese fleets dominated East Asian waters. The Lung-chiang shipyard at Nanking continued to function, and the plans for the treasure ships survived into the 1470's, but only the eunuch establishment continued to favor further naval expeditions. Confucian opposition was stronger and more persistent. The reconquest of the north up to the Great Wall had, after all, removed the defense considerations that had prompted the Southern Sung to create their navy in the first place, and Yung-lo himself had radically curtailed the construction of oceangoing ships after the Grand Canal had proved effective in supplying Peking. When the Ming court next faced a naval crisis, in the Wakō (Japanese pirate) raids of the sixteenth century, it responded unimaginatively and ineffectively with coastal defense measures.[28]

After the shogun Yoshimochi's severance of diplomatic and trading relations between Japan and China, Yung-lo several times tried unsuccessfully to restore relations, and Hsüan-te continued this policy. Yoshimochi's successor Yoshinori (r. 1429–41) was sympathetic to reviving Sino-Japanese relations on the basis that had prevailed under Yoshimitsu. In 1432 Hsüan-te sent a mission to Japan, headed by the eunuch Ch'ai Shan, that proposed restoration of relations and an increase in the amounts of permitted trade.

Yoshinori's acceptance inaugurated a long period of diplomatically regulated trade that lasted to 1549 and was marred only by squabbles over prices and by Chinese complaints that Japanese authorities had failed to suppress piracy completely. Under this revived tally trade, all of the actual missions came from Japan and landed at Ningpo; as had previously been the case, Japanese Buddhist monks played a major role in the negotiations, and the trade served to keep Japan abreast of current developments in Chinese society and culture without causing any corresponding growth in awareness in China of Japanese affairs.[29]

Despite Hsüan-te's usual obedience to Confucian opinion as represented by his grand secretaries, the latter were never able either to destroy the eunuch establishment or to confine it to its "proper" function of service within the palace. Frequent notices during the Hsüan-te reign record the abolition of eunuch-directed procurements—timber cutting, shipbuilding, and certain other economic activities. The repetition of such notices indicates that eunuch operations, terminated in one area, tended to reappear in another, and in fact the use of eunuchs to superintend activities of personal concern to the emperor was on the increase throughout the reign. In 1426 the six offices of scrutiny, as part of their general duty of monitoring the flow business in the Six Ministries, were ordered to memorialize for confirmation before permitting the enforcement of any decree transmitted to them by a eunuch. This provision, faithfully observed until the fall of the dynasty, failed to provide the expected barrier against eunuch participation in government; emperors were willing to provide the required confirmation, since they were using the eunuchs for their own purposes. In 1429 Hsüan-te established a school in the palace to teach literary skills to young eunuchs, and eunuchs also served him as generals and diplomats and in other responsible positions. It was becoming apparent that of all the alternative elites of the early Ming period, only the eunuchs were able to master the secret of bureaucratic organization; that capability alone enabled them to develop into an institutionalized rival of the civil service in the competition for imperial attention and political power.[30]

The highest levels of the civil service continued to be dominated by the same small group that had gained control of the government in 1424, many of whom had been appointed to office as early as 1402. They resisted the entry of new members into their circle. In 1426 the vice-minister of rites Chang Ying was made a grand secretary, and in 1427 the same honor went to the vice-minister of revenue Ch'en Shan.* They were both dismissed on 13 November 1429, Chang to be minister of rites at Nanking and Ch'en to a lesser post. No more grand secretaries were appointed until 1440, so after the death of Chin Yu-tzu in 1431 the Grand Secretariat consisted only of Yang Shih-ch'i, Yang Jung, and Yang P'u. The two grand secretaries appointed in 1440, Ma Yü and Ts'ao Nai, had been first in the chin-shih examinations of 1427 and 1433, respectively, and their appointments established a custom, lasting for the rest of the dynasty, that linked high place in the examinations to quick advancement to the Grand Secretariat.[31]

In 1428 Chin Ch'un, the minister of justice, was accused of drinking and feasting during the triennial capital evaluations of officials, was briefly imprisoned, and was forced to retire from office. In the same year the extent of Liu Kuan's corrupt activities as chief censor came to light. He was sent to tour the provinces, and in his absence he was dismissed and Ku Tso appointed chief censor. At his subsequent interrogation, Liu pleaded his record of long service but confessed his crimes and was imprisoned until his death the following year. Liu's crimes were deserving of death, according to prevailing standards, but Hsüan-te hated to execute anyone. The generals and officials found responsible for the loss of Vietnam were let off with brief terms of imprisonment, and Wang T'ung even kept his noble title. Obviously, the court was a pleasanter place for officials than it had been in Hung-wu's reign; Chin Ch'un and Liu Kuan were the only officials of ministerial rank to lose their offices as punishment, and no ministers received a more severe punishment. The emperor's mercy extended down to common subjects caught up in the judicial process, and he frequently ordered the three legal offices (Ministry of Justice, Censorate, and Grand Court of Revision) to review criminal cases with the aim of reducing sentences. Only toward eunuchs was a harsh standard of punishments maintained, the outstanding example of which was the execution of Yüan Ch'i and ten eunuch accomplices in 1431 for corrupt activities.[32]

---

* Ch'en Shan, curiously, became the head of the palace eunuchs' school.

In the autumn and winter of 1434 the emperor led the army patrolling the frontier, and Arughtai's son came to the emperor's camp to submit formally. After his return to Peking Hsüan-te fell ill. He was unable to hold court on the lunar New Year's Day, and he died two days later on 31 January 1435. His heir was a young boy born in 1427. Hsüan-te's will consequently ordered that his own mother, Empress Dowager Chang, wife of Hung-hsi, be consulted on all matters of state. Her cooperation with the grand secretaries ensured that the hand of the dead Hung-hsi, which had been the strongest political force throughout the Hsüan-te reign, would continue to direct the Ming state until the 1440's.[33]

If the passing of Hsüan-te scarcely disturbed the continuity of normal Confucian government, it nevertheless marked the end of the early Ming period in a significant sense. Hsüan-te was the last Ming emperor who was both attentive to his duties as head of state and reasonably impartial in his treatment of the groups that composed the ruling elite. Although he usually deferred to the senior civil officials inherited from his father, he also treated his eunuchs and military officers generously and attempted to be fair in his decisions. Later emperors either withdrew completely to the pleasures of the palace or entered the political world as vigorous partisans either of the civil officials or, more often, of the eunuchs; they ceased, in other words, to be a stabilizing element within the Ming system. Little wonder, then, that subsequent generations of Ming officials looked back nostalgically on the Hsüan-te period as a golden age of good government that stood in sharp contrast to the institutional decay and bitter political conflicts with which they were familiar.

EIGHT

Ming History: The
Roads Not Taken

In the preceding pages we have traced the evolution of the Ming regime from an obscure band of dislocated peasant soldiers in the 1350's to the mighty empire that dominated eastern Asia in the 1430's. However, growth in size had led to change in kind, so the Ming empire of the 1430's was no longer capable of the achievements that had characterized the earlier Ming regime. The Chinese tradition had triumphed over the Mongol inheritance, and civil bureaucrats had replaced military men in control of the state, just as the development of gentry society had ended the plurality of elites. China remained passive in its military posture and hidebound in its attitudes throughout the remainder of the Ming period. When the Ming empire collapsed in 1644, its political and military institutions and the structure of gentry society on which they rested were essentially those that had emerged by 1435, though the size of the Chinese population and the scale of the economy had increased many times over. The early Ming leadership had decided matters in response to urgent contemporary necessities; their decisions had led to institutional and social changes that often turned in unforeseen directions.

The concluding chapter goes beyond the contemporary background in order to place the early Ming period in a broader historical perspective. The first part summarizes the state of the

Ming empire around 1435, and then considers the mature Ming period in order to show the lasting influence of early Ming solutions. The second gives some alternative scenarios of historical development that are suggested by other periods of Chinese history but that were preempted by the actual course of the early Ming; it concludes with a discussion of the role of early Ming history in bringing to an end the "medieval economic revolution" of the Sung and Yüan periods.*

Early Ming Outcomes and the Shape of Ming History

Chapter 1 defined five principal areas of concern for early Ming emperors and leadership. In descending order of importance these were warfare, the geographical basis of power, military institutions, foreign affairs, and the civil service and governmental administration. Although one may distinguish analytically between these areas, in practice decisions affecting a given area were often carried out by several different sets of officials, so cause and effect and lines of responsibility may be blurred. Furthermore, in making their decisions, Ming emperors were usually responding to a contemporary situation in which a problem in one area might call for a decision in another. Thus wars were undertaken in order to defend or extend the territorial base of Ming power, the civil service was established to provide logistical support for the army, and foreign contacts were tightly controlled to prevent future wars. In the spirit of Croce's observation that all history is contemporary history, Chapters 2 through 7 have emphasized the immediate circumstances at each stage in the development of the Ming state. But this contemporary emphasis tends to obscure the totality of the changes during the early Ming period. By about 1435 the five areas had all been transformed in comparison to 1355, and Chinese society as a whole had changed in response.

Warfare. The military history of the early Ming divides naturally into six subperiods. From 1355 to 1364 the Ming regime was engaged in a precarious fight for survival against the other

---

* This term is applied by Mark Elvin to the changes that took place in China from mid-T'ang to about 1200 in farming, water transport, money and credit, marketing and urbanization, and science and technology. See Elvin, *The Pattern of the Chinese Past* (Stanford, Calif., 1973).

Chinese-dominated regimes of the Yangtze valley; a single defeat might have extinguished Ming hopes. From 1364 to 1372 the Ming was preoccupied by the campaigns to expel the Mongols from the Chinese-inhabited parts of the Yüan empire. From 1372 to 1381 defeats by the Mongols led to the regime's adopting a premature policy of passive defense. The conquest of Yünnan inaugurated a new period; from 1381 to 1393 a phase of expansion on the frontiers and of military activism was associated with the rise of a new class of powerful generals. The elimination of this group and the transfer of military command to the imperial princes begins a fifth period; from 1393 to 1402 growing rivalry among the princes produced instability and civil war. Finally, Yung-lo's victory in the civil war led to a period of military adventurism; from 1402 to 1427 the emperor personally initiated a series of expansionist campaigns that lasted until the collapse of the Chinese position in Vietnam.

The overall theme of the military history of the early Ming is the decline in the importance of offensive warfare. It was vital for the Ming to destroy their lower Yangtze rivals and to expel the Mongols if they were to claim the Mandate of Heaven. The need for further territorial conquest was debatable, and it was regularly opposed by the civil officials, who after 1427 had the Vietnam fiasco as an argument against either further wars of conquest or the revival of autonomous military power. The early Ming state, like the early Ottoman Empire, had been oriented and organized to wage offensive warfare on a regular basis; in this respect the early Ming period came to an end in 1427.

Geographical basis of power. Even in time of peace Ming leaders had to concern themselves with maintaining control of the territory from which troops were recruited and supplies gathered, and with thwarting the centrifugal tendencies of the regional armies.

Conquering and holding the necessary amount of land was the major problem facing the Ming before 1364, and the conquest of Kiangsi that was completed that year provided the margin of victory in the struggle for the lower Yangtze region. Afterwards the Nanking army under Chu Yüan-chang was always strong enough to overawe any regional Ming force, and it served simultaneously as the principal expeditionary army.

After 1364 troops from the vanquished armies were drafted into Ming expeditionary forces and sent to make further conquests while Chu Yüan-chang retired from field command and settled his old soldiers as military colonists in the Nanking area. Thereafter, the ability of the capital guards to counterbalance the expanding and combat-ready field armies steadily declined, and first the nobles and then the princes became increasingly indispensable links in the chain of command.

In 1398 Chien-wen faced independent and insubordinate field armies commanded by his princely uncles, and he provoked civil war by attempting to recentralize military authority. Yung-lo's victory and seizure of the throne in 1402 meant that the new imperial power base was no longer in Nanking but rather at Peking, the heart of Yung-lo's original military command. He concentrated troops there, reopened the Grand Canal to supply them, and used the city as the base for his Mongolian expeditions.

The transfer of the capital to Peking in the winter of 1420–21 marks the attainment of the internal military-geographical balance characteristic of the rest of the dynasty. Except for skeletal units, the capital guards at Nanking were transferred to the new capital, and the training functions once performed in the provincial military units were transferred to the training camps in Peking. The capital's share of the overall troop total increased, its percentage of the combat-trained total rose still higher, and it became a huge garrison city linked to the rice-growing areas by the Grand Canal. Because of its location it was overly sensitive to the military needs of northern frontier defense.

Military institutions. The early Ming period saw the rise and fall of the military nobility and the flowering and withering of the wei-so system. The original Ming armies were formed of units that had coalesced through accidents of war in the period of general turmoil in the 1350's. Because of this, the troops were personally loyal to their commanders, and succession to command in each unit tended to follow hereditary lines. Chu Yüan-chang had little control over these features of the system. He developed the military colonies to provide supplies, and in 1364, after his decisive victory in the P'oyang campaign, he reorganized his troops into the wei-so units and assigned new officers' ranks on the basis of the number of troops in each unit, but he also explicitly confirmed hereditary ranks for the officers and a hereditary obligation for the soldiers. Later regulations provided that about 70 percent of the troops should be engaged in farming during peacetime, so the military colony system made it possible to "deactivate" the armies without subjecting them and the state to the social and economic stress of large-scale demobilization. A group of about three dozen military nobles provided a pool of higher commanders who could be summoned to active duty as required. This organization was completed by the 1370's, but the purges of 1380 and 1393 eliminated most of the nobles, who were replaced by princes; the functioning of the system at its lower levels was left unchanged.

Yung-lo's accession in 1402 led to the creation of the capital training camps that afterwards dominated the combat-training function. The wei-so units retained only the duties of supplying raw conscripts and administering the military farmlands. As officers turned the military colonies into quasi-private estates, soldiers increasingly deserted the military registers, producing the forms of corruption characteristic of the Hsüan-te period. After Hsüan-te's death, the civil officials sought and partially captured operational and administrative control within the military establishment, control that they shared reluctantly with the eunuchs throughout the mature Ming period.

Foreign affairs. Before 1364 foreign affairs did not go beyond generally unsuccessful attempts at alliances with one or another of the contending warlords. After 1364, as the Ming regime became imperial, it faced the traditional concern of fitting non-Chinese peoples into a foreign-relations system characterized in principle by Chinese predominance. However, like their predecessors, Ming rulers did not view foreign affairs from a single perspective. Rather, there were three distinct areas toward which Ming policy gradually diverged.

In the north, frontier defense was the main policy goal. After a period of passive defense, Ming armies under Lan Yü shattered the Mongols' central power in 1388. Military colonies were planted in Manchuria and Inner Mongolia, and the next decade saw the high point of Ming power in these areas. When he rebelled, Yung-lo had won the support of some of the Mongols by withdrawing military forces from Inner Mongolia. When he became emperor, he attempted to dominate Mongolia by military expeditions. From 1424 throughout its mature imperial period, the Ming relied chiefly on passive defense; its rulers exerted little influence on Mongol politics, but Mongol coalitions were usually not strong enough to break through the Great Wall and its defenses.

In the south and west, Ming policy was to conquer and assimilate tribal lands and non-Chinese peoples. The traditionally Chinese province of Szechwan had to be annexed, and the Mongol regime in Yünnan and Kweichow had to be liquidated. Although the tribal peoples were never assimilated, the Ming were generally able to maintain control despite rebellions. It was with these successes in mind that Yung-lo embarked on the campaign in Vietnam that led to the disaster of 1427.

Toward the states of East and Southeast Asia, foreign policy was concerned with the regulation of trade and tributary embassies. The founding of the Ming had been greeted with the hope that the centralized tributary trading system of the T'ang would be restored. After a long period of restriction under Hung-wu, Yung-lo actively promoted both trade and embassies through Cheng Ho's maritime expeditions. However, his moving the capital to Peking undermined the institutional basis for these activities and they shortly lapsed.

The foreign policies of the mature Ming period can be discerned as early as the 1370's, but their stabilization had to wait until Yung-lo's death permitted the termination of his personal foreign policy initiatives. When Cheng Ho's last fleet returned in 1433, the foreign relations stance of the mature Ming was in full effect. China afterwards remained closed and hostile to foreign contact as long as the traditional society could make its will felt.

Civil service and government administration. The growth of the civil service and the restoration of Confucian gentry society under the protective umbrella of the early Ming military state is possibly the most important theme of early Ming history. Civil service and gentry society required a long period of sheltered growth before they were able to seize control of Ming China.

Civil administration was rudimentary before 1364, but from then until 1380 there was a steady growth of the civil service and a steady differentiation of civil from military functions. The Six Ministries and the provincial civil governments were created, and regular administration was restored at the prefectural and county levels. During this period of growth, officials were recruited chiefly by recommendation. Hung-wu had tried and rejected civil service examinations, feeling that they would not recruit practical talents.

After the 1380 purge of Chancellor Hu Wei-yung and the dismantling of his political machine, Hung-wu sacrificed every other consideration to his desire for personal control. The chancellorship was abolished; the Six Ministries, the five Chief Military Commissions, and the three commissioners in each province were all placed directly under the emperor. The revival of the civil service examinations in 1384–85 should be seen against this background. Whatever their defects, the examinations prevented any single minister from controlling the entire recruitment process. During these years, Hung-wu sent out his army to survey the land and count the people, a process completed in 1393, and the tax quotas assigned at this time served as the basis of Ming fiscal structure for the rest of the dynasty. Increased land revenues made income from other sectors of the economy less necessary, and this reinforced Confucian prejudices in favor of agriculture.

Characteristically, later Confucians took for granted Hung-wu's revival of the examinations, but blamed him for promoting despotism by abolishing the chancellorship. In fact, after 1385 the examinations dominated the civil service recruitment process to an unprecedented degree, and this greatly enhanced the ideological cohesiveness and esprit de corps of the civil officials vis-à-vis other elites. The Grand Secretariat emerged in the Yung-lo reign, and from 1402 until the 1440's the grand secretaries and the ministers of the Six Ministries served very long terms, a marked contrast to the Hung-wu period. When the succession in 1435 brought a weak child emperor to the throne for the first time in Ming history, the civil service—recruited by examination for the past fifty years—possessed greater unity and continuity of purpose than any potential competing group, and so was ideally placed to seize power in the state. In the later development of Chinese society, examination degrees grew in importance as marks of status while hereditary military ranks and noble titles declined in importance. Gentry society until 1905 was based on the recruitment of officials, the regulation of social status, and the indoctrination of society as a whole by means of the examination system.

In terms of the above themes, the Ming after 1435 saw little change. Warfare was begun only for defensive reasons; the Ming would respond if invaded or rebelled against (or, as in the 1590's, when its loyal tributary Korea was attacked), but there were no new attempts to annex territory. Peking continued as the capital and military center of the empire, although its inappropriateness for that role was suggested by the T'u-mu crisis of 1449 and the invasions of Dayan Qan and Altan Qan, and then was confirmed by the circumstances of the fall of the dynasty in 1644.[1] Military effectiveness remained at a low level, but military institutions were not reformed or significantly altered. Foreign policy continued to be isolationist. The civil service continued to dominate the state and the degree gentry to dominate society. In all of these respects, the situation was much the same in 1644 as it had been in 1435.

With the alternative elites of military officers, nobles, and imperial clansmen thus demoralized and ineffective, the political stage was dominated by the civil officials. Two later emperors, Ching-t'ai (r. 1450–57) and Hung-chih (r. 1488–1505), accepted this state of affairs as normal and ruled generally in accordance with the advice of their officials.[2] Most of the later Ming emperors, however, although lacking the imagination and experience to conceive an ·alternative to civil service rule, nevertheless chafed under the Confucian tutelage it imposed. Their reactions indicated impotence and frustration; they occasionally employed public humiliation, flogging, or even execution in individual cases, but they did not resort to measures against the civil officials as a class. These emperors either responded with indifference to government affairs, thus severely disrupting the orderly conduct of government business, or else delegated virtually total power to favored eunuchs, who then exercised quasi-dictatorial authority over palace and state alike. The eunuch establishment, working through the secret police in the Chin-yi Guard and certain other army units, kept the organs of governmental terror in imperial hands and carried out certain special assignments, but for the most part the civil service ran the state in accordance with bureaucratic routines.

Hsüan-te's immediate successor was his young son Cheng-t'ung (r. 1436–49, restored as T'ien-shun, r. 1457–64), and Hsüan-te's officials retained political power under the regency of his mother, the grand dowager empress Chang, until her death in 1442. In these years civil dominance over the military was finally secured by the institutionalization of the hsün-fu system. By the 1440's civil service government had become routine, but since the officials responsible for this development had mostly passed from the scene, Cheng-t'ung's personal rule after 1442 led to the emergence of the first of the eunuch dictators, his childhood playmate Wang Chen (d. 1449). Wang as director of ceremony (*szu-li t'ai-chien*) was in control of the palace eunuch establishment; his eunuch henchmen supervised the capital training camps, and nobles and military commanders, especially the officers of the Chin-yi Guard who had charge of secret police functions, were drawn into the system. The bureaucratized eunuch establishment thus served as the means of linking together the demoralized hereditary elements of the Ming elite: emperor, nobles, and military officers.

These elements were united in their resentment of civil service dominance, but collectively they were unable to develop alternative policies. The use they made of their power was therefore essentially parasitic. Appointments and other important government business had to be cleared through Wang Chen. He and his associates therefore amassed substantial fortunes, and the emperor also benefited from the diversion of state funds to palace purposes. This was the pattern of subsequent eunuch dictatorships; it was reproduced by Ts'ao Chi-hsiang in the T'ien-shun period, Wang Chih in the Ch'eng-hua period (1465–87), Liu Chin in the Cheng-te period (1506–21), and, most elaborately of all, Wei Chung-hsien in the T'ien-ch'i period (1621–27).[3]

Eunuch dictators thus emerged in four of the six reigns from 1435 to 1521 (counting Cheng-t'ung and T'ien-shun as different reigns), and so at least until 1521 eunuch dictatorship was a more usual state of affairs than the idealized relationship of minister and ruler so beloved of Confucians. Normal or not, the emergence of a eunuch dictator was certain to provoke an outraged chorus among the civil officials. Politics would then be polarized, with emperor and eunuchs (and the officials supporting them) on one side and principled civil officials on the other. At tension-charged court conferences officials would accuse eunuchs of usurping the emperor's authority and accumulating fortunes through corruption, often suffering death or lesser punishment for their temerity. The charges of usurpation were false. No eunuch dictator survived the death of his imperial patron, and the eunuchs maintained their power by pandering to the emperor's whims, not by reducing him to tutelage. If the eunuch dictators grew wealthy through corruption, the civil officials themselves were no strangers to self-serving financial irregularities.[4]

In fact, the eunuch establishment was the only possible viable alternative to civil service rule in the mature Ming period. The emergence of a eunuch dictator posed the threat that the emperor himself might seize the political initiative and once again drive the state toward goals repugnant to Confucian orthodoxy. In the early Ming period the eunuchs had aided the emperors in the pursuit of such goals; fear of a recurrence lay behind the almost hysterical response of many Confucians to eunuch influence in the government.*

A different pattern of imperial rule emerged under Chia-ching (r. 1522–66) and his successors Lung-ch'ing (r. 1567–72) and Wan-li (r. 1573–1620). These emperors confined themselves to private concerns and pleasures within the palace compounds, but retained control and did not permit the rise of a eunuch dictator with unchallenged authority over the eunuch establishment. If the emergence of a eunuch dictator had tended to unite officialdom against eunuch rule, the subsequent pattern of imperial passivity tended to divide the civil officials into quarreling factions. Government routines were severely disrupted, resuming a semblance of normal functioning only when certain of the grand secretaries were able to establish working relations with the leading eunuchs, whose demands were implicitly backed by the authority of the emperor. This usually required bribing the eunuchs and paying for extraordinary palace expenditures out of state funds. In times of military crisis such as the 1590's, this did not sit well with the rank and file of civil officials, who protested frequently and vociferously.

Matters were not helped by the distinct career patterns of the grand secretaries, who after 1440 were usually chosen from among

---

* A clear example of this is Liu Ta-hsia's destruction during the ascendancy of Wang Chih of the records of the Vietnam campaign of 1407 and of the Cheng Ho voyages, including the plans of the treasure ships. See L. Carrington Goodrich and Chaoying Fang, eds., *Dictionary of Ming Biography* (New York, 1976), pp. 958–62.

those who had passed at or near the top of their chin-shih class and had then served in the Han-lin Academy and other central literary agencies. Their career experience was thus isolated from that of most civil officials, who in consequence tended to be suspicious of them. Grand Secretary Yen Sung could reconcile himself to collecting bribes from civil officials in order to finance his own bribery of the eunuchs, but Chang Chü-cheng, who received abuse from both directions, could only lament that he had the responsibilities of a chancellor without the corresponding authority.[5]

Nevertheless, despite these permanently dysfunctional factors, the eunuchs, grand secretaries, and lower-ranking civil officials were often able to work together to keep the government going, at least until the decade of the 1590's. The bitter conflicts between eunuchs and officials that broke out then were occasioned by the diversion to palace use of funds urgently needed for the war in Korea. Beginning with these conflicts, the hostility of the more idealistic of the civil officials to the palace and the eunuchs grew steadily more intense throughout the remainder of the Wan-li reign. The Tung-lin party emerged to lead the civil officials, and Wei Chung-hsien became the last of the eunuch dictators after the ephemeral T'ai-ch'ang reign (1620). It was political polarization that prevented the Ming from coping effectively with the crises of the 1620's, chief of which was the rise of the Manchu state and its conquest of the Chinese garrisons in the Liao River valley.[6]

The last Ming emperor, Ch'ung-chen (r. 1628–44), tried to escape from the influence of both eunuchs and civil officials. After eliminating Wei Chung-hsien, he ruled personally, executing and dismissing ministers and generals in numbers not reached since the days of Hung-wu. But it was now too late. Wrecked by over a century of maladministration, the Ming regime in the interior could not withstand the peasant rebellions of Li Tzu-ch'eng and Chang Hsien-chung that devastated the North China plain. While his border armies successfully held the Great Wall against the Manchus, the emperor hanged himself as the rebels poured into a largely undefended Peking.[7]

In the early Ming period the emperors held the political initiative and transformed Chinese institutions and society; in the mature Ming period the dominant civil service ended by paralyzing whatever it could not convert to routine. There was certainly no lack of opportunity after 1435 for the kinds of policy initiatives characteristic of the early Ming, but the invasions of Dayan Qan and Altan Qan did not lead to any imperially commanded expeditions against them, and the Wakō troubles did not lead to the revival of the navy. The attempts of Chang Chü-cheng and others to reform the empire's military and fiscal institutions were thwarted by the intransigent opposition of lower-ranking civil officials. This was typical; the civil service was consistently able to veto policy innovations, whether they came from the grand secretaries or the so-called eunuch dictators. If reform was to be initiated at all, it had to be carried out piecemeal by the provincial officials in the manner of the single-whip taxation reforms. Moving the capital away from the dangerously exposed site of Peking should have been a priority concern after 1621, but though it was proposed, the step was never taken.[8]

During the mature Ming period, despite the control over the administrative machinery and the veto power over policy change held by the civil service, it was exceptional for government at the highest level to be conducted in accordance with Confucian norms. There was regularly a high degree of eunuch participation in the relations between sovereign and minister, either in the form of eunuch dictators ruling through delegated imperial authority, or of eunuch bureaucrats transmitting the imperial will and implementing imperial policies that were themselves distasteful to Confucians. Confucian officials, for all their internal disagreements, consistently opposed the imperial policies characteristic of the early Ming period, while the interconnected elites of imperial clansmen, nobles, and military officers failed to preserve their political cohesion into the mature Ming period. But to some extent the eunuchs provided an institutional memory of the policies and achievements of the founding emperors of the dynasty, and inspired some of the post-1435 emperors to try to emulate them. Thus Cheng-t'ung's personally led expedition against Esen in 1449, which ended in the T'u-mu disaster, was undertaken on Wang Chen's urging, and Wang Chih urged the revival of the naval voyages. But the survival of early Ming attitudes as represented by the eunuchs was only vestigial; the civil service managed to thwart all substantive attempts to revive early Ming policies.

Alternative Scenarios from Chinese History

The early Ming period had lasting effects on the subsequent social, economic, and political history of China. Political unification made civil service rule and gentry society possible, and military success made intellectual complacency and population growth possible. Possible does not mean necessary, so subsequent history might conceivably have taken different paths, given the early Ming outcome as background; however, the specific outcome of early Ming political history was at least a necessary precondition for the path actually followed. Conversely, given a different outcome for the early Ming period, alternatives to the state and society of the mature Ming and Ch'ing periods were possible. Some speculation about alternative consequences in three key areas of early Ming history—political unification, the destruction of the power of the elite of military officers and nobles, and the transfer of the capital to Peking—will help to illuminate some of these contrasting possibilities.

Political unification. The Mongols conquered all of China by 1279, reunifying the Chinese cultural area after a period of division that had lasted since the latter half of the T'ang dynasty. They created an empire that the Ming were able to restore in 1368 and the Manchus in 1644, in each case with only a brief interregnum. Political and military unity was thus a fact in the last six centuries of imperial China; the government was not usually challenged either by rival emperors or by generals usurping local power behind a facade of loyalty to the throne.

For Chinese historians this state of affairs was both normal and normative; there could be but one sun in Heaven and one emperor in human society. Drawing on the accepted traditions of the mythical Hsia dynasty and the historical Shang and Chou dynasties, the historians constructed a theory explaining the cyclical breakdown of dynasties and justifying the transfer of power to new ruling houses. Western historians have attempted to apply this theoretical dynastic cycle to all of Chinese history, generalizing backward from the Ch'ing, Ming, and Yüan; the result has been to create an image of a society remaining politically and institutionally stagnant for over two millennia until it began to respond to the West. According to this theory, if a dynasty fell, someone would come along sooner or later and found a new one; the details of any particular case were not important.[9]

The dynastic cycle theory may to some extent be an appropriate explanation of the Yüan, Ming, and Ch'ing, but it simply does not apply to earlier centuries. In the first 1,500 years of Chinese imperial history (211 B.C.–A.D. 1279), the sort of political unity characteristic of the post-1279 era prevailed only during the periods 221 B.C.–A.D. 190, 280–317, and 589–755, a total of 614 years (41 percent of the total) that includes the brief interregna following the fall of the Ch'in, the Hsin, and the Sui dynasties, and a spate of civil war in the Chin after 290. Periods of division, on the other hand, total 886 years (59 percent of the total). These include two periods (190–220, 755–907), during which an imperial court presided in name over an empire in which political and military power had in fact passed to regional warlords, plus three periods (220–80, 317–589, 907–1279) in which two or more dynasties existed side by side, each claiming to possess the sole legitimate imperial title.* The Yüan dynasty had reunified China briefly after a long period of division, and its fall might have been expected to precipitate the sort of extended disunity that had in fact been characteristic of most of the imperial period until then.

The comprehensive nature of Chu Yüan-chang's military victories permitted a speedy reunification of the empire; he survived two apparent assassination attempts in 1362 and 1380, attempts which, if successful, would have shattered this unity; and the total victory of his son Yung-lo in the civil war following his death ended the threat to unity posed by the princes.

Previous Chinese history suggests what might have happened if events had gone differently. By 1360 most of China was under the control of military regimes nominally loyal to the Yüan. If Chu Yüan-chang and the other avowed rebel leaders had been de-

---

* The Han empire never recovered its unity after the Yellow Turban rebellion, and after about 190 the emperor was merely the puppet of Ts'ao Ts'ao. Similarly, the T'ang never succeeded in entirely suppressing its northern warlords, despite partial success in the reign of Hsien-tsung (see p. 284, n. 10). Although some might find it contentious to refer to the Sung as a period of disunity, it remains a fact that the Sung never incorporated the Chinese-inhabited areas immediately south of the Great Wall, and that this was a permanent source of military weakness for the dynasty. See E.A. Kracke, *Civil Service in Early Sung China, 960–1067* (Cambridge, Mass., 1953), pp. 9–11.

stroyed in the wars of the 1360's, the result would have been nominal reunification under the Yüan, but in fact the situation would have resembled that of the late Eastern Han from 190 to 220, or of the middle and late T'ang from 755 to 907: a weak or powerless dynasty would have ruled in name over a group of actually independent and mutually hostile regional warlords. Judging from the late T'ang example, such a state of affairs could have gone on for generations.[10]

Chu Yüan-chang's major rival until 1363 was the ruthless adventurer Ch'en Yu-liang, who had advanced his career by murdering his original patron in 1355, a principal subordinate in 1359, and his nominal emperor in 1360. The last murder caused his ally, the warlord of Szechwan, to break away. Ch'en's entire career was plagued by distrust between himself and his inferiors. This fact suggests that, had he been victorious in 1363, his subsequent career might have been similar to that of Chu Wen (r. 907–15), founder of the Later Liang dynasty, whose rise to power was also based on a personal army under his direct command, and whose assumption of the throne precipitated declarations of independence from all of South China and inaugurated the Five Dynasties, a type period in Chinese historiography for instability and political division. Conditions in the Five Dynasties permitted the Khitans to seize and hold part of North China, and full political unity was not restored until the completion of the Mongol conquest in 1279.[11]

Finally, Chu Yüan-chang's delegation of military authority to his sons recalls the similar practice of Szu-ma Yen, founder of the Chin dynasty (265–420). The civil war among the princes following the founder's death in 290 led directly to the barbarian revolts of the early fourth century, which in turn resulted in the division of China between northern and southern dynasties that lasted until 589.[12]

The establishment and maintenance of imperial unity in the early Ming therefore seems to be an exceptional accomplishment, one that was achieved in the face of threats similar to those that had destroyed political unity on earlier occasions.

Military officers and nobles. One of the defining characteristics of the early Ming period was the leading role played by an elite whose social function was to command troops and whose social position was hereditary. The emperors and imperial princes headed this elite, with the nobles, hereditary after 1370, coming next and the wei-so officers, hereditary after 1364, last. This elite controlled the separate military colonies that were farmed by hereditary soldier-tenants. Successful commanders could expect promotion and even ennoblement. The ranks and salaries of military officers were set several grades higher than those of civil officials of corresponding degrees of responsibility, and the nobles were elevated to a position above the nine ranks so that they stood above all officials, civil or military. The situation was unprecedented in Chinese history.

The effective social dominance of this elite of military officers and nobles did not survive the early Ming period. Civil dominance over the military was the eventual outcome of the conflict in the Yung-lo reign over the emperor's Mongolian campaigns and the Vietnam war. As previously related, control of military command and administration at all levels was granted more or less formally to civil officials in the years 1435–40, and never subsequently relinquished. The fall of the professional officers was compounded by their failure to avert disaster in the T'u-mu crisis of 1449, which permitted the civil bureaucrat Yü Ch'ien to take control. Afterwards, in the mature Ming and Ch'ing periods, a non-Banner Chinese military elite always existed alongside the civil service elite, sustained to some extent by military examinations conceived in imitation of the civil service examinations (this was true after 1478), but always largely hereditary in theory and practice. Even though holders of the military examination degrees belonged formally to the degree gentry, the military elite after 1435 had little actual social prestige or political influence, at least in comparison to civil officials and civil degreeholders. Although regimental officers came largely from the military elite or by promotion from the ranks, the determination of policy, the control of the military supply system, and the higher field command itself all came to be virtually monopolized by civil officials. Tso Tsung-t'ang and his late-nineteenth-century colleagues thus stand at the end of a long tradition inaugurated in the fifteenth century by such Ming officials as Yü Ch'ien.[13]

However, it is an error of perception to read this pattern of civil-military relationships into the pre-Ming period. Early Ming emperors and officials could look back only on a historical record in which military and aristocratic elites had rivaled the civil service—often successfully—in the struggle for political influence and its accompanying social rewards, frequently becoming so strong as to threaten the security of the throne.

Military elites had been associated with an aristocratic tradition and with autonomous regional power. This association began in the Western Han (206 B.C.–A.D. 9) when the Huo, Li, Wei, and Wang families gained power by marriage with the imperial line and exercised this power by commanding armies. Huo Kuang ruled as dictator with the title of grand general, and Wang Mang went so far as to usurp the throne and found the Hsin dynasty (9–23). In the Eastern Han (23–220) the Teng and Tou families repeated the pattern of imperial marriage relationships and military command, with the Tou sponsoring Pan Ch'ao's campaigns in Central Asia. When the Yellow Turbans rebelled in 184, the throne was compelled to turn to the local magnates in order to raise an army for their suppression.[14]

For the next four centuries, South China was ruled by quasi-dynasties of local magnates that exercised both civil and military power in the areas under their control and were able to defy, rival, and sometimes replace the emperors reigning at Nanking. Imperial unity was reestablished by the Sui (589–618) and T'ang (618–907) dynasties, under which a class of aristocratic families (partly of non-Chinese origin) from the Kuanchung area was socially and politically prominent, controlling the military system and, to a large extent, the civil service through their right of hereditary entry through "protection" (*yin*).[15] These noble classes represent the aristocratic tradition that developed after Confucianism was accepted as the official ideology of the bureaucratic imperial state of Western Han; they are thus not continuations of the nobility of pre-Han China but creations of the imperial period itself. The survival of these aristocratic elites was to some extent logically antithetical both to the Confucian demand that officials be chosen on the basis of moral worth rather than class or parentage, and to the bureaucratic requirement that local administrators be removable and subservient. Nevertheless, the nobles existed quite well alongside the Confucian civil service, playing their imperial connections and local power into patronage rights that buttressed their influence on the composition of the civil bureaucracy and their domination of the military establishment.

The An Lu-shan rebellion (755–763) marked the end of aristocratic dominance of the armies—though not of the aristocracy itself—and the coming to power of regional militarists of much lower social origins. The officers of the armies of An Lu-shan and his rivals had been promoted from the ranks of the frontier garrison forces. The imperial need for armies to suppress the rebellion meant that the commanders of forces that remained loyal were able to extort autonomous appointment powers as their price for supporting the throne. For the rest of the T'ang dynasty, military units in certain important areas, chiefly Hopei and Shantung, were run by a closed (hereditary and/or co-optative) officer class that also controlled civil administration in its areas. The kind of autonomous regional power that these units wielded was a constant example and temptation to other units that were under tighter imperial control. However, their hereditary status did not lessen the social distance between the new-style military officers and the imperial clan, and marriage ties to the court did not develop. Instead of competing with aristocratic and bureaucratic elements for influence within the central government, the post-rebellion military officers sought local power to a degree that disrupted the cohesion of the empire.[16]

This tendency culminated in the Five Dynasties and Ten Kingdoms period (907–60) of ephemeral "imperial" houses in the north and solidly entrenched local regimes in the south. The founding emperors of the Sung dynasty (960–1279) pursued a generally successful conciliatory policy of persuading commanders to give up local power in return for high status at court. Even so, the persistence of autonomy and hereditary recruitment in the officer class was a source of major concern to the emperors, even in the midst of the debacle caused by the twelfth-century Jurchen invasions.*

In the early Ming period there existed both an embryonic nobility and a class of hereditary military officers, and the way was

---

* See Helmut Wilhelm, "From Myth to Myth: The Case of Yüeh Fei's Biography," in Arthur F. Wright and Denis Twitchett, eds., *Confucian Personalities* (Stanford, Calif., 1962), p. 160, where Emperor Kao-tsung of Sung (r. 1126–62) is quoted as saying, "What makes me happy is not that Ch'i has been defeated, but that the generals obeyed orders."

open to the re-creation of powerful noble families connected to the dynasty by marriage, a class of territorial magnates, or a combination of the two. The way in which military units had come into existence in the 1350's and the relationships of personal loyalty obtaining among officers and between officers and men had made the wei-so units virtual patrimonies of their commanding officers. Chu Yüan-chang was forced to recognize this state of affairs, hoping to regularize it by formally granting officers hereditary ranks, succession to which required confirmation by the throne. Any attempt to abolish the hereditary and personal nature of military authority would have led to massive defections to the enemies of the Ming in the wars of unification. The nobles included Chu Yüan-chang's original companions, some relatives, and some important military leaders who had joined him at critical phases in the civil wars. They originally owed their positions to Chu Yüan-chang's trust in them, and they came to serve as his delegates in the exercise of field command as the Ming armies grew too large for control by a single general.

Chu's withdrawal from active field command after 1364 changed this situation. By the 1370's, after another decade of leading the same troops in successive campaigns, the nobles had won the loyalty of the officers and men in their particular commands, but at the price of losing the trust of the emperor. The latter might have attempted to secure the loyalty of the nobles by wedding their daughters to his growing flock of sons, at the risk of creating a powerful class of imperial in-laws wielding military authority as in Han times; or he might have attempted to reverse his original policy by depriving the nobles of their field commands and turning them into hereditary sinecurists, but at the risk of creating a class of provincial military officers very much detached from the throne and from the main body of Chinese society as in Sung and post-755 T'ang times.

The actual responses of the early Ming emperors to the problem of officer recruitment and military command differed from both of the foregoing, and they were less than conspicuously successful. They led indirectly to such a degree of civilian control over the military as to vitiate the ability of the military to perform its legitimate functions. How this came about has already been discussed; here the important point is that there was still open at the beginning of Ming the option of creating a class of military officers and nobles powerful enough to serve as a political and social counterweight to the class of civil officials and degree gentry. Judging from the experience of previous dynasties, such a development might have been the more normal course for Ming institutions to follow.

The location of the capital. For dynasties of Chinese origin, changes in the location of the capital have reflected both long-term shifts in the overall population distribution and the more immediate issue of each dynasty's geographical origins. Thus, the location of the capital at Ch'angan during the Western Han and T'ang dynasties symbolized the conquest of China by military power generated in the Kuanchung area, and the location of the capital at Loyang during the Eastern Han and at K'aifeng during the Northern Sung resulted from the fact that both dynasties had come to power by first unifying the North China plain. On the other hand, the location of the capital at Nanking during the Six Dynasties and at Hangchow during the Southern Sung was a consequence of the loss of the North China plain to barbarian invaders; the Chinese remnant regime had no choice but to base itself on the Yangtze delta area, which was the population center of South China.[17]

Political factors sometimes dictated and sometimes skewed the placement of capitals in relation to key economic areas. The Sui and T'ang reunified China from Kuanchung even though that area had for centuries been declining in population relative to China as a whole. Kuanchung's production was insufficient for the needs of the capital, and grain transportation to Ch'angan from other regions was so difficult that the court had to move to Loyang for long periods, yet the capital was not formally transferred there until 904, the very eve of the fall of the T'ang. When the Sung restored a measure of unity in 960, its capital also was not located in China's economic center of gravity, and grain had to be transported from South China in order to maintain it. Here also special politico-military circumstances were operating; Chao K'uang-yin (Emperor T'ai-tsu of Sung, r. 960–76) was attempting to solve the twin problems of warlordism and barbarian invasion by concentrating the armies in the capital, where he could watch them, and maintaining the capital in the north, where its armies would shield the rest of the empire from attack.[18]

Nanking and Hangchow, in contrast, actually were in the economic heartland of both the Six Dynasties and the Southern Sung; and when the Ming, coming to power as a result of their conquest of the lower Yangtze area, established their capital at Nanking, political and economic factors once again coincided. Apparently this was the logical culmination of the historical processes that had caused first China's demographic center and later China's imperial capital to migrate in uneven stages from the Kuanchung area to the North China plain, and then to the lower Yangtze region in South China.

Regimes of non-Chinese origin tended to locate their capitals near the Great Wall in the transition zone between arable and pasture land. Such regimes were based on a balance between the military power of an aristocrat-ruled nomadic society and the wealth of bureaucrat-administered Chinese sedentary society; the location of their capitals in the borderlands between the two societies was the index of this balance. Increasing dependence on a fixed capital located further south reflected a rise in the power of the Chinese component sufficient to upset the original social balance. Beginning with the Former Yen dynasty in the fourth century, the site of Peking has been a favored location for the capitals of such regimes. The Khitan Liao placed their southern capital there, and it was the main capital of both the Jurchen Chin and the Mongol Yüan. The Manchu Ch'ing, who were fond of evoking their heritage from the Liao, Chin, and Yüan, also made Peking their capital after 1644.[19]

When they did this they were following a Ming precedent, that of Yung-lo's making Peking his main capital in 1420–21. In the light of previous history as summarized above, Yung-lo's was a distinctly anomalous decision, since it was the first time a dynasty of Chinese origin had located its capital in the Sino-barbarian transition zone, or indeed anywhere outside the road from Ch'angan to Hangchow along which both the capitals of the native Chinese dynasties and the center of the Chinese population had traveled up to then. In its walls and streets and palaces Peking was much the same city under the Manchus as under the Ming, but as the capital its significance was very different. The Manchu emperors could hold audience with their Chinese officials in the traditional Chinese manner in Peking and then, only a few days later, could be north of the Great Wall receiving their subject tribal princes in splendid fêtes in which Chinese Son of Heaven was forgotten in a revival of the image of Mongol qaghan. The Ming, on the other hand, had to defend a northern frontier along the Great Wall, as had the T'ang and the two Han dynasties before them; for them the lands beyond the wall were a source of danger, not of strength. The location of the capital at Peking meant that both the government and the armies on the northern border had to be supplied by grain transport whose capacity was not excessive for either task.

Although North China's percentage of the total Chinese population increased from the founding of the Ming onward, even today the majority lives in South China; clearly the reversal of the demographic trend did not in itself require a change in capitals. Later Ming emperors sometimes played at war, but only Cheng-t'ung in 1449 attempted to follow Yung-lo's example of personal military leadership against the Mongols. Far from being well situated to supervise the defense of the northern frontier, the Ming emperors at Peking were the prisoners of local military crises, of which Cheng-t'ung's capture at T'umu was only the most extreme example. And without denying the gravity of the combined peasant rebellions and Manchu invasions that destroyed the Ming dynasty in 1644, the truth is that most of the empire was unaffected by either. Had the capital remained at Nanking, it is probable that the Ming empire would have survived, though possibly only in a truncated form reminiscent of the Southern Sung.[20]

The location of the capital at Peking resulted from Yung-lo's rise to power in that area and his use of Peking to marshal forces for his Mongolian campaigns, and from Hung-hsi's failure, due to his early death, to return the capital to Nanking. It is the outstanding example of a decision being taken in early Ming for specific political and military reasons and then hardening into a permanent dysfunction in the mature Ming system. If the capital had remained at Nanking, the society and politics of the mature Ming might have differed significantly in at least two respects.

In the first place, Nanking was in the area of the Yangtze valley and the southern coastal urban culture that had grown so greatly in population and importance during the Southern Sung. Locating the imperial court and the body of capital officials there would have enabled them to share more readily the concerns of this culture. For instance, the considerable expansion of seaborne foreign trade that the mature Ming witnessed might have remained at least formally legal, possibly even becoming an object of official solicitude if the capital officials and the imperial court had had greater opportunities to profit directly from it. In fact, overseas trade in the mature Ming period developed as a result of the efforts of native and foreign merchants who often were in collusion with some of the officials, but it was in violation of the government policy of closing the country to foreign contact.[21] An imperial court based in South China would also probably have been less willing to give up the Vietnam adventure and more concerned with an active military and diplomatic policy in Southeast Asia. Naval expeditions on the scale of those organized by Cheng Ho would still doubtless have depended on imperial sponsorship, but such sponsorship might have been more consistently forthcoming as successive generations of emperors were bred in the city where the ships were built. The effect of all this on the early stages of Western colonial expansion would have been striking.

In the second place, although emperors in Nanking might have neglected the northern frontier, supplying the armies would have been easier, and the consequences of military defeat would have been less. Yung-lo's campaigns against the Mongols would not have occurred, and the military stance in the north would have remained defensive, as it was during the mature Ming period. However, even a defensive strategy would have required a standing army on the northern frontier. Under the T'ang dynasty the combination of such a standing army and an imperial court increasingly indifferent to either its welfare or its control had led to the rebellion of An Lu-shan and the ensuing regional warlordism. This in turn had presaged the economic and technological developments of the Sung "medieval economic revolution."

The actual outcome of early Ming history preempted all alternative scenarios. The course of mature Ming and Ch'ing history was that described by Elvin as the "high-level equilibrium trap." Commercial and industrial sectors of the economy declined in comparison to agriculture, and the scale of the economy as a whole, although it expanded greatly, was unaccompanied by significant technological or social change. Elvin contrasts the high-level equilibrium trap with the medieval economic revolution preceding it, which had seen the development of scientific farming carried out more and more on rationally managed estates, technological innovation that included the invention of cannon and great advances in shipbuilding, interregional trade in grain and other commodities (all based on greatly expanded water transport and the development of the necessary credit facilities and commercial organization), and large-scale urbanization. The watershed between these two periods came in the early Ming. The Chinese economy fell into decline, and when it recovered in the sixteenth century, its further growth was in scale only, which is a defining characteristic of the high-level equilibrium trap. Elvin describes the "fourteenth-century turning point" in terms of three main features: a reversal of the demographic trend, constant since Ch'in-Han times, of an increase in the percentage of the Chinese population living in South China; the increasing isolation of China from the rest of the world; and a change in the nature of intellectual activity, that resulted in intuition and literary scholarship being valued more highly than empiricism and the study of the real world.*

These developments are contrary to Western experience and are "still largely inexplicable" in terms of social and economic history.[22] They become a good deal clearer when related to the political and military history of the early Ming period.

Demography. The rate of increase in South China's share of the total Chinese population had tapered off considerably by the beginning of the tenth century. Had all of China up to the Great Wall remained at peace under Chinese rule, the existence of fertile and undercultivated lands in the south would nevertheless have ensured a continuous increase in the proportion of the total population living in the south, even though the rate of increase would

---

* *The Pattern of the Chinese Past* (Stanford, Calif., 1973), especially pp. 203–34. Some of Elvin's interpretations, especially those concerning the extent and persistence of serfdom, are considered overdrawn, but it is difficult to quarrel with his concept of the fourteenth century as a watershed between different *types* of development.

have continued to decrease as the southern lands filled up. However, the Khitan, Jurchen, and Mongol invasions—which first turned large sections of the North China plain into military frontier zones and then killed millions of Chinese and turned millions more into refugees who fled south—ensured that the demographic predominance of South China would go on increasing at an accelerated rate during the period described as the medieval economic revolution.[23] To some extent, both the medieval economic revolution and the rate of increase in South China's share of the population stemmed directly from the protracted wars against the invaders.

The Ming expulsion of the invaders was both a necessary precondition to the growth of the population in the north and a stimulus to deliberate attempts at resettlement. Hung-wu was the first emperor of Chinese origin since the eighth century to control all the territory up to and including the Great Wall. He began the resettlement of the northern provinces by transferring large numbers of both civilian and military colonists from the Yangtze delta area. Yung-lo continued the process by transferring several hundred thousand troops and their families to Peking when he moved the capital. Since the north was not seriously disrupted by war or invasion until the fall of the dynasty, natural increase filled up the empty lands.

Ming statistics from the sixteenth century indicate this process. Hung-wu's provision for an annual census had been one of the first casualties of the Confucian takeover of government, and later Ming statistics do not reflect the considerable increase in the total population that took place during the long Ming peace. They do show increases in both population and registered land in the north, where the government promoted resettlement. The majority of the population remained in the south, where the Chinese continued to take land from the tribal peoples. In the already densely populated areas such as the Yangtze delta and the Canton region modest improvements in technique and great increases in the amount of human fertilizer available led to substantial improvements in yield per acre.[24] Growth in population thus tended to increase the relative preponderance of the agricultural sector of the economy and to reinforce the official tendency to treat agriculture as the only proper economic activity.

Isolation. The separation of China from the rest of the world resulted from imperial policy complementing Confucian preference. Hung-wu reacted to the threat of Japanese piracy by increasing the number of coastal garrisons and restricting travel by sea. Confucian preference in this area had crystallized in the ninth-century reaction against Buddhism, in which Chinese fascination with foreign things and ideas had been blamed for the An Lu-shan rebellion and the subsequent collapse of the T'ang empire. Later material and spiritual imports, mostly arriving in the train of the Jurchen and Mongol conquerors, had not lessened literati dislike of things foreign. While Yung-lo sponsored the voyages of Cheng Ho, he also permitted the growth of a civil service establishment ideologically hostile to such undertakings. Even during his lifetime the transfer of the capital to the north diverted his attention from them, and after his death, no significant institutional voice regularly contested the policy of closing the country.

In the specific context of the early Ming period, the ending of offensive war and the closing off of China to foreign contact were policies motivated both by general Confucian ideology and by the specific circumstances of the civil officials' rise to power in 1402–35. However, by the mid-sixteenth century these policies had functioned with apparent success for some 150 years, and Confucian officials could cite practical utility as well as ideological orthodoxy as reasons for maintaining them. Thereafter they would counter any temporary breakdown of the system by attempting to restore it as it had been. Institutional or technological change was unnecessary, since existing methods had proved perfectly adequate. And, of course, isolationism and defensiveness tended to minimize the foreign contacts and military crises that might have provided the impetus for intellectual change. This self-reinforcing cycle continued for most of the Ming and Ch'ing periods; it could not have come into existence had not the early Ming emperors succeeded in establishing unity, peace, and secure frontiers.

Thought. The marked pragmatism of the Sung mind, and the relative absence of pragmatism in Ming thinking, parallel the fact that the Sung empire had a permanent military problem while the Ming frontier defense system was on the whole remarkably successful. Permanent crisis during the Sung bred a group of scholar-

officials who remained continuously available as potential ini-
tiators of reform. In contrast, in the mature Ming period the
successes of the early Ming had induced a certain complacency.
The solution to most crises was seen basically as a matter of
returning to the original institutions of the dynasty, and this
required effort and character rather than original thought. A Ming
figure like Wang Shou-jen could be a pragmatic and successful
statesman-general in his official life, and a philosopher of intuitive
awareness in his scholarly life; in Sung times he would have been
more likely to devote both sides of his mind to the real world.

The complacency that comes with success tended to exaggerate
and reinforce the stereotyping of intellectual life encouraged by
the examination system. In reviving that system in 1384–85,
Hung-wu raised the examinations to a more important place in the
recruitment of officials than they had ever held before. By the early
fifteenth century the examinations were emphatically the most
important route of social mobility in China. Rising in the military
usually involved some original hereditary rank, and few cared to
join the eunuch establishment, but success in the examinations
might transport a man of relatively humble social origins to
heights of wealth and power as an official—even gaining one of
the lesser degrees could help to preserve an old fortune or make the
way easier for the son of a rising family. The officials themselves
were thus only the apex of the hierarchy of vested interests represented by the examination system. Below them stood the local
degreeholding elite, ranging from wealthy landowners down to
poor students, who collectively constituted a base of public opinion that the government ignored at its peril. Still farther down
were all of those who had not yet won even the lowest examination degree, but hoped to—those who had invested time and
capital in education directed to that end.

As educational levels and literacy rose during the Ming, it
became increasingly difficult to contemplate challenging all of
these vested interests by making even minor changes in the examination system—not that officials who were themselves products of
the system were often minded to do so. The power of the civil
officials guaranteed the efficacy of the examination degrees as
indicators of social status. The effectiveness of the examination
system as a ladder of social mobility made it highly likely that

Chinese education and thought would become closely tied to and constrained by the content of the examinations, as actually happened. Finally, the expanded educational opportunities made possible by prolonged peace and prosperity meant that those intellectual restrictions were not confined to a small elite but were increasingly widespread in the Chinese population as a whole.[25]

Under the early Ming emperors, political conflict had led to institutional change, and in approximately eighty years Chinese society had altered markedly in response. Military unification and military success had led to civil peace and civil rule. The leadership of Chinese society in the 1350's had been in the hands of a socially and intellectually diverse elite composed of Chinese and barbarians, soldiers and civilians, illiterates and Confucian literati. By 1435 the ruling elite was much more narrowly defined—socially by the possession of an examination degree and intellectually by the possession of an orthodox Confucian viewpoint. The formal elite status of military officers, nobles, and imperial clansmen was essentially vestigial; these groups lived well but had little influence on society.

After 1435 political conflicts were fought out within a restricted arena whose shape had been fixed by the outcome of the early Ming period. The resolution of these conflicts did not lead to institutional change. As Chinese society grew in population and faced new and severe challenges, the Ming state remained largely paralyzed, unable to relocate its capital, to change its military or fiscal systems, or to make reforms in other areas. Naturally the history of the mature Ming period is itself so complex that it cannot be fully understood without the study of specific later circumstances, but the influence of the two great early Ming emperors reaches beyond Ming history into the gentry society that attained its full growth as a result of their deeds.

Reference Matter

Notes

Complete authors' names, titles, and publication data for all items cited in the Notes are given in the Bibliography, pp. 285–93. The following abbreviations are used in the Notes:

CLHP   Shen Chieh-fu, *Chi-lu hui-pien*
DMB   Goodrich and Fang, *Dictionary of Ming Biography*
ECCP   Hummel, *Eminent Chinese of the Ch'ing Period*
HHSL   Yang Shih-ch'i, *Jen-tsung Chao-huang-ti shih-lu*
HLTTS   Cheng Chen-to, *Hsüan-lan-t'ang ts'ung-shu*
HMCS   Chang Lu, *Huang-Ming chih-shu*
HTSL   Yang Shih-ch'i, *Hsüan-tsung Chang-huang-ti shih-lu*
HWSL   Hu Kuang, *T'ai-tsu Kao-huang-ti shih-lu*
MS   Chang T'ing-yü, *Ming-shih*
TMHT   Shen Shih-hsing, *Ta-Ming hui-tien*
YLSL   Yang Shih-ch'i, *T'ai-tsung Wen-huang-ti shih-lu*
YS   Li Shan-ch'ang, *Yüan-shih*

CHAPTER ONE

1. For Szu-ma Ch'ien's view of Han Wu-ti, see Watson, pp. 30–36; and Dubs, 2: 1–13, 16–17. For Sui Yang-ti as a negative role model, see Rogers, pp. 40–51; and Wright, "Sui Yang-ti."

2. The T'ang obsession with the exotic is treated exhaustively in Schafer. The intellectual history of the critical post–An Lu-shan period is discussed in Pulleyblank, "Neo-Confucianism and Neo-Legalism"; Twitchett, "Lu Chih"; and McMullen.

3. The military history of the late T'ang and Five Dynasties is discussed by Wang Gungwu in his works *Structure of Power* and "Middle Yangtze"; and by Peterson in his works "Restoration Completed" and "Regional Defense." Yüeh Fei's career and legend, the paradigm for official fears of too-successful generals, are analyzed in Wilhelm; and Haeger.

4. Wang Yü-ch'üan, "Outline of the Central Government"; Pulleyblank, *An Lu-shan*; des Rotours, *Traité des examens* and *Traité des fonctionnaires*; and Kracke.

5. On civil service examinations, see Ho, *Ladder of Success*; on Yüan government, see Ratchnevsky.

6. On the Ottoman system, see Gibb and Bowen; on the Mughals, see Hodgson.

CHAPTER TWO

1. Vernadsky, pp. 138–232, summarizes these developments. On Iran, see Boyle, pp. 303–421, 483–537.

2. Martin summarizes earlier studies of the rise of the Mongols. On the Yüan empire at its height, see Schurmann's "Mongolian Tributary Practices" and *Economic Structure*; and Dardess, "Mongol Empire."

3. Mote, "Confucian Eremitism."

4. Dardess, "Transformations."

5. On the Northern Wei, see Eberhard. On the Ch'ing, see Michael; and, for a more recent discussion, Wakeman.

6. MS, 123: 11b–13b; YS, 39: 8a–9a, 13b–14a; DMB, pp. 433–35.

7. Muramatsu Yūji; Shigematsu Toshiaki summarizes these developments.

8. MS, 122: 3b–6a; Dardess, "Transformations"; Dreyer, "Emergence," pp. 30–44, 60–74, and sources cited therein.

9. Dardess, *Conquerors and Confucians*, pp. 95–105; Nakayama Hachirō, "Shisei jūichinen."

10. DMB, pp. 485–88, 600–602; Dardess, *Conquerors and Confucians*, pp. 103–5.

11. Dreyer, "Emergence," pp. 30–32, 60–63, 144.

12. Militarization as a social response to the breakdown of political order is discussed in Kuhn, pp. 10–36, 64–92; many of Kuhn's conclusions apply to the fourteenth century.

13. Dreyer, "Emergence," pp. 45–48; MS, 123: 6a–7b; DMB, pp. 99–103; Takahashi Takuji.

14. Dardess, *Conquerors and Confucians*, pp. 105–9, 119–22.

15. MS, 1: 1b–2a, 122: 1a–3b; HWSL, 1: 2a–4b; DMB, pp. 777–80; Taylor, "Social Origins."

16. Dreyer, "Emergence," pp. 144–45.

17. DMB, pp. 381–92; Taylor, "Social Origins"; Wu Han, *Chu Yüan-chang*, pp. 1–40.

18. Ku Chieh-kang cites numerous examples of this attitude.

19. T'an Ch'ien, pp. 262–64.

20. Dreyer, "Emergence," pp. 109–12.

21. MS, 1: 2a; HWSL, 1: 4b.

22. Dardess, *Conquerors and Confucians*, pp. 119–28.

23. Dreyer, "Emergence," pp. 74–85.

24. MS, 123: 6b–8a.

25. Dreyer, "Emergence," pp. 46–52; Otagi Matsuo; Mote, *Kao Ch'i*, pp. 23–25, 36–37, 64–65, 89–114.

26. Dreyer, "Emergence," pp. 56–58; MS, 124: 7a–12a.

27. Dreyer, "Emergence," pp. 52–56; MS, 123: 11b–15b; DMB, pp. 433–35.

28. Dreyer, "Emergence," pp. 32–35; MS, 123: 1a–6a, 15b–21a; HWSL, 8: 5a–6b; DMB, pp. 600–602, 1069–73.

29. Dreyer, "Emergence," pp. 34–36; MS, 123: 1a–6a; DMB, pp. 185–88.

30. Dreyer, "Emergence," pp. 34–36.

31. Dreyer, "Emergence," pp. 36–42; HWSL, 7: 3b–6a.

32. Dreyer, "Emergence," pp. 42–44.

33. Dreyer, "Emergence," pp. 62–66; MS, 122: 4b–5b.

34. Ibid.

35. Dreyer, "Emergence," pp. 67–68; MS, 122: 6a, 124: 1a–b; YS, 46: 5b, 141: 4a–15a.

36. MS, 1: 2a–b; HWSL, 1: 4b–7b.

37. MS, 1: 2b–3b; HWSL, 1: 7b–9a, 2: 1a–5a; DMB, pp. 1248–51.

38. MS, 1: 3b; HWSL, 2: 5a–b; Wada Sei, "Min no Taisō"; Dreyer, "Emergence," pp. 68–73.

39. MS, 1: 3b–4b; HWSL, 3: 1a–6a; DMB, pp. 908–10, 1618–20; Dreyer, "Emergence," pp. 74–84.

40. MS, 1: 4b–5a; HWSL, 4: 1a–3a.

41. On Nanking, see Farmer, pp. 51–57.

42. MS, 1: 5b; HWSL, 4: 3a–4a. For the organization of the Ming state at this time, see Dreyer, "Emergence," pp. 77–79, 98–120; and Taylor, "Social Origins." I disagree with the belief expressed by Wada Sei in "Min no Taisō" that Chu became duke of Wu only in 1361; cf. Dreyer, "Chi-shih-lu." On the yi, see Aoyama Jirō.

43. MS, 1: 5b–6a; HWSL, 4: 4a–5b, 5: 1a–4b.

44. MS, 1: 5b–7a; HWSL, 5: 1b–2a, 3a–4b, 6: 2b–3a, 5b–7b; DMB, pp. 115–20, 629–31, 1277–80.

45. On the Yangtze situation in 1360, see Dreyer, "Emergence," pp. 83–84, 88–98, 459–68; and Mote, Kao Ch'i, pp. 8–37.

46. Dreyer, "Emergence," pp. 98–120, 383–89; Taylor, "Wei-so System."

47. Dreyer, "Emergence," pp. 139–57; Dreyer, "Poyang Campaign."

48. MS, 1: 7a; HWSL, 8: 2b–3a; Dreyer, "Emergence," pp. 168–77; DMB, pp. 115–20.

49. MS, 1: 7a–b; HWSL, 8: 3a, 5a, 6b; Dreyer, "Emergence," pp. 177–91.

50. MS, 1: 7b; HWSL, 8: 6a–7b.

51. MS, 1: 7b; HWSL, 8: 6a–7b; DMB, pp. 694–96. See also MS, 129: 14b–16a, 130: 3b–5a, 12a–13a, 133: 11b–14b; Nakayama Hachirō, "Chin Yū-ryō"; and critiques of Nakayama in Dreyer, "Emergence," pp. 479–87, 511–14, and Dreyer, "Chi-shih-lu."

52. MS, 1: 7b–8a; HWSL, 8: 7b–8b; Dreyer, "Emergence," pp. 191–212.

53. MS, 1: 8a, 133: 9b–11b; HWSL, 8: 8a.

54. MS, 1: 8a, 133: 6a–9a; HWSL, 8: 8b–9a; DMB, pp. 629–31.

55. HWSL, 8: 9b–10b, 9: 1a–3b; Dreyer, "Emergence," pp. 215–24.

56. MS, 1: 8b; HWSL, 9: 3b–4a; DMB, pp. 1277–80.

57. MS, 1: 8b; HWSL, 9: 4a–5a.

58. MS, 125: 1a–11a; HWSL, 9: 5a–b; Dreyer, "Emergence," pp. 225–42.

59. MS, 1: 8b, 125: 11a–17a; HWSL, 9: 5a–6b.

60. MS, 1: 8b, 129: 16a–18a; HWSL, 9: 7a–b, 10: 1a–2b.

61. HWSL, 10: 6a–b.

62. MS, 1: 8b–9a, 133: 6a–9b; HWSL, 10: 2b–6a; DMB, pp. 629–31; Dreyer, "Emergence," pp. 242–56.

63. MS, 1: 9a; 126: 1a–8a; HWSL, 10: 6a–b, 11: 1a–2b; DMB, pp. 881–87.

64. MS, 1: 9a; HWSL, 10: 6a–b, 11: 1a–2b; Dreyer, "Emergence," pp. 256–72.

65. MS, 1: 9a; HWSL, 11: 2b–3a; Dreyer, "Emergence," pp. 527–28.

66. MS, 1: 9a; HWSL, 11: 3a–b.

67. HWSL, 11: 3a; YS, 46: 5b–6a, 141: 9b; Dardess, *Conquerors and Confucians*, pp. 145–46.

68. MS, 1: 9b; HWSL, 12: 1b–2b, 4b–5a; DMB, pp. 485–88; Wada Sei, "Min no Taisō"; Dreyer, "Emergence," pp. 282–87.

69. MS, 1: 9b; HWSL, 12: 3a; DMB, pp. 185–88; Dreyer, "Poyang Campaign"; Dreyer, "Emergence," pp. 287–99.

70. MS, 1: 9b; HWSL, 12: 3b–4b.

71. MS, 1: 9b; HWSL, 12: 3a–b, 13: 4b; Dreyer, "Emergence," pp. 300–304.

72. MS, 1: 9b; HWSL, 12: 5a–b; Dreyer, "Emergence," pp. 304–11.

73. *T'ien-huang yü-t'ieh*, in CLHP, 12: 5a. See also the discussion of numbers in Dreyer, "Emergence," pp. 469–78.

74. MS, 1: 9b; HWSL, 12: 6a–b; Dreyer, "Emergence," pp. 312–19.

75. MS, 1: 9b–10a; HWSL, 12: 6b–7a; Dreyer, "Emergence," pp. 319–37.

76. MS, 1: 10a–b; HWSL, 12: 7a–b; *P'ing-Han lu*, in CLHP, 28: 8b; DMB, pp. 909–10, 1618–20.

77. MS, 1: 10a–b; HWSL, 12: 7a–b.

78. MS, 1: 10a–b, 125: 13a, 133: 4b; HWSL, 12: 7b–9b; Dreyer, "Emergence," pp. 337–57.

79. MS, 1: 10b–11a; HWSL, 13: 1a–b.

80. Dreyer, "Poyang Campaign," especially pp. 202, 239–40.

81. The ideological significance of Chang's regime is the theme of much of Mote, *Kao Ch'i*; compare DMB, pp. 99–103. For Chu's general conservatism, see especially Taylor, "Social Origins."

82. MS, 1: 11a; HWSL, 13: 5a.

83. MS, 1: 11a, 123: 11b–21b, 124: 7a–12a; HWSL, 14: 1a; DMB, pp. 433–35, 1069–73; Dreyer, "Emergence," pp. 407–18.

84. MS, 1: 11a–b; HWSL, 13: 4b–5b, 14: 2a–4a, 10a, 15: 2b–3a; Dreyer, "Emergence," pp. 373–78, 389–406.

85. HWSL, 15: 3b–4a, 5a–6a, 7b–8a, 16: 2a, 4a, 6b.

86. HWSL, 15: 2a–4b, 6b–7b, 16: 1a–2b, 6a.

87. HWSL, 15: 9a, 16: 2b–4b.

88. HWSL, 16: 6b, 17: 1a–b.

89. HWSL, 13: 5a–b.

90. MS, 1: 11a, 90: 1a–2b, 76: 20a–b; HWSL, 14: 4b–6b, 7a–b, 10a–b; Aoyama Jirō; Taylor, "Wei-so System."

91. See n. 90; and Dreyer, "Emergence," pp. 379–89. The order relating to retirement is in HWSL, 17: 4b–5a; MS, 1: 12a. No source spells out the way in

which surrendered troops were reassigned; the version given here is inferred from scattered references in HWSL.

92. HWSL, 15: 6a–b, 7b, 16: 2b; Dreyer, "Emergence," pp. 419–32.

93. MS, 1: 11b, 126: 1a–8b; HWSL, 16: 4b–6a, 18: 7b (Hsü Yi's refusal to fight); DMB, pp. 881–87.

94. MS, 1: 12a–b; HWSL, 18: 2a–3a, 4a–5a; 19: 3a–b, 7a–8b, 20: 1a–b.

95. MS, 1: 12a–b; HWSL, 20: 1a–b, 2b–3a, 6a–7a.

96. HWSL, 18: 4b–5a.

97. MS, 1: 12b–13a; HWSL, 21: 1a–3b, 5b–8a.

98. MS, 1: 13a, 14a, 123: 6a–11a, 125: 1a–11a, 133: 3a–6a; HWSL, 21: 8a–b, 23: 3a–b, 7a–b; DMB, pp. 99–103, 603–8, 1618–20.

99. MS, 1: 14a, 123: 10b; HWSL, 24: 1a–2b, 25: 1b–3a.

100. YS, 141: 4a–15a; Dardess, *Conquerors and Confucians*, pp. 132–39.

101. YS, 45: 15b, 16b; Dardess, *Conquerors and Confucians*, pp. 134–46.

102. YS, 45: 19a–20b, 46: 2a–3a.

103. Ch'üan Heng, pp. 38a–39a; MS, 1: 9a; HWSL, 11: 3a, 4b–5a; YS, 46: 5b–6a.

104. MS, 124: 1a–7a; DMB, pp. 724–28.

105. Dardess, *Conquerors and Confucians*, pp. 147–56.

106. MS, 1: 14a–15b, 132: 1a–2b; HWSL, 24: 6a–7a, 25: 1a, 4b, 7a, 9b, 26: 2a, 3a, 11b–12a, 27: 1a, 2b–3b, 5a, 28A: 3a–b.

107. MS, 1: 14b–15a, 129: 16a–18a; HWSL, 26: 6b–8b; Dreyer, "Emergence," pp. 433–39.

108. MS, 1: 15a–b, 2: 1a–2a; HWSL, 28A: 4a, 6a–b, 28B: 17b–18a, 29: 5a–b, 9a–b, 13b–15a, 30: 4b–5a, 31: 4b, 32: 1b–2a, 4b–5a; DMB, pp. 504–5.

109. MS, 1: 15a–b, 2: 1a–2a; HWSL, 28A: 4a, 28B: 1a, 29: 13a, 30: 10a–b, 11b–13b, 31: 1a, 2a–4b, 7b–8a, 9a, 10a–12a.

110. MS, 2: 2a–3b; HWSL, 31: 11b–12a, 32: 1b, 2b–4b, 7a–9a, 33: 1a–2a, 7b–10a, 34: 1a–2b, 7a–8a, 9b, 11a–12a; DMB, pp. 15–17, 602–8, 1290–93.

111. MS, 1: 13a, 129: 10a–14a; DMB, pp. 485–88, 909–10.

112. HWSL, 21: 9a.

113. HWSL, 27: 4a–b, 28A: 5a–b, 28B, 29: 1a–3b.

CHAPTER THREE

1. For varying interpretations of Hung-wu's general character and attributes, see DMB, pp. 381–92; Mote, *Kao Ch'i*, pp. 30–37, 234–43; and Wu Han, *Chu Yüan-chang*, especially pp. 1–32.

2. DMB, pp. 381–92; Mote, *Kao Ch'i*, pp. 30–37, 234–43; Wu Han, *Chu Yüan-chang*, especially pp. 1–32; see also Ku Chieh-kang, pp. 254–311. The quoted passage is from Chu Yüan-chang, 1: 481. This and other passages are analyzed in Dardess, "Autocrat Remolds Society."

3. MS, 2: 1b; HWSL, 30: 9a–10a.

4. Wu Han, *Chu Yüan-chang*, pp. 103–9; see also Wada Sei, "Min no Taisō," pp. 278–302; and Wu Han, "Ming-chiao," pp. 235–78.

5. Jordan's book replaces previous work on the subject. A study of the KMT leaders' explicit evocation of the Ming founding, which is clear from their choice of terms, might be useful.

6. Wu Han, *Chu Yüan-chang*, pp. 103–9; Wada Sei, "Min no kokugō," pp. 592–97.

7. MS, 2: 3b–4b; HWSL, 34: 11a–12a, 35: 2b–3a, 37: 1a–b, 38: 12b–13a, 40: 1a, 4b–5b, 41: 3b–5b, 42: 1a–b.

8. MS, 2: 4b–5a, 125: 11a–17a; HWSL, 41: 1a–b, 43: 2b–3a, 5b, 44: 6b–7a; DMB, pp. 115–20.

9. MS, 2: 5a–b, 123: 15a–21a; HWSL, 43: 6b–7a, 44: 2a–b, 46: 2a–3a, 48: 1a–2a; DMB, pp. 1069–73.

10. MS, 2: 5b–7a, 126: 1a–8b; HWSL, 49: 7a, 52: 4b, 6a, 53: 4b–6a; DMB, pp. 881–87.

11. MS, 2: 6a, 133: 6a–9a; HWSL, 51: 7b, 52: 1a, 8b–9a; DMB, pp. 629–31.

12. MS, 2: 5a–b, 129: 14b–16a; HWSL, 46: 2a–3a.

13. MS, 2: 7a–8b, 126: 12a–17a, 129: 5b–14b; HWSL, 54: 5b–6a, 60: 1a–b, 64: 1a–b, 66: 1a, 2b–4a, 5a, 67: 2a–b; DMB, pp. 466–71, 909–10, 1248–51.

14. MS, 2: 7a–b, 9a; HWSL, 57: 3a–b, 59: 2b, 71: 5b–6a; DMB, pp. 15–17.

15. MS, 2: 9a–10a; HWSL, 73: 2b, 7b–8a, 74: 2b–3a, 8b, 9b–10a, 75: 1a–b. The campaigns of this year and the nature of the Ming reverse are also stressed in the biographical accounts: MS, 124: 1a–7a, 125: 1a–11a, 126: 1a–8b, 129: 1a–5b, 132: 5b–12a; DMB, pp. 453–55, 602–8, 724–28, 788–91, 881–87.

16. MS, 2: 10a, 11b; HWSL, 77: 5a–6a, 93: 2a–3a; DMB, pp. 1293–94.

17. For general evolution of the wei-so system, see MS, 90: 1a–4a (including lists of wei and so). See also Dreyer, "Emergence," pp. 469–78; Taylor, "Wei-so System," pp. 23–40; and Aoyama Jirō, pp. 91–116.

18. MS, 1: 8b; HWSL, 9: 7a–b.

19. MS, 129: 1a–5b, 10a–14b; DMB, pp. 453–55, 908–10.

20. MS, 1: 11a–b; HWSL, 14: 4b–7b, 10a–b; Dreyer, "Emergence," pp. 383–89; see also MS, 90: 1a–4a; Taylor, "Wei-so System," pp. 23–40; and Aoyama Jirō, pp. 91–116. The considerable materials on Yüan and Sung military organization (for instance, YS, 98–101; *Sung-shih*, 187–98) need further study; Hsiao Ch'i-ch'ing is a recent work on the Yüan. For the T'ang, des Rotours, *Traité des fonctionnaires*, pp. xiii–lxxi, 747–904, remains standard.

21. MS, 76: 6a–8a, 19a–b; HWSL, 14: 5a–b. See below, chap. 4, n. 70, for analysis of the civil-military rank discrepancy. Hucker outlines the military in "Governmental Organization," pp. 56–63.

22. The number of guards is extracted from the tables in MS, 90: 4a–7b.

23. HWSL, 6: 1b–2a, 12: 1b; Shimizu Taiji, "Eiden kō," pp. 355–65.

24. Summarized from Wang Yü-ch'üan, *Chün-t'un*, pp. 11–26; see also Shimizu Taiji, "Gundon no tenkai," pp. 269–328.

25. For the cultivated land, see TMHT, 17: 1a–13a. For the military colony lands, TMHT, 18: 1a–8a, gives the raw figures that are the starting point for analysis. I have followed Wang Yü-ch'üan, *Chün-t'un*, pp. 98–113, in revising the overall totals to the figures indicated and in assigning the "original quotas" to 1502 and the "present quotas" to 1578. These problems are also dealt with by Shimizu Taiji in his "Mindai no tonden," pp. 235–68.

26. HWSL, 223: 6b–7a.

27. MS, 76: 2a–21a, and TMHT, 227–28, describe the military chain of command. MS, 77: 1b–5b, outlines the registration system, which is analyzed in

Wei Ch'ing-yüan. Ho, *Ladder of Success*, pp. 54–67, is able to cite many instances of men escaping the chün-chi classification, but this merely emphasizes the point that persons so classified were at a relative disadvantage compared to commoners (min-chi).

28. Dreyer, "Emergence," pp. 102–12, 217–19, 262–64; see also Taylor, "Wei-so System."

29. The analysis is derived from the tables in MS, 105, by comparing men awarded noble titles while still alive with their date of entry into Ming service. This point is developed at greater length in Dreyer, "Chu Yüan-chang." See also Taylor, "Ming T'ai-tsu."

30. MS, 2: 7a, 16a, 105: 1a–35b; HWSL, 58: 2b–7a, 127: 1a–b.

31. For these systems of nobility, see des Rotours, *Traité des fonctionnaires*, pp. 42–50; Hsin T'ang-shu, 46: 7a–10a; Sung-shih, 163: 6b–8b.

32. For stipends of nobles, see MS, 2: 7a, 16a, 105: 1a–35b; HWSL, 58: 2b–7a, 127: 1a–b. For salaries of the nine ranks, see MS, 72: 13a, and Table 2 above. The use of the nobles as generals is evident in many of the campaigns described in this book.

33. The fourteen were T'ang Ho, T'ang Sheng-tsung, Lu Chung-heng, Chou Te-hsing, Hua Yün-lung, Ku Shih, Keng Ping-wen, Ch'en Te, Kuo Hsing, Wang Chih, Cheng Yü-ch'un, Fei Chü, Wu Liang, and Wu Chen; see MS, 105: 2a–14a, and above, chap. 2, n. 19.

34. MS, 126: 12a–17a; DMB, pp. 1248–51.

35. MS, 131: 11b–14a, 308: 3a.

36. MS, 130: 6a–8b; DMB, pp. 713–18.

37. The nine were the aforementioned K'ang Mao-ts'ai, Hu Mei, and Fu Yu-te, as well as Chu Liang-tsu, Han Cheng, Huang Pin, Ts'ao Liang-ch'en, Mei Szu-tsu, and Lu Chü; see MS, 105: 16b–21a.

38. The original followers were Lan Yü, Hsieh Ch'eng, Chang Lung, Ts'ao Hung, Ts'ao Chen, and Chang Wen; the Lake Ch'ao leaders were Ch'iu Ch'eng, Wu Fu, Chin Ch'ao-hsing, Yeh Sheng, Chou Wu, and Wang Pi; see MS, 105: 24b–29b.

39. MS, 2: 1a, 6a, 14b–15a; HWSL, 29: 3a–b, 51: 1a–5a, 117: 1a.

40. The ideal system is set out in MS, 76: 2a–21a, and Hucker, "Governmental Organization," pp. 56–63. Judging from the notices in HWSL, however, new wei and higher units frequently were created without the full prescribed complement of officers.

41. Summary accounts of local government include Kracke, pp. 54–63; des Rotours, *Traité des fonctionnaires*, pp. 646–746; and Yang Lien-sheng. Wang Yü-ch'üan treats local government only peripherally.

42. Derived from YS, 58–64.

43. Derived by comparing the organization of North and South China in YS, 58–64. Northern lu usually had subordinate chou, but southern lu controlled their hsien directly.

44. See the description of Hsü Ta's capture of the Yüan capital in YS, 125: 5a–b. Other examples are listed on pp. 44–45, 54–55 above; and in Dreyer, "Emergence," pp. 400–403.

45. For examples, see MS, 1: 4b–5a, and HWSL, 4: 1a–2b (for Nanking); MS,

1: 6a–b, and HWSL, 6: 5b–8a (for Chinhua); MS, 1: 8b, and HWSL, 10: 1a–2b (for Nanch'ang); MS, 1: 11a, and HWSL, 14: 2a–4a (for Wuch'ang); MS, 1: 11b, and HWSL, 15: 2b–3a, 17: 6b (for Luchou); and MS, 2: 2b–3a, and HWSL, 34: 1a–2b (for Peking).

46. MS, 75: 19b–21b; Hucker, "Governmental Organization," pp. 44–45.

47. For documentation on eleven of the provinces, see MS, 41: 1a (Shantung), 41: 5a (Shansi), 42: 1a (Honan), 42: 11a (Shensi), 43: 1a (Szechwan); 43: 22a–b (Kiangsi), 44: 1a (Hukwang), 44: 20b–21a (Chekiang), 45: 1a (Fukien), 45: 8b (Kwangtung), and 45: 18b–19a (Kwangsi). See also MS, 40: 3a for Peip'ing province.

48. HWSL, 10: 1a; see also n. 3 above.

49. HWSL, 4: 3a–4a; MS, 127: 1a–6a, 135: 6b–7a; Dreyer, "Emergence," pp. 78–79, 102–5; DMB, pp. 850–54.

50. MS, 128: 1a–16b; DMB, pp. 90–94, 932–38, 1225–31; Dreyer, "Emergence," pp. 164–65.

51. DMB, pp. 932–38.

52. See MS, 2: 1b; and HWSL, 30: 1a–4b, 10a, for decrees on ritual and dress. See DMB, pp. 696–99, 1225–31; and Mote, *Kao Ch'i*, pp. 145–80, for an account of the responses of intellectuals to the Ming founding. T'ao An was the official chiefly responsible for matters connected with ritual and sacrifice; see MS, 136: 1a–3b; and DMB, pp. 1263–66.

53. See MS, 1: 11a, 2: 1a; and the tables in MS, 109: 2a–3a.

54. See MS, 2: 1a; and HWSL, 29: 7a–8b, for honorific appointments to the crown prince's household. See Table 1 and MS, 109: 2a–4a, for the rising influence of civil officials. MS, 72: 4b–5a, 76: 18b, give descriptions of the formal organization of the chancellery and the provincial military agencies in the first several years of the dynasty.

55. MS, 72: 6a–32a. Hucker, "Governmental Organization," pp. 31–36, summarizes the ministries, whose formal status and organization were until 1380 similar to that described in detail for T'ang in des Rotours, *Traité des fonctionnaires*, pp. 32–130.

56. See MS, 72: 9a, 10a, for these ranks.

57. MS, 2: 13b, 75: 10b; HWSL, 106: 5b.

58. MS, 2: 3b, 5b–6a; HWSL, 35: 2a–b, 36A: 1a–b, 46: 9a–b, 49: 6b–7a, 52: 4b, 53: 1a. The decree on schools is dated 29 November in MS, but HWSL places it in proper sequence with other dates, ten days earlier.

59. MS, 2: 6a–b, 7b–8a, 10a–b, 127: 6a–b; HWSL, 52: 5a–6a, 54: 6a–7a, 60: 1a, 8a, 62: 1a, 78: 3b, 79: 4a–b; DMB, pp. 1389–92.

60. See the tables in MS, 73: 4b–5a, 111: 1b–6a; and Hucker, *Censorial System*, pp. 47–50.

61. MS, 75: 11a–12b, 13b–15b; Hucker, *Censorial System*, pp. 53–54.

62. See Wu Han, *Chu Yüan-chang*, pp. 190–203; and Wang Yü-ch'üan, pp. 143–46, for the historical development of the chancellorship. See also MS, 308: 2a–5b; DMB, pp. 638–41; Wu Han, "Hu Wei-yung," pp. 163–77; and pp. 122–40 below.

63. See n. 62.

64. Wang Yi-t'ung, pp. 10–26; Wolters, pp. 64–72; and pp. 114–22 below.

65. See MS, 124: 12a–13a, for the prince of Liang; and DMB, pp. 1083–85, for Naghachu.
66. See n. 62. Much of this discussion anticipates issues raised in Chapter 4. Wu Han, *Chu Yüan-chang*, pp. 158–70, has another summary of the purges.
67. MS, 2: 16a; HWSL, 128: 3a–4b, 129: 1a–4a.
68. See nn. 62, 67.
69. See MS, 308: 4b, for the 30,000 figure. From the tables in MS, 105, it is clear that most of the people involved in the Hu Wei-yung case, and all the victims of the Lan Yü case, were killed or posthumously degraded after the reopening of the general purge in 1390.
70. MS, 2: 16a; HWSL, 129: 5a–6b.
71. HWSL, 239: 2b; Wu Han, *Chu Yüan-chang*, p. 161.

CHAPTER FOUR

1. MS, 124: 12a–13a.
2. *Ibid.*
3. MS, 2: 9b–10a; HWSL, 74: 8b, 75: 5b–6a, 76: 5b.
4. MS, 2: 11b; HWSL, 88: 6a.
5. MS, 2: 14a–15b, 126: 8b–12a, 17a–27a; HWSL, 111: 8a, 115: 3b–4a, 116: 1b–4a, 121: 1b; DMB, pp. 1079–83, 1277–80.
6. MS, 2: 14b–15a, 134: 12b–13a; HWSL, 116: 5a, 117: 5a–b.
7. MS, 2: 15a–b; HWSL, 119: 2a–b, 121: 1a–b.
8. MS, 2: 15b; HWSL, 122: 2b, 3b, 125: 5a–b.
9. MS, 2: 16a; HWSL, 126: 3b, 127: 1a–b; chap. 3, n. 38 above.
10. MS, 2: 17a, 128: 8b–13a; DMB, pp. 1225–31.
11. MS, 2: 17b–18a, 124: 12a–13a, 129: 5b–10a; HWSL, 139: 1a–b, 140: 1a, 5a–8a; DMB, pp. 466–71.
12. MS, 3: 1a–2b, 126: 17a–27a; HWSL, 141: 2a–b, 3b–4a, 142: 1b–2b, 3b–5b, 143: 2a–3a, 8a–9a, 144: 2a, 146: 6a, 153: 1a; DMB, pp. 1079–83.
13. MS, 3: 4a; HWSL, 174: 3b–4a, 175: 3b, 176: 2b–3a.
14. MS, 3: 7a–b, 10a, 12b–13a; HWSL, 193: 7b, 195: 3b, 214: 4b–5a, 235: 4a, 236: 2b–3a.
15. MS, 6: 12a; YLSL, 137: 1a–2b.
16. MS, 3: 4a, 6b, 7b–8a, 15a, 314: 20b–34b; HWSL, 176: 5a, 188: 1b–2a, 198: 2a–3a, 255: 2a–b; DMB, pp. 1208–14.
17. For Kwangsi, see MS, 45: 18b–31b; for the population of Yünnan, see MS, 46: 1b; for the t'u-kuan, see MS, 76: 21a–22a.
18. MS, 46: 20a–34a.
19. For Szechwan, see MS, 43: 1a–22a; for Hukwang, see MS, 44: 1a–20b; for Yünnan, see MS, 46: 1a–20a.
20. MS, 76: 21a–22a.
21. For a standard account of the Yi, see Fairbank, Reischauer, and Craig, pp. 298–304; see also MS, 320.
22. For the Tran and Le dynasties, see Hall, pp. 169–75; see also MS, 321.
23. Sansom, pp. 3–126, offers a standard treatment of the split in the imperial line and the rise of the Ashikaga; see also MS, 322.

24. The background implications of the tribute system are discussed in Fairbank, pp. 1–33.

25. MS, 2: 5b, 7b, 8b; the figures are extracted from the year-end summaries of tribute missions in MS, 2–3.

26. MS, 323: 1b–11a, details the history of the relationship between Ming and Liuch'iu and the changes in the Liuch'iu kingdoms.

27. MS, 320: 1a–6b; DMB, pp. 1598–1603.

28. MS, 321: 1a–4a; DMB, pp. 797–801.

29. See n. 28.

30. MS, 75: 18b–19a. Wolters, pp. 8–38, 61, discusses the economic impact of the tributary trade for Southeast Asia; see also MS, 324–25.

31. Wolters, pp. 1–7, 39–48.

32. *Ibid.*, pp. 49–66.

33. *Ibid.*, pp. 66–76.

34. Wang Yi-t'ung, pp. 10–12; MS, 322.

35. Wang Yi-t'ung, pp. 12–14.   36. *Ibid.*, pp. 14–16.

37. *Ibid.*, pp. 16–20.   38. *Ibid.*, pp. 20–21.

39. MS, 91: 10a–11a.   40. TMHT, 105: 1a–b.

41. MS, 77–78, and TMHT, 17, 19–20, are two of the basic sources. The subject is treated in an extensive literature, including Ho, *Population of China*, pp. 3–23; Huang, *Taxation and Governmental Finance*, pp. 32–63; Huang, "Fiscal Administration"; Wei Ch'ing-yüan; and Elvin, who provides a controversial summary of the Japanese literature.

42. HWSL, 9: 1a, 12: 2b–3a; Dreyer, "Emergence," pp. 132–36.

43. HWSL, 26: 1a.

44. The population of Soochow fu was less than 4% of the empire's (in 1393 it was 2.4 out of 60.5 million; in 1491, 2.0 out of 53.3 million; in 1572, 2.0 out of 60.7 million), but its autumn-grain tax in 1393 was over 11% (2.74 out of 24.72 million shih); see TMHT, 19, 24.

45. MS, 2: 8a–b; HWSL, 62: 3a, 66: 6b–7a.

46. Ho, *Population of China*, pp. 3–7.

47. *Ibid.*, pp. 7–8; Wei Ch'ing-yüan. HWSL, 140: 8b–9b, preserves the enumeration of 1381, broken down by provinces; the numbers are 1–2% less than those of the more commonly cited census of 1393 (TMHT, 19); in only one case, Kiangsi, are they identical.

48. Liang Fang-chung, *Liang-chang chih-tu*; Huang, *Taxation and Governmental Finance*, pp. 36–38; TMHT, 29: 1a–b.

49. Wu Han, *Chu Yüan-chang*, pp. 109–18. Wada Sei, *Minshi shokkashi*, presents a Japanese translation and analysis of the economic chapters of MS. The work of Shimizu Taiji collected in *Mindai tochi seidoshi kenkyū*, especially pp. 1–90, 385–458, presents detailed arguments for the emergence of a manorial order in the countryside as a result of governmental policies. See also n. 48.

50. Ho, *Population of China*, pp. 107–8. See also Huang, *Taxation and Governmental Finance*, pp. 40–42. Both writers stress that registration was not carried out in a uniform manner nationwide.

51. Ho, *Population of China*, pp. 24–35, 101–23.

52. *Ibid.*, p. 10; TMHT, 17: 1a, 19: 1a–b.

53. TMHT, 24: 4a–b; Huang, "Fiscal Administration," p. 87.

54. HWSL, 9: 1a, 12: 2b–3a; Dreyer, "Emergence," pp. 132–36; TMHT, 32–34; Huang, *Taxation and Governmental Finance*, pp. 189–224.

55. TMHT, 35: 8b–54a; Huang, *Taxation and Governmental Finance*, pp. 231–33.

56. Huang, "Fiscal Administration," pp. 94–99; see also n. 54.

57. Huang, "Fiscal Administration," pp. 89, 99; Schurmann, *Economic Structure*, pp. 80, 170.

58. HWSL, 165: 2b–3a; the entry, dated 9 October 1384, refers to the period from 29 September to 6 October of that year.

59. Extracted from the tables appended to T'an Ch'ien; and MS, 111: 1b–6a.

60. See n. 66 for material on the chin-shih examinations. Ho, *Ladder of Success*, especially pp. 215–17, deals with the factors behind early Ming official recruitment; see also MS, 3: 2b–3a; HWSL, 160: 1a–2a.

61. TMHT, 78: 1a–22b, 156: 1a–8a; MS, 74: 22a–b, 75: 21b–22b; Ho, *Ladder of Success*, pp. 171–75.

62. See n. 61.

63. Ho, *Ladder of Success*, pp. 255–66, especially p. 261.

64. On academies in the Sung, see Terada Gō; on their place in Chinese history generally, see Taga Akigoro; on Ming perceptions of the role of academies, see Meskill.

65. Grimm; Ho, *Ladder of Success*, pp. 26–27.

66. HWSL, 62: 1a–b, 172: 1a–b, 189: 1a, 208: 1b–2a, 232: 1a, 251: 1a.

67. This is my estimate; for others, all within the same range, see Hucker, "Governmental Organization," p. 12.

68. Ho, *Ladder of Success*, pp. 216–17.

69. On Mongol social organization, see Iwamura Shinobu; Meng Szu-ming. On fiefs awarded to princes and high officials, see Hambis.

70. MS, 105: 2a–35b, gives original stipends and later increments for nobles of the Hung-wu period: MS, 77: 11a–b, gives office lands. See also Shimizu Taiji, *Mindai tochi seidoshi kenkyū*, pp. 157–204. Amounts of land given to individual nobles and princes varied.

71. TMHT, 38: 1a–17b; Hucker, "Governmental Organization," pp. 8–9.

72. MS, 2: 16b–17b; HWSL, 131: 6a–b, 134: 4b–5b, 135: 1a, 137: 1a, 2b–3a, 138: 7a.

73. DMB, pp. 15–17, 1293–94.

74. MS, 3: 5a; HWSL, 179: 8b–9a, 180: 1a–b.

75. DMB, pp. 115–20, 602–8, 850–54, 881–87, 1248–51, 1277–80.

76. DMB, pp. 466–71, 788–91.

77. MS, 3: 5b–6a; HWSL, 181: 1a, 185: 2a.

78. DMB, pp. 305–7.

79. MS, 3: 5b–6a; HWSL, 182: 1b–2b, 4b, 5b–8b.

80. MS, 3: 6a; HWSL, 184: 1b–2a, 3b–6b; DMB, pp. 453–55.

81. MS, 3: 6a; HWSL, 185: 5b.

82. MS, 3: 6b, 132: 4a–12a; HWSL, 190: 2a–b.

83. DMB, pp. 1293–94.

84. HWSL, 190: 4b.

85. MS, 3: 7a; HWSL, 190: 6a–7a, 193: 3b–4b.
86. MS, 127: 1a–6a, 132: 5b–12a, 308: 2a–5b; DMB, pp. 638–41, 788–91, 850–54; chap. 3, n. 63 above.
87. MS, 3: 8b; HWSL, 202: 3a, 4b–5a. See also the tables in MS, 105: 2a–35b; and individual biographies in MS.
88. MS, 3: 3b–4a; HWSL, 172: 6b.
89. MS, 3: 8a–b, 9b; HWSL, 199: 1a–b, 4a, 200: 5b–6a, 6b–7a, 208: 5b–6a.
90. MS, 3: 9b, 10b; HWSL, 208: 4b, 217: 2a.
91. MS, 3: 11a; HWSL, 220: 4a; Shimizu Taiji, *Mindai tochi seidoshi kenkyū*, pp. 157–74.
92. MS, 3: 10b–11a; HWSL, 217: 3b, 5a–b, 218: 4a–5a, 220: 1b, 4a–b, 222: 4b–5a.
93. DMB, pp. 788–91.
94. MS, 3: 11b–12a; HWSL, 225: 1b–2a.
95. MS, 3: 12b–13a; HWSL, 235: 4a, 5b, 236: 3a–5a; DMB, pp. 453–55, 466–71.
96. For Lan Yü, see MS, 132; for Hu Wei-yung, see MS, 308. See also Wu Han, *Chu Yüan-chang*, pp. 158–73.
97. Wu Han, "Hu Wei-yung."
98. MS, 3: 10b, 115: 1a–5a; HWSL, 217: 4b–5a; DMB, pp. 346–48.
99. Summarized from MS, 100–102.
100. For the organization of the princes' establishments, see MS, 75: 7a–9a.
101. MS, 73: 17a–19a, gives the changes made during the Hung-wu period in the establishments of the crown prince and the princes; the military tutors were abolished in 1376.
102. On the princes, see Farmer, pp. 73–79; and Chan, "Problem of the Princes."
103. See Table 4, extracted from MS, 90: 4a–7b.
104. MS, 3: 8a–b, 9b, 11b; HWSL, 199: 1a–b, 4a, 200: 4b–5a, 208: 5b, 226: 1b.
105. MS, 3: 10b; HWSL, 217: 2a.
106. But compare MS, 3: 11b; HWSL, 226: 1b, where the prince of Tai is described as leading troops of a hu-wei.
107. There are discussions in Farmer, pp. 94–98; Chan, *Usurpation*, pp. 4–8.
108. MS, 3: 12b; HWSL, 232: 4b.
109. MS, 3: 14a–b; HWSL, 245: 1a, 249: 2a.
110. MS, 3: 15b–17a; HWSL, 257.
111. For intepretations of Chu Yüan-chang, see, for example, DMB, pp. 381–92; Wu Han, *Chu Yüan-chang*; and Mote, *Kao Ch'i*.

CHAPTER FIVE

1. See pp. 148–52 above; Chan, "Problem of the Princes," pp. 183–93; Chan, *Usurpation*, pp. 9–21; Farmer, pp. 71–97; and DMB, pp. 397–404.
2. MS, 4: 1b–2a; DMB, pp. 224–27, 426–33.
3. Chan, *Usurpation*, p. 14.
4. MS, 4: 2a; DMB, pp. 350–54.
5. MS, 4: 2a.

6. MS, 4: 3a; DMB, pp. 350–54, 381–91; Chan, *Usurpation*, pp. 17–21.

7. Chan, *Usurpation*, pp. 25–41; DMB, pp. 1561–65. Chan includes the story of the prince of Yen's visiting Nanking at this time, which I have omitted; in this I follow Wang Ch'ung-wu.

8. MS, 4: 3a, 5: 1b–2a.

9. Text of the letter in YLSL, 2: 2a–4a; see also MS, 4: 3a–b, 5: 1b–2a; and YLSL, 2: 4b–6b.

10. MS, 4: 3b–4a, 5: 2a; YLSL, 3: 1a; DMB, pp. 713–18.

11. MS, 4: 4a, 5: 2a–b; YLSL, 3: 1a–4a.

12. MS, 4: 4a–b, 5: 2b; YLSL, 4A: 1a; DMB, pp. 305–7.

13. MS, 4: 4a–b, 5: 2b; YLSL, 4A: 1a–b; DMB, pp. 881–87.

14. MS, 4: 4b, 5: 2b–3a: YLSL, 4A: 1b–2a, 4B: 1a–2a.

15. MS, 4: 4b, 5: 3a–b; YLSL, 5: 1a–2a.

16. MS, 4: 4b, 5: 3a–b; YLSL, 5: 6a–b, 6: 1a–4a.

17. MS, 4: 4b–5a, 5: 3a; text of letter in YLSL, 5: 2a–4a; the life of Fang Hsiao-ju, in DMB, pp. 426–33, offers some speculation as to what these reforms might have meant in practice.

18. MS, 4: 5a, 5: 3b; YLSL, 6: 4a.

19. MS, 4: 5a, 5: 3b–4a; YLSL, 6: 4a–6b.

20. MS, 4: 5a, 5: 4a; YLSL, 6: 6b–7a, 7: 1a–2a.

21. MS, 4: 5a, 5: 4a; YLSL, 7: 2a; DMB, pp. 1196–98, 1284–86.

22. MS, 4: 5b, 5: 4b; YLSL, 7: 3b–5b.

23. MS, 4: 6a.

24. MS, 5: 4b; YLSL, 7: 6a–b.

25. MS, 4: 6a, 5: 4b–5a, YLSL, 7: 7a–9b, 8: 1a–2a.

26. MS, 4: 6a, 5: 5a; texts of Yen letters in YLSL, 8: 2a–5a.

27. MS, 4: 6a–b, 5: 5a–b; YLSL, 8: 5a–9a.

28. MS, 5: 5b; YLSL, 8: 9a–b.

29. MS, 4: 6b–7a, 5: 5b–6a; YLSL, 8: 9b–10a, 9A: 1a–b.

30. MS, 4: 7a, 5: 5b–6a, YLSL, 9A: 1b–4b.

31. MS, 4: 7a, 5: 6a–b; YLSL, 9A: 4b–5b.

32. MS, 4: 7a–b, 5: 6b; YLSL, 9A: 5b–8a.

33. MS, 4: 7b, 5: 6b–7a; YLSL, 9A: 8a–9b, 9B: 1a.

34. MS, 4: 7b; Chan, *Usurpation*, pp. 80–83.

35. MS, 4: 7b–8a, 5: 7a–b; YLSL, 9B: 1a–4b. DMB, pp. 394–404, summarizes the growth of legends concerning Chien-wen's alleged escape.

36. MS, 5: 7a–b; YLSL, 9B: 4b–7b. The purging of the Chien-wen loyalists also gave rise to legendary elements; cf. DMB, pp. 426–33.

37. Standard references are Gibb and Bowen; Hodgson; Boyle.

CHAPTER SIX

1. MS, 5: 7b; YLSL, 10A: 1a–4b.

2. See MS, 5: 8a–b; the genealogical tables of Yung-lo-period nobles in MS, 106: 1a–40b; and YLSL, 12A: 1a–7a.

3. MS, 6: 2a.

4. MS, 6: 1b; YLSL, 18: 1b–2a.

5. See MS, 6: 8a; the description of the Oirats in MS, 328: 1a–8a; YLSL, 92: 13b–14a; and DMB, pp. 1035–37.

6. See Fletcher, pp. 206–24, and his extensive bibliography.

7. MS, 6: 7b–8a; YLSL, 88: 5b–8b, 89: 1a–2a. For general background, see Farmer, pp. 107–14; and Franke, "Feldzüge," pp. 1–54.

8. MS, 6: 8a–b; the description of the Mongols in early Ming in MS, 327: 1a–9a; YLSL, 94: 1a–2a, 95: 2b–4a, 96: 2a–b; DMB, pp. 12–15, 1128–31.

9. MS, 6: 9a–b; YLSL, 100: 1a; 101: 1a–2b, 3b–4a, 5a–6b, 102: 1a.

10. MS, 6: 9b–10a; YLSL, 103: 1a–b, 2b–5a, 104: 1a–6a, 105: 1a–5b, 106: 1a–2a, 3b–6a, 107: 2b, 4b.

11. MS, 6: 12b–13a, 328: 1b (which places Bunyashiri's death in 1412) ; YLSL, 139: 1a, 141: 1a, 145: 1a–2b.

12. MS, 7: 1a–b, YLSL, 148: 1a–b, 149: 3b–5a, 150: 1a–5b.

13. MS, 7: 1b–2b; YLSL, 151: 2b–4a, 152: 1a–4a, 154: 1a, 160: 1b–2a.

14. MS, 7: 2b–4a; DMB, pp. 12–15; Farmer, pp. 114–28.

15. MS, 7: 7b–8b; YLSL, 239: 1b, 243: 1a–2a, 246: 1b–2a; DMB, pp. 531–34, 1483–85.

16. MS, 7: 8b; YLSL, 247: 2a–3a, 248: 2a, 249: 1a–3b, 250: 1a–b.

17. MS, 7: 8b–9a; YLSL, 250: 2a–9b, 251: 1a–3a.

18. YLSL, 251: 2a–3a; DMB, pp. 1535–38.

19. MS, 7: 10a–b; YLSL, 261: 2b–4a, 262: 1a–4a, 263: 1a–2b, 264: 1a–3b.

20. MS, 7: 10b–11b; YLSL, 267: 1b, 269: 1b–2a, 270: 2a–3a, 271: 1a–5a, 272: 1a–3a, 273: 1a–2b.

21. MS, 6: 1a–b; YLSL, 17: 1b–2a; Farmer, pp. 114–28.

22. See Farmer, pp. 148–62; and Hoshi Ayao.

23. Summarizes MS, 89: 1b–17a, on the capital camps and imperial guards; I have derived the information on specific changes from comparisons of the wei-so lists in MS, 90: 4a–7b, 8a–16b.

24. MS, 6: 4a, 5b–6a, 7a; YLSL, 38: 4b, 39: 5a, 59: 3a, 66: 4b, 80: 1a. Farmer, p. 118, traces Yung-lo's physical location during his reign.

25. MS, 6: 10b; YLSL, 113: 4b–5a, 116: 4b–5a; DMB, pp. 157–59, 1224–25; Farmer, p. 118. The military organization of the Grand Canal boats is described in detail in Hoshi Ayao, pp. 95–146, 179–240.

26. MS, 6: 11b, 12a, 7: 2a, 3a–b, 5b; YLSL, 126: 4a, 137: 4a–b, 154: 1a, 165: 2b, 167: 1b, 172: 1a, 178: 1a, 213: 1b.

27. MS, 7: 2b, 3b–4a; YLSL, 162: 1a–b, 164: 2b–3a, 179: 3a, 182: 1b–2b.

28. MS, 7: 4a–b; YLSL, 184: 2b, 185: 2b, 186: 2a, 3b–5a, 187: 1b–2a, 188: 1a; Farmer, pp. 114–28.

29. MS, 7: 6b–7a; YLSL, 229: 1a, 2a–b, 232: 1a–3a, 233: 1a–5b.

30. MS, 7: 4b, 118: 16b–21a; YLSL, 186: 3b–4b; DMB, pp. 340–43.

31. My data are derived from the wei-so lists in MS, 90: 4a–7b (dated 1393 and summarized in Table 4), and 90: 8a–16b. The second list is dated simply "later"; Hucker, in his "Governmental Organization," p. 59, placed it in the early fifteenth century. However, comparison of this list with the wei-so list in TMHT, 124, shows that the TMHT list is entirely included in the MS list, while the MS list also records changes occurring after the last revision of the TMHT (1587). The second MS list is thus intended to provide a comprehensive record of all wei-so

changes up to the fall of the dynasty. Nevertheless, most of the important changes after 1393 were made in the Yung-lo reign, that is, in the early fifteenth century.

32. See n. 31.

33. MS, 89: 1b–17a, 90: 4a–7b, 8a–16b; Hucker, "Governmental Organization," p. 59.

34. For Nanking, see MS, 76: 10a–11a, 90: 12a–b, 16a–b.

35. MS, 90: 15a–b.

36. MS, 90: 15b–16a.

37. MS, 89: 1b–17a, 90: 4a–7b, 8a–16b.

38. *Ibid.* This topic is treated at greater length in Dreyer, "Military Reorganization."

39. For population figures, see MS, 40: 4a–b; for an analysis of the role of Peking under the Manchus, see Rozman.

40. MS, 76: 4b–6a, 90: 20b–24a. The latter describes the system of troop rotation between the local guards and the camps in the capital.

41. MS, 89: 1b–11a, describes the organization and history of the three main camps as a unit.

42. *Ibid.*, especially p. 2b.

43. *Ibid.*, especially pp. 2b–3a.

44. MS, 89: 17a–19a.

45. On border defenses, see MS, 91: 1a–9b, and TMHT, 129–32; on the state of the border later, see Mote, "T'u-mu Incident."

46. Listed in MS, 76: 12b–15b; and in Hucker, "Governmental Organization," pp. 62–63. The subject is treated at length in TMHT, 129–32.

47. For these persistent rumors, see DMB, pp. 397–404; they are also mentioned at the beginning of Cheng Ho's biography in MS, 304: 2b–5b.

48. Needham, pp. 476–540, has a long account of the Cheng Ho episode that summarizes the earlier literature. On the dating of the expeditions, see Duyvendak. On the ships, see Pao Tsun-p'eng, whose study summarizes his own substantial previous work on the subject. On the Indonesia-Malaya area in this period, see Wolters. See also Cheng Ho-sheng; and DMB, pp. 144–45, 194–200, 440–41, 522–23, 1026–27, 1198–1202, and 1364–1366, which provide extensive additional bibliography.

49. See especially DMB, pp. 194–200; Needham, pp. 515–16; and MS, 326: 5b–7b.

50. See especially Needham, pp. 489–90, 515–16; and MS, 325: 10a–12b.

51. See especially Needham, p. 530; and Duyvendak.

52. See especially Needham, p. 490.

53. Needham, pp. 476–79.

54. DMB, pp. 397–404; MS, 304: 2b–5b.

55. Wolters, especially chaps. 4, 7, and 11, analyzes the role played by Chinese policy in the rise of the Indonesian trading states and, in particular, the role of the Yung-lo voyages in the rise of Malacca.

56. Needham, pp. 524–28.

57. MS, 304: 2b; Pao Tsun-p'eng; Needham, pp. 479–82.

58. The Lung-chiang shipyard is described in detail in Li Chao-hsiang, *Lung-chiang ch'uan-ch'ang chih*, in HLTTS, 117–19. Unfortunately, by the time of Li's

incumbency the plans of the treasure ships and the other large classes of vessels were already long lost. See Li's biography in DMB, pp. 804–5.

59. Needham, pp. 479–80.

60. Needham, pp. 315–16, 480, 525–26; DMB, pp. 157–59, 1224–25. There is an extensive discussion in Hoshi Ayao, pp. 15–30.

61. Needham, p. 484. For sources relating to the Nanking garrison, see MS, 76: 10–11a, 90: 12a–b, 16a–b.

62. For the title shou-pei, see MS, 76: 10a.

63. Needham, pp. 476–540, also goes into considerable detail on the diplomatic aspect of the voyages.

64. Wang Yi-t'ung, pp. 20–25. See also above, pp. 119–22.

65. *Ibid.*, pp. 34–38.   66. *Ibid.*, pp. 38–47.

67. *Ibid.*, p. 47.   68. *Ibid.*, pp. 47–53.

69. MS, 323: 1b–11a.   70. Fletcher.

71. MS, 6: 4b; YLSL, 52: 3b. For the tea and horse trade, see Rossabi.

72. For the ambiguities in the Vietnam-China relationship, see Woodside, pp. 7–59.

73. MS, 321: 1a–3b.

74. MS, 321: 1a–3b, 324: 1a–3b. See also Lo Jung-pang, "Policy Formulation," pp. 55–60; and DMB, pp. 797–801.

75. MS, 6: 3a–4b; YLSL, 33: 5b–6a, 10b–11b, 38: 3b–4a, 43: 4a–b, 49: 2b–3a, 52: 6a–b.

76. MS, 6: 5a–b; YLSL, 56: 1a–3b, 60: 1a; DMB, pp. 64–67.

77. MS, 6: 5b–6a; YLSL, 60: 1b–8b, 61: 1a, 62: 2a–4a, 63: 2a–b, 67: 1b–2b.

78. MS, 6: 6a–7a, 321: 8a–11b; YLSL, 68: 1a–6a, 81: 2a–6b.

79. MS, 6: 7a–b; YLSL, 82: 5a–7b, 86: 6b–7b, 88: 5b.

80. MS, 6: 8b–9a; YLSL, 95: 9a, 96: 1b, 98: 1b–2a; DMB, pp. 64–67.

81. MS, 6: 10a–b, 13a, 7: 1a–b, 4a, 321: 11b–12b; YLSL, 111: 6a, 112: 2b, 117: 2b–3a, 121: 1a–b, 131: 1a, 146: 1a–b, 149: 2a–b.

82. MS, 7: 4b–6a, 321: 12b–13a; YLSL, 185: 2a–b, 186: 1b.

83. MS, 7: 4b–6a, 321: 12b–13a; YLSL, 189: 1b, 196: 1b, 197: 2a–b, 212: 1a, 215: 1a–b; DMB, pp. 793–97.

84. MS, 7: 6a, 7a; YLSL, 220: 1a, 230: 2a.

85. MS, 7: 7b, 8a, 9b; YLSL, 237: 2a–b, 245: 1a, 255: 1b.

86. MS, 72: 1a–2a, 4a–6a; Hucker, "Governmental Organization," pp. 27–31; Grimm, "Neiko."

87. MS, 5: 8a, 8: 2b, 109: 4a, 6a–b, 9b–10a (tables), 150: 3a–4a; YLSL, 88: 4b–5a; HHSL, 1B: 1b–2a; DMB, pp. 234–36, 665–67, 1535–38.

88. MS, 147–48; DMB, pp. 340–43, 554–58, 641–43, 1519–22.

89. See n. 88.

90. MS, 149: 1a–3b, 151: 7a–9a; DMB, pp. 234–36.

91. MS, 111: 7a–11b (tables), 151: 10a–11a; DMB, pp. 531–34, 1483–85.

92. MS, 111: 7a–11b (tables), 150: 4a–5a, 154: 7a–10a; DMB, pp. 653–56, 1224–25.

93. MS, 111: 7a–11b (tables), 151: 5a–6a, 7a–9a, 10b–12b, 157: 1b–2a, 160: 1a–2b, 308: 5b–10a.

94. Discussed and documented in Farmer, pp. 114–28, 134–38, 144–47.

95. MS, 75: 3a–b, 76: 10a, 154: 7a–15a; DMB, pp. 145–48, 653–56.

96. MS, 153: 1a–4a; DMB, pp. 1224–25.

97. The chin-shih totals are given in YLSL, 29: 1a, 52: 6a, 114: 1a, 126: 1a, 162: 1a, 198: 1a, 235: 1b, and 269: 2a.

98. See nn. 88, 90–92. For the closing of alternate entry routes after the 1430's, see Ho, *Ladder of Success*, pp. 14–15, 215–17.

CHAPTER SEVEN

1. MS, 8: 1a–2a; DMB, pp. 338–43.

2. MS, 8: 2a–b; HHSL, 1A–1B; DMB, pp. 531–34, 1483–85.

3. MS, 8: 2b; HHSL, 1B: 1a–5a.

4. MS, 8: 2b–4a; HHSL, 1B: 5b–6a, 2A–2C; on Hung-hsi's character, see Hucker, *Censorial System*, pp. 109–17.

5. HHSL, 3A: 4a–10a.

6. MS, 8: 5a–6a. See also HHSL, 4A: 9a–b, 9A: 3b–4a.

7. MS, 8: 5a.

8. MS, 8: 5b–6b; HHSL, 9A–10.

9. Hucker, *Censorial System*, pp. 109–17; Hucker, "Governmental Organization," pp. 5–6.

10. MS, 9: 1a–b; HTSL, 1: 11b–15b.

11. DMB, pp. 279–89.

12. MS, 8: 3a; HHSL, 2A: 2b–3a.

13. MS, 8: 3a, 4a, 5b, 321: 14b–15a; HHSL, 2A: 3b–4a, 2B: 5a–b; DMB, pp. 653–56, 793–97.

14. MS, 9: 2b, 321: 15a–b; HTSL, 15: 3a–b, 16: 1a; DMB, pp. 145–48.

15. MS, 9: 2b–3a, 321: 15b–16b; HTSL, 17: 1b–2b, 22: 12a–b.

16. MS, 9: 3b; HTSL, 23: 1b–2a, 9a–b, 11a.

17. MS, 9: 3b–4a; HTSL, 25: 3b–4a, 27: 2a–b, 8a–b, 29: 4a.

18. MS, 9: 4a–b, 321: 17a–18b; HTSL, 31: 2a–4b, 32: 8b, 33: 1a–2b.

19. MS, 9: 4a–b, 321: 17a–18b; HTSL, 32: 7b, 33: 1a–2b; Lo, "Policy Formulation," especially pp. 56–60.

20. MS, 321: 18b–20a; DMB, pp. 793–97.

21. MS, 321: 18b–20a; Hall, pp. 159–75.

22. MS, 321: 18b–20a; Hucker, *Censorial System*, pp. 108–51.

23. MS, 9: 2a, 73: 9a–13b.

24. MS, 73, 9a–13b, for these offices.

25. MS, 9: 3a; HTSL, 20: 1a–16a; DMB, pp. 340–43.

26. MS, 9: 5a–b, 327: 7b–8a; HTSL, 47: 1a–4a.

27. Needham, pp. 490–91, 524–28; Lo, "Early Ming Navy."

28. On the Wakō, see Hucker, "Hu Tsung-hsien's Campaign"; and So.

29. Wang Yi-t'ung, pp. 60–81.

30. MS, 9: 2b–3a, 74: 31b, 304: 1a–2a; HTSL, 19: 3b–4a.

31. MS, 9: 3b, 6a, 8b, 109: 10a–13a.

32. See Hucker, *Censorial System*, pp. 108–51.

33. MS, 9: 10a–b; HTSL, 113–15.

CHAPTER EIGHT

1. Mote, "T'u-mu Incident"; on the fall of the dynasty, see Parsons; and DMB, pp. 6–9, 17–20, 416–20.

2. DMB, pp. 294–98, 375–80.

3. For the five eunuch dictators, see DMB, pp. 941–45, 1298–99, 1347–49, 1357–58; and ECCP, pp. 846–48.

4. On the polarization of politics during periods of eunuch rule, see Hucker, *Censorial System*, pp. 152–234; and the ECCP entries for the period 1620–27.

5. DMB, pp. 53–61, 315–22, 324–38, and 365–67, offer summary accounts of these reigns.

6. See Huang, "Fiscal Administration," pp. 113–23; and ECCP, pp. 176–77, 190, 846–48, 892–93.

7. Parsons; ECCP, pp. 37–38, 191–92, 491–93.

8. For the implementation of the single-whip reforms, see Liang Fang-chung, *Single-Whip Method of Taxation.*

9. By now the classic statement of this viewpoint in Western textbooks is that in Fairbank, Reischauer, and Craig, pp. 70–75.

10. On the T'ang after 755 see Peterson, "Regional Defense"; Peterson, "Restoration Completed"; and Wang Gungwu, "Middle Yangtze."

11. For the background of the Five Dynasties, see Wang Gungwu, *Structure of Power.*

12. On the Chin, see Rogers.

13. On Yü Ch'ien, see DMB, pp. 1608–12; and Franke, "Yü Ch'ien."

14. These examples are discussed in Ch'ü.

15. On the extent of hereditary definition of the T'ang ruling class, see, for example, Twitchett, "T'ang Ruling Class."

16. See nn. 10–11.

17. This theme is treated at length in Chi.

18. Kracke, pp. 8–23.

19. For an elaborate treatment of the Khitan regime that stresses the accommodation between Chinese and non-Chinese ways, see Wittfogel and Feng.

20. See n. 2.

21. This contradiction between officials' interests and official policy is developed in Hucker, "Hu Tsung-hsien's Campaign."

22. Elvin, p. 203.

23. Elvin, pp. 204–15, discusses and quotes some of the literature on population in this period.

24. This is the theme of Perkins.

25. Widespread acceptance of the values expressed in the examination system is a major theme of Ho, *Ladder of Success.*

Bibliography

With one or two exceptions, the following Bibliography lists only works actually cited in the Notes. This restriction is imposed mainly for space considerations; the Ming was a period of expansion in publishing and of rising literacy, and much of the literary production of the time has survived to the present day, despite the Ch'ing literary inquisition. In addition to the extensive bibliographic studies in Chinese and Japanese, information on Ming materials is readily available to western scholars in Wolfgang Franke's *Introduction to the Sources of Ming History* and in the bibliographies appended to individual entries in the *Dictionary of Ming Biography*.

The ninety-five-year gap between the fall of the Ming (1644) and the appearance of the official *Ming History* (1739) created a market for unofficial histories of the Ming period. But despite the historical persistence of the competition, the high quality of the official history has led to its general acceptance as the most authoritative history written in the standard composite form. Of the unofficial histories, I have found T'an Ch'ien's *Kuo-ch'üeh* (ca. 1653) and Ku Ying-t'ai's *Ming-shih chi-shih pen-mo* (1658; correctly titled *Ming-ch'ao* but usually indexed as *Ming-shih*) to be the most useful.

The multiplicity of independent histories masks an underlying dependence on one basic source, the *shih-lu*, or "veritable records," of the several Ming reigns. In the research leading to this book, I have examined numerous later unofficial histories and found them to give identical accounts of the same event, usually copied word for word from the shih-lu. The first four shih-lu—*T'ai-tsu Kao-huang-ti shih-lu* (HWSL; 1352–98), *T'ai-tsung Wen-huang-ti shih-lu* (YLSL; 1398–1424), *Jen-tsung Chao-huang-ti* (HHSL; 1424–25), and *Hsüan-tsung Chang-huang-ti shih-lu* (HTSL; 1425–35)—are therefore bound to provide the basic documentation for any account emphasizing the political and military affairs of the early Ming. In the Notes I have usually also cited the official *Ming History* (MS), as representative of the best thinking of later traditional Chinese historiography. And certain entries in the *Dictionary of Ming Biography* (DMB) are indicated as well, generally because reference to them will supply needed bibliographic guidance or identify significant problems in the sources. I have also cited modern secondary literature where appropriate.

Our dependence on the shih-lu naturally raises questions about the completeness, objectivity, and reliability of their surviving versions. Of the four shih-lu that concern us, YLSL (1430), HHSL (1430), and HTSL (1438) were produced under the chief editorship of Yang Shih-ch'i, the dominant grand secretary of the 1420's and 1430's; the sole surviving version of HWSL (1418) came out under the chief editorship of Yang's grand secretarial colleague Hu Kuang. The four shih-lu were thus produced within the span of a generation by a close-knit, long-lived group of men who spearheaded what I have described in Chapter 6 (pp. 212–20) as the "Confucian takeover" of the Ming state, so one might expect the shih-lu to mirror the concerns and values of high-ranking civil officials rather than those of emperors, peasants, military officers, barbarians, or others who also played important parts in making the history of the period.

It is also clear that immediate political considerations influenced the composition of the shih-lu. Yung-lo could not recognize his predecessor Chien-wen as a legitimate emperor, so YLSL incorporates the events of his reign under the separate title "Feng-t'ien ching-nan" (Heavenly-authorized suppression of troubles) and describes them from the viewpoint of the then prince of Yen rather than of the emperor. HWSL was revised at least twice, first of all in the Chien-wen reign, perhaps to play down Chu Yüan-chang's Red Turban connections (obnoxious in the hyper-Confucian atmosphere of the Chien-wen court), or perhaps to remove references that suggested Chu Yüan-chang was intending to name the prince of Yen as his heir. Its final winnowing in the Yung-lo reign was presumably occasioned by the need to incorporate or reinstate passages that would enhance the legitimacy of Yung-lo's seizure of the throne.

The mode of transmission of the shih-lu has also given rise to questions regarding their accuracy. The official sets of the several Ming shih-lu were destroyed after the publication of the official Ming History, in accordance with the established practices of traditional Chinese official historiography. However, unauthorized hand copies circulated widely during the Ming and survived in private collections to recent times. Modern versions are photographic reproductions of such unofficial copies. They contain copyists' errors, which often can be corrected by collation, and occasionally omit entire chapters.

Despite these problems, the shih-lu constitute a reliable source in most of the cases where they can be brought to bear. They were created by successive reduction of primary source materials, a process that usually preserved the wording of those materials. Despite omissions, they retain more detail than any alternative source while maintaining internal consistency with respect to chronology and other matters. Although the biases of traditional Chinese historical thinking affected the choice of detail, the same biases affected the alternative sources as well, and the abundance of detail in the shih-lu helps the modern historian to make allowance in his analysis for the predispositions of the compilers and to identify deliberate falsification. Defects attributable to the process of transmission are not numerous enough to compromise the usefulness of the shih-lu as a source. In general, the shih-lu should be the standard against which alternative sources are judged in matters of detail, especially for dates and similar questions of fact.

Some of the foregoing would not be necessary were it not for the widespread acceptance of Wada Sei's 1923 attempt to revise the basic sequence of events in the founding of Ming. I have dealt with this question in *Journal of Asian Studies* (1972), and it is enough to repeat here that I consider Wada and his disciples to be letting their case rest on a single alternative source—Yü Pen's *Chi-shih-lu*—whose chronology is impossible.

Aoyama Jirō 青山治郎. "Shu Go-koku yoku gensuifu kō" 朱吳国 翼元帥府 考 (A study of the wing commanders' headquarters in the Chu Wu-state). *Sundai Shigaku*, vol. 13 (March 1963).

Boyle, John A., ed. *The Cambridge History of Iran. Volume V: The Sāljūq and Mongol Periods.* Cambridge, 1968.

Cha Chi-tso 查繼佐. *Tsui-wei-lu* 罪惟錄. *Szu-pu ts'ung-k'an* ed. Shanghai, 1936.

Chan, David B. "The Problem of the Princes as Faced by the Ming Emperor Hui (1399–1402)." *Oriens*, vol. 11 (1958).

———. *The Usurpation of the Prince of Yen.* San Francisco, 1976.

Chang Lu 張鹵, ed. *Huang-Ming chih-shu* 皇明制書. 20 chüan. N.p., 1579.

Chang T'ing-yü 張廷玉 et al., eds. *Ming-shih* 明史. 4 + 332 chüan. N.p., 1739.

Cheng Chen-to 鄭振鐸, ed. *Hsüan-lan-t'ang ts'ung-shu* 玄覽堂叢書. 1st series: 32 works in 120 ts'e. Shanghai, 1941. 2nd series: 20 works in 120 ts'e. Nanking, 1947. 3rd series: 12 works in 32 ts'e. Nanking, 1948.

Cheng Ho-sheng 鄭鶴聲. *Cheng Ho* 鄭和. Chungking, 1945.

Chi Ch'ao-ting. *Key Economic Areas in Chinese History, as Revealed in the Development of Public Works for Water Control.* London, 1936. Reissued New York, 1963.

Chu Yüan-chang 朱元璋. *Tzu-shih t'ung-hsün* 資世通訓. In Chang Lu, ed., *Huang-Ming chih-shu*, listed above.

Ch'ü, T'ung-tsu. *Han Social Structure.* Seattle, Wash., 1972.

Ch'üan Heng 權衡. *Keng-shen wai-shih* 庚申外史. Taipei, 1967.

CLHP, see Shen Chieh-fu.

Dardess, John W. "An Autocrat Remolds Society: Psychological and Behavioral Rectification Under Ming T'ai-tsu." Paper presented at Western Conference, Association for Asian Studies, Albuquerque, N. Mex., 1973.

———. *Conquerors and Confucians: Aspects of Political Change in Late Yüan China.* New York, 1973.

———. "From Mongol Empire to Yüan Dynasty: Changing Forms of Imperial Rule in Mongolia and Central Asia." *Monumenta Serica*, vol. 30 (1972–73).

———. "The Transformations of Messianic Rebellion and the Founding of the Ming Dynasty." *Journal of Asian Studies*, vol. 29 (1970).

DMB, see Goodrich and Fang.

Dreyer, Edward L. "The *Chi-shih-lu* of Yü Pen: A Note on the Sources for the Founding of the Ming Dynasty." *Journal of Asian Studies*, vol. 31, no. 4 (1972).

———. "Chu Yüan-chang and His Higher Military Command." Paper presented at Western Conference, Association for Asian Studies, Albuquerque, N. Mex., 1973.

————. "The Emergence of Chu Yüan-chang, 1360–1365." Ph.D. dissertation, Harvard University, 1970.

————. "Military Reorganization in the Yung-lo Period." Paper presented at Mid-West Conference, Association for Asian Studies, Lawrence, Kans., 1974.

————. "The Poyang Campaign, 1363." In John K. Fairbank and Frank A. Kierman, eds., *Chinese Ways in Warfare*, listed below.

Dubs, Homer H. *History of the Former Han Dynesty*. Vols. 1–3. Baltimore and London, 1938–55.

Duyvendak, J.J.L. "The True Dates of the Chinese Maritime Expeditions in the Early Fifteenth Century." *T'oung Pao*, vol. 34 (1938).

Eberhard, Wolfram. *Das Toba-Reich Nordchinas*. Leiden, 1949.

ECCP, see Hummel.

Elvin, Mark. *The Pattern of the Chinese Past*. Stanford, Calif., 1973.

Fairbank, John K., ed. *The Chinese World Order: Traditional China's Foreign Relations*. Cambridge, Mass., 1968.

————, and Frank A. Kierman, eds. *Chinese Ways in Warfare*. Cambridge, Mass., 1974.

————, Edwin O. Reischauer, and Albert M. Craig, eds. *East Asia: Tradition and Transformation*. Cambridge, Mass., 1973.

Farmer, Edward L. *Early Ming Government: The Evolution of Dual Capitals*. Cambridge, Mass., 1976.

Fletcher, Joseph F. "China and Central Asia, 1368–1884." In John K. Fairbank, ed., *The Chinese World Order*, listed above.

Franke, Wolfgang. *An Introduction to the Sources of Ming History*. Kuala Lumpur, 1968.

————. "Yü Ch'ien, Staatsmann und Kriegsminister." *Monumenta Serica*, vol. 11 (1946).

————. "Yunglos Mongolei Feldzüge." *Sinologische Arbeiten*, vol. 3 (1945).

Gibb, H.A.R., and Harold Bowen. *Islamic Society and the West: Volume I, Parts 1 and 2*. London, 1950.

Goodrich, L. Carrington, and Chaoying Fang, eds. *Dictionary of Ming Biography*. New York, 1976.

Grimm, Tilemann. "Ming Education Intendants." In Charles O. Hucker, ed., *Chinese Government in Ming Times*, listed below.

————. "Das Neiko der Ming-Zeit von den Anfängen bis 1506." *Oriens Extremis*, vol. 1, no. 2 (1954).

Haeger, John W. "Between North and South: The Lake Rebellion in Hunan, 1130–1135." *Journal of Asian Studies*, vol. 28, no. 3 (1968–69).

Hall, D.G.E. *A History of South-East Asia*. New York, 1955.

Hambis, Louis, *Le chapitre CVIII du Yüan Che*. Leiden, 1954.

HHSL, see Yang Shih-ch'i, *Jen-tsung Chao-huang-ti shih-lu*.

HLTTS, see Cheng Chen-to.

HMCS, see Chang Lu.

Ho, Ping-ti. *The Ladder of Success in Imperial China*. New York, 1962.

————. *Studies on the Population of China*. Cambridge, Mass., 1959.

Hodgson, Marshall. *The Venture of Islam*. 3 vols. Chicago, 1974.

Hoshi Ayao 星斌夫. *Mindai sōun no kenkyū* 明代漕運の研究 (A study of grain transport in the Ming period). Tokyo, 1963.

Hsiao, Ch'i-ch'ing. *The Military Establishment of the Yüan Dynasty*. Cambridge, Mass., 1978.

Hsieh Chin 解縉. *T'ien-huang yü-t'ieh* 天潢玉牒 (ca. 1400). 1 chüan. In Shen Chieh-fu, *Chi-lu hui-pien*, listed below.

HTSL, see Yang Shih-ch'i, *Hsüan-tsung Chang-huang-ti shih-lu*.

Hu Kuang 胡廣 et al., eds. *T'ai-tsu Kao-huang-ti shih-lu* 太祖高皇帝實錄. 257 chüan. N.p., 1418.

Huang, Ray. "Fiscal Administration During the Ming Dynasty." In Charles O. Hucker, ed., *Chinese Government in Ming Times*, listed below.

————. *Taxation and Governmental Finance in Sixteenth Century Ming China*. Cambridge, 1974.

Hucker, Charles O. *The Censorial System of Ming China*. Stanford, Calif., 1966.

————. *Chinese Government in Ming Times: Seven Studies*. New York, 1969.

————. "Governmental Organization of the Ming Dynasty." *Harvard Journal of Asiatic Studies*, vol. 21 (1958).

————. "Hu Tsung-hsien's Campaign Against Hsü Hai." In John K. Fairbank and Frank A. Kierman, eds., *Chinese Ways in Warfare*, listed above.

Hummel, Arthur W., ed. *Eminent Chinese of the Ch'ing Period*. Washington, D.C., 1943.

HWSL, see Hu Kuang.

Iwamura Shinobu 岩村忍. *Mongoru shakai keizaishi kenkyū* モンゴル社会経済史研究 (Researches into the social and economic history of the Mongols). Kyoto, 1968.

Jordan, Donald A. *The Northern Expedition: China's National Revolution of 1926–1928*. Honolulu, 1976.

Kracke, E.A. *Civil Service in Early Sung China, 960–1067*. Cambridge, Mass., 1953.

Ku, Chieh-kang. "A Study of Literary Persecution During the Ming Dynasty." *Harvard Journal of Asiatic Studies*, vol. 3 (1938).

Ku Ying-t'ai 谷應泰. *Ming-shih chi-shih pen-mo* 明史紀事本末. 80 chüan. N.p., 1658.

Kuhn, Philip. *Rebellion and Its Enemies in Late Imperial China*. Cambridge, Mass., 1970.

Li Chao-hsiang 李昭祥. *Lung-chiang ch'uan-ch'ang chih* 龍江船廠志. In Cheng Chen-to, *Hsüan-lan-t'ang ts'ung-shu*, 2nd series, listed above.

Li Shan-ch'ang 李善長 et al., eds. *Yüan-shih* 元史. N.p., 1369. Cited from 1739 ed.

Liang Fang-chung 梁方中. *Ming-tai liang-chang chih-tu* 明代糧長制度 (The tax-captain system of the Ming period). Shanghai, 1957.

————. *The Single-Whip Method of Taxation in China*. Cambridge, Mass., 1956.

Lo, Jung-pang. "The Decline of the Early Ming Navy." *Oriens Extremis*, vol. 5, no. 2 (1958).

————. "Policy Formulation and Decision-Making on Issues Respecting Peace and War." In Charles O. Hucker, ed., *Chinese Government in Ming Times*, listed above.

McMullen, David. "Historical and Literary Theory in the Mid-Eighth Century." In Arthur F. Wright and Denis Twitchett, eds., *Perspectives on the T'ang*, listed below.

Martin, Henry Desmond. *The Rise of Chinggis Khan and His Conquest of North China*. Baltimore, 1950.

Meng Szu-ming 蒙思明. *Yüan-tai she-hui chieh-chi chih-tu* 元代社會階級制度 (The social class system of the Yüan dynasty). Peiping, 1938.

Meskill, John. "Academies and Politics in the Ming Dynasty." In Charles O. Hucker, ed., *Chinese Government in Ming Times*, listed above.

Michael, Franz. *The Origin of Manchu Rule in China*. Baltimore, 1942.

Mote, Frederick W. *The Poet Kao Ch'i, 1336–1374*. Princeton, N.J., 1962.

———. "Confucian Eremitism in the Yüan Period." In Arthur F. Wright, ed., *The Confucian Persuasion*, listed below.

———. "The T'u-mu Incident of 1449." In John K. Fairbank and Frank A. Kierman, eds., *Chinese Ways in Warfare*, listed above.

MS, see Chang T'ing-yü.

Muramatsu, Yūji. "Some Themes in Chinese Rebel Ideologies." In Arthur F. Wright, ed., *The Confucian Persuasion*, listed below.

Nakayama Hachirō 中山八郎. "Chin Yū-ryō no dai-ikkai Nankin kōgeki" 陳友諒の第一回南京攻撃 (Ch'en Yu-liang's first attack on Nanking). In *Suzuki Shun kyōju kanreki kinen tōyōshi ronsō* 鈴木俊教授還曆紀念東洋史論叢. Tokyo, 1964.

———. "Shisei jūichinen ni okeru kōkin no kiji to Ka Ro no kakō" 至正十一年に於る紅巾の起事と賈魯の河工 (The Red Turban rising of 1351 and Chia Lu's dredging work). In *Wada hakase koki kinen tōyōshi ronsō* 和田博士古稀記念東洋史論叢. Tokyo, 1960.

Needham, Joseph. *Science and Civilization in China*. Volume IV, Part 3. Cambridge, 1971.

Otagi Matsuo 愛宕松男. "Shu Go-koku to Chō Go-koku: shoki Min Ōchō no seikaku ni kansuru ichi kōsatsu" ·朱吳国と長吳国初期明王朝の性格に関する一考察 (Chu's Wu-state and Chang's Wu-state: an inquiry into the character of the early Ming dynasty). *Bunka*, vol. 17, no. 6 (1953).

Pao Tsun-p'eng 包遵彭. *Cheng Ho hsia Hsi-yang chih pao-ch'uan k'ao* 鄭和下西洋之寶船考 (A study of the treasure ships of Cheng Ho's voyages in the western ocean). Taipei, 1961.

Parsons, James B. *The Peasant Rebellions of the Late Ming Dynasty*. Tucson, Ariz. 1970.

Perkins, Dwight. *Agricultural Development in China, 1368–1968*. Chicago, 1969.

Peterson, Charles A. "Regional Defense Against the Central Power: The Huai-hsi Campaign, 815–817." In John K. Fairbank and Frank A. Kierman, eds., *Chinese Ways in Warfare*, listed above.

———. "The Restoration Completed: Emperor Hsien-tsung and the Provinces." In Arthur F. Wright and Denis Twitchett, eds., *Perspectives on the T'ang*, listed below.

Pulleyblank, Edwin G. *The Background of the Rebellion of An Lu-shan*. London, 1955.

———. "Neo-Confucianism and Neo-Legalism in T'ang Intellectual Life." In Arthur F. Wright, ed., *The Confucian Persuasion*, listed below.

Ratchnevsky, P. *Une code des Yüan*. Paris, 1937.

Rogers, Michael C. *The Chronicle of Fu Chien: A Case of Exemplar History*. Berkeley and Los Angeles, 1968.

Rossabi, Morris. "Ming China's Relations With Hami and Central Asia, 1404–1513: A Re-examination of Traditional Chinese Foreign Policy." Ph. D. dissertation, Columbia University, 1970.

des Rotours, Robert. *Traité des examens*. Leiden, 1932.

———. *Traité des fonctionnaires et Traité de l'armée*. 2 vols. Leiden, 1947–48.

Rozman, Gilbert. *Urban Networks in Ch'ing China and Tokugawa Japan*. Princeton, N.J., 1973.

Sansom, George. *A History of Japan: 1334–1615*. Stanford, Calif., 1961.

Schafer, Edward H. *The Golden Peaches of Samarkand: A Study of T'ang Exotics*. Berkeley, Calif., 1963.

Schurmann, H. Franz. *The Economic Structure of the Yüan Dynasty*. Cambridge, Mass., 1956.

———. "Mongolian Tributary Practices of the Thirteenth Century." *Harvard Journal of Asiatic Studies*, vol. 19 (1956).

Shen Chieh-fu 沈節甫. *Chi-lu hui-pien* 紀錄彙編. 216 chüan. N.p., 1617.

Shen Shih-hsing 申時行, ed. *Ta-Ming hui-tien* 大明會典. 228 chüan. N.p., 1587.

Shigematsu Toshiaki 重松俊章. "Sō-Gen jidai no kōkingun to Gen-matsu no Miroku-Hakuren kyōhi ni tsuite" 宋元時代の紅巾軍と元末の弥勒白蓮教匪に就いて (Concerning the Red Turban armies of the Sung-Yüan period and the Maitreya–White Lotus religious bandits of the late Yüan). *Shien*, vol. 24 (November 1940); vol. 26 (November 1941); vol. 28 (December 1942).

Shimizu Taiji 清水泰次. "Eiden kō" 営田考 (A study of the *ying-t'ien* colonies). In *idem, Mindai tochi seidoshi kenkyū*, listed below.

———. "Mindai no gundon" 明代の軍屯 (Military colonies of the Ming period). In *idem, Mindai tochi seidoshi kenkyū*, listed below.

———. "Mindai no tonden" 明代の屯田 (Agricultural colonies of the Ming period). In *idem, Mindai tochi seidoshi kenkyū*, listed below.

———. *Mindai tochi seidoshi kenkyū* 明代土地制度史研究 (Researches on the history of the land system of the Ming dynasty). Tokyo, 1968.

———. "Minsho ni okeru gundon no tenkai to sono soshiki" 明初に於る軍屯の展開とその組織 (The development of military colonies at the beginning of the Ming period and their organization). In *idem, Mindai tochi seidoshi kenkyū*, listed above.

So, Kwan-wai. *Japanese Piracy in Ming China During the 16th Century*. East Lansing, Mich, 1975.

Taga Akigoro 多賀秋五郎. *Chūgoku kyōikushi* 中国教育史 (A history of Chinese education). Tokyo, 1955.

Takahashi Takuji 高橋琢二. "Gen-matsu Chō Shi-sei seiken no kōbō" 元末張士誠政権の興亡 (The rise and fall of the late Yüan regime of Chang Shih-ch'eng). *Shigaku*, vol. 31, nos. 1–4 (1958).

T'an Ch'ien 談遷. *Kuo-ch'üeh* 國榷 (ca. 1653). 4 + 104 chüan. Peking, 1958.

Taylor, Romeyn. "Ming T'ai-tsu and the Nobility of Merit." *Ming Studies*, vol. 2 (1976).

———. "Social Origins of the Ming Dynasty." *Monumenta Serica*, vol. 22, no. 1 (1963).

———. "The Yüan Origins of the Wei-so System." In Charles O. Hucker, ed., *Chinese Government in Ming Times*, listed above.

Terada Gō 寺田剛. *Sōdai kyōikushi gaisetsu* 宋代教育史概説 (Outline of the history of education in the Sung period). Tokyo, 1965.

TMHT, see Shen Shih-hsing.

T'ung Ch'eng-hsü 童承敘. *P'ing-Han-lu* 平漢錄 (16th century). 1 chüan. In Shen Chieh-fu, *Chi-lu hui-pien*, listed above.

Twitchett, Denis. "The Composition of the T'ang Ruling Class: New Evidence from Tunhuang." In Arthur F. Wright and Denis Twitchett, eds., *Confucian Personalities*, listed below.

———. "Lu Chih (754–805): Imperial Adviser and Court Official." In Arthur F. Wright and Denis Twitchett, eds., *Confucian Personalities*, listed below.

Vernadsky, George. *The Mongols and Russia*. New Haven, Conn., 1953.

Wada Sei 和田清. "Min no kokugō ni tsuite" 明の国号に就いて (On the dynastic name "Ming"). *Shigaku zasshi*, vol. 42, no. 5 (1931).

———. "Min no Taisō to kōkin no zoku" 明の太祖と紅巾の賊 (Ming T'ai-tsu and the Red Turban rebels). *Tōyō gakuhō*, vol. 13, no. 2 (1923).

———. *Minshi shokkashi yakuchū* 明史食貨志訳註 (Annotated translation of the economics monograph of the Ming History). Tokyo, 1957.

Wakeman, Frederic. *The Fall of Imperial China*. New York, 1975.

Wang Ch'ung-wu 王崇武. "Ming ching-nan shih-shih k'ao-cheng kao" 明靖難史事考証稿 (Analysis of the historical sources of the Yung-lo usurpation in the Ming). In *Academia Sinca, Institute of History and Philology, Monograph No. 25*. Hong Kong, 1969.

Wang, Gungwu. "Early Ming Relations with Southeast Asia: A Background Essay." In John K. Fairbank, ed., *The Chinese World Order*, listed above.

———. "The Middle Yangtze in T'ang Politics." In Arthur F. Wright and Denis Twitchett, eds., *Perspectives on the T'ang*, listed below.

———. *The Structure of Power in North China During the Five Dynasties*. Kuala Lumpur, 1963.

Wang, Yi-t'ung. *Official Relations Between China and Japan, 1368–1549*. Cambridge, Mass., 1953.

Wang Yü-ch'üan 王毓銓. *Ming-tai chün-t'un* 明代的軍屯 (Military colonies in the Ming period). Peking, 1965.

———. "An Outline of the Central Government of the Former Han Dynasty." *Harvard Journal of Asiatic Studies*, vol. 12 (1949).

Watson, Burton. *Ssu-ma Ch'ien: Grand Historian of China*. New York, 1958.

Wei Ch'ing-yüan 韋慶遠. *Ming-tai huang-ts'e chih-tu* 明代黃冊制度 (The Yellow Register system of the Ming period). Peking, 1961.

Wilhelm, Helmut. "From Myth to Myth: The Case of Yüeh Fei's Biography." In Arthur F. Wright and Denis Twitchett, eds., *Confucian Personalities*, listed below.

Wittfogel, Karl A., and Feng Chia-sheng. *History of Chinese Society: Liao (907–1125)*. Philadelphia, 1949.

Wolters, O. W. *The Fall of Srivijaya in Malay History*. Ithaca, N.Y., 1970.

Woodside, Alexander Barton. *Vietnam and the Chinese Model: A Comparative Study of Nguyen and Ch'ing Civil Government in the First Half of the Nineteenth Century*. Cambridge, Mass., 1971.

Wright, Arthur F. "Sui Yang-ti: Personality and Stereotype." In *idem*, ed., *The Confucian Persuasion*, listed below.

———, ed. *The Confucian Persuasion*. Stanford, Calif., 1960.

———, and Denis Twitchett, eds. *Confucian Personalities*. Stanford, Calif., 1962.

———, and Denis Twitchett, eds. *Perspectives on the T'ang*. New Haven, Conn., 1973.

Wu Han 吳晗. *Chu Yüan-chang chuan* 朱元璋傳 (Biography of Chu Yüan-chang). Peking, 1949.

———. "Hu Wei-yung tang-an k'ao" 胡惟庸檔案考 (The case of Hu Wei-yung). *Yen-ching hsüeh-pao*, vol. 15 (1934).

———. "Ming-chiao yü Ta-Ming ti-kuo" 明教與大明帝國 (The Religion of Light and the Great Ming empire). In *idem, Tu-shih cha-chi* 讀史劄記. Peking, 1956.

Yang Lien-sheng. "Ming Local Administration." In C.O. Hucker, ed., *Chinese Government in Ming Times*, listed above.

Yang Shih-ch'i 楊士奇 et al., eds. *Hsüan-tsung Chang-huang-ti shih-lu* 宣宗章皇帝實錄. 115 chüan. N.p., 1438.

———. *Jen-tsung Chao-huang-ti shih-lu* 仁宗昭皇帝實錄. 10 chüan. N.p., 1430.

———. *T'ai-tsung Wen-huang-ti shih-lu* 太宗文皇帝實錄. 274 chüan. N.p., 1430.

YLSL, see Yang Shih-ch'i, *T'ai-tsung Wen-huang-ti shih-lu*.

YS, see Li Shan-ch'ang.

Character List

A-tzu 阿資
Ahmad 阿合馬
Altan Qan 俺答汗
Anch'ing 安慶
Anfeng 安豐
an-fu shih 安撫使
Anlu 安陸
An Lu-shan 安祿山
Arughtai, prince of Honing
　　和寧王阿魯台
Ashikaga Yoshimitsu 足利義滿
Ashikaga Yoshimochi 足利義持
Ashikaga Yoshinori 足利義敎
Ayushiridara 愛猷識里達臘
Basalawarmi 把匝剌瓦爾密
Batu Bolod 把禿孛羅
Bolod Temür 孛羅帖木兒
Bunyashiri 本雅失里
Buyur Lake 捕魚兒海
Chaghan Lake 察罕腦兒
Chaghan Temür 察罕帖木兒
Ch'ai Shan 柴山
Chan Hui 詹徽
chan-shih fu 詹事府
Chang, grand dowager empress
　　誠孝張皇后
Ch'angan 長安
Changchou 漳州
Ch'angchou 常州
Chang Chü-cheng 張居正

Chang Fu, duke of Ying 英國公張輔
Chang Hsien-chung 張獻忠
Chang Hsin, marquis of Lungp'ing
　　隆平侯張信
Ch'anghsing 長興
chang-kuan szu 長官司
Ch'ang Mao 常茂
Chang Ping 張昺
Ch'angsha 長沙
Ch'ang Sheng 常昇
chang-shih 長史
Chang Shih-ch'eng 張士誠
Chang Shih-hsin 張士信
Chang Shih-te 張士德
Ch'angshu 常熟
Changte 彰德
Chang Ting-pien 張定邊
Chang Yi 章溢
Chang Ying 張瑛
Chang Yü 張玉
Ch'ang Yü-ch'un 常遇春
Ch'ao, Lake 巢湖
Chao Chü-jen 趙居任
Chao Chün-yung 趙均用
Chao Chung-chung 趙仲中
Chao Hung 趙宏
Chao K'uang-yin 趙匡胤
ch'ao-p'in 超品
Chao P'u-sheng 趙普勝
Chao Shu 趙述

chao-t'ao chih 招討使
Chao Te-sheng 趙德勝
Chao Yung 趙庸
Ch'en Chao-hsien 陳兆先
Ch'en Ch'ia 陳洽
Chenchiang 鎮江
Ch'en Chih, earl of Yungch'ang
　榮昌伯陳智
Ch'en Esen 陳埜先
Ch'en Hsüan, earl of P'ingchiang
　平江伯陳瑄
Ch'en Hui 陳暉
Ch'en Kuei, marquis of T'aining
　泰寧侯陳珪
Ch'en Mou, marquis of Ningyang
　寧陽侯陳懋
Ch'en Ning 陳寧
Ch'en Shan 陳山
Chenting 眞定
Ch'en Tsu-yi 陳祖義
Ch'en Ying 陳瑛
Ch'en Yu-jen 陳友仁
Ch'en Yu-liang 陳友諒
Ch'en Yu-ting 陳友定
Ch'en Yung, marquis of Linchiang
　臨江侯陳鏞
ch'eng 丞
Cheng Ho 鄭和
ch'eng-hsiang 丞相
ch'eng-hsüan pu-cheng szu 承宣
　布政司
Ch'eng-hua 成化
Cheng-te 正德
Ch'engtu 成都
Cheng-t'ung 正統
Cheng Tz'u 鄭賜
cheng yi-p'in 正一品
Cheng Yü-ch'un 鄭遇春
Chian 吉安
Chichou 薊州
Chi Kang 紀綱
ch'i-lin 麒麟
Chining 濟寧
Ch'i-shou wei 旂手衞
Ch'ishui 蘄水
Ch'i T'ai 齊泰
Chiyang 濟陽

chia 甲
Chia-ching 嘉靖
Chiaho 夾河
Chialing River 嘉陵江
Ch'iang 羌
Chiangche 江浙
chiang-chi 匠籍
Chiangling 江陵
Chiangtung Bridge 江東橋
Chiangyin 江陰
Chiaochih 交阯
Chiaochou 交州
chiao-shou 教授
chiao-yü 教諭
Chiehchou 階州
Chiench'ang 建昌
ch'ien-hu 千戶
ch'ien-hu so 千戶所
chien-sheng 監生
Chien-wen 建文
Chien Yi 蹇義
chih-chou 知州
Ch'ihchou 池州
chih-fu 知府
chih-hsien 知縣
chih-hui ch'ien-shih 指揮僉事
chih-hui shih 指揮使
chih-hui t'ung-chih 指揮同知
chih-li chou 直隸州
Chinch'uan Gate 金川門
Chin Ch'un 金純
ch'in-chün 親軍
Chin Chung 金忠
Chinhua 金華
Ch'inhuai yi 秦淮翼
chin-shih 進士
ch'in-wang 親王
ch'in-wang fu 親王府
Chin-yi wei 錦衣衞
Chin Yu-tzu 金幼孜
Chingchiangk'ou 涇江口
Ch'ingchiangp'u 清江浦
Chingchou 靖州
Ch'ingchou 慶州 (Inner Mongolia)
Ch'ingchou 青州 (Shantung)
Chinggis Qan 成吉思汗
Ching-nan Army 靖難軍

Ching-t'ai 景泰
ching-wei 京衛
ching-ying 京營
Ch'ingyang 慶陽
Chiuchiang 九江
Ch'iu Fu, duke of Ch'i 淇國公邱福
ch'iu-liang 秋糧
chiu-pien 九邊
chou 州
Chou Te-hsing 周德興
Chu Chan, prince of Ch'ing 慶王
　朱㮵
Chu Chan-chi 朱瞻基
Chu Chen, prince of Ch'u 楚王朱楨
Chu Ch'i 朱杞
Chu Chih, prince of Liao 遼王朱植
Ch'üching 曲靖
Ch'uchou 滁州 (Anhwei)
Ch'uchou 處州 (Chekiang)
Chuch'üan 諸全
Chu Ch'üan, prince of Ning 寧王
　朱權
Chu Ch'un, prince of Shu 蜀王朱椿
Chu Fu, prince of Ch'i 齊王朱榑
chü-jen 舉人
Chu Kang, prince of Chin 晉王朱棡
Chu Kao-chih 朱高熾
Chu Kao-hsü, prince of Han 漢王
　朱高煦
Chu Kao-sui, prince of Chao 趙王
　朱高燧
Chu-ko Liang 諸葛亮
Chu Kuei, prince of Tai 代王朱桂
Chu Liang-tsu 朱亮祖
Chu Neng, duke of Ch'eng 成國公
　朱能
Chu Piao 朱標
Chu Po, prince of Hsiang 湘王朱柏
Chusan Islands 舟山
Chu Shuang, prince of Ch'in 秦王
　朱樉
Chu Su, prince of Chou 周王朱橚
Chu T'an, prince of Lu 魯王朱檀
Ch'üt'ang Gorge 瞿塘峽
Chu Ti, prince of Yen 燕王朱棣
Chu Tsung 祝宗
Chu Tzu, prince of T'an 潭王朱梓

Chu Wen 朱溫
Chu Wen-cheng 朱文正
Chu Ying, prince of Su 肅王朱楧
Chu Yüan-chang 朱元璋
Chu Yün-wen 朱允炆
Chu Yung 朱榮
Chüyungkuan 居庸關
Ch'üan Chin 權謹
Ch'üanchou 泉州
chün-chi 軍籍
chün-hsien 郡縣
chün-min fu 軍民府
chün-wang 郡王
Ch'ung-chen 崇禎
Chung-chün 中軍
Chungking 重慶
chung-shu-sheng 中書省
Chungtu 中都
Dai Viet 大越
Dalai Lake 達里湖
Dash Badulugh 荅失八都魯
Dash Temür 達識帖睦邇
Dayan Qan 達延汗
Dazaifu 太宰府
Engke Temür 安克帖木兒
Esen 也先
Esentü Qan 也先土汗
fang 方
Fang Chao 房昭
Fang Cheng 方政
Fang Hsiao-ju 方孝孺
Fang Kuo-chen 方國珍
Fang Pin 方賓
Fei Chü 費聚
Fei River 淝水
Fen River 汾水
Feng Ch'eng 馮誠
Feng Kuo-yung 馮國用
Feng Sheng 馮勝
Fengyang 鳳陽
Foochow 福州 (Fukien)
Fouliang 浮梁
fu 府
fu chiang-chün 副將軍
fu ch'ien-hu 副千戶
Fuchou 撫州 (Kiangsi)
Fu-chün ch'ien-wei 府軍前衛

fu tsung-ping kuan 副總兵官
Fuyü 富峪
Fu Yu-te 傅友德
Godaigo 後醍醐
Hami (Qomul) 哈密
Hanchou 漢州
Hanchung 漢中
Han Lin-erh 韓林兒
Han River 漢水
Han Shan-t'ung 韓山童
Hantung 罕東
Han Wu-ti 漢武帝
Hanyang 漢陽
Han Yü 韓愈
Hangchow 杭州
Haochou 濠州
Henghai wei 橫海衛
Ho Chen 何眞
Hochien 河間
Hochou 和州
Ho Fu 何福
hou 侯
Hsining 西寧
Hsia 夏
hsia-shui 夏稅
Hsia Yü 夏煜
Hsia Yüan-chi 夏原吉
hsiang 廂
Hsiangyang 襄陽
hsiao Ming Wang 小明王
Hsieh Chin 解縉
Hsieh Kuei 謝貴
Hsinch'eng 新城
Hsinch'eng Gate 新城門
Hsinho 新河
Hsink'an 新淦
hsing chung-shu-sheng 行中書省
Hsingho 興和
hsing hou-chün tu-tu fu 行後軍
　　都督府
Hsinghua 興化
hsing-pu 行部 (Branch Ministry)
hsing-pu 刑部 (Ministry of Justice)
hsing shu-mi-yüan 行樞密院
hsing t'ai-p'u szu 行太僕寺
hsing-tsai 行在
hsing yü-shih-t'ai 行御史臺

Hsiung T'ien-jui 熊天瑞
Hsüchou 徐州
Hsü Hui-tsu 徐輝祖
Hsü K'ai 徐凱
Hsü Shou-hui 徐壽輝
Hsü Ta 徐達
Hsü Yi 徐義
Hsüyi 肝胎
hsüan 玄
Hsüanfu 宣府
hsüan-fu shih 宣撫使
Hsüan-te 宣德
hsüan-wei shih 宣慰使
Hsüanwu Lake 玄武湖
hsüeh-cheng 學正
Hsüeh Kuei 薛貴
hsün-chien szu 巡檢司
hsün-fu 巡撫
hsün-tao 訓導
Huchou 湖州
Huk'ou 湖口
Hu Kuang 胡廣
Hu Mei 胡美
hu-pu 戶部
Hu Ta-hai 胡大海
Hu Te-chi 胡德濟
Hut'o River 滹沱河
hu-wei 護衛
Hu Wei-yung 胡惟庸
Hu Yen 胡儼
Hua Kao 華高
Hua Yün 花雲
Hua Yün-lung 華雲龍
Huaian 淮安
Huaich'ing 懷慶
Huailai 懷來
Huai River 淮河
Huangchou 黃州
Huang-chüeh-szu 皇覺寺
Huang Fu 黃福
Huang Huai 黃淮
Huang Pin 黃彬
huang-t'ai-sun 皇太孫
huang-t'ai-tzu 皇太子
huang-ts'e 黃冊
Huang Tzu-ch'eng 黃子澄
Huichou 徽州 (Anhwei)

Huichou 會州 (Inner Mongolia)
Hun-chiang-lung 混江龍
Hung-chih 弘治
Hung-hsi 洪熙
Hunghsien 雄縣
Hung-wu 洪武
huo-ch'ung 火銃
Huo Kuang 霍光
Imagawa Ryōshun 今川了俊
Jaochou 饒州
Jehol 熱河
Juning 汝寧
K'aifeng 開封
K'aip'ing 開平
kai-t'u kuei-liu 改土歸流
Kanchou 甘州 (Kansu)
Kanchou 贛州 (Kiangsi)
k'an-ho/kangō 勘合
Kan River 贛江
Kanenaga 懷良親王
K'anglangshan 康郎山
K'ang Mao-ts'ai 康茂才
K'ang T'ai 康泰
Kaoch'eng 藁城
Kaoyu 高郵
Kenchū Keimi 堅中圭密
Keng Ping-wen 耿炳文
Keng Tsai-ch'eng 耿再成
ko 閣
K'o-chin 克勤
Kökö Temür 擴廓帖木兒
Koryŏ 高麗
Ku Shih 顧時
Ku Tso 顧佐
Kuyüan 固源
K'uanho 寬河
Kuanghsin 廣信
kuang-lu-szu 光祿寺
Kuangning 廣寧
Kuangp'ing 廣平
Kuangyang wei 廣洋衞
K'ueichou 夔州
K'unlun Mountains 崑崙山
kung 公
Kungch'ang 鞏昌
kung-pu 工部
Kuo Chi 郭驥

Kuo Tzu 郭資
kuo-tzu-chien 國子監
Kuo Tzu-hsing 郭子興
Kuo Ying 郭英
Kyōto 京都
Kyūshū 九州
Lanchou 蘭州
Lan Yü, duke of Liang 涼國公藍玉
Lang So'n 諒山
Le Hao 黎澔
Le Lo'i 黎利
Le Qui Ly 黎季犛
li 里
Li An, earl of Anp'ing 安平伯李安
li-cheng 里正
li-chia 里甲
Li Ch'ing 李慶
Li Ching-lung 李景隆
Li Pin, marquis of Fengch'eng 豐城侯
　孝彬
Li Po-sheng 李伯昇
li-pu 吏部 (Ministry of Personnel)
li-pu 禮部 (Ministry of Rites)
Li Shan-ch'ang 李善長
Li Szu-ch'i 李思齊
Li Tzu-ch'eng 李自成
Li Wen-chung 李文忠
Li Yüan 李遠
liang-chang 糧長
liang-shui fa 兩稅法
Liaoning 遼寧
Liaotung 遼東
Liao Yung-an 廖永安
Liao Yung-chung 廖永忠
Linch'ing 臨清
Lin Hsien 林賢
Lint'ao 臨洮
Lingpei 嶺北
Lingpi 靈璧
ling-sheng 廩生
Liu Chi 劉基
Liu Chiang 劉江
Liu Chin 劉瑾
Liuch'iu 琉球
Liu Chun 劉儁
Liu Fu-t'ung 劉福通
Liu Kuan 劉觀

liu-kuan 流官
Liu Pang 劉邦
Liu Pei 劉備
liu-pu 六部
Liu Sheng, marquis of Anyüan
　安遠侯柳升
Liu Ta-hsia 劉大夏
Loan-chou 樂安州
Loyang 洛陽
lu 路
Lü Chen 呂震 (minister)
Lü Chen 呂珍 (Wu general)
Luchou 廬州
Lu Chü 陸聚
Luch'uan 麓川
Lu Chung-heng 陸仲亨
Lulungshan 盧龍山
Lu principality 魯
Lü Yüan 呂淵
Luan Feng 欒鳳
Lung-chiang Shipyard 龍江船廠
Lung-ch'ing 隆慶
Lungwan 龍灣
Ma Ch'i 馬騏
ma-ch'uan 馬船
Ma Yü 馬愉
Mahmud 馬哈木
Maidiribala 買的里八剌
Manzi Qarajang 蠻子哈剌章
Manzi Qaya 蠻子海牙
Maochou 茂州
Mao Kuei 毛貴
Mei Szu-tsu 梅思祖
Miao 苗
Miyün 密雲
Mienyang 沔陽
min-chi 民籍
Min River 閩江 (Fukien)
Min River 岷江 (Szechwan)
Ming-chiao 明教
Ming Sheng 明昇
Ming Wang 明王
Ming Yü-chen 明玉珍
Mochou 鄭州
Mu Ch'un 沐春
Mu Sheng, duke of Ch'ien 黔國公
　沐晟

Mu Ying 沐英
Namboku-chō 南北朝
Naghachu 納哈出
Nanch'ang 南昌
Nan Chihli 南直隸
Nanhutsui 南湖觜
Nank'ang 南康
Nanking 南京
Nanyang 南陽
Nayur Buqa 乃兒不花
nei-ko 內閣
Nghe An 乂安
Ni Liang 倪諒
Ni Wen-chün 倪文俊
nien-hao 年號
Ninghsia 寧夏
Ningkuo 寧國
Ningpo 寧波
Omeishan 峨眉山
Ordos 鄂爾多斯
Orkhon River 阿魯渾河
Ōuchi 大內
Pai 白
Pai River 白河
Paikouho 白溝河
Paishih River 白石江
pa-ku wen 八股文
Pan Ch'ao 班超
P'an Yüan-ming 潘元明
Pao Chao 暴昭
pao-ch'uan 寶船
Paoting 保定
P'ei 沛
Pei Chihli 北直隸
Peip'ing 北平
P'eng Ta 彭大
P'eng Ying-yü 彭瑩玉
P'ing An 平安
p'ing-chang cheng-shih 平章政事
P'ingliang 平涼
ping-luan 兵亂
ping-pu 兵部
po 伯
Pochou 亳州
po-hu 百戶
po-hu so 百戶所
P'oyang Lake 鄱陽湖

pu-cheng shih 布政使
pu tz'u-shih 部刺史
P'u Ying 濮英
Qaidu 海都
Qara Qorum 和林
Qubilai 忽必烈
Qulan Qushwan 忽蘭忽失溫
Ryūkyū. *See* Liuch'iu
Sanch'ien ying 三千營
san ta ying 三大營
Semu 色目
Shan 撣
Shanhaikuan 山海關
Shan Shou 山壽
shang-shu 尚書
Shangtu 上都
Shaohsing 紹興
Shao Jung 邵榮
shao-pao 少保
shao-shih 少師
Shaowu 邵武
Shen-chi ying 神機營
sheng 省
sheng-yüan 生員
Sheng Yung, marquis of Lich'eng
　歷城侯盛庸
shih 石
Shihhuishan 石灰山
shih-kuan 世官
shih-lu 實錄
Shih-mo Yi-sun 石抹宜孫
shih-po szu 市舶司
shih-po t'i-chü szu 市舶提舉司
Shimazu Hisatoyo 島津久豐
shogun 將軍
shou-fu 首輔
shou-pei 守備
shou-yü ch'ien-hu so 守禦千戶所
shu-chou 屬州
Shui-chün tso-wei, yu-wei 水軍左衞
　右衞
Shunte 順德
Shunt'ien 順天
Sian 西安
so chen-fu 所鎮撫
Soochow 蘇州
Sorai 祖來

Suchou 宿州 (Anhwei)
Sui Yang-ti 隋煬帝
Sun Chien 孫堅
Sun Te-yai 孫德崖
Sun Yen 孫炎
Sung Chung 宋忠
Sung Hui-tsung 宋徽宗
Sung Kao-tsung 宋高宗
Sung Li 宋禮
Sung Lien 宋濂
Sungp'an 松潘
Sung Szu-yen 宋思顏
Szuchou 泗州 (Kiangsu)
Szuchou 思州 (Kweichow)
Szu family 思
szu-li t'ai-chien 司禮太監
Szu Lun-fa 思倫發
Szu-ma Yen 司馬炎
Szu-wei ying 四衞營
ta chiang-chün 大將軍
ta hsüeh-shih 大學士
Tali 大理
ta-li-szu 大理寺
Taming 大名
T'an principality 潭
Taning 大寧
Tashengkuan 大勝關
Tatu 大都
Tatu River 大渡河
ta tu-tu fu 大都督府
Tat'ung 大同
Ta-t'ung-kuan t'i-chü-szu 大通關
　提舉司
T'ai-ch'ang 泰昌
t'ai-ch'ang-szu 太常寺
t'ai-chien 太監
T'aichou 台州 (Chekiang)
T'aichou 泰州 (Kiangsu)
t'ai-fu 太傅
T'aip'ing 太平
T'ai-p'ing 太平
t'ai-shih 太師
t'ai-shou 太守
T'aits'ang wei 太倉衞
t'ai-tzu 太子
t'ai-tzu shao-fu, shao-shih, shao-pao
　太子少傅少師少保

t'ai-wei 太尉
T'aiyüan 太原
T'ang Ho 湯和
T'ang Sheng-tsung 唐勝宗
tao 道
Taochou 道州
Tao-yen 道衍
Techou 德州
Temür 鐵木耳
Teng Yü 鄧俞
Tenryūji 天龍寺
Thanh Hoa 清化
t'i-chü-szu 提舉司
t'i-hsing an-ch'a-shih szu 提刑按察
　使司
t'i-tu hsüeh-tao 提督學道
T'ieh Hsüan 鐵鉉
tien 殿
T'ien-ch'i 天啓
t'ien-ch'iao 天橋
T'ien-chieh-szu 天界寺
T'ien-shun 天順
T'ien-wan 天完
Tingchou 定州
Tinghsi 定西
ting 丁
Ting P'u-lang 丁普郎
Ting Yü 丁玉
Tingyüan 定遠
Toghon Temür 妥懽貼睦爾
Toghtō 脫脫
Toghus Temür 脫古思帖木兒
Tra Long 茶籠
Tran 陳
Tran Cao 陳暠
Tran Nguy 陳頠
Tran Qui Khoang 陳季擴
Ts'aishih 采石
ts'an-cheng 參政
ts'an-chiang 參將
ts'an-chih cheng-shih 參知政事
tsan-li chün-wu 贊理軍務
ts'an-tsan chi-wu 參贊機務
ts'an-yi 參議
Ts'angchou 滄州
Ts'ao Chi-hsiang 曹吉祥
Ts'ao Nai 曹鼐

Ts'ao Ts'ao 曹操
tseng-sheng 增生
Tsinan 濟南
Tso Chün-pi 左君弼
Tso-shao 左哨
Tso Tsung-t'ang 左宗棠
Tso-yi 左掖
Tsou P'u-sheng 鄒普勝
Tsu-shan 祖闌
Tsunhua 遵化
tsung chiu-p'in 從九品
tsung-kuan fu 總管府
tsung-ping kuan 總兵官
tsung-tu 總督
tu-ch'a yüan 都察院
T'u Chieh 涂節
t'u chih-chou 土知州
tu chih-hui ch'ien-shih 都指揮僉事
tu chih-hui shih 都指揮使
tu chih-hui shih szu 都指揮使司
tu chih-hui t'ung-chih 都知揮同知
tu chuan-yün yen shih szu 都轉運鹽
　使司
t'u-kuan 土官
T'umu 土木
Tuan Te-kung 段得功
Tula River 土剌河
tu-tu 都督
tu-tu ch'ien-shih 都督僉事
tu-tu fu 都督府
tu-tu t'ung-chih 都督同知
tu-wei 都衛
Tuan-li Gate 端禮門
Tunhuang 敦煌
t'un-t'ien 屯田
Tunga 東阿
Tungch'ang 東昌
t'ung-cheng szu 通政司
T'ungchou 通州
T'ungkuan 潼關
Tunglin 東林
Tungp'ing 東平
Tzuching Pass 紫荊關
Uriyangqad 兀良哈
Wakō/wo-k'ou 倭寇
Wanch'üan 萬全
Wan-li 萬歷

Wang Chang 王彰
Wang Chen 王振
Wang Chih 汪直
Wang K'ai 王愷
Wang Kuang-yang 王廣洋
Wang Mang 王莽
Wang Pao-pao 王保保
Wang Pi, marquis of Tingyüan 定遠侯王弼
Wang P'u 王溥
Wang Shou-jen 王守仁
Wang T'ung, marquis of Ch'eng-shan 成山侯王通
Wang Wei 王禕
Wang Yu, marquis of Ch'ingyüan 清遠侯王友
wei 衛
wei chen-fu 衛鎮撫
Wei Ch'ing 衛青
Wei Chung-hsien 魏忠賢
wei ju liu 未入流
Wei River 渭水
wei-so 衛所
Wenchou 溫州
Wenshang 汶上
Wuch'ang 武昌
Wu Chen 吳禎
Wu Chieh 吳傑
Wuchou 梧州
Wu Ch'un 武淳
wu-chün tu-tu fu 五軍都督府
Wuchün ying 五軍營
Wu Chung 吳中
wu-fu 武傅
Wu Han 吳晗
Wu Kao 吳高
Wu Liang 吳良
Wu Yün 吳雲
Xu'ong Giang 昌江
Yang Ching 楊璟
Yangchou 揚州
Yang Hsien 楊憲
Yang Jung 楊榮
Yang Öljei 楊完者

Yang P'u 楊溥
Yang Shih-ch'i 楊士奇
Yang Yen 楊炎
Yao Kuang-hsiao 姚廣孝
Yeh Ch'in 葉琛
Yeh Sheng 葉昇
Yenan 延安
Yenchou 嚴州 (Chekiang)
Yenchou 兗州 (Shantung)
yen-k'o t'i-chü szu 鹽課提舉司
Yenmen Pass 雁門關
Yenp'ing 延平
Yenshan wei 燕山衛
Yensui 延綏
Yen Sung 嚴嵩
Yi 繇
yi 翼
Yiling 夷陵
Yi Songgye 李成桂
Yitu 益都
yi yüan-shuai-fu 翼元帥府
yin 廕
Yin Ch'ing 尹慶
ying 營
Yingch'ang 應昌
Yingchou 潁州
ying-t'ien shih 營田使
yu-chi chiang-chün 遊擊將軍
Yü Ch'ien 于謙
Yülin 榆林
yü-lin t'u-ts'e 魚鱗土冊
yü-shih chung-ch'eng 御史中丞
yü-shih-t'ai 御史臺
Yu-shao 右哨
Yü T'ung-hai 俞通海
Yü T'ung-yüan 俞通源
Yu-yi 右掖
Yüan Ch'i 袁琦
Yüanchou 沅州
yüan-shuai 元帥
Yungchou 永州
Yung-lo 永樂
Yungp'ing 永平

Index

312 *Index*

1982
STANFORD UNIVERSITY PRESS
STANFORD, CALIFORNIA

 *Early Ming China*